A Very Dangerous Woman

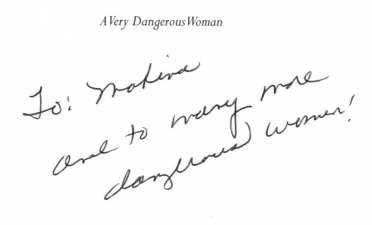

To: Matina
and to many more
dangerous women!

Sherry & Jim

A
VERY
DANGEROUS
WOMAN

Martha Wright and Women's Rights

SHERRY H. PENNEY
AND JAMES D. LIVINGSTON

University of Massachusetts Press

Amherst and Boston

Copyright © 2004 by University of Massachusetts Press
All rights reserved
Printed in the United States of America
LC 2003027702
ISBN 1-55849-446-4 (library cloth ed.); 447-2 (paper)
Designed by Milenda Nan Ok Lee
Set in Perpetua
Printed and bound by The Maple-Vail Book Manufacturing Group

Library of Congress Cataloging-in-Publication Data

Penney, Sherry H.
  A very dangerous woman : Martha Wright and women's rights / Sherry H. Penney
and James D. Livingston.
       p. cm.
  Includes bibliographical references and index.
  ISBN 1-55849-446-4 (library cloth : alk. paper)—ISBN 1-55849-447-2 (pbk. :
alk. paper)
    1. Wright, Martha Coffin, 1806–1875. 2. Feminists—United States—Biography.
3. Suffragists—United States—Biography. 4. Women social reformers—United
States—Biography. 5. Women's rights—United States—History. I. Livingston,
James D., 1930– II. Title.
  HQ1413 .W753P46 2004
  305.42'092—dc22

                                                                2003027702

British Library Cataloguing in Publication data are available.

To our children:
Joan, Susan, Barbara, Mike, and Jeff

Contents

CONTENTS

Illustrations follow page 80.

Acknowledgments

We spent many hours working with letters and other material in the Garrison Family Papers of the Sophia Smith Collection at Smith College, and we are especially thankful to Sherrill Rodman and her staff, especially Kathleen Nutter and Susan Boone, for their help. We are also grateful to Carolyn Davis, Terry Keenan, and their colleagues in the Bird Library at Syracuse University, who assisted us with our research in the Osborne Family Papers. Our work in Syracuse was greatly facilitated by the cooperation of Claire White Putala of SUNY Oswego, whose familiarity with this collection helped to make our time there more fruitful.

Christopher Densmore, curator of the Friends Historical Society at Swarthmore College, Sarah Hutcheon of Radcliffe's Schlesinger Library, Kevin Gallagher, archives assistant at Westtown School, and John Heiser, park ranger and historian at the Gettysburg National Military Park, each contributed important information. Deanne Blanton of the National Archives kindly provided information on the military records of Julius Catlin and Peter Pelham. Thanks are also due the research staffs at Harvard's Lamont and Houghton Libraries, the American Antiquarian Society, Massachusetts Historical Society, Boston Public Library, New York Public Library, New York State Library at Albany, Stowe-Day Library in Hartford, Bancroft Library of the University of California, Berkeley, and the Library of the University of North Carolina at Chapel Hill.

ACKNOWLEDGMENTS

Especially helpful were local historians in the area of upstate New York in which Martha Wright spent most of her life. Judy Furness, historian of the town of Ledyard, generously sought and provided much information pertinent to Martha's years in Aurora, and Sheila Edmunds, Aurora historian, provided additional information. Mary Gilmore of the Local History Room in the Seymour Library in Auburn assisted us in numerous ways, providing access to her file on Martha Wright and helping us to locate the site of Martha's home. Also aiding our research in Auburn were Collin Sullivan and Gina Stankivitz of the Cayuga Museum, the late Martha Shosa, resident expert on Martha Wright, Mike Long, city planner, Thomas Eldred, county historian, and staff at the Cayuga County Community College. Erik Osborne of Auburn, a descendant of Martha Wright, provided us with a copy of the will that Martha wrote in 1821, and kindly showed us the portraits of Martha and her mother, husband, sister Lucretia, and daughter Eliza that hang in his home. In Seneca Falls, Anne Derousie, historian of the Women's Rights National Historical Park, and David Malone, park ranger, were cooperative and helpful, as was the staff at the Seneca Falls Historical Association. Mary Watkins of the Cayuga & Owasco Lakes Historical Society provided information on the location of David Wright's farms in Moravia. Bunny Fuller, a descendant of Eliza Wright Osborne, kindly provided us access to a schoolbook of Martha Coffin's and two paintings of Martha's in her possession.

Numerous historians expert in the period were generous with information, suggestions, and encouragement. These notably included Ann Gordon of Rutgers University, editor of the Stanton and Anthony papers, who provided us copies of important material from early newspapers, and Beverly Palmer of Pomona College, editor of the Lucretia Mott letters, who allowed us to see her book in page proof. Harriet Alonso was kind enough to send us material from her book on Garrison's children, *Growing Up Abolitionist*, prior to publication. We have also profited from discussions with Margaret Hope Bacon, biographer of Lucretia Mott, Carol Faulkner of SUNY Geneseo, researcher on the Mott Project, Jean Humez of the University of Massachusetts Boston and Kate Clifford Larson, experts on Harriet Tubman, Kathryn Kish Sklar of SUNY Binghamton, Nancy Cott of Yale University, Paula Doress-Walters of Brandeis, director of the Ernestine Rose Society, Sally Roesch Wagner, director of the Matilda Joslyn Gage Foundation, and Laurie Carter Noble, studying xiii

ACKNOWLEDGMENTS

Olympia Brown. We thank Andrea Hawke for providing us with a copy of her master's thesis on Elizabeth M'Clintock.

We are also thankful to all who provided us information concerning the Pelhams. These include Wilfried Roeder, William Pelham, Randolph and Elizabeth Pickell, Julius Gordon, Thomas Hubert, Nancy Britton, Sandra Mathews-Lamb, Wendy Wright, and Peggy Vogtsberger of the John Pelham Historical Association.

Very special thanks are owed to friends and colleagues who read all or part of our manuscript and made helpful suggestions. These included James Gould, whose genealogy of Martha Wright's family was extremely helpful (and who first called our attention many years ago to the Garrison Family Papers at Smith), and Irving Bartlett, an expert of the period and biographer of Wendell Phillips, Daniel Webster, and John C. Calhoun. Judith Smith of the University of Massachusetts Boston provided many helpful comments and suggestions, as did Christopher Densmore of Swarthmore and Judith Wellman, former historian at Seneca Falls and author of *The Road to Seneca Falls: Elizabeth Cady Stanton and the First Woman's Rights Convention*. We have especially appreciated the enthusiastic support and encouragement of our project provided by Judy, who for some time has been, like us, enchanted with the life and personality of Martha Coffin Wright.

We are especially grateful to Paul Wright of University of Massachusetts Press, who acquired our manuscript and guided it skillfully through the review process. After our manuscript was accepted, managing editor Carol Betsch, with great care and the assistance of copy editor Deborah Smith, helped to transform our manuscript into the finished product. We acknowledge with sincere thanks all the staff of the University of Massachusetts Press who contributed to this project.

A Very Dangerous Woman

Introduction

> We hold these truths to be self evident: that all men and
> women are created equal; that they are endowed by
> their creator with certain inalienable rights; that among
> these are life, liberty, and the pursuit of happiness.[1]

IN JULY 1848, sixty-eight women and thirty-two men in Seneca Falls, New York, signed the Declaration of Sentiments, a document modeled after the Declaration of Independence, which had been written and adopted seventy-two years earlier. To many contemporaries, the addition of "and women" to Thomas Jefferson's famous sentence was as revolutionary as the original Declaration. Another seventy-two years would pass before the Nineteenth Amendment to the Constitution enfranchised women, the majority of the U.S. population; only one of the female signers of the Seneca Falls declaration lived to see it. Even today, full gender equality has not been achieved in American society. However, tremendous progress has been made since 1848, thanks to the organized movement for woman's rights triggered by the historic meeting at Seneca Falls.

The importance of the Seneca Falls Convention to the history of America was formally recognized in 1980, when Congress established the Women's Rights National Historical Park. The park's Visitor Center today features a group of life-size bronze statues representing key participants in the 1848 convention. One statue is highly unusual; it is of a woman who is obviously pregnant. She is Martha C. Wright, one of the five women who planned the convention. That July Martha was forty-one years old and six months pregnant with her seventh child. Her statue is testimony for the ages that the bearing of children does not necessarily preclude women from making important public contributions to society. Martha's condition limited her role during the convention sessions, but she was responsible for adding something distinctive to the proceedings—a touch of humor.

Discussions at the Seneca Falls woman's rights convention were mostly very serious, but the official convention report notes at least one light moment: "LUCRETIA MOTT read a humorous article from a newspaper, written by MARTHA C. WRIGHT."[2] Lucretia Mott was a well-known Quaker preacher and antislavery activist, the only person whose name had appeared in the published announcement of the meeting; the organizers knew that Lucretia's name would help to draw an audience. Martha was Lucretia's sister, and the two had met with Elizabeth Cady Stanton, Mary Ann M'Clintock, and Jane Hunt a few days earlier to plan the convention, the Declaration of Sentiments, and a series of resolutions on woman's rights. At the convention, Martha sat quietly in the audience while Lucretia, one of the few women in America who had become comfortable with speaking in public, amused the audience with Martha's "humorous article." Some months later, in response to a letter from Lucretia, Martha explained her limited participation in the discussions at Seneca Falls.

> I plead guilty to being very stupid & dispirited at Seneca Falls—the prospect of having more *Wrights* than I wanted tending materially to subdue the ardor & energy that wd. [would] doubtless have characterized me "at another time" but I was glad of the privilege of looking on and shrinking, as far as *shrinking* was practicable, into the insignifance [sic] that under the circumstances [pregnancy] was appropriate for me.[3]

This excerpt reveals the humor that characterized her letters and published writings, including her newspaper article read at Seneca Falls. But Martha was much more than a clever writer. She remained active in the woman's rights movement throughout her life, presiding over numerous conventions and serving, before her death in 1875, as president of the National Woman Suffrage Association. Active also in the antislavery movement, she was one of a handful of women present at the 1833 founding of the American Anti-Slavery Society in Philadelphia. At her home in conservative Auburn, New York, she welcomed fugitive slaves and antislavery leaders, such as William Lloyd Garrison, Frederick Douglass, and Harriet Tubman, as well as feminist leaders, including her sister Lucretia Mott and her friends Elizabeth Cady Stanton and Susan B. Anthony. Stanton and Anthony often sought Martha's advice on strategies for advancing woman suffrage and woman's rights. Because Martha's outspoken promotion of woman's rights, abolition of slavery, and a freethinking approach to religion challenged the status quo and the contemporary view of "woman's sphere," her neighbors in Auburn called her "a very dangerous woman."[4]

Ann D. Gordon, editor of *The Selected Papers of Elizabeth Cady Stanton and Susan B. Anthony,* describes Martha as "a stalwart of the state antislavery society and, after attending the meeting at Seneca Falls, one of the inner circle of woman's rights leaders until the end of her life. An avid letter writer and a wit, she left a valuable archives of correspondence on woman's rights and woman suffrage."[5] Martha's diaries and many of her papers, including nearly two thousand of her letters, fortunately have been preserved. Most are in the Sophia Smith Collection of Smith College and have been used extensively by historians studying nineteenth-century reform and by biographers studying the lives of Martha's better-known associates. Of the five women who organized the Seneca Falls Woman's Rights Convention, only three remained active in the woman's movement in the decades following—Lucretia Mott, Elizabeth Cady Stanton, and Martha Wright. Of the sixty-eight women who signed the Declaration of Sentiments, only these three women, according to Judith Wellman, foremost expert on the convention, "became figures of national importance."[6] The lives and contributions of Mott and Stanton have been described in numerous biographies, but Martha has been relatively neglected. As Robert Riegel points out, "The eminence of Lucretia Mott threw the career of her sister Martha C. Wright into the shadow. . . . Her influence, however, was widespread and important."[7] It is time to allow Martha to emerge from her sister's shadow.

As many earlier biographers and historians have found, Martha's thoughtful, amusing, and provocative letters provide revealing insights into the lives and personalities of her colleagues in reform. As we studied Martha's letters, however, we also became convinced that her life was full of interest beyond any reflected glory from her famous friends and colleagues. As a prominent participant in the woman's rights and antislavery movements, she was caught up in the timeless conflict between tradition and societal change. Like all reformers of the time, Martha drew hostility and ridicule from politicians, press, pulpit, and public. She faced the threat of physical harm from angry mobs when she attended antislavery meetings and derision from neighbors when she entertained blacks in her home or sought signatures on petitions for woman's rights. Her early personal trials included expulsion from her Quaker meeting, shipwreck, and a harsh life at a frontier fort. She was widowed at nineteen and later experienced the deaths by drowning of a fiancé and her oldest son, the deaths of two other children, and the near-fatal wounding of her second son at Gettysburg. Her life was not easy, but it was interesting and important.

Martha Wright's sense of humor and the support of a strong family network helped her to overcome her many difficulties, serve her husband and children devotedly as wife and mother, and make important public contributions to the advancement of human rights. Martha's relative inactivity at Seneca Falls caused by her pregnancy is only one of numerous examples of the competition between her private roles as wife and mother and her public commitment to reform. In child rearing, she balanced sensitivity to woman's rights issues with the practical concerns of a realistic and pragmatic mother who wanted her children to lead happy lives in contemporary society.

Martha's views differed from those of her neighbors not only on the issues of abolition and woman's rights but also with regard to organized religion. Although Martha considered herself a Christian, she was accused, she told her sister, of being "infidel" and having "a want of reverence" because of her dislike of orthodox religion, especially church leaders who condoned or ignored slavery and those who used Bible passages to justify the subordination of women.[8] With the coming of the Civil War, Martha's hatred of slavery and her pride in her son's service in the Union army led her to discard her Quaker-taught pacifism and support the war with vehemence. She had earlier abandoned other Quaker constraints and grown to enjoy music, art, and theater, while retaining a strong disapproval of revealing female dress, alcohol and tobacco, and capital punishment.

Martha Wright's letters contain so much detail that numerous historians have used them to reveal to present-day readers the daily lives of nineteenth-century middle-class American women.[9] And they are full of wit. Lucretia

Mott charged that her sister Martha had "cultivated Mirthfulness,"[10] and Elizabeth Cady Stanton wrote that she was "certainly guilty of being a wit."[11]
Martha's sense of humor and her good sense added spice and balance to the
woman's rights movement and make her letters, from which we will quote
generously, a delight to read. Another notable quality of Martha's letters is her
frankness. We suspect that there were other women of her time who were
unhappy to find themselves pregnant in their forties, others who found it
difficult to maintain order with several small children underfoot, others who
became bored with the tedium of daily household chores. But few recorded
their feelings in such detail, or in such a lively and readable manner, as she did.
This biography, like Martha's letters, covers both her public activities in behalf
of woman's rights and abolition and her private activities within her family.

Martha's stance as an ardent abolitionist also makes her correspondence
with her slaveholding relatives in the South of particular interest. During the
Civil War, one brother-in-law served briefly as the Confederate governor of
New Mexico, several nephews fought in the Confederate army, and one became a hero of the South with his exploits at the Battle of Fredericksburg.
Another became a "reconstructed reb" and a Congressman after the war, proud
that some of his father's former slaves had voted for him when he ran for
public office. But Martha's personal interest in the Civil War centered mostly
on one of her sons, an officer in the New York artillery unit that played a
central role at Gettysburg in repelling the famous "Pickett's Charge."

The dramatic life story of Martha C. Wright is interwined with the history
of American reform before, during, and after the Civil War. Her life spanned
the period between the presidencies of Thomas Jefferson and Ulysses S. Grant,
when America experienced relentless and unsettling change, including westward expansion, industrialization, explosive population growth fueled by surg-
ing immigration, and conflict over the "peculiar institution" of slavery. Her life
story shows how various historical events—the War of 1812, the U.S. acquisition of Florida, the opening of the Erie Canal, the growth of the railroads,
the California gold rush, the Fugitive Slave Law, the birth of the Republican
Party, John Brown's raid, and the Civil War and Reconstruction—affected one
middle-class family. It shows how a discerning wife and mother dealt with the
stark contrast between society as she felt it should be and society as it was and
how, armed with the power of laughter, she met challenges and tragedies and

learned how to balance the competition between her public and her private commitments.

In the interest of full disclosure, we should note that we have a personal interest in Martha—she is Jim's great-great-grandmother. During those long hours in various research libraries, this relationship provided an extra impetus to tackle yet another box of papers. Jim took special interest in Martha's later letters, in which she refers lovingly to her granddaughter Mabel, whom he knew many years later as his paternal grandmother. At a separation of four generations, Jim can neither claim credit nor accept blame for any of Martha's opinions or actions, so this family connection should not limit our objectivity as biographers. Any bias we have toward our subject is more likely to arise from the fact that, like Martha, we are feminists and political and religious liberals.

One further point: Martha spent her days moving back and forth between her family and her political obligations. In the morning, after washing, dressing, and feeding her younger children, she may have answered letters from Susan B. Anthony and Elizabeth Cady Stanton on woman's rights issues, written to an older child away at boarding school, made beds, swept the parlor, and prepared some Nantucket corn pudding. In the afternoon, she may have mended clothes for her family, walked to the newspaper office with a notice of the coming antislavery meeting, visited her daughter's home to help with her latest grandchild, and discussed politics and religion over tea with her friend Frances Seward. In the evening, she may have settled an argument between her children, darned socks while listening to her husband, a lawyer, describe his day in court, and drafted a letter to a New York newspaper about woman suffrage. Although our description of Martha's life is roughly chronological, for clarity we separate out the various activities she regularly intermixed. Some chapters, or sections of chapters, focus on her woman's rights or her antislavery activities, while others focus more on her private life and family. To fully appreciate Martha Wright, one of America's feminist foremothers, however, one must understand both her public and her private life.

I

Origins and Influences

Out of Nantucket

MARTHA COFFIN was born in Boston on Christmas Day, 1806. Yet after her death, even her close friends Susan B. Anthony and Elizabeth Cady Stanton mistakenly wrote that she was born in Nantucket.[1] Each probably thought that Nantucket was Martha's birthplace because it was her older sister Lucretia's, and in her adult years, Lucretia Coffin Mott often spoke of how her childhood on the island had developed her interest in abolition and woman's rights. Moreover, all of Martha's siblings were born on Nantucket, as her father, Thomas Coffin, and her mother, Anna Folger Coffin, had been. Thomas and Anna were descendants of two of the men who had settled Nantucket in 1659, Tristram Coffin and Peter Folger. (Anna's grandfather Abisha Folger was a first cousin of Benjamin Franklin's, whose mother was a Nantucket Folger.) Six generations of Coffins and Folgers had lived on the tiny island twenty-five miles south of Cape Cod, Massachusetts, and were imbued with the ideas and values that developed there. So, too, through her parents and siblings, was Martha Coffin Wright.

Within a half century of its founding, Nantucket had become the center of the American whaling industry. Many Nantucket husbands sailed off on whaling or trading expeditions to places as far away as China, which kept them away from home for many months, often for a year or more. While their husbands were away at sea, Nantucket wives were required to maintain their households on their own, and many also operated shops and stores to generate income. So many shops of the village were managed by women that the main street became known as Petticoat Row. Thomas Coffin was a ship captain when he married Anna Folger in 1779, and Anna became one of Nantucket's many female shopkeepers. Like these other women who managed a household and a business during their husbands' long absences, she became an independent, self-reliant woman. Through Anna's example, her daughters, including Martha, grew up with the belief that a woman need not be a helpless, subordinate creature, permanently dependent on the care and protection of a man.[2]

Another important influence on the Coffins and Folgers, including Martha, was the Quaker religion. For several decades after its founding, Nantucket had no organized church; the only religious observances on the island were those of the Wampanoag Indians. But early in the eighteenth century, Mary Coffin Starbuck, the dominant social figure on the island, was converted by a visiting missionary to the Society of Friends, commonly called Quakers. Soon Quakerism became the dominant religion of Nantucket, and the religion of many Coffins and Folgers.[3] The Quaker religion places a strong emphasis on the individual and holds that each person, male and female equally, has an Inner Light that shows the way of God. Thus, historically, Quaker women have played a more important role in church affairs than women in most other religions. Also among the Quaker teachings in the nineteenth century were pacifism, temperance, simplicity in dress, and opposition to slavery. (As early as 1729, Anna Coffin's Folger cousin Benjamin Franklin had published Quaker tracts in Philadelphia against slavery and the slave trade.) These beliefs and values remained with Thomas and Anna Coffin and their family after they moved from Nantucket to Boston in 1804, two years before Martha's birth. As an adult Martha gradually discarded some of these Nantucket Quaker values. Others remained an important part of her character throughout her life, including temperance, a belief in sexual equality, an individualistic approach to religion, and a deep hatred of slavery.

The Coffins' move to the mainland resulted primarily from a disastrous voyage that took a heavy financial and emotional toll on the family. A few years earlier, Thomas had purchased a ship of his own, called the *Trial*, and soon set sail for the Pacific. His ship had rounded Cape Horn and sailed over a thousand miles along the coast of Chile when it was seized by a Spanish man-of-war, charged with "violation of neutrality," forced into the port of Valparaiso, and impounded by the authorities.[4] For many months, Thomas argued his case in Chilean courts, having learned enough Spanish to serve as his own attorney. But his attempts to regain his ship were ultimately unsuccessful. He gave up his case and his ship, crossed east over the Andes into Argentina, and eventually reached Brazil and found passage home. He returned to Anna and his family nearly three years after his departure on the *Trial*. The entire family was pleased when Thomas, probably under the urging of Anna, decided to leave his sailing career behind him and seek a new start in Boston.[5]

Thomas Coffin became a merchant, partnering with an established Boston trader, Jesse Sumner. The firm of Sumner and Coffin sold a wide variety of imported goods, and Thomas soon became successful enough to buy, for the then very substantial sum of fifty-six hundred dollars, a newly built brick house on Round Lane, near the city center.[6] And on Christmas Day 1806, Martha was born, the last of the eight children born to Anna Folger Coffin and the only member of her family born outside of Nantucket. Two daughters had died in infancy, but Martha grew up with four older sisters—Sarah, Lucretia, Eliza, and Mary—and one brother, Thomas.

Boston was not as comfortable an environment for a Quaker family as Nantucket had been. Although over a century had passed since the Puritans had hanged four Quakers in Boston, religious intolerance remained strong.[7] In contrast, Philadelphia had been founded as a Quaker settlement, and Quaker influence still permeated the city. When the opportunity arose in 1809 for Thomas to purchase a factory for the manufacture of cut nails on the outskirts of Philadelphia, he invested all his newly acquired wealth in the project and moved his family there. Martha arrived in Philadelphia when she was only two, and this would be her home for the next fifteen years. Although she was born in Boston and would live most of her adult life in upstate New York, Martha spent her formative childhood years in Philadelphia.

When the Coffins arrived in Philadelphia, Martha's brother, Thomas, and her sisters Eliza and Mary were enrolled in Westtown, a coeducational Quaker boarding school outside the city.[8] The oldest sister, Sarah, about whom little is known, remained at home. Lucretia had for several years been a star pupil at

Nine Partners, a Quaker boarding school in Dutchess County, New York. She had done so well there that at the age of fifteen she had been offered a job as an assistant teacher, a position she had filled with distinction. But she now rejoined her family in Philadelphia and persuaded her father to take into his business a young teacher from Nine Partners named James Mott, of whom she had become very fond. Within a year, Lucretia and James had received parental consent for their engagement and had applied to their Meeting of Friends for permission to marry. They were married in April 1811, with 175 family and friends signing their wedding certificate. The youngest of the signers was four-year-old Martha, who amused the bride and groom at the ceremony with the probing question, "Is this a wedding?"[9]

Yet all was not well in Martha's home. Her father's cut-nail business failed, and he went into debt. A deeper tragedy soon followed; he contracted typhus and died in 1815 at the age of forty-eight. Anna Coffin once again became a shopkeeper and vowed to pay off her husband's debts. Once again, she operated as an independent, self-reliant woman, generating an income and supporting her family on her own. And this time Martha was there. From the age of eight, Martha Coffin grew up in a home in which a woman was the head of the family, and her views on woman's role in society began to crystallize.

Soon after Thomas Coffin's death, Thomas Mott, James and Lucretia Mott's first son, died. He was not yet three. Martha, then ten, had become very fond of her nephew, and the death of her little playmate was a severe shock. Many years later, she wrote, "after little Tommy Mott's death, I would fancy him returned, & wake to disappointment. No one knew how long I mourned that darling child—nor the self reproaches I felt for years, for childish acts of neglect or inattention toward him."[10] (In contrast, we have no found no mention in her letters of her father's death, which occurred shortly after her eighth birthday. Perhaps his business affairs had severely limited the extent of his contact with his youngest daughter.) Martha's immediate family circle continued to grow smaller as other sisters married and left home to start their own families, Eliza with Benjamin Yarnall and Mary with Solomon Temple. Now only Sarah and Martha remained at home with their mother, who had developed a new source of income by turning their large and now emptier home into a boardinghouse. Anna, Sarah, and Martha shared one bedroom, leaving the remainder of the house available to boarders.

Although the Coffins were now dispersed throughout the city, they often gathered in each other's homes for meals and social evenings. In their family discussions, Lucretia had always been the most outspoken and articulate. Now that she had started to raise a family, and particularly after she had lost her first son, she began to read intensively about religion and became intimately familiar with the Bible and the writings of William Penn. In Quaker meetings, Lucretia more and more often found the courage to break the silence and stand up to express herself whenever the spirit moved her. Her wide reading enabled her to support her thoughts with telling quotations, and the members of the meeting became more and more impressed with her calm, clear voice, her simple, unassuming manner, and the spiritual power of her words. In January 1821 she was inaugurated into the ministry of the Society of Friends, an unusual honor for a woman of only twenty-six.[11] Martha had long been in awe of Lucretia's keen intelligence and wide knowledge, and now she had another reason to admire her sister.

In years to come, Lucretia Mott would speak many times a year to audiences far larger than those in her local Quaker meeting house and would eventually become nationally and internationally known as a leader of the antislavery and woman's rights movements. In a woman suffrage convention held a half-century later in New York, Susan B. Anthony introduced Lucretia as "the mother of us all." Today, the U.S. Capitol building contains many sculptures honoring men in American history, but few honoring women. The first to be placed there, carved by Adelaide Johnson, features Susan B. Anthony, Elizabeth Cady Stanton, and a diminutive woman in a prim Quaker cap in front of them both—Lucretia Mott. This position is very suitable, because Lucretia was the leader who inspired them both. But no one was more influenced and inspired by the tiny but powerful Quaker preacher than her youngest sister, Martha.

We know little of Martha's early childhood activities except that she attended the same neighborhood Quaker day school for ten years. Her siblings and Mott and Yarnall nieces and nephews provided plenty of playmates, and as she grew older, she was called on to help her mother at home. The earliest document of record written by Martha herself is a will that she wrote in April 1821, when she was only fourteen.[12] Writing a will is not a typical act of a teenage girl, but the death of her young nephew had made her very aware of human mortality. The document's formal legal language is presumably based on a family will she had seen. "Be it remembered," she wrote, "that I Martha Coffin spinster now sojourning in the city of Philadelphia, the state of Pennsylvania, of sound and well disposing mind, memory and understanding, do make and ordain that my last will and testament in manner and form following, that is to say, first I will that my just debts be paid. Item, I give and bequeath to my sister Sarah the book which is in my trunk entitled 'A Father's Legacy to His Daughters.'"

Also included in Martha's will are her sister Eliza and "brother Benjamin" (Eliza's husband), her sister Mary and "very dear brother Solomon" (Mary's husband), her sister Lucretia (who was bequeathed both love and a basket), and several cousins and friends. Most, like her bedmate and oldest sister, Sarah, then thirty, were left specific items belonging to Martha. But by the age of fourteen, Martha appears to have accumulated very few possessions to distribute to her heirs, so that some, like "brother T.M.C." (Thomas Mayhew Coffin), were bequeathed only love. Her niece Maria Mott, aged three, was to receive a china bird and a small Bible, "hoping she will make a good use of the latter." Maria's sister Anna Mott, aged eight, was pointedly disinherited: "I had intended to have left something to my niece Anna but have recalled it in consequence of a KICK and a PINCH just received from her." Martha's mother and her sister Mary were appointed executors, and the will was duly witnessed by two friends. Forty-three years passed before Martha, then no longer a spinster, wrote another will.

Quaker Schools and the Spirit of Mischief

The Nantucket Quaker values Martha absorbed from her family and from attendance at Quaker meetings were supplemented by the lessons she received during her many years spent in Quaker schools, first in a Philadelphia day school and later at boarding school. Once Anna Coffin had paid off her husband's debts, she could afford to send Martha in 1821 to Westtown, the boarding school outside of Philadelphia Thomas, Eliza, and Mary had attended a decade earlier.[13] Martha's time at Westtown was apparently quite memorable, since letters she wrote as an adult contain many references to her student days there. The education she received at Westtown was probably representative of her education at the Quaker day school in Philadelphia.

Westtown was founded by Philadelphia Quakers in 1799 with the expressed purpose of "creating a hedge" around Quaker children to free them for a time from the immoral influences of Philadelphia, America's largest port. And to Quakers, these "immoral influences" included drinking, fighting, swearing, prostitution and other crimes, as well as theater, dancing, music, fanciful dress, and ostentatious display of any kind. The school also was intended to build within the children a strong Quaker identity and an introspective thoughtfulness that would build their characters and help guide them through life. Their time at Westtown was to be simple and quiet, with much time for silent contemplation. Teachers were sober and committed members of the Society of Friends, serving as examples to the children of a way of life to emulate.

Because of the Quaker emphasis on the individual, independent of sex, Quaker girls had more exposure to education than most other girls in early nineteenth-century America. Westtown School, coeducational from the beginning, enrolled about two hundred students when Martha attended, the youngest of which were nine. There were girls as old as twenty-four, but the boys were no older than sixteen, because older male teens had been found too difficult to discipline. The school building and the entire campus were divided through the middle into "Girls' Bounds" and "Boys' Bounds." Boys and girls were normally in the same room only during the silent Worship Meetings and during meals, when they sat in silence at opposite ends of the room.[14]

Girls and boys nevertheless received the same basic education. The major difference in their curricula was that the girls attended sewing school two weeks out of every six while the boys studied trigonometry and surveying. The subjects all students studied included arithmetic, algebra, geometry, bookkeeping, botany, astronomy, geography, and grammar. Sciences were taught with a focus on observation, in keeping with the Quaker emphasis on the experiential rather than the abstract. Reading was mostly of Biblical extracts, religious poetry, and inspirational and informational nonfiction prose. Students did not read prose fiction or drama and did not study music or art. History was taught sparingly because so much of it tended to dwell on wars and monarchs.

The original library booklist, "Catalogue of Books belonging to Friends Boarding School at Weston," included many Bibles, William Penn's *Call to Christendom*, John Bunyan's *Pilgrim's Progress*, John Milton's *Paradise Lost*, and other titles such as *Power of Religion on the Mind*, *Necessity of Silent Worship*, *Buds and Blossoms of Piety*, and *Fox's Book of Martyrs*.[15] No novels or plays or collections of romantic poetry appear on the list. Students could learn about slavery from *A Poetical Epistle to the Enslaved Africans*, *Cause of the Negroes*, and *Considerations on Keeping Negroes* and about American Indians from *Mission to the Indians of North America* and *Account of a Visit to the Quakers by Pompoonah an Indian Chief*. The Quaker belief in the Inner Light of God within every person led logically to abhorrence of slavery, and the Quakers' own history of being subjected to persecution made them more sensitive than most to the plight of oppressed peoples.[16] A teacher at Westtown, Enoch Lewis, published one of the first abolitionist newsletters in the United States, the *African Observer*.[17]

All students at the school were taught penmanship, a basic and useful skill that many kinds of work required. Indeed Martha developed a beautiful and legible style of writing that makes her letters much easier and more pleasant to read than those of most of her reformist colleagues.[18] Martha also became an avid reader, although as an adult she preferred novels and romantic poetry to religious tracts of the type emphasized at Westtown. Another skill taught at school that Martha used extensively in her adult life was sewing. Her letters refer often to her sewing clothes for her family, by hand in her early married years, later with the help of a machine, suggesting that of her various household chores, it was her favorite—or, perhaps, her least disliked.

Martha described her life at Westtown in a letter she wrote to her husband after a visit to the school in 1871.

it was great fun to see so many familiar things—It is just *half a century* since I was there, but the chambers & meeting room & many things were just as they were, & the prim teachers & plain little girls & the dinner tables & the oaken floors & the very same stairs that I had run up, two steps at a time (not near so wide & imposing as I tho't they were) were all very pleasant to see. . . . It sounded so natural when the teacher said, after all were collected in solemn silence, waiting the signal to go 2 by 2 to dinner, "I shall expect to see the girls that were late, after dinner." I had told her when the girls were collecting, how well I used to like to keep hold of another girl till the very last minute, for the 2nd bell to ring, & then rush to be in time. "I expect so," said she with a grim smile, "they do it yet."[19]

From Martha's adult letters, one can infer that she was a lively young girl, inclined sometimes to test the limits of the school's regulations. Consistent with her unladylike assault on the school's stairs, she recalled that her teachers had criticized her for her "awkward, ungainly, outlandish manner." "The teachers are just as prim & repelling," she reported in another letter after her visit to the school in 1871, "but not half so majestic and awe-inspiring."[20]

Martha also visited Swarthmore College on the same day and reported that Westtown suffered in comparison.[21] "Everything was beautiful in both places," she wrote to her husband, "at Swarthmore however there was life & freedom." "All seemed well & happy—a certain joyous freedom that was lacking at West-town with their narrow orthodox restrictions & limitations."[22] On balance, Martha apparently had pleasant memories of her Quaker boarding school, which she described as "the scene of so many happy and a few unhappy moments."[23] Despite her lifelong love of learning, however, she had resented the rigid regimentation of school. "Schools *are* horrid places," she wrote once to Lucretia, "I never pass one without being glad *I have done going* nor see the little urchins creeping like snails unwillingly to school without rejoicing that I am not one of them—Think of people saying they would willingly live their days over again!!"[24]

Martha recalled exchanging with friends at school her vision of her future, which included a husband and three children, a much smaller family than her mother's (and also a much smaller family than her future would actually hold). She also recalled school-age pranks. In 1841, Martha wrote to Lucretia about meeting one of her old schoolmates, who "looked as if she remembered the dead mouse that Anna & I found & put in her desk."[25] She later accounted for another prank by noting that "people do very childish things sometimes through the promptings of the Spirit of Mischief."[26] The Spirit of Mischief, which never completely left her, may have played a role in her first romance.

In the summer of 1822 Martha, now a lively, inquisitive, and attractive girl, left the protective hedge of Westtown School to return to her mother's boardinghouse in Philadelphia and her mother's more familiar form of Quaker restrictions and limitations. Her time away from home and her interactions with other students may have stimulated the rebellious and adventure-seeking part of her personality. She may have learned more at Westtown than penmanship, sewing, and the "necessity of silent worship." Having experienced the excitement of testing the limits set by her school, she soon found herself testing the limits set by her mother and by her Quaker meeting. A few months after her return from school, during the winter of 1822–23, Martha fell in love with one of Anna Coffin's boarders, a non-Quaker named Peter Pelham.

2

First Love

The War Veteran and the Fair Quakeress

IT WAS an unusual match. Martha, barely sixteen when she fell in love with Captain Peter Pelham, had spent most of her life in Philadelphia. She had been infused both at home and at school with Quaker values, which included pacifism and a strong dislike for the military. Pelham, thirty-seven, was a non-Quaker who had traveled widely and had spent most of his adult life serving in the army. Martha's family was opposed to slavery, while Pelham had been raised on a Kentucky plantation worked by slaves. Perhaps the prospect of leaving the boredom of her daily chores at her mother's boardinghouse and the constraints of her tightly-knit Quaker family and escaping to far-off places with a handsome, well-read, and articulate man appealed to her adventurous and romantic nature—to her "Spirit of Mischief." We do know that they discussed books she borrowed and read from his personal library that were more worldly than the moralistic religious tracts that she had been exposed to at Westtown. (Peter's books included works by Plutarch, Samuel Johnson, and his favorite, Oliver Goldsmith, author of *The Vicar of Wakefield* and the lively comedy *She Stoops to Conquer*.)[1] Whatever the source of the attraction, future events made it clear this was not simply a passing infatuation. Who was this mysterious captain, the first man to win Martha's heart?

Captain Pelham's grandfather and great-grandfather, both also named Peter Pelham, had emigrated together from England to Boston a century earlier.[2] Peter the older was an engraver and portrait painter. He married a widow and helped to train her son, John Singleton Copley, today recognized as the premier artist of colonial America. Peter the younger married Ann Creese and later moved to Williamsburg, Virginia, where he became renowned as a church organist.[3] Their second son, Charles, born in 1748, was Captain Pelham's father.

Charles Pelham had a military bent and served for several years as a midshipman on a British warship.[4] In 1776 he resigned from the British Navy to join the Continental army and saw considerable action in the Revolutionary War as an infantry officer. Captured when the British took Charleston, he was paroled a few months later and went to visit his older brother Peter, who lived in Petersburg, Virginia. There Charles met and courted Isabella Atkinson. He was thirty-seven, and she was eighteen. They married in Caswell County, North Carolina, in 1784, and Peter, the first of their many sons, was born there in December of the following year. Soon thereafter, probably in fall 1786,[5] Charles and Isabella settled permanently in Maysville, Kentucky. For most of their years there, they lived on a plantation along the Ohio River called Cottonwood.[6] There they raised "cotton, corn, tobacco, slaves, and eleven sons and daughters."[7] Of the eleven children, Martha would come to know four sons—Peter and his brothers Atkinson, William, and John.

In his early twenties, Peter lived for some time with an uncle in Boston, and he joined the army in 1812 shortly before President James Madison declared war on England.[8] The boundary between Canada and the United States was the location of much of the action in the War of 1812, which ended inconclusively after two years of bitter conflict. Peter, then a lieutenant in the Twenty-first Infantry, was among the American troops moving east along the Saint Lawrence River in November 1813 with the goal of joining with another American force for an attack on Montreal. At the battle of Crysler's Farm,[9] on the Canadian side of the river about twenty miles northeast of Ogdensburg, New York, Peter Pelham was wounded by a bullet in the upper thigh. Repeating the experience of his father in the Revolutionary War, Peter was captured by the British and paroled two months later as part of a prisoner exchange.

However, his wound, incurred in a nearly forgotten battle in an inconclusive war, left internal injuries from which he never fully recovered.

After his release, Peter was promoted to captain and remained in the army for another eight years. His duties included finding recruits throughout the Northeast and commanding frontier forts in the Great Lakes region. But complications from his battle injury continued to plague him. In the fall of 1820 he traveled south along the Missouri and Mississippi Rivers to St. Louis and later to New Orleans, seeking warmer weather and better medical attention. The following year he was discharged with an invalid pension based on "fatigues and privations on the upper Missouri" and "painful irritation and spasm of the bladder, sphincter, and urethra," the lasting effects of the British bullet that had wounded him at Crysler's Farm.[10] But his experience in dealing with Indians along the northern frontier and his preferred status as a disabled war veteran soon gained him appointment as subagent for Indian affairs in Florida by Secretary of War John C. Calhoun.[11]

Florida had just been acquired from Spain, and there was considerable pressure in Congress to remove the Seminole Indians from the new territory and open it to white settlement. Peter's position required, among other challenges, solving numerous problems concerning blacks enslaved by the Indians such as obstructing their sale to "unauthorized persons."[12] In early 1822, he was stationed in St. Augustine, but by fall he obtained a furlough from the War Department, citing "the precarious state of my health since my arrival in Florida."[13] He sought medical help in Philadelphia, where his younger brother Atkinson was studying at the Jefferson College of Medicine. By the end of the year, Peter had moved in with Atkinson at 44 S. Sixth Street, the rooming house operated by Anna Coffin. There he met her daughter Martha.

Peter's poor health often confined him to his room, and perhaps Anna assigned Martha the task of bringing him food and other necessities. If so, Anna soon regretted it. Peter declared his love for Martha, Martha declared her love for him, and Anna immediately took steps to separate them. Whatever other reservations Anna may have had, marriage to a non-Quaker was strictly forbidden by the rules of their meeting. Peter learned that Martha was being sent away and wrote to her immediately: "I cannot forgive myself for shocking your gentle feelings in the manner they were last night. . . . Suffer me, my dear

Martha, to repeat that I have never loved any woman as I love you & am convinced that I cannot long live after the extinction of the hope of a nearer connection."[14]

Martha was sent to live at her sister Eliza's house several blocks away and was forbidden to see Peter, but he continued to send her books, with secret love letters hidden within the pages, pleading his case. He praised her "beauty united with wit & taste." He assured her, "I have never loved, until I knew you" and "nothing in the world would so effectually secure my happiness as to pass the rest of my days in your society." He countered her family's arguments against him. Admitting Martha's "youth and inexperience," he argued that women mature faster than men, and "they are of course as capable of judging correctly at sixteen as a man is at 20 or 21." Furthermore, he wrote, "there was about the same disparity of age between my own parents, and I have never thought my mother less happy on that account." Aware that his being non-Quaker was the biggest obstacle to the relationship, he offered, "Never having embraced the dogmas or been educated according to the forms of any religious sect, I am simply a Christian, and why then may I not under your instructions adopt the discipline & forms of your society?" Martha put Peter's secret letters in a box she hid up a chimney.

After weeks of enforcing separation, Anna began to allow the couple occasional brief chaperoned meetings. She and other family members liked Captain Peter Pelham. Nonetheless, she continued to oppose the proposed marriage because of Martha's youth and, more important, because of the restrictions against marrying a non-Quaker. Then another complication arose. Maria Spence, whom Peter had met during his stay in Boston when he was only twenty, sent him several letters and agreed to marry him. Although she was ten years older than Peter, in the intervening years he had more than once proposed marriage. She had refused each time, but now she relented. Her letters referred to Martha as "your fair Quakeress" and cautioned him to "take care of how you arrange your ideas of female loveliness lest you should shut out a long-tried friend of yours."[15] When Martha, aware of the letters, released Peter from his commitment to her, he wrote to Maria Spence that after her repeated refusals he felt himself at liberty to form another attachment and pursued his suit with Martha.

While Peter Pelham focused his diplomatic skills on Martha and her family in Philadelphia, the Secretary of War called on him to use them on the Seminole Indians in Florida. In April, Calhoun wrote: "You will consider St. Augustine as your place of residence, to which you will return as soon as the state of your health will permit."[16] In June, he urged Peter's immediate return to Florida "in consequence of the treaty which is proposed to hold with the Indians in the course of the summer."[17] Peter remained in Philadelphia and in so doing lost his job as subagent for Indian affairs in Florida. His lack of employment added a new obstacle to marriage. In September 1823, however, a treaty negotiated with the Seminoles created another opportunity for him,[18] and he traveled to Washington that fall to report an improvement in his health and to seek another position.

The treaty limited the Seminoles to a reservation several miles inland from the Gulf and Atlantic coasts. To offer security to potential settlers army posts would be constructed along the coast. In October Peter Pelham was appointed "sutler"—the official source of provisions—for a fort that was to be located on the shores of Tampa Bay. He was told that the total annual salary of the two hundred soldiers to be stationed there would be over twelve thousand dollars and his trade with them would probably net him an annual profit of at least twenty-five hundred dollars. There was also the prospect of extending his trade to the local Indians and, eventually, to settlers. Peter wrote to Martha in November, "I have exchanged my late place for one 2 or 3 times as profitable."[19] He soon headed south to establish his store at Fort Brooke and his business connections with suppliers in New Orleans, Mobile, and elsewhere.[20]

He wrote to Martha throughout his travels, but these letters were more discreet than his secret love letters of the previous year because he knew that they would be read by Anna Coffin and other members of Martha's close-knit family. In May 1824, however, he ended a letter written from New Orleans with "testimonies of love esteem and affection that I should have expressed to you in person 12 months gone by." On his way north the following October, he wrote to Martha, "I shall unfortunately have but a short time to remain in Philadelphia and sincerely hope you will be prepared to decide agreeably to my desire on the important subject."[21] She was indeed. Their love had survived over a year of separation, Martha was now almost eighteen, and her mother and family no longer objected to her marriage. Peter Pelham and Martha Coffin were married in Philadelphia on November 18, 1824, by a Methodist clergyman.[22] Peter wrote about his wife and her family to his father, Charles, then seventy-six years old and still living in Maysville, Kentucky.

> In my wife you will find a daughter worthy of your esteem and affection—a daughter who will feel for you as well as for my mother the warmest attachment . . . I have the strongest pledge of her being endowed with all the virtues essential in forming an intelligent friend and an amiable wife, capable of appreciating her duties, and competent to the task of discharging them with credit for herself and with honor to my choice. It is highly satisfactory to find that her relations, altho' strict disciplinarians of the Quaker's society, have promptly and cordially given me assurance of their approbation of our union, and to me personally tendered those marks of confidence and esteem which at once assures me that I have not only obtained an inestimable wife, but secured the regard of valuable and affectionate friends.
>
> My dear Martha will leave these relations (including her mother, a brother & two sisters married in this city) and share with me the inconveniences and dangers of a voyage, as well as submit to all the privations attending a first residence in an unsettled country. And when it is recollected how full of ease, and how many enjoyments attend a city life, the place of one's birth [sic] & the abode of one's relations, this is no paltry sacrifice. I am now an inmate in the family of her mother, for whom I already feel the affection of a son, and who gives daily proofs of kindness and liberality in supplying her daughter with every article required to furnish our future home in a style more like a city domicil than a wilderness hut.[23]

Martha was leaving her family and the city of Philadelphia for an army fort on Tampa Bay, where the only residents were two hundred soldiers and a few of the officers' wives. The closest Indian village was ten miles away, and the local wildlife included an abundant supply of insects, spiders, wild hogs, and alligators. Martha indeed faced the promise of a new life in a "wilderness hut" in "an unsettled country," but her first challenge was to survive the "inconveniences and dangers of a voyage" to Florida on a sloop named Hope. Their voyage turned out to be more inconvenient and more dangerous than Peter and Martha had expected.

Shipwreck of Hope

The *Hope* carried Martha and Peter to Florida, along with the goods they had assembled for their new home, plus goods intended for sale to the soldiers at Fort Brooke. But the *Hope* never reached Tampa Bay. One night off the Florida coast, the ship ran aground in the shallow waters surrounding a small offshore island and began to take in water. Peter later wrote his brother, "Martha retains her cheerfulness under all disappointments, and actually exhibited more calmness and self-possession in the trying moments, I may say hours of our danger, than any person on board. It was midnight when our vessel filled, and we were driven from the cabin to the Quarter deck where we sat until daylight."[24]

When morning came, passengers and crew abandoned the sloop and waded to the island, where they were forced to wait for two weeks, sleeping under tents, until rescued. Although Peter and Martha completed their journey to Fort Brooke on a small boat, most of their furniture, clothing, and other goods were damaged in the shipwreck. It was not an auspicious start for their new life together. In her adult years, Martha would refer to the trip as her "Sinbad voyage" and would recall feeling a "spirit of adventure." But the young bride who left the city of Philadelphia and friends and family behind must have had a few moments, while lying under a tent on that isolated island off the coast of Florida, when she questioned the wisdom of what she had done.

The next blow, not unexpected, arrived in the form of a letter to Martha from the Philadelphia Monthly Meeting of Friends, dated January 7, 1825. Since "thy marriage was accomplished contrary to the order of our discipline, and by the assistance of an hireling minister, thou canst not, consistently therewith, be continued in religious membership, unless thou should believe it thy duty to condemn the act, and canst do so to the satisfaction of the meeting."[25] In Quaker parlance, any non-Quaker minister, receiving pay, was considered a "hireling minister." Quaker "discipline" included four main causes for expulsion—drunkenness, fighting, fornication, and "marrying out of meeting."[26] It took some months for this letter to reach the remote outpost at Tampa Bay, but Martha's April reply was succinct: "I do not feel willing to condemn the act of which you speak, but can truly say that I have much regretted the existence of a rule admitting of but one alternative."[27] Martha's expulsion from her family's religious group, for the simple act of following her heart and marrying a non-Quaker, contributed to her lifelong aversion to the prescripts and dogmas of organized religion.

How did Martha enjoy her early married life at the frontier fort on Tampa Bay? No letters of hers from Tampa Bay seem to have been preserved. But letters she wrote more than forty years later when one of her sons contemplated moving to Florida report conflicting memories. "During my residence in Florida," she wrote in one letter, "I enjoyed the escape from conventionalities that continually interfere with ones freedom of action."[28] Throughout her life, Martha resented restrictions on her "freedom of action." In other letters she referred to Florida as "that dismal spider & scorpion country" and recalled, "The Winters are delightful, but the annoyance of swarms of fleas & mosquitos all the year round & cockroaches in your chambers & in your food, without the greatest care, made it anything but pleasant to me as a permanent residence."[29]

Shortly after arriving at Tampa Bay, Martha learned that she was pregnant. By May, she had left Peter in the Florida wilderness and returned to her family in Philadelphia to prepare for the birth of their baby. Despite their very limited funds, Martha was accompanied on this return voyage by a servant named Sarah. Sarah became ill while they were at sea, however, and died soon after they arrived in New York, her death attributed to yellow fever. Martha reported Sarah's illness and death to Peter, whom she addressed as "my dear Pelham," in a letter from New York. If she was afraid of contracting yellow fever from Sarah, she did not say so in her letter.[30]

Martha had also been accompanied on her journey by a pet flying squirrel named Puss. About "little Puss," she wrote, "He was very well satisfied with his accommodations on board the vessel and was not incommoded by the motion, except when he had fixed himself at the foot of the berth with a nut and the vessel would roll and make him tumble over. It appeared to him very incomprehensible. He was very good and slept in the berth with me all the time."[31] No letters survive that describe how Anna Coffin responded when her daughter arrived in Philadelphia accompanied by a flying squirrel.

Once again at home, Martha wrote loving letters to her husband, lamenting her separation from him and noting that "somehow it is pleasanter to wake and find thee by me."[32] As the time for her delivery approached and it was not clear when Peter could join her, she wrote, "The thought of being absent from thee another month is almost insupportable. . . . O how I long to see thee— to dream of being with thee and then awake and find it but a dream is very tantalizing. Come to me, my love."[33] To one letter, she added a postscript: "Do be careful of thy health, my love, and don't go into the river at Tampa. I lay awake an hour the other night thinking of alligators."[34]

Peter's letters to Martha during this second separation were also loving, but they became more and more filled with poor reports on his health and on his business. He was growing disheartened with "chicanery and extortion," "the deception, knavery, envy, dissimilation and falsehood of the trading world," and "the designing, narrow minded, selfish and avaricious herd."[35] He complained about sharks and alligators and "legions of mosquitoes." In July, he was in "low spirits & infirm health" and was finding it impossible to locate a vessel going north to allow him to be with Martha in time for the birth of their baby. On August 26, he wrote from Pensacola that he had finally attained passage on a ship leaving for New York, but on that same day, over a thousand miles away, Martha gave birth to Mary Anna Pelham. By the time Peter reached Martha, Mary Anna (Martha would later change the spelling to Marianna) was already a month old. The baby's name combined the names of Martha's mother, Anna, and Martha's married sister Mary Coffin Temple, who had died at the age of twenty-four the previous summer. (Her oldest sister, Sarah, had died from a fall the same year, leaving Martha with just two surviving sisters—Lucretia Mott and Eliza Yarnall.)

The Pelhams, now a family of three, sailed back to Tampa Bay, this time uneventfully. But Peter's health and his business continued to deteriorate. The lingering effects of his wounds from the War of 1812, the strains of much travel, and the climate and "legions of mosquitoes" in Florida probably all contributed to his death in Pensacola on July 10, 1826. Martha was only nineteen, a new mother, and far from the comfort of her family. Peter's death after less than two years of marriage was a shock from which she never fully recovered. Throughout her life, martial music would bring tears to Martha's eyes, arousing memories of her brief life on an isolated army base with Peter Pelham, her first husband and her first love.

Martha reported Peter's death to his brother Atkinson, expressing regret that she had traveled to Philadelphia the previous year, thereby being separated from her husband for almost a third of their short married life. Atkinson, who by then had completed his medical studies and moved to North Carolina, assured her that Peter had wanted her to have her baby in Philadelphia. He added, "The death of my affectionate brother would, at any time, grieve me, and I feel it the more on your account, your situation must have been unhappy beyond description—left alone without one kind friend to aid or assist you in the least."[36] Martha would continue to correspond with Atkinson, and with other relatives of Peter's, for many years.

A few days before Peter's death, on the fiftieth anniversary of the signing of the Declaration of Independence, America lost two of its founding fathers, Thomas Jefferson and John Adams. Adams's son, John Quincy Adams, was then President, despite having received in 1824 fewer popular votes and fewer electoral votes than Andrew Jackson. None of the candidates had won an electoral majority, and the election moved into the House of Representatives, where Henry Clay threw his support behind Adams. Jackson was furious, and in July 1826 was already hard at work campaigning to unseat Adams in the next election. America was on the threshold of a new era, and Martha was on the threshold of a new adventure.

In September, Martha sailed back to Philadelphia on a voyage plagued with bad weather that took over a month. One night, off Cape Hatteras, the ship was discovered to have sprung a leak that flooded the cargo hold and required many hours to plug. The next night they encountered a severe thunderstorm during which several sailors on deck received shocks when lightning struck the ship. The captain later told Martha that if they had not discovered the leak before the storm, "we should not have seen another day."[37] When they finally came within sight of New York, the wind was so strong and the waves so high that they were forced to remain at sea for five days until the storm subsided and a pilot could come on board to take them into port. With Martha's earlier shipwreck, and with her knowledge of the close call off Cape Hatteras, those five days on a ship tossing and turning in an angry sea must have been a very frightening time for the young widow holding a baby in her arms.

During this long and unsettling journey, Martha was comforted by the company of a young army lieutenant named Julius Catlin, who was returning north after a tour of duty in Arkansas Territory. One of the officers at Tampa Bay had written to Catlin and described Martha as "a lady of no common stamp. Her mind of the highest order naturally is well cultivated and refined. Her disposition is tempered by all the virtues which serve to render the other sex so accessory to our happiness and comfort. She left at Tampa many friends, among them myself and wife, who felt much interested in her welfare."[38] Lieutenant Julius Catlin apparently developed a strong bond with Martha during their journey north. He was destined to become the next chapter in Martha's romantic life.

3

Dawn in Aurora

ALTHOUGH MARTHA was born in Boston, grew up in Philadelphia, and lived briefly in Florida, she spent most of her life as a resident of upstate New York. She first moved to New York, to the tiny village of Aurora on the east shore of Cayuga Lake, one of the largest of New York's Finger Lakes, in November 1827. This region had earlier been home to the Cayugas, one of the Six Nations of the Iroquois Confederacy. But the Iroquois had sided with the British during the Revolution, and soon after the war most of them departed to Canada or were confined to reservations. This exodus opened central and western New York State to settlement, a process greatly accelerated by the opening in 1825 of the Erie Canal linking the Hudson River and Lake Erie and providing easy transportation between the Atlantic coast and the region today called the Midwest. This region of New York also became known as the "burned-over district" because of the proliferation of religious movements, experimental utopian communities, and reform activities that occurred there in the antebellum years.[1] In Seneca Falls, a city not far from Aurora, Martha would later make her own contribution to the reputation of the district as a center for reform.

Many of the early settlers in the Finger Lakes region were Quakers, and a

Quaker school for girls that became known as Brier Cliff had been established in Aurora in 1815. Anna Coffin left Philadelphia to take over management of the school early in 1827.[2] The village of Aurora, named after the Roman goddess of the dawn, had only a few hundred residents in 1827 (and is not much more populous today, discounting the students at Wells College). Martha reported her move to Aurora in a letter to her father-in-law, Charles Pelham.

> About a year since my mother very unexpectedly concluded to remove here, to take the superintendence of an old established school; my cousin, Miss Bunker, who taught school in Philadelphia, came with her as principal teacher. After remaining in Philadelphia long enough to acquire a knowledge of drawing and painting, with a view of taking that branch of instruction, I left there and arrived here in November last accompanied by my brother-in-law, Mr. Mott, who returned immediately to Philadelphia. My time is now fully occupied with attending to painting in the morning and to writing in the afternoon. Knowing that it is necessary that I should do something towards my own support and that of my little girl, reconciles me to the confinement here, and separation from my sisters and most of my friends.[3]

Martha went on to describe teaching as "an occupation that I exceedingly dislike" and, furthermore, "I do not think I can bear the confinement of a school many years." To Peter's brother Atkinson, she wrote, "You ask if I take pleasure in teaching. To tell the '*real truth*' I take not the least—but as it is a duty, I can submit to it with a tolerably good grace." She admitted, however, that her duties were light compared with those of her cousin Rebecca Bunker, who was the primary teacher at the school. Rebecca's job required "instilling knowledge into those heads whose thickness renders an over abundance of patience necessary," whereas she had only "to attend to painting in the morning and writing in the afternoon, and as none paint but those who have an inclination or talent for it, I find it no difficult task, and any goose, let her head be of what thickness it may, can learn to write, for that requires no talent." She admitted, however, that teaching one of her painting students "might be a delightful task if she were not preeminently dull and unteachable."[4]

About fifty girls were enrolled in the school each year, but some for only part of the year, so that there were seldom more than thirty in attendance at any one time. Anna Coffin's account book for the school records that one father donated a horse in lieu of the standard eighty-five-dollar fee for one year's board and tuition.[5] Also recorded were the day in the spring when the school's cows were let out to pasture and the day when they were brought in for the winter. The name Martha Pelham appears on numerous pages, usually for the purchase of painting supplies, once for purchase of shoes for herself ("$1.50") and for Marianna ("62½¢").

About her new location, Martha wrote Atkinson that "Aurora is not Philadelphia!!—*by a jugfull*—yet I believe I like it tolerably well." She had, she said, a "larger circle of acquaintances than I had there, and visit more than I ever did." But, "Last winter was horrible . . . the mud was two yards deep, poetically speaking, and there was consequently an embargo on every house. If it should be so this winter I will not stay another but will blow away."[6]

Ill-Fated Artist

In September 1828, Martha received a visit from Julius Catlin, the young man who had accompanied her on her return trip from Florida after her husband's death. Through correspondence, Julius had maintained regular contact with her since, and their relationship had grown to the point that they wished to become engaged. Only part of one of his letters to Martha has been preserved. It ends with, "Believe me my friend, you are constantly remember'd in fondest wishes and *hopes*."[7]

Like Peter Pelham, Julius Catlin had been a military man. He graduated from West Point in 1824 and received an appointment as a second lieutenant in the First U.S. Infantry. After spending two years' duty on a fort in Arkansas Territory, he resigned from his commission to pursue portrait painting.[8] Julius greatly admired his older brother George, who had already achieved success as a portrait painter and urged his brother to try to do the same. In those days before cameras or daguerreotypes, skilled portraitists were much in demand. Julius was an aspiring artist when he met Martha on that long voyage north, and it seems likely that Martha's decision to study painting when she returned to Philadelphia was influenced by their shipboard conversations.

George Catlin yearned to travel west to paint Indians of different tribes in their own habitats. He encouraged Julius to go with him, for Julius had become interested in Indians during his military assignment in Arkansas. George would eventually make painting and writing about American Indians his life's work; a large collection of his Indian portraits is on display today at the Smithsonian Institute in Washington, D.C. Julius, however, would not accompany him on his trips West. Nor would his plans to marry Martha come to fruition.

In September 1828, Julius set out for Rochester, New York, to deliver a portrait his brother George had painted of New York Governor DeWitt Clinton to the Franklin Institute of Rochester. On his way to Rochester, Julius stopped in Aurora to give Martha some unpleasant news. Although he had done successful portraits of a growing number of people, he had so far found it difficult to generate much income. Because of his very limited financial means, his father did not approve of his plans to wed a young widow and assume the responsibility of supporting her and her two-year-old child. Julius was told to wait until his financial situation was more secure; the engagement must be put on hold. Martha's mother had similar reservations. After informing Martha of his father's decision, Julius continued on to Rochester to deliver his brother's painting, but promised to return to Martha in three weeks to discuss their future options.

Five days later, however, an article appeared in the *Rochester Daily Advertiser* under the heading "An Ill-Fated Artist." "Considerable excitement was produced here yesterday," it announced, "by the sudden death of a young gentleman named Julius Catlin, brother of the celebrated artist of that name." Julius had been sketching a waterfall from the edge of the Genesee River, which ran north through Rochester and into Lake Ontario. According to a witness, Julius had descended the steep banks into the river for a swim but soon thereafter called for help and disappeared under the fast-moving waters. His body was carried far downstream and was found only after a long search. The article concluded: "The inquest, after a protracted investigation, returned a verdict of death by drowning. Mr. Catlin was educated mostly, we understand, at West Point, was an intelligent and accomplished gentleman, and proficient in the Arts in which his brother is such a distinguished master. His untimely death, falling literally a martyr to his favorite study, in the very rigour of manhood, has created a deep sensation through the village."[9] Julius Catlin was buried in Rochester with no friend or family at his funeral. The sad occasion inspired a young man in Rochester to write a poem, "The Stranger's Burial," which was published in another Rochester paper.[10]

Martha heard the news several days later and just two years after the death of Peter Pelham. She immediately wrote a note of condolence to Julius's sister Mary.

Aurora Oct. 5th, 1828

My dear friend,

Although a stranger to you, permit me to address you by this title, in assuring you of my participation in your sorrow for the loss of an affectionate brother, of whose sudden and most unfortunate death I have this moment been informed.

His kindness to me in affliction, when almost a stranger to me, and his subsequent attentions during an unpleasant voyage, endeared him to me, and this unlooked for intelligence deeply affected me, for I have felt for him the affections of a sister, and as such let me again assure you of my sincere sympathy.

On the 17th of Sept. he spent about two hours with me, and left with the expectations of returning at the expiration of three weeks. I had begun to look for him when the paper containing the melancholy account was this morning handed me.

You will not, I trust, consider this letter as an intrusion, but believe me, Mary, very sincerely

Your friend
Martha C. Pelham[11]

Martha's letter to Mary crossed in the mails with a letter to Martha from Julius's father, Putnam Catlin, who made it clear that Julius's family were well aware that Martha's relationship with Julius involved more than "the affections of a sister." He wrote: "In the convulsive agonies of grief for this irreparable loss to them, the parents, brothers, and sisters of that most amiable and ill-fated youth desire the sympathy of your friendly and most feeling heart on this solemn occasion. From the frank statement of the lamented deceased, they have long known the origin and the sincerity of his attachment to you, & they hope you will continue to cherish the remembrance of one so dear to them."[12] She did. Martha lamented Julius's death throughout her life and continued corresponding with Putnam Catlin and with Mary Catlin Hartshorne for many years. Putnam's later letters were full of pride in the growing public interest in George Catlin's exhibits of his Indian paintings. Martha maintained an interest in George's career but apparently never met him.

A few months after Julius's death, Martha visited the Catlins in Montrose, Pennsylvania, and later wrote to Mary about her homeward trip to Aurora by stagecoach. At one stop, she wrote, they exchanged their "good horses for four snails, with which we went on a moderate creep to Ithaca." The road from Ithaca to Aurora along the bank of Cayuga Lake was very uneven, and she reported being "well pounded" from the "jolting of the stage." Martha added, "I could not help laughing once to find myself very comfortably and gently seated on the straw in the bottom of the stage."[13] This occasion provides an apt metaphor. Martha's readiness to laugh in the midst of misfortune helped to ease the pain of her life's many "bumps along the road."

Mr. Wright

The archives of the Village of Aurora contain a small, thin, and worn diary of an unidentified student at Brier Cliff School, covering only ten days of August 1829 and two weeks in the summer of 1830.[14] The 1830 entries record a visit to Aurora by Lucretia Mott and her attendance at Quaker meetings with her mother and, on one occasion, with her sister Martha. The entries for August 1829 indicate that the student was studying writing with Martha that summer. On the eighth, she wrote, "We had five compositions one was in poetry and was Mrs. Pelhams which was very pleasing." Several other entries that week report "Mrs. Pelham quite pleasant." But the entry for August 5, 1829, is of special importance. On that day, the student recorded, "M Pelham and

D Wright went to take a walk." Martha's walking companion that day was a young law student she had met in Aurora in June named David Wright. Within a few months after this diary entry, they were married.

David Wright, who was born in Bucks County, Pennsylvania, grew up there and was educated for several years at a Quaker school in the village of Fallsington, a few miles from his father's home. Although he and his father, Amos Wright, were not Quakers, his mother, Elizabeth Pennington, who died when David was still an infant, had been a member of the Society of Friends. David was very familiar with Quaker teachings because he had been required at school to attend weekly Quaker meetings. In writing a brief autobiography late in his life, he declared, "I have ever believed that it was, and yet is, the most reasonable, and the best for the welfare of the individual and of the community, of any of the many forms of faith and practice."[15]

After leaving school, David worked for a while at his father's farm and tried several trades, including carpentry, milling, and tanning. None of these trades appealed to him as a life's work. After a visit to an uncle in the Finger Lakes region, he decided that this rapidly developing area held more promise for him than Bucks County. In 1826, with twenty-five dollars in his pocket, he left Pennsylvania and traveled north on the Hudson River from New York City to Albany on a barge towed behind a steamboat. From Albany, he traveled west on the Erie Canal, which had just opened the previous year. He reports in his autobiography, "I came very near being finally stopped in my career while on the canal-boat." At one of the many low bridges over the canal, David did not hear the steersman's traditional warning, "Bridge ahead!"[16] He was struck on the head by the bridge timber and knocked down. The blow was so severe that other passengers feared he had been killed, but he survived without serious injury, and continued on to a village near Aurora.

David started as a clerk in a country store. He later worked with the engineer corps constructing the Cayuga and Seneca Canal that linked the two lakes, and when the canal was completed, became a teacher in the district school. But he finally found work that suited him when he left the school in the spring of 1829, at the age of twenty-three, and took a job in a law office in Aurora, with the expectation of becoming a lawyer.[17] Soon he met Martha and fell in love with the attractive young widow with a four-year-old daughter.

The courtship lasted five months. (Years later, when their twelve-year-old daughter Eliza learned this, she said, "that all! I should want to be acquainted with a man longer than that, *six months at least*.")[18] With no objections from Anna Coffin, David and Martha were married by a justice of the peace in Aurora on November 18, 1829, five years to the day after her first marriage.[19] This marriage lasted until Martha's death in 1875.

The couple lived for a while at Brier Cliff School, but soon, with nearly a thousand dollars of Martha's, largely from Peter Pelham's estate, and some help from Anna Coffin, they purchased and furnished a small house on a one-acre lakeshore lot containing an apple orchard. Located near the north end of the village, the property was just a short walk from the school.[20] This house was to be their home for the next ten years and the birthplace of Eliza in 1830 and Matthew Tallman (later called just Tallman) in 1832. David continued his study of law, working under established local lawyers, but with little income. He and Martha tended a vegetable garden, purchased a cow to provide milk, and kept bees for honey. In late 1832, on the basis of three and a half years of apprentice law practice, David was admitted to the bar and gradually began to build up his own law practice and his income. But Martha would later look back at their early marriage years as some of the most difficult years of her life.

David's law business started to take him away on frequent trips, but he and Martha communicated regularly through letters, in which they expressed their loneliness. David wrote, "You cannot imagine my anxiety & desire to be with you or rather to have you with me. I almost continually think of you & the children."[21] Martha responded:

> You complain of feeling lonely, in a crowd, surrounded by the gaieties of a city, how then do you suppose I now feel, the children all asleep, mother gone to meeting . . . I sometimes find myself, in the stillness of the evening, giving way to gloomy forebodings, which it requires a considerable effort to dispel . . . but I had not anticipated that you would feel lonely, for I thought your mind would be so much occupied with constant change of scene during your absence that you would scarcely send a wish or thought after me, but you do, my love, don't you?"[22]

She reported eagerly waiting for the stagecoach hoping that it might bring a letter from him. When David was returning from a business trip on the steamboat that regularly plied the lake, she would listen with anticipation for the ringing of its bell. Friends were surprised that Martha was not afraid to sleep in the house without a man present. She told David, "It is only those who have never known *real terror* who yield to the influence of imaginary ones."[23]

Despite such brave statements, Martha suffered during David's absences, particularly during the Aurora winters when severe weather confined her and the children to the cramped quarters of their small house. After her mother returned to Philadelphia in 1832, she felt even more isolated. Now her mother, brother, and sisters were all many miles away, and Martha deeply missed the companionship of her close-knit family. In November 1833, she and Marianna traveled to Philadelphia for a visit of two months, staying with James and Lucretia Mott. The rest of the family was left in the care of David's sister Sarah, about whom, David wrote to Martha, "between ourselves she is not the best cook in the world but a very cheap one." With regard to her skill with Eliza and Tallman, he said, "I doubt Sarah's being a first rate hand to manage such creatures."[24]

While Martha was away in Philadelphia, David's letters made it clear that her presence was keenly missed. "I guess you won't want to be absent another winter, however often I may be called away, or however long I may stay . . . life at best is but short, and the company of those we loved is the sweetest joy known in that short time, then why should we not enjoy each other's society as much as possible."[25] "I was not aware before of how much I loved you Dearest, but your absence leaves such a blank in my existence. . . . [H]ow very pleasant it is to love and be beloved."[26] His letters were often written over several evenings, and each entry ended with "Good night my Love" or "Good night Dearest."

One of David's letters outlined their financial situation. In 1833, his income was over $2,000, while their expenses were $1,090, with $368 for professional expenses, $370 for family expenses, $252 for house and grounds, and $100 for her journey to Philadelphia. He estimated their property as worth at least $3,000, his law library $300, and other personal property $400. He gave further details, probably considerably more detail than most husbands gave their wives at that time, but warned "the above is for your own satisfaction, please be *very* careful who sees it or hears it as it is our own *private* affairs."[27] Comparison of 1830s dollars with current dollars has its pitfalls, but their overall purchasing power was over twenty times that of current dollars. This is the last year for which such a detailed overview of their family finances is available. As David's law business grew, his income appears to have increased substantially, probably doubled, but family expenses similarly increased. The Wrights eventually became a comfortable middle-class family, able to afford household help and send their children to boarding schools, but never accumulated substantial wealth.

Martha's letters to David from Philadelphia were filled with enthusiastic descriptions of happy family gatherings and excursions, though she wrote that she could not "help feeling anxious away from so many who are dear to me."[28] And she complained about Lucretia, who was fourteen years older and accustomed to controlling her youngest sister's behavior. Martha "had a great desire" to go to the theater to see Fanny Kemble, then a very popular actress, but after mentioning it to Lucretia, "I had to haul in my horns she made such a fuss." Lucretia maintained her Quaker displeasure over other frivolities, including such a slight departure from plain dress as a colored handkerchief. Martha reported to David that Lucretia "was so dissatisfied with my red handkerchief that she insisted on presenting me with a white one . . . I have no objections, as long as the expense is not mine, to being *friendified* to their heart's content."[29] Although no longer a Friend, and now a twenty-seven-year-old married woman and mother of three, Martha bowed to Lucretia's wishes and submitted to being "friendified" while she was a guest in her home.

By this time, Lucretia had become widely recognized as a very effective preacher and was often invited to distant Quaker meetings to present her sermons. Although she was more pious than Martha, the two women had similar basic views toward religion despite very different degrees of outward practice. The Quakers had split into two main factions, the Orthodox and the Hicksites, the latter inspired by a stirring preacher named Elias Hicks. Over the years, Orthodox Quakers had more and more emphasized the importance of the divinity of Jesus and the inspiration of the Scriptures, but to Hicks, it was the "Inner Light" emphasized by the early Quakers that was most important, and the literal truth of the Bible was secondary. Many other issues were involved in the controversy, including the authority and power of church elders. Lucretia had admired Hicks from the time she had heard him preach at Nine Partners School during her student days. Like Hicks, she felt strongly that religion was a very individual matter that came from within and should not be directed by church authorities. With regard to such concepts as the virgin birth, miracles, and the resurrection of Jesus, Lucretia liked to quote from William Penn: "Men are to be judged by their likeness to Christ, rather than their notions of Christ."[30] To Orthodox elders, such a statement was almost blasphemous, despite its source. They felt that one's "notions of Christ" should adhere strictly to the text of the New Testament. When the situation within Lucretia's Quaker meeting required taking a stand, both she and her husband, James, sided with the Hicksites.

Martha's other sister, Eliza Yarnall, remained firmly Orthodox, as did most of the other Yarnalls. Eliza's mother-in-law, disturbed by Martha's interest in attending the theater and her generally liberal attitude, said to her, "Martha dear, I want thee to remember that we never can be happy without religion." Martha responded, "most people were agreed on that point, the difficulty with them appeared to be in what constituted religion."[31] Even more strongly than Lucretia, Martha felt that religion was a very individual matter and should not be based on dogma, even the dogma of a relatively liberal church like the Society of Friends. She subscribed fervently to one of Lucretia's favorite sayings, "Take Truth for authority, not authority for Truth." If Martha had not married "out of meeting" and had remained a Quaker, she would surely have been a Hicksite.

Another issue that divided the Orthodox and Hicksite Quakers was activism on social issues, including the hottest issue of the day, slavery. Quakers had eliminated slavery within their own ranks in the previous century, and for most Orthodox Quakers, that was enough. Hicks, however, felt that slavery was a grievous sin, and that its presence in America should not be ignored. Lucretia also had grown to abhor slavery, and had started to preach against it. Martha's days of social activism were still ahead of her, but her visit to Lucretia that year exposed her to the most controversial reform movement of the time, abolitionism.

4

Philadelphia Story

The Lion and the Jackals

MARTHA WRIGHT'S 1833 visit to Philadelphia coincided with the founding meeting of the American Anti-Slavery Society.[1] As the guest of James and Lucretia Mott, Martha had her first direct exposure to the moral fervor of William Lloyd Garrison and other leaders of the growing abolitionist movement. James and Lucretia had earlier become enthusiastic participants in the movement.

In the first decades of the nineteenth century, many antislavery reformers had focused on the idea of "colonization." The American Colonization Society, formed in 1816, financed the purchase of slaves from their owners and the emigration of the freed blacks to a colony in West Africa that later became the nation of Liberia. But even though the slave trade to the United States had ceased by 1808, as prescribed by the Constitution, the slave population in the country continued to increase, and the development of the cotton industry made slavery more and more important to the economy of the South. By 1830, Garrison had become convinced that the only solution to the problem of slavery in America was abolition—the immediate emancipation of all slaves.[2] In the following year, he began publishing the *Liberator*, an uncompromising weekly journal devoted to promoting of the abolition of slavery. In his first issue, he stated, "I do not wish to think, or speak, or write, with moderation. . . . I am in earnest—I will not equivocate—I will not excuse—I will not retreat a single inch—AND I WILL BE HEARD."[3] And he was, attracting many supporters, but also many detractors, not all of whom were in the South. In 1832 he formed the New England Anti-Slavery Society, and in 1833 he chose Quaker Philadelphia as the site for the formation of a national society.

At an early age, Martha had developed a deep hatred of slavery. Before this visit to Lucretia's, however, she appears to have devoted little thought to the relative merits of competing approaches to solution of the problem. On December 5, Martha wrote to David about "a Convention that was to meet here for the purpose of forming a society favorable to immediate emancipation and opposed to Colonization . . . Sister L. called on Wm Lloyd Garrison *the* great man the lion in the Emancipation cause and invited him to tea here . . . innumerable jackals were also invited. Yesterday was spent in preparation— there were about 50, counting our own family."[4] About Garrison, "the lion," Martha wrote, "I had always supposed he was a coloured brother but he isn't." The "jackals" were Garrison's followers in attendance at the party, and they included both black and white supporters of abolition. For the event, Lucretia had placed on her center table an "imposing array of Anti Slavery pamphlets," including one "representing a coloured woman rampant [actually kneeling, hands clasped and chained] and the words 'Am I not a woman & a sister.' " This was a feminine variation on the more usual image on anti-slavery pamphlets of a black man in chains with the message, "Am I not a man and a brother?"[5]

The Motts' home that week was the center of many antislavery discussions, and some visitors tended to dominate the conversation. In response to the "profound conversation" of one man, Martha reported that she "dispensed the proper quantity of assenting nods, all the time thinking Sister L's 'indeeds' and 'possibles' quite supererogatory."[6] Although Martha's formal education ended at fifteen, her letters reveal an extensive vocabulary, presumably a result of her wide reading.

"The Convention met yesterday to organize themselves," Martha wrote, adding, "no females present." But that was remedied the next day, when "just as I had seated myself to commence this letter," an abolitionist "came to say that he and others were dispatched to invite 'the women' to meet with the

Convention, and Mother Sister L. and Anna [Mott] quickly clapped on their bonnets to accept the gallant invitation. Mother urged me to accompany them, thinking my poor letter of no consequence but I thought I should enjoy myself more with you than with them." However, Martha did "clap on her bonnet" later and attend sessions of the convention, "which I found quite interesting . . . For two evenings there has been a public controversy or rather discussion between a Colonization advocate and an anti Colonization. I attended and became interested in the course of the debate, tho' as the intentions of both appear good, I feel indifferent which succeeds."[7] This visit to Philadelphia, however, would soon turn her into a committed abolitionist, like her sister Lucretia.

Later that week Martha attended a meeting where Samuel J. May, a Unitarian from Connecticut, "delivered an address in favor of immediate & unconditional emancipation. Setting aside the merit of his cause of which I don't pretend to judge, it was the most beautiful discourse I ever heard and beautifully delivered."[8] May would later accept a Unitarian pulpit in Syracuse, New York, providing Martha and David many opportunities to hear and meet with him over the years. He would remain one of Martha's favorite speakers on reform issues, including temperance and woman's rights, in addition to abolition, and would later preside at the wedding of one of her daughters.

David Wright, although strongly antislavery, was initially in favor of colonization. Martha continued to declare herself "neutral—willing to hear either side provided they don't talk too long."[9] Her enthusiastic response to May's lecture suggests, however, that he, Garrison, the Motts, and other abolitionists Martha encountered during that visit to Philadelphia had begun to win her over. Perhaps particularly convincing were the black abolitionists she met at Lucretia's, who were firmly against colonization. Most had spent their entire lives in the United States and had no interest in being transported to Africa. Before long, both David and Martha were committed abolitionists, actively involved in the movement, even to the extent of assisting fugitive slaves.

Few Americans, even in the North, where slavery was not the integral part of the economy and culture that it was in the South, supported the cause of abolition in the 1830s. Belief in black inferiority was widespread, Northern business was very dependent on trade with the South, and even Northerners who were troubled by slavery feared that calling for its abolition would break up the Union. The U.S. Constitution had recognized slavery and even gave states extra representation based on their slave population through the notorious "three-fifths clause."[10] The nation had been held together since then only by a series of delicate political compromises between the slave states and the free states, and Garrison's *Liberator* clearly did not preach compromise. He not only attacked slave traders and slave owners, he attacked anyone who supported colonization. In 1835 a crowd of anti-abolitionists in Boston seized Garrison and nearly lynched him. Anti-abolition mobs included men of all social classes and were often led by prominent citizens.[11] Two years later, an abolitionist editor in Illinois, Elijah Lovejoy, was shot and killed trying to defend his printing press from an angry mob. The Motts themselves barely escaped violence the following May in Philadelphia. A crowd of many thousands, incensed by the sight of black and white women meeting together at an antislavery convention, burned down the building in which the meeting had been held and raced through the streets looking for abolitionists' homes to attack. Fortunately, a friend misdirected the mob and the Motts and their home were spared.[12] Although Martha was not in Philadelphia at the time, she too would face angry mobs at future antislavery conventions.

Extended Family

Many of the fifty people who attended Lucretia Mott's 1833 tea party for Garrison were, as Martha described them, "our own family." They included Anna Coffin, Lucretia and James Mott, Eliza and Benjamin Yarnall, Martha and her brother Thomas, Marianna and several of the Mott and Yarnall children, and numerous Coffin, Folger, Mott, and Yarnall cousins, as well as several local antislavery friends of the Motts' who became so close to the family that they were treated as cousins.[13] Even when there were no visiting dignitaries to meet and entertain, the Philadelphia "family" centered on Lucretia and James Mott gathered together often throughout the years, at different houses.

In January 1834 Anna Coffin, then sixty-two, wrote to David that, it had been "very pleasant" to have Martha's company, especially, she said, because "I have thought perhaps this would be the last time that the three sisters &

brother would meet. I consider Lucretia in delicate health."[14] Anna's worries were misplaced. Lucretia, who was perennially ill with digestive problems, would outlive her mother and all of her siblings, including the much-younger Martha.

During this and later stays in Philadelphia, Martha developed strong bonds with Lucretia's four daughters, two of whom were closer in age to Martha than Lucretia herself was. Another niece close to Martha was Anna Temple, daughter of Martha's deceased sister Mary. Anna later married Walter Brown. Martha once described the Motts' extended Philadelphia family as going through the alphabet, "beginning with the Browns and ending with the Yarnalls." Some of the Mott children moved out of Philadelphia after marriage, and even Lucretia and James later moved to Roadside, a country estate a few miles outside the city. But most remained near Philadelphia, making Martha's home in upstate New York a distant family outpost.

The Motts and others made frequent visits to Martha, usually in the summer, and Martha made frequent visits to Philadelphia, usually in the winter. Throughout the rest of the year Martha kept in touch with her family by writing letters, mostly to Lucretia. But Martha's letters were considered "family sheets" and circulated from house to house around the Philadelphia-based family circle, which later included homes in Orange, New Jersey, and Brooklyn, New York. When Martha's letters had completed these rounds, they were forwarded to Nantucket for the Coffin and Folger cousins. Most started with no salutation. The few that varied from this pattern opened with "Dear sisters," "My darling sisters, daughter, etc.," "My dear sister & Patty & Eliza & Ellen & Fanny," or simply "Dear Everyone." Many of Martha's and Lucretia's family sheets have fortunately been preserved and provide a remarkably detailed story of the lives of a middle-class extended family of the nineteenth century.[15]

Martha's next, briefer, visit to her family in Philadelphia was in the winter of 1838. Once again, David's letters from Aurora complained of his loneliness without her, and her letters to him were full of enthusiastic reports of family activities, including a visit with Lucretia to a phrenologist, who declared that Lucretia's head showed "her moral feelings were stronger than common." A fad of the day, phrenology claimed that much could be learned about character by examining the shape of a person's head. Reading Martha's head, the phrenologist found "much combativeness" and divined that "this lady would be more likely to love a second time than the other." Very likely, the phrenologist had learned a bit about the sisters before their visit. Martha declared herself "quite pleased with the evening's amusement."[16]

In March 1844, Anna Coffin died on the day following her seventy-third birthday. As a shopkeeper on Nantucket's Petticoat Row and later shopkeeper and landlady in Philadelphia, she had held the family together through many difficult years. Managing the school in Aurora, she had provided a home and financial support for Martha and Marianna after Peter Pelham's death and had helped Martha and David during the birth of Eliza and Tallman. Even after her return to Philadelphia, Anna made frequent visits to Martha and her growing family in upstate New York. Until her death, Anna Folger Coffin remained vigorous in body and mind, the recognized head of the family, and an important source of strength and support to Martha.

All three daughters were deeply affected by Anna's death. Lucretia and Eliza were both ill at the time and neither was able to attend the funeral service. Lucretia became even sicker and extremely despondent. One of her daughters wrote to Martha, "If Aunt Martha does not come on, we are afraid the effect will be unfavorable to Mother, as it seems to be the only bright spot that she looks forward to."[17] But from her sickbed Lucretia asked her daughter to assure Martha that she or Eliza would make annual visits to New York in place of Anna's visits. She apparently felt that she had inherited the responsibilities of the family matriarch. Martha reached Philadelphia in time for her mother's burial and afterward took over the job of nursing Lucretia back to health. Later that year Martha herself was confined to bed with a lengthy illness. She wrote to Philadelphia, "Is it not singular that we should all three have suffered so much since Mother's death?"[18]

During the year Anna died, some of Martha's grief is revealed in her poetry, which grew serious and introspective. From her school days, Martha had enjoyed writing verse, usually bright and comic, to add to the fun of family gatherings and later to entertain her children. One of her more serious poems is dedicated to Anna, and another, focused on her own life's journey, and entitled "Philosophy of Life's Noon," reveals an attempt to respond with guarded optimism to this latest of her many personal tragedies.

Let me blot from the record of memory—the past
    Its illusions, so soon overwhelmed by pain
And forgetting the radiance so soon overcast
    In the present and future, be happy again

Be happy, tho' youth with its freshness is gone
    Be content with the blessings that still may be mine
My children's enjoyment still feel as my own
    And, forgetting the past, let me cease to repine

Let me rather rejoice that life's noon is serene
    Rejoice that the day in tranquility flows
And tho' clouded and stormy the morning has been
    In brightness and splendor the evening may close[19]

Martha's "morning" had brought her shipwreck, expulsion from the Society of Friends, and the deaths of her parents, her two sisters, and her first two loves, Peter Pelham and Julius Catlin. Her "afternoon" would indeed provide her with times of tranquility and moments of brightness and splendor. She would soon meet Elizabeth Cady Stanton and Susan B. Anthony and make major contributions to the advancement of woman's rights. But not all the clouds and storms in her life were behind her. One cloud appeared even while Martha was in Philadelphia for her mother's burial. She learned that her oldest daughter, Marianna Pelham, was very unhappy and needed her attention.

Marianna Pelham

Marianna had received her early schooling in Aurora, but when she turned twelve in 1837, Martha and David sent her away to Kimberton, a Quaker boarding school about thirty miles from Philadelphia. There she spent two years, broken by occasional visits to the Mott family and by visits from Martha. While Marianna was away at school, Martha wrote to her regularly, reporting the doings at home but also dispensing plenty of loving sentiments and parental advice, including "never allow yourself to deviate from the truth," "never slight those who are younger than yourself," and the familiar "do as you would be done by."[20] Martha would follow this pattern when each of her children went off to school. Her characteristic humor shows up in most of the letters. When Marianna wrote about a bird that had distracted her during a Quaker meeting at Kimberton, for example, Martha responded, "The incident of the bird singing in meeting was rather a singular one, he should have chosen some other society that approved of *Church Music*."[21] (Quaker services included no music.) In another letter, she told Marianna that David had gone to pick wild strawberries, but "it wouldn't be I that wd. want to pick them, they are so much smaller than *tame* ones."[22] (To ensure that the reader would not miss her jokes, Martha often underlined the key words, here rendered as italics.)

Marianna's father Peter Pelham had died before her first birthday, and she had grown up with considerable curiosity about her Pelham uncles, aunts, and cousins in the South that she had never met. Martha's correspondence with the Pelhams had lapsed, but in 1838, she was surprised and pleased to receive a letter from one of Peter's brothers, written from Philadelphia.[23] William Pelham had become surveyor general of Arkansas, and his official duties required him to make occasional trips to Washington and other cities in the East. On a brief visit to Philadelphia, he had searched the city directory for Pelhams in an unsuccessful attempt to locate his young niece Marianna. He wanted to meet her and invite her to travel with him to meet her father's family. William's planned itinerary included Maysville, Kentucky, the Pelham homestead where her father was born and had grown up, and Arkansas, where William now lived.

Martha and Marianna responded to William's letter favorably but told him that Marianna wanted first to finish her schooling at Kimberton and then return to New York for a year to get reacquainted with her Wright family before she met the Pelhams. Three years passed before William finally visited Marianna and the Wrights in upstate New York in 1841. Shortly before William arrived, Martha wrote and told him, "You will find Marianna grown almost as tall as her mother—As to her mother, you will find some difference between your Ideal of a girl of 16 that your brother fancied and the matron of 34 on whom Time has laid a somewhat ungentle hand."[24] The family would decide during the visit whether Marianna, then fifteen, could travel with him to Kentucky and Arkansas. William made a good impression on all, Marianna was eager to go, and Martha was favorably inclined, but David disapproved. Lucretia and most of the Philadelphia clan also disapproved. To the argument one family member made that the trip would have been more appropriate if Marianna were younger, Martha replied that Marianna was unlikely to get any younger! And she told David that she "felt very bad at not letting Marianna go. . . . Her grandmother is 75 and might not live, and after his [William Pelham] taking so long a journey it did not seem right."[25] David finally gave in. Marianna spent several months in Kentucky and Arkansas with the Pelhams and enjoyed herself immensely.

Martha's reconnection with the Pelhams brought together the incompatible worlds of slavery and abolitionism. In Marianna's first letter to her Uncle William, she had asked whether he had slaves. Martha recorded his answer in a letter to Lucretia: "And my dear sister, he has *only* eight slaves, 4 grown and 4 children, which he means to free at his death. He was amused to find M.A. [Marianna] and the other children such strong abolitionists and talked very fully on the subject."[26] William's brothers also held slaves. Further friendly contacts between the slaveholding Pelhams and the abolitionist Wrights and Motts would follow and even included a public antislavery speech Lucretia Mott delivered when she and Martha visited the Pelhams in Maysville, Kentucky, in the 1850s. But as tensions between North and South steadily increased and the Civil War approached, the letters Martha received from her Pelham relatives became distinctly less friendly. When war finally arrived, one of Martha's Pelham nephews and her own son, named after William Pelham, would both become artillery officers, facing each other across several bloody battlefields.

When Marianna left on her trip to the South with her uncle, she was only a few months younger than Martha was when she first fell in love, and so was Lucretia's daughter Elizabeth. Speaking from her experience of marriage at an early age, Martha wrote at the time to Lucretia, "I hope with Sister L that Elizabeth & Marianna too will keep themselves 'fancy free' for several years & enjoy the sunshine of life, before cares throw their shadows around them."[27] Years later she expressed the same cautious attitude towards early marriage in a letter to Lucretia in which she wrote about seeing some young girls playing a game. "I asked what game they were playing. She said 'Matrimony'. Poor little souls. It is to be hoped their pleasure will not be as abruptly ended as when they come to play it in earnest."[28]

Soon, however, Marianna was considering marriage and once again became the focus of family controversy and decision making. She had spent much of her time with the Motts since her return from the South and while there had become engaged to a Philadelphia Quaker named Rodman Wharton. When Martha came to Philadelphia for her mother's burial and stayed to care for Lucretia, she was surprised to find that Marianna had cause for unhappiness beyond the death of her grandmother. Although she was engaged to Rodman, Marianna confided to her mother, she was deeply in love with her first cousin, Thomas Mott. Martha wrote to David for advice about the "struggle" Marianna "had had to maintain between what she considered her duty & her inclination." The Motts and Wrights had earlier noticed a growing attachment between Marianna and Thomas but "had supposed it to be a mere transitory & childish passion." The Motts warned Thomas against it, and both sets of parents believed that the relationship had cooled, particularly after Marianna became engaged to Rodman. Marianna had accepted Rodman Wharton's proposal only because she had assumed that since she and Thomas were first cousins they would not be permitted to marry, and, Martha explained to David, "she thought it would be best to place an insurmountable barrier to it, by accepting Rodman."[29] But feeling miserable about her decision, Marianna sought advice from her mother.

Martha told her daughter that it was unjust to give Rodman "a divided heart." Martha had hoped to withhold the details from Lucretia until she recovered from her illness, but when Lucretia herself raised the topic of Marianna's depression, Martha explained its source. Lucretia was upset that Marianna and Thomas had not been more open with her. "How little Marianna knew us," said Lucretia, "to suppose we should oppose them if their hearts were so deeply interested."[30] Both mothers then agreed that Marianna should break her engagement with Rodman. She did, and Rodman accepted the rejection graciously, but David wrote to Martha that Marianna should "utterly refuse even for a moment to harbor the most remote expectation of ever becoming the bride of her Cousin."[31] As with the matter of Marianna's trip to the South with William Pelham, Martha eventually wore down David's resistance. He reluctantly gave his approval, and Marianna and Thomas were married in 1845 with the blessings of all.

The wedding announcement read: "Thomas Mott of Philada. to Miss Marianna Pelham, daughter of the late Capt. P. Pelham U.S.A. and adopted daughter of D. Wright Esq. of Auburn." Lucretia and Martha were now not only sisters but also in-laws, and would eventually share three grandchildren. David and other family members had worried that the young couple risked producing children with mental defects, but Martha dismissed their concerns with the trenchant observation, "I know a good many simpletons in the world whose parents are not cousins."[32]

5

Auburn

192 Genesee Street

MARTHA HAD gone to Aurora to teach at Brier Cliff, and David had moved there to study at a local law office. But Martha's teaching years were behind her, and David's law business continued to grow and required more and more travel, which was not easy from tiny, isolated Aurora. By 1839, after ten years in their lakeside home, they decided to move to Auburn, the county seat about fifteen miles to the northeast.[1] Much of David's business was conducted there in the county courthouse, and Auburn also was becoming convenient for more distant travel. A railroad line had just been completed connecting Auburn to Albany, and Albany offered connections by Hudson River steamboat (and later by railroad) south to New York City. Travel westward from Auburn was still by stagecoach, but the rail link to Rochester was soon to be completed.[2] Like Aurora, Auburn was not Philadelphia "by a jugfull." But while the population of Aurora was only a few hundred, Auburn's was already over five thousand, and the advent of the railroads would stimulate further growth. The Wrights sold their Aurora home and moved to a rental house in Auburn that fall. The following year, they moved to another rental home, this time on Orchard Street, which then "was an assembling place for cows and was all hills and valleys like a country road."[3] But in 1841, they purchased for thirty-five hundred dollars a brick house at 192 Genesee Street that would be Martha's home for the rest of her life.[4]

Genesee Street was Auburn's main business thoroughfare, wider and more citified than Orchard. The Wrights' house at 192 was only a few blocks west of the city center and, most important to David, was close to the county courthouse. His law office had several locations on Genesee Street over the years, all close to the courthouse and an easy walk from home.[5] The train depot, which he would use more and more often as his law business grew, was only a short ride away by horse-drawn hack, for a fee of one shilling (twelve and a half cents). Once the westward train was in service, he used it to travel to Rochester and to make the short trip to meet the Cayuga Lake steamboat, which took him back to Aurora, where he still had a few clients. "The expense of going to Aurora by R.R. and S. B. is seven shillings," wrote Martha, "less than the stage fare and I suppose less than a hired conveyance."[6]

The new Auburn house, as Martha's daughter Eliza described it, was set far back from Genesee Street. It was large, with seven bedrooms and several fireplaces.

> There was the loveliest one in the parlor. Mother attended to it herself, keeping a pot of potter's clay, mixed with a brush, ready, and after there had been a fire she whitened the sides and back, laid the wood and kindling all ready for next time. The andirons were beauties she found at a second hand store in the town, costing 75 cents. In the dining room there was a crane and pothooks where was boiled many a bottle of molasses for candy. The kitchen had also a large fireplace, with crane, and there was a brick oven, of course, which was used when the family was increased by our Philadelphia relatives coming. Every summer several of them visited us. If roses were in bloom, Mother always put one on the pillow of an expected guest.[7]

The house had ample room for the frequent family guests from Philadelphia. "Quilts were generally put into the frames when the Aunts and Cousins came for a visit," Eliza wrote, "and such a merry visiting time there would be over the quilting." The Wright home would also later serve as a haven for fugitive slaves and for visiting leaders in the abolition and woman's rights movements, including Frederick Douglass, William Lloyd Garrison, Wendell Phillips, Elizabeth Cady Stanton, Matilda Joslyn Gage, Ernestine Rose, and Susan B. Anthony, who, years later, wrote nostalgically about her "many, many calls and visits at the dear old family home on Genesee St."[8] But the main reason Martha and David moved into a larger house in 1841 was to provide more space for their growing family.

Martha's third daughter, Ellen, had been born in 1840. Shortly after the move to Genesee Street, Martha wrote to Lucretia, good-humoredly describing her busy morning, which included a rare error in the kitchen.

> Auburn Nov. 19th. 12 o'clock & I have not had time since breakfast to rest, having the dining room to sweep, my bed room &c &c—After which I left Ellen in Eliza's care, & made some gingerbread which was very good with the slight omission of *ginger*, so I went to work & made another batch, remembering that important ingredient. . . . Ellen is 15 mo. old to-day, & the snipe is just waking when she has only slept while I wrote the above.[9]

Eight years had passed between the births of Tallman and Ellen, an unusually large gap between births at the time. In her memoir of Martha written in the 1890s, Eliza reported that Martha had suffered several miscarriages during those years. It is also possible that Martha had used some early form of birth control to slow the growth of their family.[10] The family's funds were very limited during the 1830s, and Martha's first three children had already crowded their small house in Aurora. In Auburn in the 1840s, they had a larger house and a larger income. Whatever the reason underlying the birth gap between Tallman and Ellen, more children now arrived in rapid order. Martha's second son was born in 1842 and, at Marianna's urging, was named after her uncle, William Pelham. Two years later, Francis, called Frank, was born. He was Martha's sixth child, her fifth with David. She once again had three small children to take care of, and this time two of them were boys. As she noted in one family letter, "boys rhymes with noise."[11]

In spring 1846, Frank was a little over one year old; William, called Willy, was three; and Ellen was five. In a letter to Lucretia, Martha said, "I have no prospects but pleasant ones just at this present, and it is the first May for the six years that we have lived in Auburn that I have not had a young infant *or worse*. I want time to pass as fast as ever it can . . . so that I can be 55 and bestow all my *pity* on other people's "prospects."[12] (In family letters, a pregnant woman was discreetly referred to as having "prospects.") When Martha wrote this, she was thirty-nine and felt that her family—three sons and three daughters—was already quite large enough. But she also clearly recognized that she was still young enough for further prospects. Her next was only two springs away.

With her three young children demanding much of Martha's energy and attention, Tallman became a rebellious young man, creating other challenges. When he was thirteen, he expressed his desire for a gun that a neighbor offered to sell David. "I told him I *shouldn't* let Pa get it," Martha wrote to Lucretia. "I didn't want him to own a gun—they were dangerous things—he replied with great earnestness 'well I know if *I* was Pa, you wouldn't be Boss.' I was so amused that he soon recovered from his ire—nothing so soon puts one in good humor than finding one has unintentionally said something comical."[13] Humor, including encouraging the ability to laugh at oneself, was one of the tools Martha used to maintain order. She employed other techniques of parental authority but avoided corporal punishment, of which she firmly disapproved. The question of guns remained a problem, however, particularly in the spring when large flights of pigeons encouraged the men of Auburn to "go forth to commit havoc on the innocent travelers."

> David I see has quite a struggle between respect for my prejudices against guns and the associations of boyhood when his greatest happiness was in his dog & gun, having no mother to make home cheerful—and he gives me little help in my endeavors to inspire Tallman with my own aversion to such a cruel amusement. My descriptions of the wounded & suffering birds that do not fall at once, call forth only a curl of the lip & a shrug from Tallman, who I suppose thinks it a matter of course that a woman should be afraid of a gun. . . . Tallman often wishes for a gun . . . but he will have to wait till he has a house of his own to keep it in."[14]

On this issue, clearly Martha intended to remain the "Boss."

While David kept busy with his law practice, Martha was responsible for managing the household. In the early years in Aurora, David's sister Sarah had helped, but she was married now and had a family of her own. (Martha was unimpressed with Sarah's husband, Nathaniel Kniffen, about whom she wrote, "I never saw a more vacant mind.")[15] Martha did the majority of the household work herself, caring for her children, sewing and mending clothes for the family, cleaning the house, tending the garden, planning the meals, and doing much of the cooking. Each fall, she made soap and candles, preserved vegetables and fruits, and made wine. (The Wrights, like the Motts, disapproved of alcohol, but used wine in modest amounts for flavoring and medicinal purposes.) Eliza praised her mother's many household skills.

> No one else could make such sweet cottage cheese, or such delectable Nantucket corn pudding, or broil a steak better and many other toothsome dishes. . . . The sewing and mending and baby tending went on and was marvelously well done. . . . She took all the care of her babies, made all the garments worn by the family with very little outside help.[16]

Martha's daughters assisted with some household chores, but she also had hired help. She usually had a "girl" to help in the kitchen, and a "man" who helped with repair of the house and barn, maintenance of the grounds, and care of the cow and chickens. Getting and keeping good kitchen help was a continual problem that Martha often complained about in her letters. The best "girls" always seemed to have suitors, and many departed for marriage soon after their kitchen skills had developed to the point that they were more boon than burden. About keeping a cow, Martha once wrote, "Somebody has to work hard, whenever there is a cow—tho' it is elegant to have one, if you can find that somebody."[17] As for the chickens, she wrote in 1847, "We are going to part with all our hens this spring, they are so troublesome in the garden and it costs as much to feed them as to buy eggs."[18]

One of the Wrights' more unusual adventures with keeping animals was their raising of silkworms, then a local fad. Silkworms are caterpillars of a moth whose cocoon consists of a single thread of silk hundreds of meters long. Although the Wrights lost many of their silkworms to hungry rats and to their cow, each moth that emerges lays several hundred eggs, and their silkworms multiplied rapidly. However, the mulberry leaves on which they feed were costly, as was paying the Auburn State Prison for inmates to perform the tedious task of unwinding the cocoons and producing the thread. (This project had been introduced to keep the prisoners usefully occupied and to defray the costs of operating the prison.) Eliza later estimated that the resulting silk cost about twice as much as it would have cost from the store.

One aspect of Auburn that Martha commented on frequently in her letters was its severe winters. One January she wrote, "How elegant Auburn is in the spring & summer, and how horrid in winter."[19] She was even less positive that March: "We have but two seasons, two months summer and ten months winter."[20] Located at the northern tip of Owasco Lake, the community had developed around Auburn State Prison, established there in 1816, and Auburn Theological Seminary, founded two years later by the Presbyterian Church.[21] These two institutions contributed to making the people of Auburn largely conservative in religion and politics, but Martha and David soon formed strong friendships with several families with liberal opinions close to their own.

Most noteworthy among their early Auburn friends were the Sewards. William Henry Seward had recently been elected governor of New York State, but David had known him earlier through his law practice. Seward's wife, Frances, and her sister Lazette Worden became two of Martha's closest Auburn friends and exchanged frequent visits with her.[22] Like Martha, Frances and Lazette ardently supported the abolition of slavery. They later also took great interest in Martha's activities in the woman's rights movement, although they never became actively involved themselves. On one occasion, Martha called on Frances to return some books and found the governor at home dealing with applications for executive clemency. Seward asked Martha's opinion on one case that aroused her sympathy, a youth of twenty who had already served over half of his sentence for theft, and whose mother had petitioned for his release because his father was seriously ill and near death. "I told him," she wrote, "that I thought the power to pardon in a case like that must be a source of great happiness to him—but he seemed to think it was 'on the contrary, quite the reverse' and he mentioned several cases where sympathy & duty conflicted." Martha clearly leaned toward sympathy. "I had the honor of the Governors' arm on the way home," she added. "He came in and talked with David till near dark."[23]

After Seward completed his term as governor, he and David served together on some local legal cases, resulting in several lengthy visits by Seward to the Wrights' home. "Mr. Seward came up on Sunday and sat two hours," Martha wrote. "When Eliza took him into the parlor he asked if he might smoke. She hesitated, said why she didn't know—she didn't know what Ma would say, but she guessed he might smoke out of the window—which he did. I was amused when she told me [and] . . . I apologized as he was going out. . . . He said that it was all right—that they were very strict with him at home."[24]

Teenaged Eliza had been strict with Governor Seward, well aware that Martha and David disapproved of smoking. They disapproved even more strongly of drinking; David was very active in local temperance organizations. One evening they were invited to the Sewards' home after an evening concert, and Martha was disturbed to find that champagne was among the refreshments offered. She reported disapprovingly to Lucretia, "There was a time, while Mr. S. was governor, that he professed to be a 'cold water man,' but I perceive he now places wine before his guests."[25] The former governor had further political ambitions, and he wanted the support of both drinkers and nondrinkers.

Underground Railroad

Like other abolitionists, Martha and David could contribute to the antislavery cause by assisting fugitive slaves on their journey north. Since slaves were the legal property of their owners, assisting their escape was illegal, and contemporary accounts of the harboring of fugitive slaves are very rare. Thus Martha's family letter describing a visit by a runaway slave in 1843 is of special interest. She reported that he arrived with a paper directed to "the 'spiritually minded' recommending a runaway slave to the care of whom it may concern," adding, "I went down & talked a little with him & left him to eat a comfortable supper." He left after supper, promising to return. Martha described the rest of his visit:

Our slave returned about 9 last evening & sat alone in the kitchen & read till David came. He went down & talked with him—he said he was from Baltimore

& had paid his master 300 dollars—he asked 800—being sold to go south he
ran away to Pittsburg . . . & was on his way to Massachusetts where his people
lived. As I didn't fancy having him go up stairs he had D's old cloak, & slept by
the kitchen stove on *my settee*—how little I imagined to what use it was to be
applied. After getting him to put a stick in the furnace D. left him & fastened
the door at the head of the kitchen stairs—he gave him 50¢ as he wanted to
get a ride part way. Early this morning David saw him & got some bread &
butter for him as he wished to be off before it was very light. So after putting
in more wood & tying up a couple of shirts & bosoms [garments to cover the
chest] that we gave him, he cleared. Tallman came down early to have some
interesting conversation with him about the land of chains & was much disappointed to find that he had left—he had to go to the Post Office then, but
could not find his tippet [scarf] which he knew he hung in the kitchen with his
cap, and as David noticed it in the evening the inference was that early morning
walks made warmer clothing desirable & the slave had taken Gerritt Smith's
advise & *the tippet*—But we didn't say so to Tallman, David said it would give
such a shock to his philanthropy & as to Eliza, she was as afraid as could be of
him before, & hardly dared to go to bed & if she should know it she would
hardly dare stay in the house if another came—David didn't relish it much &
said if his master came for him he would not defend him—I suppose he would
willingly have given him the tippet if he had asked. I told him we must consider
that he had had no one to teach him better.[26]

Unlike Martha, who was clearly more forgiving than he of the slave's appro-
priation of Tallman's scarf, David lived by a very strict code of behavior and
expected others to do likewise. Tallman, ten, and Eliza, twelve, also had very
different responses to their overnight guest.

This story of the fugitive slave who slept on a settee in the kitchen con-
trasts with the romantic stories of the Underground Railroad that feature
hidden cellar rooms and secret tunnels. And it is unlikely that this was the only
time that Martha and David harbored a fugitive slave in 192 Genesee Street. A
half-century later, Eliza would write that "a branch of the underground railway
came through Auburn, and our house was one of the stations."[27] But after this
1843 letter, David probably gave Martha firm lawyerly advice that she should

not detail their illegal activities in family letters that were so widely circulated, for we have found no later descriptions of overnight visits in their home by fugitive slaves.

The Wrights also aided others in Auburn who harbored fugitive slaves, including a black minister who was himself an escaped slave. Their help included contributions of cash and clothing, as Martha described in an 1857 letter to Ellen.

> Rev. Mr. Eastup called here a few weeks ago, to say that there were six fugitives at his house. Pa gave him what money he cd. spare, and yesterday I went to see whether they had got to Canada yet. Had quite a pleasant call. Mrs. E. was anxious to form a sort of fugitive aid or Anti-Slavery society among the colored people, to make up & repair garments for those that they have to clothe. I contributed *a mite* and she hopes to accomplish something this wk. I had quite a pile of coats & things that had been waiting to be judiciously disposed of, so I got Mr. E. to come for them, & while he was here got him to give me a history of his own escape, wh. was very interesting—his wife is a genuine Native American, being of Indian extraction—was never in the South. He left a wife & 10 children there—his wife died three years after he left, & two of his children were sold to go to Georgia. He is quite a good looking man.[28]

Murder and Madness

Martha's interest in reform also included the issue of capital punishment. In 1843, she wrote to Lucretia, "Yes, I have been very glad to see the feeling against Capital Punishment gradually spreading."[29] But Martha and Lucretia and others opposed to capital punishment remained very much in the minority.[30] The topic became of strong local interest in Auburn a few years later, when the city was abuzz over the murder trials of two black men.[31] Seward, then no longer governor and not yet senator, defended both men on the grounds of insanity. The prosecutor for both cases was John Van Buren, state attorney general and son of former President Martin Van Buren. The star power of the contending lawyers, the defense strategy, the race of the defendants, and the nature of the crimes drew large audiences to the courtroom.

The first defendant was Henry Wyatt, a prisoner accused of murdering a fellow convict. Martha and David attended several sessions, watching their friend Seward in action. Seward later told Martha that "it did him good to see my Quaker face among so many." Although most of the crowd was eager to see Wyatt hanged, Seward was well aware of Martha's sympathy toward blacks and her Quaker sensibilities against capital punishment. A friend discussing the case with Martha and referring to the defendants quoted the Biblical injunction "Thou shall not kill." "I replied," Martha wrote, "that that text was equally binding on those who would hang him. . . . I told her that I did not think that the power to take life had ever been delegated to man."[32]

Wyatt's first trial ended in a split jury, but he was convicted in a second trial and sentenced to hang.[33] David, convinced that Wyatt was insane, was angered at the verdict and argued with the local Methodist minister about the propriety of hanging an insane man. The minister was "very earnest that he [Wyatt] be hanged. David said he didn't believe there was a sheriff or deputy in the County that would undertake the office. 'I would hang him myself' said this follower of Jesus."[34] This is one of many examples in Martha's life when church leaders angered her by taking positions that she considered immoral.

Martha reported the hanging in another letter to Lucretia: "Do you want to hear about the judicial Assassination of Wyatt? . . . He was hanged on Monday somewhere in the jail, near the cell. Fainted twice, and from the fact of his pulse ceasing the moment he was swung off I presume he fainted at the time. It seems to me a refinement of cruelty to restore a man who has fainted at such a time. Why not hang them while insensitive to suffering? How such barbarous laws can exist for a day I cannot see."[35]

The second accused murderer was William Freeman, who had a history of insanity in his family. In 1840, at age sixteen, he was convicted of stealing a horse and sentenced to Auburn Prison for five years. Convinced of his innocence, he suffered miserably under the harsh conditions of the prison and refused to cooperate with the guards. They frequently brutalized him, and once hit him so hard on the head with a board that his skull was cracked and he was deafened. After he was released from prison in September 1845, he wandered about Auburn mumbling that he was going to have his "pay" for the work he had been required to do while in prison. He asked the justice of the peace for a warrant to sue for this pay but was told that was impossible.

He then chose, apparently at random, the family of John Van Nest, a farmer living a few miles south of Auburn, on which to wreak his revenge. He entered their house and with a knife killed four people—Van Nest, his pregnant wife, her mother, and a sleeping child. He also wounded a hired hand, who survived and identified the murderer. The crime was so abhorrent that when Freeman was captured and returned to Auburn, he barely escaped lynching by an angry mob. Officials promised the public that this time there would be no insanity plea and no Seward to defend the murderer. But the officials were wrong; Seward did take the case and did employ an insanity defense. David Wright was assigned by the judge to assist Seward, and he accepted under the urging of Martha, Seward, and a local magistrate who said of David that "he's the only man who has the heart to dare."[36]

David's legal practice was usually devoted to patent and contract disputes and other civil cases and only rarely dealt with criminal cases. One of his specialties is clear from the title of his book published in 1844: *Executor's Administrator's and Guardian's Guide*.[37] (As the book neared publication, Martha wrote, "David's book is not out yet—they get on very slowly & make vexatious mistakes sometimes—the word 'facts' they changed to 'parts' making the sentence unintelligible. David told them he wondered they did not retain the 'f' instead of 'p.'")[38] When David did take criminal cases, the decision was guided by his strict moral principles. He once declined to defend a man charged with the illegal sale of liquors, and the man angrily said, "You would defend a murderer, would you not?" David replied, "Yes, for I do not believe in hanging, but I do believe in punishing men for the illegal sale of liquor."[39] David helped Seward defend Freeman because he opposed capital punishment, but this did not make him popular among the Auburn public eager to avenge a horrible crime. The fact that Freeman was black intensified feelings of the generally racist public but also intensified the determination of both Seward and David to see that Freeman received a competent defense. They each committed almost three months to the case, without receiving any compensation from the court. Seward argued that they would be paid from the "exchequer of heaven." Martha said that was fine, but she would prefer that David be paid from an earthly one as well. He worked "without any other reward than a clear conscience, which does not make pots boil."[40]

There was first a sanity trial to determine whether Freeman was sane enough to be tried for murder. The defendant exhibited no understanding of what was going on, or what role Seward and David were playing. The two lawyers called several doctors who testified that Freeman was clearly insane, but the prosecution called many more who testified that he was not. Witnesses sent to Freeman's cell to interrogate him reported that he always willingly admitted that he had killed the Van Nest family—to get his "pay." The fact that he had a memory of the event was used as evidence of his sanity. The jury decided that Freeman was "*sufficiently* sane"[41] to be tried for murder.

After that decision, Martha wrote that David felt "it was a mockery of justice to try such an imbecile wretch and he would have nothing to do with it" but added she "rather urged David to continue, lest his withdrawal might look like a want of moral courage, for there is great excitement and the counsel for the prisoner are promised tar & feathers & even hanging."[42] Once again, David consented. During the murder trial, emphasis shifted from Freeman's present sanity to whether he was sane at the time of the murders; no one was surprised when he was found guilty and sentenced to be hanged. Seward and David entered an appeal based on prejudicial actions and statements made by the judge, and the Supreme Court reversed the decision and ordered a new trial.[43] But the defendant's condition had further deteriorated, and the circuit judge declared him incapable of standing a new trial. Freeman died in prison from consumption the following year. A postmortem examination revealed serious brain damage that David was convinced had resulted from his beating in prison. Two years later, David turned down an invitation from the district attorney to assist him in a murder trial. As Martha reported to Philadelphia, "he said he would never assist on the side of the people in the case of life and death."[44]

Infidelity and the Trammels of Sect

Martha differed from her conservative Auburn neighbors not only on the issue of capital punishment but also in her attitude toward organized religion and the teachings of Christianity. Students at the Auburn Theological Seminary often delivered religious tracts from door to door throughout the city. Martha kept a pile of pamphlets of the American Anti-Slavery Society near her door and would agree to read the seminarians' pamphlets if they would read hers. She engaged them in debate and had answers for all their arguments. In a letter to Lucretia in 1846, she described one such visit.

> I told him I would accept it [his tract], though I totally disapproved of the doctrines that they took pains to inculcate in them, and a much longer talk than I anticipated was the result. He said in some astonishment: "Are you a member of no Christian Church?" I told him we were independent of all sects, that we endeavored to instill the precepts that Christ taught, and I considered that all sufficient, without burdening children's minds with any of the absurd dogmas of any sect. He wanted to know if I didn't think they were more inclined to do wrong than right. I replied that their judgement being immature they were very troublesome and had to be guided, but not because they were wicked. He didn't know, he thought it was only through grace that he was able to resist the evil tendencies of his nature. His promptings were more for evil then for good. I told him *mine* were *not* nor were my children's. Perhaps the doctrine originated with those who were thus inclined and who therefore supposed everybody else was so. Didn't I consider the Bible the only rule of faith and practice?—By no means! I considered the old testament a very unfit book for children to read. He began to speak as if there were to be sure some *indelicate passages*. I told him I had no reference to that, but that revenge and all the evil passions were encouraged by some parts of that book, that while Christ commanded forgiveness to enemies, David said, "I hate thy enemies, O Lord," with perfect hatred. "O," said he, "he meant that he hated their evil actions." "Then he should have said so," said I.[45]

Apparently stimulated and challenged by this first exchange, the seminarian returned within a few weeks for another visit. Once again, the conversation focused on whether or not people are inherently wicked, a concept Martha continued to reject. By asking the seminarian about his personal experience with the Quakers he knew, she reveals that she judged people by their behavior, and not by their theological beliefs.

On Saturday, just as I had finished my gingerbread, my little Divine called with his tract. I quite begin to like him for he can talk rationally. . . . I told him I supposed he was too much startled by my heresies to come again. He said not at all—he was pleased with my frankness, and in many things could agree with me. The only thing that he could not get along with, was my idea as to children not being naturally wicked. He did not know how anybody could help seeing that they were. I told him they were all exceedingly troublesome, but not because they meant to be wicked, but because their reason was not matured. He said if I thought every one could be good I did away entirely with the necessity of atonement. "Certainly," said I, "I think it a most preposterous idea that an innocent person should suffer for another's sins, but you were brought up to consider those things essentials." "Yes," said he, "my parents were Con-gregationalists, and I am one." "My parents," said I, "were Quakers, and I am one." He said he knew a great many Quakers in Vermont where he was brought up. "Well," said I, "what did you observe as the result of their teachings. Were their children less moral, less regardful of the rights of others, less honest, than the children of those taught according to your views?" (I didn't tell him that a portion of the Quaker Society [the Orthodox, as opposed to the Hicksites] were quite as Presbyterian as he was himself.) He replied that there was not a more honest class of men anywhere, than those neighbors of his. "Then," said I, "let that teach you charity and make you willing to believe that they may be as near right as yourself." When he left, it was with the wish that each of us might do as near right as we could, and let the result show which was best, or something to that effect, to which I agreed.[46]

Despite having been expelled from her Quaker Meeting in Philadelphia for marrying Peter Pelham, and despite claiming to be "independent of all sects," Martha in her conversation with the seminarian called herself a Quaker. Once Ellen, aged five, asked, "Ma you ain't a Quaker are you?" "Yes," said I, "who said I was?"[47] Ellen's playmates had raised the issue. Martha felt that she was a Quaker because she had been raised a Quaker, gone to Quaker schools, and felt comfortable with most of the liberal views of the Hicksite Quakers. But when friends in 1839 asked Lucretia whether Martha was a Quaker, she said no—and asked Martha whether she objected. She responded, "You also ask if you did me wrong in saying I was no Quaker. . . . I liked vastly to hear the conversation and was not in the least wounded by your imputations on my quakerism—them 'testimonies' I don't think much of 'which go to constitute the quaker'."[48] Martha's credentials as a Quaker were certainly weak in the eyes of Lucretia, a practicing Quaker minister in regular attendance at Quaker meetings, who formally subscribed to the few "testimonies" required of Hicksites, which Martha did not. She considered any such requirements or restrictions, certainly the dictum against marrying a non-Quaker, as the "trammels of sect." In an 1846 family letter, she reported a discussion about theology with a friend who argued that "she did not think it was right for people to feel the obligations of their sect a burden, to feel that they were trammeled. She did not feel so. I told her that sister L. [Lucretia] thought she did not, but they were both mistaken."[49] Martha's highest priority was freedom of thought. Despite the great admiration and respect that she felt for her sister, and despite the liberality of Lucretia's religious beliefs compared with those of most other Christians of the time, Martha firmly believed that Lucretia was "trammeled" by her strict adherence to the Quaker "sect."

In the 1840s, the city of Auburn had seven churches—an Episcopal, a Methodist Episcopal, a Baptist, a Roman Catholic, a Universalist, and two Presbyterian.[50] Shortly after their arrival in Auburn, David purchased a pew in the First Presbyterian Church, but, as he reported in his autobiography, "we could not comfortably listen to the doctrine then preached in that church, it was too *lurid* for us. We then took a pew in the Universalist Church and found the preaching much more to our taste." Even there, Martha rarely attended services. However, once after a visiting Universalist minister had preached in Auburn, Martha described the sermon to a friend. When the friend heard what the minister had preached about "the duties of the rich toward the poor," she said, according to Martha's report to Lucretia, "'Yes these Universalists always preach moral sermons'—'What sort does your Episcopal minister preach?' said I—'The Episcopalians preach gospel sermons' said she. I asked her what a gospel sermon was, but she declined enlightening me."[51] Martha had an especially negative view of the Episcopal Church, which she once described as "that gloomy incomprehensible faith, so utterly at variance with the dictates of reason."[52] On another occasion, a neighbor was shocked when

Martha praised a visiting Unitarian minister. "She said 'They deny the Divinity of our Savior—and when they take away that from us, they take away everything.' Not feeling qualified to be the exponent of their faith, I merely said 'They consider him a perfect example and are guided by his precepts as set forth in the New Testament.' 'But they don't take the Bible as their rule of faith,' said she plaintively. . . . I admitted the beauty of parts of the Bible but there was a great deal in it I don't believe & in the new there was enough for our guidance—and then for her edification I told her that I took for my text those lines of Alexander Pope:

> 'For modes of faith let graceless zealots fight
> His can't be wrong, whose life is in the right'[53]

a favorite quotation that I have hurled at the heads of our theologians & saints so often that if it was not imperishable, would have worn out."[54]

One reason that Martha admired many Universalist and Unitarian ministers was that they were often most outspoken in discussing what she and David considered the most important moral issue of the time—slavery. Since Martha's exposure to William Lloyd Garrison and other abolitionists at the 1833 American Anti-Slavery meetings in Philadelphia, the Wrights had diligently read the *Liberator* and other antislavery literature and had become more and more committed to the abolitionist cause. To Martha, one's "life is in the right" only if one is openly opposed to slavery. Most leaders of the more conservative Christian churches in both North and South were silent on the subject. Those who defended slavery often used quotations from the Bible to justify their position. The attitudes of these church leaders fueled Martha's hostility toward much of organized religion. That hostility, combined with her views on the "trammels of sect" and her infrequent attendance at local church services, led many of her conservative Auburn neighbors to label her an "infidel."

The term *infidel* was also frequently applied to Garrison and other abolitionists who promoted the antislavery cause outside the churches. In 1847, Martha was angered by an article by a minister, published in *New York Evangelist*, that described Garrisonian abolitionists as "irreligious," questioning their credentials as Christians. By the late 1840s, it had been become a habit for Martha to reply in print to articles that offended her. This time Garrison's *Liberator* published her response, signed "M.C.W," in which she argued, "These 'irreligious' men who are doing practically, with all their might, so much for Humanity's sake, are emphatically Christians." She challenged a "pseudo-Christianity which in the formality of its worship, loses sight of the essentials, Justice, Mercy, and Humanity," "whose religion consists of barren theories," and "a church which, while loudly insisting on the forms of religion, leaves its observances to men who make no profession, preferring to be known by their fruits—men whom these writers assume to themselves the right to term 'irreligious'." Her punch line: "Mankind are beginning to see the folly of relying on the church for instruction in the simple precepts of Jesus of Nazareth."[55]

To Martha, being a Christian meant acting in a manner that followed the example and teachings of Jesus and did not depend on any "formality of worship" or declared beliefs in "barren theories." She subscribed to the statement from William Penn that Lucretia liked to quote: "Men are to be judged by their likeness to Christ, rather than their notions of Christ."[56] Martha felt deeply that Garrison and other "infidel" abolitionists, fighting slavery outside the church, were more religious and more Christian than ministers and churchgoers who ignored or condoned slavery.[57]

Martha Wright's published writings and extensive correspondence make it clear that she had deep respect for the life and teachings of Jesus. But she felt more attuned to his humanity than to his divinity. When her son Frank was only one and still often keeping her awake at night, she wrote to Lucretia, "I was looking at a beautiful picture of the Virgin Mary and the infant Jesus at Mrs. Howe's. I told Mrs. H. I wondered if he kept his mother awake half the night patting him. Doubtless she was shocked. I have often wondered whether the inexperienced Virgin had to go through with all the prose of raising an infant."[58]

6

Seneca Falls

Abolition to Woman's Rights

AMERICA WAS awash with reform movements in the nineteenth century, but the two to which Martha Wright became most committed were abolition and woman's rights. Historians recognize the 1848 Seneca Falls Convention, today the site of the Women's Rights National Historical Park,[1] as the formal beginning of the organized woman's rights movement.[2] (Although "women's rights" is in more common usage today, Martha and her contemporaries wrote and spoke mostly about "woman's rights.") As one of the planners and organizers of the Seneca Falls Convention, Martha is recognized as a pioneer in the movement. But long before Seneca Falls, there had been women who chafed at the limitations that society placed upon them. Abigail Adams complained to John Adams in 1776 that "whilst you are proclaiming peace and good will to Men, Emancipating all Nations, you insist upon retaining an absolute power over Wives."[3] Mary Wollstonecraft's *A Vindication of the Rights of Women*, published in England in 1792, was ridiculed by most men but became an inspiration for many women, including Lucretia and Martha. In calling for equal rights for women, Wollstonecraft was far ahead of her time. She warned, "Those who are bold enough to advance before the age they live in, and to throw off, by the force of their own minds, the prejudices which the maturing reason of the world will in time disavow, must learn to brave censure. We ought not to be too anxious respecting the opinions of others."[4] Through their reform activities, both Lucretia and Martha had learned to brave censure, and each kept a copy of Wollstonecraft prominently displayed in her home. Martha said she put it out "to shock guests."[5]

The organized woman's rights movement evolved from the activities of women in several American reform movements that preceded it, including the temperance and "moral reform" movements. But for Lucretia Mott and many others, it grew most directly from activities in the antislavery movement.[6] Martha's first exposure to the ideas of the abolitionists had been during her 1833 visit to her sister Lucretia, when she met William Lloyd Garrison and attended the founding meeting of the American Anti-Slavery Society (AAS). Following that meeting, Lucretia organized the Philadelphia Female Anti-Slavery Society, and work in this and in other female antislavery organizations soon amply demonstrated that women had the ability to organize and act in an effort to reform society. Two sisters who had grown up in the South in a slave-holding family, Angelina and Sarah Grimké, joined the abolition movement and began speaking in public against slavery.[7] They spoke at first to audiences that were exclusively female, but by 1837 they were lecturing in Massachusetts to "promiscuous" audiences that included men as well as women. Public speeches by women were considered anathema by much of the public and by most churches and would continue to be attacked from the pulpit for many years. However, the growing public role of women in the abolition movement began to raise awareness among both women and men that women could operate effectively outside of their assigned "sphere," the home.

This growth of public activism by women was inspiring to some, but to many others, it threatened the status quo of male-dominated society. The "woman issue" led to an angry split within the AAS at its 1840 meeting in New York. Disunion had been growing in the society over several issues, especially one of Garrison's more radical ideas, equal rights and participation of women. In the previous year, the AAS had made the highly controversial decision to admit male and female delegates on an equal basis. In 1840, they went one step further with the election of Abby Kelley, a female abolitionist lecturer, to the society's business committee. (Martha herself would later become a member of this committee.) This step was too much for many male abolitionists, who felt that allowing women to become delegates was bad enough. The abolition of slavery would not disturb their personal lives in the North, but equal rights for women certainly would. The next afternoon, the losing faction separated from AAS and formed a rival antislavery organization, the American and Foreign Anti-Slavery Association.

Garrison then left New York for an antislavery conference in London, where "the woman issue" was again hotly argued. Lucretia was sent as a delegate of the Pennsylvania Anti-Slavery Society, which had admitted female members the previous year, but she and other women delegates from Pennsylvania and Massachusetts were refused seating. The issue was discussed and brought to a vote, but seating of the women was soundly defeated. The women were required to observe the convention proceedings discreetly from a roped-off section on the edge of the convention floor. This was the first World Anti-Slavery Convention, but it is remembered today primarily as the occasion when Lucretia Mott met Elizabeth Cady Stanton.[8] Stanton had come to the convention not as a delegate but as the newlywed wife of a delegate representing the antislavery society that had just separated from Garrison's AAS. She was incensed at the refusal of the convention to seat the women delegates and was inspired by Lucretia's composure, courage, and eloquence in expressing her strongly held opinions about the role of women in promoting societal change. Stanton later recalled, "As Mrs. Mott and I walked home, arm in arm, commenting on the incidents of the day, we resolved to hold a convention as soon as we returned home, and form a society to advocate the rights of women."[9] But after they returned home, eight years would pass before their idea of holding a woman's rights convention would come to fruition.

During the 1840s, Martha began to express in her letters increasing criticism of the legal and financial status of women. In those days, a married woman had essentially no legal rights; she could not sign a contract, make a will, or sue in a court of law. Furthermore, she legally owned nothing. Any money or property she had brought into the marriage, any salary she earned, any personal belongings, even her jewelry and her clothes, were legally the property of her husband. All could be sold by him or claimed by his creditors if he went into debt. In the rare case of divorce, the man automatically received custody of the children. A married woman was essentially the property of her husband. Many of the women who fought for abolition felt that their own position in society was much like that of slaves in the South.

In March 1841, Martha praised a state legislator who "introduced a bill 'to establish and protect the right of private property of married women, and in the event of separation, to establish the rights of parents to the guardianship of children.' "[10] Later that year, when David and Martha Wright were entertaining guests, "the conversation at tea was on women having the property that their parents had accumulated for them, secured to them before marriage." (That and related problems would be addressed, to a limited extent, in the Married Women's Property Act, passed by the New York Legislature in April 1848.)[11] Some in the group sitting around the Wrights' parlor advocated the measure, while others, including David, opposed. Martha "agreed with the former, that instead of showing a want of confidence in a husband it was providing a sure means for his comfort in case of those contingencies always liable to occur where a man is engaged in business of any kind. David thought a wife shared in her husband's good fortune, & should be willing to share his reverses—& *in nine cases out of ten when a man failed in business it was traceable to a wife's extravagance.* Now I think it a great shame for David to make so ungallant a speech as that even if it was the truth which it is not. Women are very apt to . . . endeavor to avert by such arguments as they can use, the mania of speculation, the reckless endorsing for others & the thousand unprofitable schemes that are hurrying them to ruin."[12] By the 1840s, Martha had become willing to disagree openly with her husband, particularly on issues pertaining to woman's rights, including economic issues.

Unmarried working women in the mid-nineteenth century also had much to complain about, including receiving considerably lower wages than men for identical or comparable work. By 1846, finances in the Wright household were strong enough that Martha, who until then had spent countless hours making clothes for her large family, was able, happily, to hire a seamstress. "It is such a convenience," she wrote later, "to say 'Let there be dresses' and dresses are."[13] But the daily salary they paid the seamstress, Miss Soule, was less than half the daily salary they paid to their hired hand, Thomas, for outdoor work. This discrepancy bothered Martha.

I told D. this morning I would tell him how I should like to do if I was rich.
. . . It would be to pay Miss Soule exactly as much as we pay Thomas . . .
[for] steady sewing is as injurious to the health as active labor and I don't see
why a woman should not have the chances of laying up something against the
age of rheumatism and poor sight, as a man. David said such a plan would be a
curse to the community, 'why so.' Why it would raise the price of labor and
set people by the ears. I asked him why people were not set by the ears when
Thomas had six or seven shillings a day. 'Why, a man had a family to support.'
But half the laboring men's wives support the family and their husbands beside—
by taking in washing, &c. David went off to hoe his corn or cut asparagus and
wouldn't hear any more such nonsense.[14]

In the years to come, David would hear much more "such nonsense" from
Martha as she became more and more involved in working for woman's rights
after the 1848 convention. The history of woman suffrage and woman's rights
would be different if Henry and Elizabeth Cady Stanton had not moved in
1847 from Boston to Seneca Falls, a small community only fifteen miles from
Auburn. But move they did, and when Lucretia and James Mott visited Martha
the following summer, the stage was set for a historic event.

The (Second) Tea Party That Shook the World

The Boston Tea Party of 1773 ignited the movement toward American freedom from domination by England. Seventy-five years later, another tea party
would ignite the movement toward women's freedom from domination by
men. Progress in this second movement would proceed much more slowly
than in the first, but the eventual changes in the relationship between the sexes
would be profound. The newspapers in 1848 were full of reports of a series
of revolutions against authority and tradition in Europe, and something very
revolutionary was soon to take place in upstate New York as well. It started
with an invitation to Lucretia and Martha from Jane Hunt to attend a July tea
party at her home in Waterloo, just a few miles west of Seneca Falls and a

short ride from Auburn by train.[15] The Hunts were Quakers and abolitionists, and were very aware of the presence in their neighborhood of the well-known Quaker preacher from Philadelphia. Also invited were Mary Ann M'Clintock, another Quaker abolitionist in Waterloo, and Elizabeth Cady Stanton. Stanton's move from the intellectual excitement of Boston to the relative isolation of her new home in western New York had intensified her concerns about woman's rights, and conversation over the teacups led back to the discussions that she and Lucretia had had in London eight years earlier. By the end of the afternoon the women had drafted a call they sent to the *Seneca County Courier*. It was published on Tuesday, July 11.

> WOMEN'S RIGHTS CONVENTION—A Convention to discuss the social, civil, and religious condition and rights of women, will be held in the Wesleyan Chapel, at Seneca Falls, New York, on Wednesday and Thursday, the 19th and 20th of July, current; commencing at 10 o'clock A.M. During the first day the meeting will be exclusively for women, who are earnestly invited to attend. The public generally are invited to be present on the second day, when Lucretia Mott, of Philadelphia, and other ladies and gentlemen, will address the convention.[16]

A call published the week before a scheduled meeting is very short notice, but the word spread rapidly among Quakers and abolitionists in western New York. Lucretia Mott was a good drawing card and the topic of the convention was novel. Stanton recalls in her autobiography that at the tea party at which this call was written, "the chief movers and managers were Lucretia Mott, Mary Ann McClintock, Jane Hunt, Martha C. Wright, and myself."[17] Of these five pioneering women, only Elizabeth Cady Stanton, Lucretia Mott, and Martha Wright, to recall Judith Wellman's words, "became figures of national importance."[18]

Based on Stanton's autobiography, in which she gives the date for the publication of the convention call as July 14, many sources give July 13 as the date the call was written. However, since the call first appeared in the *Seneca County Courier* on July 11, it is clear that the meeting at which it was written actually occurred earlier, perhaps July 9 or July 10. *History of Woman Suffrage*, co-authored by Stanton, Susan B. Anthony, and Matilda Joslyn Gage, also records a second meeting, held on Sunday morning, July 16, at the M'Clintock home in Waterloo, "to write their declaration, resolutions, and to consider subjects for speeches."[19] Before this second meeting, Stanton drafted the general outline and form of the declaration presented at the convention, presumably drawing on discussions at the Hunts' tea party. On Friday morning, July 14, she wrote to Elizabeth M'Clintock, Mary Ann's daughter, about the declaration: "I have drawn up one but you may suggest any alterations & improvements for I know it is not as perfect a declaration as should go forth from the first woman's rights convention that has ever assembled."[20] Stanton's autobiography does not mention this second meeting, and *History of Woman Suffrage*, also written several decades after the event and dependent on Stanton's recollections, does not say who attended it. Several accounts assume that it was the same five women mentioned above as the "chief movers and managers." However, Lucretia wrote a letter to Stanton from Auburn dated Sunday, July 16, that indicates that Lucretia and Martha were not at the second meeting.[21] Furthermore, a letter of Martha's written to Lucretia several years later refers to "the meeting of Mrs. Stanton and the McClintocks previous to the first Woman Rights Convention."[22] Thus the participants at the second meeting, at which "alterations and improvements" to the declaration and resolutions were completed, were probably only Stanton and the M'Clintocks.

History of Woman Suffrage goes on to record that the women first considered the reports of various peace, temperance, and anti-slavery conventions, "but all alike seemed too tame and pacific for the inauguration of a rebellion as the world had never seen. . . . After much delay, one of the circle took up the Declaration of 1776, and read it aloud with much spirit and emphasis, and it was at once decided to adopt the historic document, with some slight changes such as substituting 'all men' for 'King George.' "[23] Stanton appears to have been the major author of the famous Declaration of Sentiments that emerged from Seneca Falls, but others surely contributed, and Martha probably played a role. Two years earlier she had written an abridgement of B. L. Rayner's 1834 *Life of Thomas Jefferson* during which exercise she had surely become intimately familiar with the words of Jefferson's Declaration.[24] And she and Lucretia had been at the 1833 meeting of the American Anti-Slavery Society, at which the "truths" Jefferson declared to be "self-evident" were cited in the founding document. That week in July 1848, Stanton clearly became very

impressed with Martha's writing skills, because immediately after the convention, she wrote to Martha, urging her, "keep your pen busy" and "[do] not let
a day by without writing something." We may never precisely know the relative roles played by the five "movers and managers" who organized the world's
first woman's rights convention in July 1848. It seems likely, however, that
Martha, already a skillful writer, contributed to the drafting of the historic
Declaration of Sentiments and the various resolutions presented there.

Self-Evident Truths

Three days before the convention opened, Lucretia wrote to Stanton: "My
sister Martha will accompany me on 4th day [Wednesday] morning—& we
will with pleasure accept thy kind invite to your house that night if you should
be not too much crowded with company."[25] On Wednesday morning, July 19,
Martha, then six months pregnant, accompanied Lucretia on the train ride
from Auburn to Seneca Falls. The convention opened in Wesleyan Chapel at
11 A.M.[26] Although the call had indicated that the first day's session would be
limited to women, several dozen men showed up, and it was decided not to
exclude them. James Mott presided. After opening remarks, Stanton read the
Declaration of Sentiments that had been drafted earlier. The delegates discussed it paragraph by paragraph, making changes and additions, and the declaration was read again that afternoon, along with a series of resolutions that
also had been drafted in advance. Martha and Lucretia spent Wednesday night
as Stanton's guests in her small home.[27] The overnight visit probably included
lively conversations about the first day's activities and some sharing of beds.
(Conveniently, Henry Stanton was out of town.) The convention reconvened
at ten o'clock Thursday morning, and the Declaration of Sentiments was then
unanimously adopted.

   The Declaration of 1848, like the Declaration of 1776, opened with the
words "When in the course of human events, it becomes necessary." But
Jefferson's next phrase, "for one people to dissolve the political bonds which
have connected them with another," was replaced by "for one portion of the
family of man to assume among the people of the earth a position different
from that which they have hitherto occupied." And Jefferson's most famous

sentence, starting with, "We hold these truths to be self-evident," was altered to conclude, "that all men and women are created equal." That statement would have sounded very revolutionary to Thomas Jefferson himself.

And it got tougher. After the preamble, the new declaration read: "The history of mankind is a history of repeated injuries and usurpations on the part of man toward woman, having in direct object the establishment of an absolute tyranny over her. To prove this, let facts be submitted to a candid world." There followed a list of the wrongs imposed on woman by man, including:

> He has never permitted her to exercise her inalienable right to the elective franchise.
>
> He has made her, if married, in the eye of the law, civilly dead.
>
> He has taken from her all right in property, even to the wages she earns.
>
> He has monopolized nearly all the profitable employments, and from those she is permitted to follow, she receives but a scanty remuneration.
>
> He has denied her the facilities for obtaining a thorough education—all colleges being closed to her.
>
> He has usurped the prerogative of Jehovah himself, claiming it as his right to assign for her a sphere of action, when that belongs to her conscience and her God.
>
> He has endeavored in every way that he could to destroy her confidence in her own powers, to lessen her self-respect, and to make her willing to lead a dependent and abject life.

After listing these and other charges, the declaration demanded for women "immediate admission to all the rights and privileges which belong to them as citizens of the United States." This inflammatory document was signed by sixty-eight women, including Lucretia Mott, Elizabeth Cady Stanton, Martha C. Wright, Mary Ann M'Clintock (and two of her daughters), and Jane C. Hunt (at whose home the tea party had been held). Among the thirty-two male signatories were James Mott, Richard P. Hunt, and Thomas M'Clintock, husbands of three of the five women at the tea party. Notably missing from the list were Henry Stanton and David Wright. The historic Declaration of Sentiments and a list of the signers is engraved on the outside "water wall" of the

Visitors Center of the Women's Rights National Historic Park, facing what remains of Wesleyan Chapel.

Most accounts estimate the attendance at the convention as three hundred, so the total of one hundred signers represents one-third of those who were present. One of the signers was Charlotte Woodward, a nineteen-year-old glove maker. In November 1920, as Charlotte Woodward Pierce, she was the only female signer of the Seneca Falls Declaration of Sentiments who lived to see the ratification of the Nineteenth Amendment, which finally granted woman suffrage. Notable among the male signers of the declaration was Frederick Douglass, the former slave who had recently started to publish in Rochester his abolitionist newspaper, *North Star.*

The resolutions read on Wednesday afternoon were debated on Thursday, and all were passed. The most controversial was the ninth: "Resolved, That it is the duty of the women of this country to secure to themselves their sacred right to the elective franchise." Stanton wrote later that many "feared a demand for the right to vote would defeat others they deemed more rational, and make the whole movement ridiculous."[28] But the resolution passed with a small majority with the help of a strong supportive speech by Frederick Douglass.

Many of those attending the Seneca Falls Convention felt that the two days were not sufficient for full discussion of all the issues raised and agreed to schedule a follow-up meeting in Rochester two weeks later in the Unitarian church. Rochester was much farther from Auburn and too long a trip for Martha, whose pregnancy was advancing. At the second gathering the women made one step closer to independence, and a woman took the chair, despite the misgivings of both Lucretia Mott and Elizabeth Cady Stanton. The Declaration of Sentiments was read and discussed again, and many new signatures were added. Much discussion this time centered on the concept of equal pay for equal work. The delegates also received Biblical injunctions directing subordination of women, such as Saint Paul's message to the Ephesians (5:22), ordering, "Wives, submit yourselves unto your own husbands, as unto the Lord," and his message to Titus (2:5), urging wives to be "obedient to their own husbands." Lucretia said that she knew of no difficulties resulting from the fact that Quaker marriage ceremonies did not require wives to promise obedience. Biblical passages would continue to be used long into the future to justify subordination of women, much as they had been used to justify slavery.

Douglass later carried a report of the Seneca Falls and Rochester conventions that appeared prominently in his *North Star* along with a strong editorial in support of woman suffrage that ended with the statement:

> All that distinguishes man as an intelligent and accountable being, is equally true of woman; and if that government only is just which governs by the free consent of the governed, there can be no reason in the world for denying to woman the exercise of the elective franchise, or a hand in making and administering the laws of the land. Our doctrine is that "right is of no sex." We therefore bid the women engaged in this movement our humble Godspeed.[29]

Much of the press coverage of the Seneca Falls and Rochester conventions, however, took a more negative view.[30] The Declaration of Sentiments had accurately predicted "no small amount of misconception, misrepresentation, and ridicule." One newspaper report headlined "Women out of Their Latitude" described the outlandish demands of the "women who attend these meetings, no doubt at the expense of their more appropriate duties" and argued that "it requires no argument to prove that this is all wrong." Others ridiculed the "Amazons" and "the reign of petticoats," whose "great effort seemed to be to bring out some new, impracticable, absurd, and ridiculous proposition, and the greater the absurdity the better." Another claimed that while "New York girls aspire to mount the rostrum, to do all the voting, and, we suppose, all the fighting too, . . . the ladies of Philadelphia . . . are resolved to maintain their rights as Wives, Belles, Virgins, and Mothers, and not as Women." (That reporter apparently was not aware that Lucretia, one of the leaders at Seneca Falls and Rochester, was from Philadelphia.) The *New York Herald* reported that "the flag of independence has been hoisted, for a second time, on this side of the Atlantic; and a solemn league and covenant has just been entered into by a Convention of women at Seneca Falls." It proceeded to ridicule the idea of equal rights for women, which would extend to seeing women such as Lucretia Mott go to war or run for President, but concluded with the comment, "We are much mistaken if Lucretia would not make a better President than some of those who have lately tenanted the White House." Although Seneca Falls and later woman's rights conventions received considerable criticism and ridicule in the press, even negative publicity raised public awareness that many women, and some supportive men, were now challenging the traditional role of women in American society.

Hints for Wives and Husbands

Martha was in strong agreement with the actions taken at Seneca Falls, but as her response to a letter from Lucretia suggests, she was, because of her pregnancy, largely silent during the discussions.[31] Her voice was heard only indirectly when Lucretia read the "humorous article from a newspaper, written by MARTHA C. WRIGHT."[32]

Until the 1840s, Martha's writing had been limited largely to her family letters. Although "private," these letters had an audience of several dozen family members. By February 1848, she had written several items for the Auburn paper and developed enough of a reputation locally as a writer of satire that a neighbor, upset over some local event, called on her to beg her "to write something 'real satirical' for the daily." "I told her," Martha wrote, "that she had quite over-rated my powers."[33] Before Seneca Falls, Martha had also written the letter to the Liberator that was published under the title "Infidelity" (see Chapter 5), the abridged biography of Jefferson, and "Hints for Wives," the "humorous article" read at Seneca Falls.[34] The article focuses on the tedium of housework, a frequent topic of her family letters. "The only way," she wrote in a letter to Lucretia in 1844, "is to grub & work, & sweep & dust, & wash & dress children, & make gingerbread, & patch & darn."[35]

"Hints for Wives" was first published on September 23, 1846, in the United States Gazette, a Philadelphia daily newspaper, and appeared again in the August 11, 1848, issue of Douglass's North Star. ("The Star comes regularly," Martha later wrote. "To think of one having that threadbare Hints for Wives in it.")[36] Presumably Douglass had enjoyed hearing Martha's article read at Seneca Falls and asked for permission to republish it. Like many of Martha's published writings, it was written in response to something she had read that angered her. Martha specialized in counterpunches. "Hints" was her response to an article that advised wives that "obedience is a very small part of conjugal duty," and that to please her husband much more was required, including "unremitting kindness" and "a cheerful smile." The wife must do all these things "as means of perpetuating her attractions and giving permanence to his affections." After quoting the offending article at length, Martha described it as

> valuable hints on the duties of wives to their lords, pointing out the modes in which they were to secure, in the husband, the chivalric devotion which had characterized the lover. The most infallible specific, or the one most strongly insisted upon in rules of this kind, is a "smiling countenance." No matter what a wife's annoyances may have been during the day, her countenance must always be wreathed in smiles on the approach of her husband. . . . It has often recurred to me, therefore, that it was rather singular that all this good advice should always come from one side. How is it that there are so few guide-posts to point the way to innocent young gentlemen who have recently submitted their neck to the "noose and the halter?" Why is it not oftener insisted upon, that the husband should always return to his fireside with a smile, and endeavor to soothe the perturbed spirit, that has for hours been subjected to the thousand annoyances of the nursery and the kitchen.

Martha went on to argue that there were married women "among my acquaintance with 'nine small children and one at the breast,'[37] who need all the soothing tenderness erst bestowed by the lover, to enable them to forget the troubles so wearing to the nerves." The article finished with a description of a typical day of such a couple.

> Compare for a moment the lot of Husband and Wife, in what is called a "well regulated family." The former takes his seat at the breakfast table, where his taste and comfort have been silently consulted, as far as is practicable—on his wife devolves the care of preparing the "nine small children" to take their seats there also, and in some degree of regulating their conduct. Breakfast ended, the husband goes forth to the workshop, his counter, his counting-house or his office, greets pleasantly his acquaintances by the way, and passes the day among the ever-varying scenes of every-day business life. The wife, meanwhile, amid incessant clamor, must renew the treadmill task of yesterday— must wash the same faces, make the same beds, sweep the same rooms; must

settle disputes in the kitchen, and quarrels among the nine fallen little sons and daughters of *her Adam*; and amid all these occupations, must find occasional moments to "stitch-stitch-stitch" the innumerable garments needed in a family.

Let her look to it, according to the sapient and oft-reiterated advice above alluded to, that she gets through this in time to clothe her harrassed and care-worn visage in those "wreathed smiles" so indispensable toward maintaining the good humor of her liege lord. He too has had troubles to encounter, for from trouble no one is exempt; but not of that petty, harrassing kind that are wearing away the spirits and the life of the partner he has chosen.

Night comes—the husband finds the repose so much needed to enable him to meet the unavoidable cares of tomorrow, and sleeps as quietly as "the babes in the wood," while the wife starts at the slightest noise, to minister to the comfort of the restless inmates of the trunnel bed and the crib, all of whom are sure to be astir at the earliest dawn, and demanding the immediate care of the mother, who rises weary and unrefreshed, again to go through the same routine—truly, she *should* smile! Whether she always can, is a debatable question. I insist, therefore, that the husband should have a full share of the advice so lavishly bestowed on the wife.

Until a better state of things can be brought about, I am firmly resolved to continue   AN OLD MAID

Hints on the duty of Obedience shall appear hereafter.

This article, written under a pseudonym like many of her published writings, implies that Martha's personal experiences with the "treadmill tasks" of raising children and running a household were a major source of her developing interest in woman's rights.

FIG. 1. Martha Coffin Wright, ca. 1830s. Daguerreotype. Courtesy Garrison Family Papers, Sophia Smith Collection, Smith College.

FIG. 2. Martha Coffin Wright with her
daughter Ellen, 1854. Daguerreotype.
Courtesy Garrison Family Papers, Sophia
Smith Collection, Smith College.

FIG. 3. Martha Coffin Wright with her son
William in uniform, 1861. Daguerreotype.
Courtesy Garrison Family Papers, Sophia
Smith Collection, Smith College.

FIG. 4. Children of Martha Coffin Wright,
ca. 1860. Left to right: Eliza, Frank, Ellen,
Marianna. Courtesy Garrison Family Papers,
Sophia Smith Collection, Smith College.

FIG. 5. Bronze statuary in Visitors Center, Women's Rights National Historical Park, Seneca Falls, New York. An expectant Martha Coffin Wright is at the right foreground, Elizabeth Cady Stanton and Frederick Douglass at the left background. The young woman next to Martha Wright represents a general convention participant, not a specific person. Courtesy National Park Service, Women's Rights National Historical Park.

FIG. 6. Lucretia Coffin Mott, ca. 1860s.
Courtesy Garrison Family Papers, Sophia
Smith Collection, Smith College.

FIG. 7. David Wright, ca. 1860s. Courtesy
Garrison Family Papers, Sophia Smith
Collection, Smith College.

FIG. 8. Genesee Street, Auburn, looking
west, ca. 1850s. Courtesy Cayuga Museum
of History and Art, Auburn, New York.

FIG. 9. Home of David and Martha Wright
(192 Genesee Street, Auburn), ca. 1875.
Courtesy Osborne Family Papers,
Department of Special Collections, Syracuse
University Library.

FIG. 10. John Pelham in West Point furlough uniform, ca. 1860. Courtesy Museum of the Confederacy, Richmond, Virginia. Copy photography by Katherine Wetzel.

FIG. 11. Elizabeth Cady Stanton, ca. 1848,
with her sons Henry and Daniel. Courtesy
Coline Jenkins-Sahlin, Elizabeth Cady
Stanton Trust.

FIG. 12. Susan B. Anthony, ca. 1850.
Enlarged from an ambrotype by William
Sherwell Ellis. Courtesy Garrison Family
Papers, Sophia Smith Collection, Smith
College.

FIG. 13. Frederick Douglass, ca. 1850.
Courtesy American Antiquarian Society.

FIG. 14. Engraving of William Henry
Seward, ca. 1850. Courtesy Garrison Family
Papers, Sophia Smith Collection, Smith
College. Lithograph published in 1855 by
C. H. Brainard, drawn by L. Grozelier from
daguerreotype by Vannerson (information
from Seward House, Auburn).

FIG. 15. Engraving of William Lloyd
Garrison by G. Kruell. Courtesy Garrison
Family Papers, Sophia Smith Collection,
Smith College.

FIG. 16. Harriet Tubman (at left) and group,
ca. 1887. The man seated to the right of
Tubman is Nelson Davis, her second
husband. Courtesy Garrison Family Papers,
Sophia Smith Collection, Smith College.

7

Arrivals and Departures

Nursing Grandmother

FROM HER upbringing and from her adult experiences with marriage and children, Martha had developed a feminist perspective that was reinforced by Seneca Falls and by increasing contacts with Elizabeth Cady Stanton. But her household responsibilities, and her immediate "prospects" of another child, would temporarily delay her public activities on behalf of woman's rights. "No one is fonder of 'children in the Abstract' than I am, but when it comes to the *concrete* it becomes suggestive of the remark of the psalmist relative to 'too much of a good thing.'" So wrote Martha in October 1848, shortly before her seventh child, Charley, was born. At the time, Eliza was eighteen, Tallman was sixteen, Ellen was eight, Willy six, and Frank four. Ellen was apparently something of a tomboy, because Martha often referred to her "three small boys." She was forty-one, and already twice a grandmother, since Marianna (now twenty-three) and Thomas Mott had two daughters. Martha went on in her letter to note that a male neighbor "was speaking of a separate tent on the Fairground, a shilling extra admission, where were exhibited a woman with three children at a birth. I told him I would sooner give a shilling *never to see one*—he no doubt thought me a monster worth two shillings for exhibition, inasmuch as he has been one who took great delight in *looking on* while his own homestead was being very thickly peopled."[1] Sarcasm came naturally to Martha, but pretense did not. She was forthright with her judgment that seven children was "too much of a good thing."

This letter to Philadelphia, completed on the day of Charley's birth, also reported her preserving fruit, repairing a fur cap, and completing other household chores: "all our quilting is accomplished—9 quilts & comforts in all . . . swept & dusted all below stairs . . . so many little jobs I have achieved that I feel reconciled to let a good many go that I had hoped to accomplish, such as carpet rags, &c." The same letter reported that she and Eliza had been distributing the official report of the Seneca Falls Convention that Elizabeth Cady Stanton had sent to her (along with the admonition from Stanton to "keep your pen busy.")

Martha's frequent accountings of problems with her children drew some comments from a cousin, as is clear from a letter of Martha's from the previous year.

> I don't wonder Phebe[2] should think I was a good deal troubled with my children. Her remarks opened my eyes to the folly of chronicling every feeling of annoyance, as I do. Other people, doubtless, have as much trouble, but they wisely keep it to themselves, and when their children are all grown up, look as placid and serene as sister Eliza does, making people believe those three boys were ministers and deacons from their birth. Still, to be honest, I don't believe hers were quite as full of mischief as my three, counting Ellen one boy, for if they had been her forehead never could have been so beautiful and unwrinkled as it is now, for troubles and care will leave their impress on the brow. I often, very often, think of her when I feel unusually nervous and worried, and wonder if she ever did feel so bad. But, I guess she is less excitable than I, of a more quiet and patient temperament.[3]

Although it is possible that Martha was more "excitable" than her sister Eliza and other mothers of the time, the major difference was that Martha expressed her feelings more openly than most. Later in the letter, she countered the image of being a complaining mother with sarcasm. "There comes my seraphic little Frank," she wrote, and since David had taken Tallman and

Willy with him for the day, she expressed her "grief at being so long deprived of the society of my blessed little boys. . . . But, 'The day drags on, tho' the clouds keep out the sun; And thus the heart will break, yet brokenly live on,' as Byron says.[4] So, I lived through the long hours of the absence of my precious little sons." Martha's reading included much poetry, and she was especially fond of quoting Byron, her favorite poet.[5]

Her letter the next month was full of details about the new baby, and she advised her readers "not to tire of this subject for it is the only one destined for the next 500 pages."[6] She soon found that being largely confined to her bedroom had its advantages: "If it is impossible to fly round the house and put everything in order and be a good housekeeper, there is decided comfort in being lazy. Here I sit, Grandmother Wright! dust reposing and a thousand things undone, nursing a tiny little boy, and sewing and knitting enough to do, if it was piled up, to reach the ceiling." Her rest also allowed her to catch up on some reading: "I have finished Omoo and Typee [seafaring novels by Herman Melville]—I think them delightful, especially the latter."[7]

Martha loved to read novels whenever she could. Lucretia, in contrast, once stated, "Made-up stories do not interest me." Martha wrote to her, "For my dear sister's sake I wish I had been constituted to take the greatest delight in Malthus on Political Economy, Adam Smith's Wealth of Nations, or that immense Folio of William Penn's so as to fill a page or two now and then with interesting comments on them. But 'whatever is—is' and I fear I shall go through life, preferring Walter Scott and Dickens to a whole basket full of the worthies I have mentioned."[8] In comparing serious reading of the type preferred by Lucretia to the novels of Dickens, she wrote, "You read one as a duty, the other as an immense pleasure after a surfeit of duties."[9]

Although Martha loved Byron, she disapproved of Walt Whitman. "There were blemishes," she wrote, "in the little that I read [of Whitman's *Leaves of Grass*], that I thought ought to exclude it from any table." The "blemishes" in Whitman's poems were open sexual references. About similar references in the Bible and Shakespeare, she wrote, "Those were written in an age when grossness was tolerated but there seemed to me no excuse for writing, in this day, what was unfit to be read."[10] Although much of Martha's thinking was radical for her times, she remained conservative with regard to sexual matters.

The year of the Seneca Falls Convention and the birth of Charley was also the year gold was discovered in California. The following year, in January 1849, Martha reported that a group from Auburn were planning to join the flood of "forty-niners" heading west to earn their fortunes: "Each one puts in $500 and they divide among them all the gold they get. They pledge themselves not to gamble or drink or work on Sundays. They are going round Cape Horn, to be absent 3 years."[11] David, she reported, was scornful: "David predicts the ruin of the country from the increase of extravagance and luxury consequent on the sudden accession of wealth, and says it wd. [would] be better if every ounce of it was in the bottom of the sea. Ruin or not, I wish I had a good lot of it. I would be willing to take the gold and let our *farm* be at the *bottom of the sea*."[12]

David had purchased several farms. One was nineteen acres and about a half-mile west of their home. (Period maps show it split by Wright Avenue, which retains that name today.) The others were much larger and in Moravia, near the southern end of Owasco Lake and about fifteen miles from Auburn.[13] David had great hope that the farms would be sources of financial gain, but Martha never shared his enthusiasm and was frequently disparaging of David's farms, including an attempt he initiated some years later to drill for oil. (She felt a farm should be described not in acres, but in "*achres*—that is the way it should always be spelled.")[14] David also became president of a company formed to construct a "plank road" between Auburn and Moravia following the passage in 1848 of a state law encouraging improvement of the public roads.[15] But this project too was largely unsuccessful. As with most other such roads built in New York, damage to the wooden planks from heavy wagons and natural decay, plus a shortage of timber, made it unprofitable. David's law business, however, continued to grow, and in that year alone he traveled six thousand miles on his various legal cases. He developed what would later be called "the leading law practice in the county," and he eventually would argue twelve cases before the United States Supreme Court in Washington.[16]

Although the gold rush in California did not appeal to David, it did to their sixteen-year-old son Tallman, which raised new worries for Martha. Tallman, who had no interest in working in his father's law office, had traveled to Philadelphia to look for opportunities. He stayed with Lucretia, to whom Martha wrote, "I appreciate fully the kindness that prompted you to offer Tallman a home with all your thousand cares & hope he can contrive some way to return it, by making himself useful."[17] But now California beckoned. When Tallman raised the issue, Martha expressed her skepticism in a letter to Lucretia: "We think he is entirely too young yet to go among such a set of ruffians as will be congregated there. He little knows the hardship and suffering he wd. be subjected to. It is probably more from the love of adventure, than for the gratification of acquisitiveness that he wishes to go, as he never has shown much of the latter disposition, but there will be time enough for adventure when he is older and his principles more firmly fixed. His father has spoken against it from the first. . . . Such immense numbers are going that there will be a better chance for situations for those who remain."[18] Parental disapproval delayed Tallman's quest for adventure in California, but not for long.

The pressure on Martha's time was somewhat relieved in 1849 when Ellen, Willy, and Frank were entered as day scholars in the Auburn Female Seminary. The school catalogue for that year lists 246 students, with Willy and Frank the only boys.[19] Martha, as a parent, was not constrained by traditional roles for boys and girls; she also taught Willy and Frank how to knit, a skill which they continued to practice after going to boarding school. But even before he reached four, Frank was aware of one important difference between men and women. After his mother mashed a potato for him at dinner one day, he asked his father to mash his next potato because "men can mash potato better than women." David and Martha were surprised and amused by Frank's pronouncement, and Martha wrote to Lucretia, "He has not been in the habit of expressing a sentiment so profound. David said he must tell Mrs. Stanton that."[20]

Tallman had left home, and it soon would be Eliza's turn. Martha wrote once that "it would be nice for Eliza to study medicine,"[21] and on another occasion, "nothing would have suited Eliza better than to be a lawyer if she had only been the boy."[22] Martha had not expressed such progressive thoughts about her oldest daughter, Marianna, five years older than Eliza. Perhaps Seneca Falls and her contacts with Stanton and others had helped to broaden Martha's views. However, like that of most women in the mid-nineteenth century, Eliza's "career" would be marriage. By 1849, Eliza was nineteen and had attracted a series of beaus. Martha described one as "a new acquaintance who has read everything she has—a 'love of a man,' Mr. Osborne, . . . a recent importation from New York."[23] Like Martha, Eliza loved reading, and a man's knowledge of literature was a definite plus in her eyes. Eliza and David Munson Osborne were married two years later. They remained in Auburn, and Munson later became highly successful in business, selling agricultural machinery.[24] Their home on South Street was within walking distance of Martha's, so Eliza and Martha remained physically close, as well as emotionally close, throughout Martha's life.

Although Martha's letters suggest that 1849 was a very busy year, she and David and Eliza did get out to a few neighborhood parties. The social scene in Auburn was lively, especially in the winter, when touches of gaiety helped to counteract the depressing impact of months and months of long, cold nights. At one party, Martha, who remained very much a Quaker in her taste in women's clothing, reported "the company beautifully dressed—except a few who were undressed—arms bare nearly to the shoulder, and bony necks generously displayed for the benefit of amateurs in anatomy."[25]

One day Martha and David received a party invitation that ended with a mysterious series of initials: R.S.V.P. This degree of continental sophistication was probably new to Auburn in the 1840s and had not yet reached the Wrights. "David thought the first must be Revised Statutes," Martha wrote Lucretia. "We sent a regret for me. . . . I was sorry I did not put on the corner of mine, to puzzle them as much as they had puzzled us, 'T.B.I.C.C.' (Too bad I can't come.)"[26]

Visiting Lecturers

Martha was also occasionally drawn away from her household duties to attend public lectures by visiting dignitaries, and she was especially interested in a lecture delivered in Auburn shortly after the Seneca Falls Convention by Frederick Douglass, the prominent black abolitionist.[27] Douglass had been a slave in Maryland until he escaped to the North in 1838 at the age of twenty-one. Originally named Frederick Bailey, he changed his name to Douglass to avoid being caught and returned to slavery. He had received a surreptitious education during his youth, and when the Massachusetts Antislavery Society discovered his skills as a lecturer, they made him an agent. Audiences found it difficult to believe that this eloquent speaker had been a slave, prompting him to write an autobiography, which was published in 1845. Abolitionist supporters then raised enough funds to purchase Douglass's freedom from his former owner, and he started publishing *North Star* in Rochester in 1847.

Martha and Douglass first became acquainted at Seneca Falls, where she was impressed with his skills as a public speaker, he with her skills as a writer. He published her "Hints for Wives" that August in the *North Star*. When she learned soon thereafter that he was speaking in Auburn, she invited him to 192 Genesee Street. Despite his widespread fame as a public speaker, Douglass was not welcome at the hotels or at most homes in Auburn because of his race. But he was welcome at Martha's. During his visit, Martha's attention was divided between her guest and her two lively sons; as she reported, "In the intervals of being agreeable I had to keep Willy & Frank straight—they were pretty wild." Douglass accepted her invitation for dinner ("nice corn and corn soup"), but not her invitation to stay overnight. His excuse was a prior commitment, but perhaps, with David out of town, Douglass was just being discreet. He did walk Martha and her daughters home that evening after his public lecture, which may have offended some of Martha's neighbors, but probably did not surprise them. About the lecture, Martha reported that "he spoke beautifully. . . . Ellen [then eight] was with us, and was very much entertained during the meeting with the demonstrations of applause—where other people laughed she did the same as heartily as if she could understand the point. She thought Douglass knew how to speak better than her Aunt L [Lucretia]."[28]

At supper one evening soon after Douglass's visit, Frank, then four, persisted in saying "nigger," a word he had apparently picked up from playmates. "After all was over & the table cleared I went up & talked to him 'a lot'," Martha wrote. "He said he wished he was dead, but if he didn't die he would say naughty words every day."[29] Raising children was never easy, but there were special challenges when the values she tried to instill in her children were so different from those of the surrounding society.

Douglass returned to Auburn to deliver another lecture the following spring. Whereas his earlier speech had been on the "free soil" political movement, which focused on keeping slavery out of newly admitted states, this time "the principal topic was the elevation of the blacks in our midst." He walked with Martha, David, and Eliza on their way home after his lecture and called on Martha the next day. "He called and sat half an hour or so," Martha wrote. But he "could not stay to dinner. . . . Eliza gave him some of her pretty roses that were just in bloom." Martha related to him a story she had received from Lucretia about the escape of some slaves from Virginia. "He held Charley while I read about the slaves to him. His wife has a daughter two weeks old."[30] Baby Charley, unlike his brother Frank, had not yet learned to be uncomfortable with blacks.

On several occasions over the years, Douglass, sometimes accompanied by other blacks, dined and stayed overnight at the Wrights' home. Although most of Martha's neighbors were not aware of the fugitive slaves occasionally harbored at her house, Douglass's visits were not clandestine and attracted considerable attention. One neighbor sought information through young Ellen and asked with considerable curiosity whether the visiting blacks had eaten at the table with them. Another approached Martha at a neighborhood party and asked her "with the slightest possible sneer after our recent *guests*, emphasizing the word, and wishing to be informed whether we gave them 'the best room.' I told him 'certainly' and informed him that in conversing with a man of superior intellect one forgot whether he was black or white."[31] During Martha's numerous visits to the Motts in Philadelphia, she had become accustomed to meeting black men and women socially, but to most of her Auburn neighbors this was very unusual and shocking behavior.

Of course not all the blacks Martha encountered were "of superior intellect" like Douglass. She often became angry with her kitchen help, who were usually either black or Irish, and once she referred to a black woman as a "baboon" and a "refractory ape."[32] However, she clearly felt guilty about that outburst and wrote, "I do not wish you to suppose, either that I am in the habit of getting so mad angry, as I can only remember two or three times in my life that I have felt even half as ferocious."[33] Over the years, Martha commented often about the women she hired. She once wrote, "My African diamond gets along beautifully & has everything so clean, instead of Irish slopping, that it is a real comfort. . . . Give me Africa over all Hibernia."[34] But about another Irish "girl" she wrote, "What a change a few days in civilized company will be made in such Emeralders. . . . Charley is good with her and we begin to like her very much."[35] In those days, prejudice against the Irish was common, and Martha was not completely immune, nor was David, who often complained about bad experiences with Irish laborers at his farm. Part of their attitude toward the Irish may have been related to Martha and David's sympathy for blacks, because many Irish were often outspoken in their contempt for blacks.[36]

Martha heard the Unitarian minister Theodore Parker, whom she much admired, and Abby Kelley Foster, speak out against slavery at lectures in Auburn in early 1852. Abby Kelley had been one of the first woman abolitionists to lecture in public, and her nomination to the business committee of the American Anti-Slavery Society in 1840 had contributed to the split in the abolitionist ranks over "the woman question." She had since married Stephen Foster, who was also an abolitionist lecturer. Both were very aggressive in attacking church leaders and churchgoers for their indifference to the evils of slavery. Abby Kelley Foster's lecture at the Universalist Church in Auburn on the first day of an antislavery meeting was so fiery that the church closed its doors to the remainder of the meeting, an action that so infuriated David that he withdrew their subscription to a pew. Even Martha felt that Foster had been a bit too harsh to be effective and told her so. She reported her conversation in a letter to Lucretia.

> [I told her] that while I didn't care how severely she rebuked the pious indifference of our people, I thought less swearing at them wd. be better, that it was not well for children to listen to such words. I thought Mr. May's [Samuel J. May] kindly manner wd. have more influence. She defended herself very ably, insisting that people wd. listen with pleasure to gentle words and go and forget them, but these very things that I complained of, were the ones that remained, made a deep impression, made the hearers very angry it was true, and were therefore remembered, and she must say that where S. J. May and Lucretia Mott had made one convert, she and her husband had made ten. . . . She went on to say, far be it from her to despise the instrumentality of the gentle zephyr, or the small summer rain; but the rushing torrent and wild Tornado had their appointed work also.[37]

Martha accepted Foster's point, conceding that "as there were all sorts of minds to influence, there must be different instrumentality." But Martha clearly differed with Foster in the relative effectiveness of the "gentle zephyr" of May and Mott and the "wild Tornado" of the Fosters in swaying public opinion.

After Theodore Parker's antislavery lecture, Rev. W. R. G. Mellen, the local Universalist minister, dropped by to discuss it with Martha and David. As she reported to Lucretia, "Mr. Mellen thought he did not quite do justice to [Saint] Paul. There was every reason to believe that Paul was a married man. I told him I had seen it asserted somewhere that he was, and if so his advice in favor of celibacy might have been in good faith, as he doubtless did as a great many other great men had done, married a simpleton."[38]

That year Martha also heard Ralph Waldo Emerson lecture, but to an audience primarily of young men and on a less controversial topic, "Success." Among his points were the importance of a determined will and repetitive drill. He supported the latter point, Martha wrote, by noting, "It was no wonder that Nature should succeed in getting up such beautiful sunsets, seeing that she had been doing it every day for so long." She was "not so much attracted toward him [Emerson], as toward Theodore Parker. Didn't feel that peculiar reverence and admiration for him, but listened nevertheless with great interest to one so renowned." Emerson made a brief visit to the Wrights after his lecture. "His manner was very pleasant. 'I am told,' said he, 'that you are sister to my friend Mrs. Mott.' I told him that was unfortunate, as it might lead him to draw comparisons."[39] Martha worried that whenever she was introduced as Lucretia's sister, as she was to Emerson, the association would create expectations of greatness that she could not live up to. She apparently was more relaxed during another visit by Emerson a few years later, which she simply reported as "very pleasant & very free & very social."[40]

Another visitor to Auburn in the 1850s was Lajos (Louis) Kossuth, who in 1848 and 1849 led Hungary's struggle for independence from Austria. Martha and other abolitionist and woman's rights activists felt that they had common cause with European revolutionaries. Like slaves seeking freedom from their masters, and women seeking freedom from the domination of men, European revolutionaries, such as Kossuth, were seeking freedom from oppression by established and traditional authority. But Kossuth, who traveled to the United States in 1852 seeking support for his cause after his movement was defeated by Russian armies, disappointed abolitionists by refusing to address the issue of slavery in America.[41] His trip included a weekend visit to Auburn, where he was the guest of William Henry Seward, now a U.S. senator and one of Kossuth's most fervent supporters. Martha and David met Kossuth at Seward's home, and the visit stimulated Martha's interest in the Hungarian fight for freedom from the Hapsburgs of Austria. That interest explains her response to a lecture delivered in Auburn that year by an Episcopal minister named William I. Kip.[42]

Kip's lecture, entitled "Recollections of Vienna," described his visit to the Austrian capital in a manner that glorified the royal family of Hapsburgs and made no mention of Kossuth and Hungary. Martha was displeased. "Instead of pointing out the oppression that must exist to keep up all this state and supply those hoards of wealth," she wrote, "his whole aim seemed to be to show how smoothly all went on, and what amiable people monarchs and Arch-dukes were." Martha was also distressed that so many others in the audience thought the lecture was wonderful. "At the close of the lecture there was as much applause as an Auburn audience ever vouchsafes, while there was not one murmur of applause when Emerson closed. . . . Mr. B. J. Hall said that was the kind of lectures that we needed here, not such as Theodore Parker and Emerson delivered, weaving in *their infidel notions.*"[43]

A few days later, a satirical poem with the same title as Kip's lecture appeared in the *Auburn Daily Advertiser* over the name "Miss Agnes Skipp." One verse ended, "E'en sullen discontent perforce is mute, / And not a rebel dares to say—Kossuth!" The poem ended:

> A *gentle despotism*, such as this
> Must surely be the height of human bliss!
> To paint its beauties all my efforts fail:
> Then Hail! Vienna! House of Hapsburg! Hail![44]

Martha called the poem "a free paraphrase that I made of the lecture and entrusted to Theodore Pomeroy to put in the daily, anticipating a little difficulty, if not a refusal, as all the Episcopalians were delighted with the lecture." But the editor "expressed himself well pleased, and it found more favor than I expected. Charles Wood said that even those who liked the lecture pro-

nounced it a good satire, and one or two said to me 'Have you read &c—
Wasn't it Capital?' Rather an embarrassing question. Mrs. Underwood looked
rather disappointed that I did not respond so heartily as she expected, but I
don't think she suspected the authorship." Many, however, had guessed it was
Martha's work, since this was by no means the first time that her satirical
writings had appeared in the Auburn daily. A few errors appeared in the first
printing of Martha's poem, so it was republished with the editor's comment
that "the stanzas are so excellent and appropriate, that they will lose none of
their interest by a re-perusal." Her satire had been gentle, because she strove
"to make it obvious enough for those to understand who saw the absurdity of
the lecture, without wounding the sense of propriety of the innocent young
gentlemen who invited the lecturer and who would feel personally any ridicule
aimed at their guest. . . . I thought likely that those who had so little discrimination as to like the lecture, would not have penetration enough to see the
intention of the satire, but enough appreciated it to answer my purpose."[45]
Although her tool was humor, her purpose was political. She was attacking
respect for tradition and established authority, and supporting rebellion.

Natural Laws

In the years following Seneca Falls, Martha suffered several family tragedies.
In July 1849, her brother Thomas, who had never married, died of cholera in
Philadelphia at the age of fifty-one. That fall Charley became very sick and
died in November, a few days after his first birthday. Infant deaths were
common in those days, but Martha had been lucky with her first six children.
She took Charley's death very hard, and one cannot help wondering whether
compounding her grief were feelings of guilt over her frequent statements
during her pregnancy about the "prospect of having more Wrights than I
wanted." Her letter reporting the news to Lucretia has not been preserved,
but we can get glimpses of it in Lucretia's response.

> My dear stricken Sister, Do I not know how to feel for a sore-wounded and
> bleeding heart? But what can I say to alleviate a mother's tender sorrow? Verily
> nothing! Tears I have almost at will, ever since our loved mother's sudden

departure from us, and a fresh fount opened when our brother went. . . . Dear little soul! How sorry I am that I did not oftener lay aside my sewing, and take him and love him. His sweet smile and intelligent eye, and his ever happy infancy will be a precious remembrance to you. . . . Why speak of "special Providences?" We can but consider them "dark and inexplicable." But when we come to look at all these seeming inflictions as the operation of the natural laws, while the pang of parting with our loved ones is none the less, we are not left so in the dark, nor do we take such gloomy views of "the ways of Providence." In thy letter thou says, "Charley's death was so decreed. It is beyond mortal power to say *why* decreed." I would ask if it is not equally impossible to *prove* it "so decreed"? . . . These partings are sad events in our lives, but how greatly do the pleasures overbalance! I do not agree with you that "life protracted is protracted woe." That is one of Young's gloomy sayings, I presume, when indulging in his morbid grief.[46] We mourn the dead, because nature has so constituted us; not on their account always, nor is the sorrow purely selfish. When people die before they have lived half their days, it seems contrary to the design of their creation; the world loses their usefulness, and they lose so much of the enjoyment of life, that all these considerations inspire sadness at their departure.[47]

Martha was very despondent indeed to write that "life protracted is protracted woe," a sentiment much at odds with her usual cheerful outlook on life. Charley's death, by what Lucretia called the "operation of natural laws," led Martha that winter even to question her long-held belief in a kind and loving God. In January, she wrote about accidents that "instead of being a Divine dispensation are only the 'impartial operation of the Natural Laws,' but how are we to view the wholesale destruction of life occasioned by sudden storms at sea and by volcanoes; it is hard to me to reconcile that with Infinite Benevolence."[48]

At a time when death was very much on Martha's mind, much public attention was drawn to a contemporary fad, a form of spiritualism based on supposed communication from the dead through mysterious rapping of tables. Kate and Maggie Fox, two young sisters living in a small town near Rochester, had received considerable publicity in 1848 from their public demonstrations of such communications. Forty years later, the Foxes were to confess it was all a fraud; they had arranged for a servant girl to rap from the cellar whenever she heard the girls' voices calling forth the spirits. At the time, however, table rapping was widely believed, particularly by people mourning the recent loss of loved ones, to be a legitimate form of messages from the dead. Among those who took the table rapping seriously was the abolitionist leader William Lloyd Garrison. When he and George Thompson, a British abolitionist, visited Martha in 1851 to "take a cup of tea," they had recently been to a spiritualist session that Martha called "the Rochester *demon*—strations." Martha reported that she "had not much good of their visit—they were so full of the knockings."[49] At a seance, Thompson had attempted to communicate not with recently departed loved ones but with Saints Paul and Luke—to ask them about Garrison's religious principles and state of health. Martha's views on "*demon*—strations" were those of a skeptic: "It is easier to think it must be delusion, than to suppose that disembodied spirits can find no better occupation that trotting tables round the room." "I think if I could not find a better mode of utterance than knocking—I would keep to the usual amusement of harping." Two years had passed since Charley's death, and Martha's sense of humor had clearly returned.

Martha was equally skeptical of another contemporary fad—spirit letters, produced by spirits who supposedly could take over a living person's hand and produce letters by "automatic writing." Benjamin Franklin was claimed to be source of several such letters, including one written to Lucretia, to whom he was distantly related through his mother, a Folger. "Sister L. received a Spirit letter from *Franklin* lately," Martha wrote to David, "postmarked Wilmington. He should have addressed her as Dear cousin, but he does not appear to recognize the relationship. The idea conveyed is that, so long as she is trammeled by her sect, she cannot attain to her full usefulness. She does not attach any more importance than I do to such manifestations."[50] (One prominent proponent of spiritualism, E. W. Capron, lived in Auburn and claimed in his 1855 book on the topic that there were then over fifty mediums in the city "in various stages of development."[51] He also lists the names of numerous Auburn residents who had observed "manifestations of the spirits"; Martha's name is, unsurprisingly, not among them.)

Although Martha did not believe in communications from the dead, she maintained a belief in an afterlife. She wrote Lucretia about an incident with Frank: "When I was washing him the other day he said 'If we say naughty words we will go to..' 'Hush,' said I 'if you say naughty words you will *not* go to Heaven and see dear little Charley.' That was a *lie* for he can't help it when he hears it every day and I believe he will see Charley just the same."[52] Frank, Willy, and Ellen were then attending Auburn Female Seminary, where they heard "every day" about heaven and hell, God and the devil. As announced in the seminary catalogue, "The School is opened each day with devotional exercises, consisting of sacred music, reading select portions of Scripture, and prayer. A Bible exercise will be required weekly."[53] "I am afraid if they go to that devout Episcopal school much longer," Martha wrote, "we shall all become very profane [in language]."[54] To Martha, "hell" and "the devil" were improper words. Furthermore, Martha did not believe in a vengeful God who would impose eternal damnation on men or women for misbehavior on Earth.

Soon after Charley's death, Martha had new cause to worry about her oldest son, Tallman. California still beckoned. In 1851, he became disenchanted with the prospects of a merchant's career in Philadelphia, paid a brief and unpleasant visit to Auburn, and immediately started west. He went first to Ohio, where Martha wrote to him, "If you can earn so much more than you could here, we have no wish to unsettle you by urging your return to a place that had become so distasteful to you." She added a message from friends that California "is not what it was, and that those who are here, do wisely to stay here."[55] Despite her advice, California remained his dream; he still had gold fever. After his arrival there, nine-year-old Frank sent him a letter with a request for a lump of gold, a lasso, and an Indian child. Unfortunately, in California Tallman found neither gold nor success with a variety of undertakings. In April 1853, he reported to Martha that he had hoped "to return to Auburn by the first of June with something over two thousand dollars in my pocket, but as it turned out I got entirely broken up, not a red, as the old saying goes."[56] He had invested eight hundred dollars in cattle, had them slaughtered, and was taking the meat by boat to San Francisco when he ran into a storm and lost all the meat when the boats sank. He had also invested six hundred dollars in hogs that he was fattening up in Sacramento, but when he returned he found the storm had washed away the corral and all the hogs were gone. He had to sell everything else he had to pay off his debts and now had "one hundred dollars only to show for eighteen months work and hard work too." "I guess he will come out right after a while," Martha wrote to David, "and learn a great deal from experience—that best of teachers they say, tho so far as *my experience* has gone, I should have preferred a gentler teacher."[57] And she would soon face another ungentle experience.

After his losses with cattle and hogs, Tallman supported himself for several months by working at a hotel, a job that provided him with room and board but not much else. Disenchanted with California, he wrote to Martha that he was considering traveling to South America to work in Chile. That plan fell through, and by summer 1854 he wrote to her from San Francisco to announce, "I may come home in the Spring in time to take charge of the farm if Father would like it. It has always troubled him so much I suppose he would be glad to get rid of it & if things go right this winter I have been thinking that would be about the only thing at home that would suit me. I have learned considerable about farming out here."[58]

Martha had not seen Tallman for over three years, and this letter raised her hopes that he would soon be returning east. It was not to be, for in September she was shocked to receive a letter informing her of Tallman's death. While working on a schooner sailing from San Francisco to Sacramento, he had been knocked overboard into the bay by a swinging boom. It was a dark night, the waves were high, and his body was never found. A neighbor expressed regret that he could not be buried, "but to me that is of no consequence," Martha wrote, "now that he is gone, it is little to me that the waves, instead of the earth, have closed over him, and that they are his only requiem."[59]

Six years earlier at Auburn, Tallman had frightened Martha by skating the length of Owasco Lake, about fourteen miles, on thin ice. "I have a horror of that lake," she then wrote, "amounting almost to a presentiment—and neither of our boys shall ever go on again if I can prevent it. I have suffered my share from such a cause."[60] This was a reference to Julius Catlin, her fiancé who had drowned in a river at Rochester in 1828. Many years later, describing her family to a relative of Julius's, she wrote, "Our oldest son was drowned in California (as tho' one such dreadful experience was not enough!)."[61] In her 1844 poem "Philosophy of Life's Noon," Martha had written, "Clouded and stormy the morning has been." With Charley's death in 1849 and Tallman's in

1854, her life's afternoon had already produced its share of clouds. "We must all love each other the more now," she wrote to Marianna.

After the deaths of Charley and Tallman, and the marriages of Marianna and Eliza, Martha's primary maternal responsibilities were narrowed to Ellen, Willy, and Frank. Soon they would be away at boarding schools, and Martha would have more opportunity to devote her energies to the causes of woman's rights and abolition.

8

The Convention Circuit

Following Seneca Falls

AFTER THE women of New York, along with Lucretia Mott, had set the precedent at Seneca Falls and Rochester in 1848, the 1850s saw a rapid explosion of conventions focused on the revolutionary topic of woman's rights.[1] One was held in Salem, Ohio, in April 1850, and that October, the first "national" woman's rights convention convened in Worcester, Massachusetts, with Paulina Wright Davis of Providence, Rhode Island, presiding. Representatives came from nine northern states, one from California, and another from Iowa. Lucretia was one of the speakers. The Worcester convention was highly successful, with over a thousand in attendance. It was followed by the second national convention a year later, again in Worcester and again chaired by Davis.

Martha's attention in the years immediately following Seneca Falls was focused mostly on family matters, but the issue of woman's rights continued to be important to her, as demonstrated in her correspondence. In 1849, two young women had approached Elizabeth Cady Stanton about their ambitions to become silk merchants in Philadelphia. One was twenty-eight-year-old Elizabeth M'Clintock, a signer of the Seneca Falls Declaration of Sentiments and daughter of one of the convention organizers. Stanton sought Lucretia's assistance. "Ah! me those woman's rights conventions have spoiled our lovely maidens," Stanton wrote. "Now instead of remaining satisfied with the needle & the school room they would substitute the compass & the exchange."[2] She asked Lucretia to prevail upon her son-in-law, Edward M. Davis, to offer a clerkship to the two young women in his wholesale business. Davis presented the suggestion to his partners and his clerks, but the idea of admitting the women to their business was soundly ridiculed and rejected. The incident generated some satirical writing by Stanton,[3] and a letter from Martha to the disappointed Elizabeth M'Clintock that included several disparaging remarks about men, plus the revelation that she was challenging traditional gender roles by teaching her sons to knit.

> In the stagnation that occurs periodically in those wholesale establishments it is not surprising that your application should have raised a "tempest in a teapot" and set Market Street in a ferment. No doubt they gladly grasped at something exciting. Men are so desperately idle, when business flags a little, having no resources of knitting and sewing to fill up odd moments, that they become inveterate *gossips* sometimes, to a degree quite painful for *women* to witness.
>
> I love Mrs. Stanton for the ardor and energy she shows in advocating our cause, and envy her the ability to clothe her thoughts in words that burn! I can only stand at a humble distance responding (mentally) most heartily to the sentiments of others, without the power to say anything myself . . .
>
> Very sincerely,
> Your friend,
> M.C.W.
>
> P.S. After a world of patient and impatient teaching as I felt nervous or otherwise, I have taught my little boys to knit. One of them has knit a garter and nearly finished the second; the other has knit three garters, and made a bag to put his marbles in, not sewed exactly like a thread case, but sufficiently neat for a beginning, and quite marvelous considering the *slow perceptions* of the sterner sex.[4]

Stanton's remarkable gift as a writer and a speaker caused Martha to envy her "ability to clothe her thoughts in words that burn." But Martha perhaps displayed a bit of false modesty in claiming that she herself was "without the power to say anything." It was Martha's fear of public speaking that kept her in awe of Stanton, her sister Lucretia, and others who had the ability to deliver fiery words effectively to large audiences. As a writer, however, Martha was quite capable herself of clothing thoughts in "words that burn." Lucretia considered Martha the writer of the family, and Stanton also admired Martha's writing skills, often seeking Martha's help with her writing for the public.

Stanton also was circulating petitions to promote woman's rights. In 1850, Martha wrote Lucretia, "I must answer a letter from Mrs. Stanton which I received a few days since, requesting me to *take charge* of this District and procure signees to a petition for the right of Suffrage for Women. What on earth shall I tell her? I should smile to see myself trotting round with a petition through this benighted region, where there are not three women who would consider it safe to touch such a petition unfumigated."[5] Martha considered the "benighted region" of Auburn too conservative for her to locate many supporters of woman suffrage. Nevertheless, within a few years she would be doing her best to collect signatures on such petitions.

Although Martha had missed the two Worcester conventions, she actively participated in the third national convention, which was held in Syracuse in September 1852. Four years earlier, Lucretia had objected to the idea of a woman presiding at a meeting where both men and women were present. Now she presided herself for the first time, with only her husband, James, objecting. "It was a singular spectacle," the *Syracuse Standard* reported, "to see the gray-haired matron presiding over a Convention with an ease, dignity and grace that might be envied by the most experienced legislator in the country."[6]

The Syracuse convention was not only the first woman's rights convention at which Lucretia presided; it was also the first at which Martha spoke in public. As one of the secretaries of the convention, Martha read the lengthy declaration of sentiments adopted that June in West Chester, Pennsylvania, at the first convention on woman's rights held in that state.[7] No longer hampered by pregnancy as she was at Seneca Falls, she overcame her fear of public speaking and also took an active part in later discussions, including one on the relevance of the Bible to the issue of woman's rights.[8] Syracuse was also important to Martha because there she met many of the women who were or would become leaders in the woman's rights movement. Among these was a woman, acting as one of the convention's other secretaries, who eventually became one of Martha's closest friends and the best known of America's fighters for woman's rights and woman suffrage: Susan B. Anthony.

Susan Brownell Anthony, thirty-two years old when Martha met her, had met Elizabeth Cady Stanton on a street corner in Seneca Falls the previous year. She had earlier become sensitive to woman's rights issues through her experience as a teacher, where women were typically paid $2.50 a week and men $10.00 a week. She left teaching in 1849, settled in her family home near Rochester, and became active in the temperance movement. Here the need for increased woman's rights was also apparent, since most drunkards were men, and their suffering wives had no legal protection against them. Anthony became frustrated with the limited role that women were allowed in the established temperance movement and helped found the Woman's State Temperance Society of New York. She also became president of the Rochester Daughters of Temperance. Through her attendance at women's temperance conventions, she befriended Amelia Bloomer of Seneca Falls, publisher of a temperance and woman's rights paper called the *Lily*.[9] In the spring of 1851, Anthony attended an antislavery convention in Seneca Falls and stayed at Bloomer's home. Walking home together after one of the sessions, they met Stanton and later called at her home to discuss the three reform movements currently attracting American women: abolition, temperance, and woman's rights. This meeting initiated a lifelong friendship between Stanton and Anthony, an alliance that remained the major force in the woman's rights movement for the remainder of the century.[10]

At the 1852 Syracuse convention Martha also met Lucy Stone and Antoinette Brown, two women who had the rare distinction of being college graduates. They had both attended Oberlin College in Ohio, the first coeducational college in the country.[11] Stone was already well known as a paid lecturer for the American Anti-Slavery Society, had lectured widely on woman's rights, and had played a prominent role in the two national woman's rights conventions at Worcester. Brown, a devout Congregationalist, had hoped to obtain a divinity degree from Oberlin, but the faculty would not accept a woman as a candidate for that degree. Nevertheless, in 1853 she became the first woman in the United States to be ordained as a minister.[12] Friends at Oberlin, Stone and Brown would later become sisters-in-law by marrying, respectively, the brothers Henry and Samuel Blackwell. At Stone's wedding to Henry Black-well, he read a statement protesting current laws limiting the rights of married women, and she pledged to "love and honor" her husband but omitted the usual pledge to "obey."[13] She also chose to retain her maiden name after marriage and objected whenever newspapers referred to her as "Mrs. Black-well." Over many years, Lucy Stone would remain one of the most effective speakers and leaders of the woman's rights movement. Many historians con-sider Stone almost as important to the movement as the "big three" honored in the U.S. Capitol—Mott, Stanton, and Anthony.[14]

The Syracuse national woman's rights convention was the first to charge admission (fifty cents), but this did not deter attendance. Interest was high, and local newspapers estimated the crowd to be nearly two thousand. Some press coverage was favorable. The *Standard* noted that "the discussions were characterized by a degree of ability that would do credit to any deliberative body in the country," and the *Daily Journal* pronounced it "the most dignified, orderly, and interesting deliberative body ever convened in this city."[15] The majority of the newspaper reports, however, were derisive. One called it the "Tomfoolery Convention" and another referred to "the mass of corruption, heresies, ridiculous nonsense, and reeking vulgarities which these bad women have vomited forth for the past three days."[16]

As at Rochester and other conventions, much discussion in Syracuse cen-tered on the interpretation of various Biblical passages pertaining to women. These included "Thy desire shall be to thy husband, and he shall rule over thee" (Genesis 3:16) and numerous dictates by Paul, such as "Let your women keep silence in the churches" (1 Corinthians 14:34). Martha is recorded as being among the women who challenged the use of such injunctions from the distant past to attack the rights of contemporary women, and Rev. Antoinette Brown offered alternative quotations as Biblical authority for the equality of men and women.[17] Lucretia at one point vacated the chair to note that at antislavery conventions, one side quoted from the Bible to prove that God opposed slavery, while the other side quoted from it to prove that God ap-proved of slavery, and much time had been wasted. With regard to woman's rights, she argued that advice given by apostles to women of their day was no longer applicable in the present, more enlightened times. Because she was known to be personally devout, Lucretia had the standing to ease the conflict between the traditional Christians and the freethinkers in the audience. But her arguments did not dissuade the *New York Herald* from reporting that "the authority of the Bible, as a perfect rule of faith and practice for human beings, was voted down" or the *Daily Star* from listing a series of "appropriate passages from God's Bible for the consideration of the infuriated gang (Bloomers and all) at the Convention."[18] The frequent use of the Bible from the press and the pulpit to attack woman's rights and to support the subordination of women further alienated Martha from orthodox religion.

Old Kentucky Home

The Seneca Falls and Syracuse conventions had been held in the vicinity of Auburn, but Martha's increasing involvement with the woman's rights movement soon required more distant travel, and more frequent lengthy absences from her home and husband. She and Lucretia, accompanied by Lucretia's husband, James, traveled to Cleveland in October 1853 for the fourth national woman's rights convention. Martha again served as secretary, a post for which her quick mind, writing skills, and clear handwriting made her especially suitable. As at Syracuse, it was a lively three-day meeting, marked with considerable controversy. After the convention, Martha, Lucretia, and James visited friends and participated in a temperance meeting in Salem, visited Folger relatives in Massilon, and then ended their Ohio trip with a stop in Cincinnati. There they met with Lucy Stone and attended a meeting at which Stone delivered what Martha called "the first lecture on Woman's Rights the people there had ever listened to—and they seemed to enjoy it."[19]

Martha and the Motts then took a slow riverboat up the Ohio River to Maysville, Kentucky, for a visit to the home where Peter Pelham, her first husband, had grown up. It was now the home of Peter's brother John and several of his sisters. Martha's daughter Marianna had visited Maysville in 1841 with her uncle William Pelham of Arkansas and again in 1851, and now it was Martha's turn to meet more of her former husband's relatives. The long trip upriver, with the free state of Ohio on their left and the slave state of Kentucky on their right, took Martha back to her distant past. She described their experiences at what she called the "old Kentucky home" in a letter to David.

We took the boat Saturday morning but the river being low, we had to go slowly and did not reach there till 11 o'clock—found John Pelham waiting for us with his carriage, and the welcome he had promised us, and there was not part of my journey more delightful to me, than the visit to these connections. We had a pleasant moonlight drive of 3 miles, over a plank road part of the way, & very smooth the other part, & the sisters all came out to meet us at the gate. We only staid that night & the next day till afternoon & John & two sisters & two nieces accompanied us to the mg [meeting] in town. John said to me he hoped Mrs. Mott wd. not allude to slavery—the notice had been given for a religious meeting. I told him that Anti Slavery was eminently religious . . . & that it was for that she came. She felt herself called of God, & it is not for me, sd I, to come between her & her convictions of duty . . . I told him no one wd. hold him responsible for her utterances. I took good care not to embarrass her by repeating the conversation and she spoke very freely & I never heard a more enthusiastic expression of assent. She was urged to speak again on Woman's Rights in the evening, & consented to, unless a boat should come along. As no one did till 11 o'clock, she had a crowded meeting in the Court House, some of the churches having adjourned their meetings.[20]

For both Lucretia and Martha, "Anti Slavery was eminently religious" and an entirely appropriate topic for a religious meeting. In fact, they both felt that it was especially appropriate, because Southern churches continued to cite Biblical references to slavery as evidence of the approval of God, a position both sisters found abhorrent. John Pelham was himself a slaveholder, but was a gracious host despite their differences. His brother William, also a slaveholder, wrote to Marianna jokingly that she loved her Uncle John more than him "perhaps because he is 'interested in the anti Slavery lectures' and 'invites the lecturers to his fireside.' Oh! Marianna have you been proselyting poor John and seducing him from his allegiance to the South? . . . I am sorry that my brother has become converted to your cause."[21]

Northern Kentucky was more liberal on the subject of slavery than most of the rest of the state, but it was probably Lucretia's gentle appearance and demeanor and her deeply religious approach to the topic that enabled her to draw from her audience what Martha described as an "enthusiastic expression of assent." Lucretia knew the Bible better than anyone in the audience and could quietly make the point that for one person to own another person, who was equally a child of God, was inconsistent with the teachings of Jesus. The argument could be applied both to abolition and to woman's rights. Not all the locals, of course, were pleased by Lucretia's visit. One writer to the *Maysville Express* called her "a female fanatic" and "a foreign incendiary" and warned that her message might be "the prelude to a heavy loss on the part of the slaveholders of the county, as a score or two of the blacks were present to behold and hear this brazen infidel."[22]

The "brazen infidel" and her husband, James, and sister Martha caught the eleven o'clock boat from Maysville, heading for Pennsylvania. A few days later they attended the annual meeting of the Pennsylvania Anti-Slavery Society in Norristown, where Lucretia described her experiences in Kentucky. Martha then returned with the Motts to their home in Philadelphia, where she stayed until January, participating in several antislavery meetings, including the Decade Meeting marking the twentieth anniversary of the 1833 founding of the American Anti-Slavery Society. She also attended a performance of a play based on Harriet Beecher Stowe's novel, *Uncle Tom's Cabin*. Martha was not overly impressed with the play but reported to David, "One is glad to hear such good sentiments & to see Anti Slavery patiently listened to where it would not have been borne a few years ago."[23]

While in Philadelphia that December, Martha was a very interested spectator at a public debate on biblical authority, where she clearly sided with Joseph Barker, the skeptic. She wrote to David that Barker, "after demolishing in a few words the assertions of his opponent, and avoiding personalities, went on clearly & briefly in explanation of his own views." As for his opponent, Rev. McCalla, "it seems impossible for an Orthodox believer ever to state an opponent fairly, & they are too apt to descend to vulgar abuse." "There would be little profit in such discussions," she added, "if the object was the conversion of either disputant to his opponent's opinions, but it gives to a large number of people accustomed to hearing but one side, the opportunity of hearing & comparing, & there is no danger of *truth* suffering." To Martha, there was never any danger in a free exchange of opinions, but many in the audience felt otherwise, reacting violently to anyone questioning strict adherence to the authority of the Bible. "It was very evident that there was a disposition to riot wh. showed itself at the conclusion in yells & execrations & an attempt to crowd around Mr. Barker but he made a hasty retreat protected by the police and reached here safely."[24] Barker stayed overnight at the Motts'.

When William Lloyd Garrison, who was also visiting Lucretia, asked Martha to write about the debate for his abolitionist paper, the *Liberator*, she instead offered him a copy of her letter to David, and Garrison published her account with only a few minor changes. One change he made is revealing. Where Martha wrote, "it seems impossible for an Orthodox believer ever to state an opponent fairly," Garrison substituted, "there is a class of minds to which fairness in argument seems an impossibility." Garrison was a very provocative writer, but Martha's words were too strong even for him. However, he was clearly impressed with her writing skills, for she reported to David, "He said he wished he could get me for a correspondent of the Liberator, but I told him I should have nothing to correspond about."[25] Martha typically discounted her own abilities, but her self-confidence was probably stronger than such statements suggest.

Elizabeth Cady Stanton, still burdened with the cares of raising many small children, was not yet able to travel the convention circuit. But Auburn was close to Seneca Falls, and Stanton began to visit Martha, and invite Martha to visit her, to confer on strategies to advance woman's rights. Although mostly homebound until the 1860s, Stanton continued to write letters to be read at the conventions, articles for publication, and petitions to present to the state legislature on woman's issues. She greatly respected both Martha's judgment and her skill with words and frequently sought her opinion on the most effective way to advance their cause. Stanton wrote in her autobiography that Martha "brought to these councils of war not only her own wisdom, but that of the wife and sister of William H. Seward."[26] Both Frances Seward and her sister Lazette Worden were close Auburn friends of Martha's and shared many of her opinions about antislavery and woman's rights. Seward himself had been elected to the U.S. Senate in 1849, and in an 1850 debate over the slavery issue, had declared, "There is a higher law than the Constitution." His "higher law" speech became widely circulated and established him as a leader of the antislavery forces in Washington.

When Stanton visited Martha in the summer of 1854, the house was being painted and Martha reported:

> I had to tell her to go around to the back door to avoid the paint. I must acknowledge that her dress, not long enough to touch the ground, was much more becoming than her former Bloomer costume. As she came around she said 'I see you have been making an improvement.' I replied 'allow me to say that you too have made an improvement.' I always meant to defend their independence in wearing a dress that commended itself for its utility, but I never said it was pretty. She is a very lovely looking unassuming woman, with all the graceful ease that characterizes one accustomed to refined society. . . . We all fell in love with Mrs. Stanton—the merry twinkle of her eye and her genuine hearty laugh would cure a misanthrope, and she talks so sensibly.[27]

In those days, women's normal dress consisted of yards and yards of heavy skirts over voluminous petticoats and whalebone stays that squeezed the waist. The lengthy skirts trailed in the mud and made walking up and down stairs or climbing into and out of carriages awkward and even hazardous. Stanton, Anthony, Stone, and many other women had since 1851 been wearing a more practical costume consisting of ankle-length trousers under a skirt ending just below the knees.[28] Amelia Bloomer promoted the costume in her paper, the *Lily,* and it had become associated with her name. However, it generated so much ridicule and scorn from the press and public that most of the women eventually returned to traditional dress. Although Martha, in her liberal spirit, approved of a woman's "independence" to wear the "Bloomer costume" if she wished, her letters make clear that she never wore it herself. In another letter she reported with shock to David about one "exaggerated Bloomer, the dress so much shorter than Lucy's used to be, that we could see the bend of the knee as she walked."[29] She nevertheless defended both the Bloomer dress "for its utility," and Lucy Stone's course in keeping her maiden name, "because I believe in people doing as they please, when there is no law agin it."[30] Such a philosophy is considered liberal even today, but it was very radical in Martha's day. And when it came to the harboring of fugitive slaves, Martha was even willing to do as she pleased when there was a "law agin it."

Although Martha had not kept her maiden name, she kept a vestige of it by signing herself Martha C. Wright. Stanton went one step further and insisted on being called Elizabeth Cady Stanton. That was further than Martha wanted to go.[31] Stanton once sent Martha a letter addressed to "Martha Coffin Wright," but Martha's only response was "it looked so funny." And although she defended Lucy Stone's right to keep her own name, Martha considered it "an absurd whim that she will outlive." Martha's practice was not as extreme as Stone's, or even as Stanton's, but she had gone one small step beyond her sister, who was always simply "Lucretia Mott," and well beyond most married women of the time, who were usually known only by "Mrs.," followed by their husband's name.

In October 1854, Martha was back in Philadelphia as one of the vice presidents of the fifth national woman's rights convention. Many of the participants stayed with the Motts, as was customary when reform meetings were held in Philadelphia. Martha reported that "there are as many here as can be accommodated by putting three in a bed in Lucy Stone's room." The Motts' guests included William Lloyd Garrison, Susan B. Anthony, and "a host of lesser luminaries (ourselves of course I include in the greater)."[32] The convention, Martha reported, "passed off very well—the citizens seemed quite astonished that women could hold a respectable meeting & speak so well."[33] One observer had commented on the plainness of many of the speakers, to which Martha responded, "Who ever thought of making want of beauty an objection in Men's Conventions. It seemed to me there was a beauty in the eloquence and earnestness of those prominent in the movement." Receipts at the door "were over $500, which leaves quite a balance for publishing tracts."[34]

As in the previous year during her stay in Philadelphia, Martha accompanied Lucretia to several antislavery meetings. She also visited Ellen and Willy, who were now students in a New Jersey school operated by the prominent abolitionist Theodore Weld,[35] his wife, Angelina Grimké, and her sister Sarah. (The Grimké sisters had created a sensation in 1837 when they addressed mixed or "promiscuous" audiences on the subject of slavery.) Martha had finally found a school for her children operated by people whose values she admired. Weld's "teachings" she described as "so beautiful that you cannot help loving him."[36]

Madame President

In March 1855, Susan B. Anthony, whom Martha jokingly referred to as "Banthony" in many of her letters, contacted Martha to engage the Court House and get out notices for a Cayuga County woman's rights meeting at which she and Stanton would speak. Martha feared that no one would attend, but afterward reported to Lucretia:

> There was quite a tolerable audience, and they listened with apparent interest to the Banthony's hard facts, and the more polished periods of Mrs. Stanton. I have heard so often that the law classes women with children and idiots, and allows six spoons &c. to widows, and that the man has the *custody* of the wife, and that the men who enforce the laws are mean men, but not meaner than the laws, that it is not quite so fresh as when I first listened to it, but I was glad for it to be driven in and clinched in the Banthony's hammer and anvil style, for the benefit of those to whom it was new. [37]

Stanton and Anthony stayed overnight at Martha's, the first of many such visits. But after this first visit, Martha's feelings about Anthony were mixed: "She is a good, worthy girl, and is doing her full part toward the promotion of the great cause to which she has devoted herself. I envy her business talent, and envy her the capacity of saying all that she does, but I hope it isn't wicked to say that people of the Gradgrind stamp do not attract me so much as some others do." [38] Thomas Gradgrind, a character in Dickens's *Hard Times*, was a grim, tedious, and humorless man obsessed with "facts." In his carefully measured world, there was no room for fun or fancy. This was Martha's first extensive exposure to Anthony, who obviously suffered in comparison to the more lively and witty Stanton, one of Martha's idols. Martha's feelings toward Anthony, however, would greatly improve over the years. Martha often likened people she encountered in her life to fictional characters, particularly those from the novels of Dickens, such as Micawber, Pecksniff, and Uriah Heep, and characters from Shakespeare, including Falstaff, Hotspur, and Lady Macbeth.

Martha submitted a brief report on the meeting to the local papers.

After expressing disappointment that Stanton's speech was not heard by a larger audience, she delivered a fervent complaint about the conservatism of Auburn, a city that she felt did not respond well to liberal speakers. "Why is it," she asked in the *Auburn Daily Advertiser*, "that while nearly every city in the Northern states has its lyceum lectures, commonly the best talent in the country, Auburn shuts itself tightly in its sectarian shell, and dares not listen to anything that savors of progress? That while in other places, eager crowds flock to listen to [Henry Ward] Beecher, [Theodore] Parker, [Ralph Waldo] Emerson, [Wendell] Phillips and others, a meagre audience is all that can be gathered here? It is a disgrace to our beautiful city that such should be the case, and that she has become a byword for all liberal people."[39] Martha was already well known in Auburn as a strong-minded advocate of woman suffrage and woman's rights, an ardent abolitionist, a woman who openly welcomed Frederick Douglass and other blacks to her home. Articles like this one, signed M.C.W., probably further convinced Martha's conservative neighbors that she was indeed what one of them had called her, "a very dangerous woman."[40]

Martha had been secretary at several woman's rights conventions, vice president at one, and organizer of another. That summer she finally took the platform and served as convention president, a position she would occupy frequently at future woman's rights and antislavery conventions, but always reluctantly.

Saratoga, New York, famed for its mineral springs, had become a fashionable place for the wealthy and not-so-wealthy to spend part of their summers. Why not hold a convention there to expose an entirely new group of people to the issues of woman's rights? The local newspaper, the *Daily Saratogian*, reported on August 15, 1855, that "the much-talked of Woman's Rights Convention is now in session in this village. It assembled at St. Nicholas Hall, at 10 ½ this morning, and organized by the appointment of Mrs. MARTHA C. WRIGHT, of Auburn, as President."[41] Martha had been very nervous about her new assignment. She wrote to her daughter Ellen, "The thought of it is a perfect nightmare, much as I want to hear those who are to speak."[42] To a friend, she wrote, "I had many misgivings as to the part assigned me, and felt somewhat like the minister who went to meeting out of *curiosity* to know what he *was going* to *say*."[43] But the convention went well, and Lucy Stone reported to Lucretia that Martha had done well as president, leading Martha to respond, "Much obliged to Lucy for her lenient judgment."[44]

Among the speakers at Saratoga were Susan B. Anthony, Lucy Stone, Antoinette Brown, and Ernestine Rose, an immigrant from Poland who had become one of the most popular lecturers on woman's rights. Samuel J. May, the Unitarian minister and abolitionist Martha had first heard and admired at the 1833 antislavery meeting in Philadelphia, also spoke. However, "they tried to applaud down Mr. May for speaking, when they preferred to listen to a woman—isn't that an advance after ridiculing woman for insisting on the right to speak and annihilating them with texts from Paul, now to insist that men must be silent & women only be heard?"[45] According to the *Saratogian*, "the audience refused to listen; but after being assured, in a mild but firm manner, by Miss Brown, Mrs. Rose, and the President, that unless Mr. M. was heard through, *the ladies would not speak*, the rowdies concluded to keep quiet, and Mr. May shortly finished his speech."

Afterward, Martha wrote, "I was very glad, you may be sure, that the convention went off so well, & that so many ventured to attend. . . . Mrs. Rose & Lucy Stone Blackwell spoke admirably and it was interesting to watch the increasing interest of those who 'came to scoff.' One lady, a perfect marvel of flounces and toilet appliances, acknowledged herself a convert, and bought some of the books, but did not wish her name mentioned. . . . Ellen accompanied me there, and was much interested—and quite delighted with T. W. Higginson."[46] Although Ellen, then fifteen, had been ill and recuperating at a health spa, she had begged her mother to allow her to attend the convention, and Martha had acquiesced.[47] Ellen's later letters make it clear that she developed a powerful crush there on Thomas Wentworth Higginson, a prominent abolitionist and Congregationalist minister who was among the speakers. After Higginson's participation in a Philadelphia convention the previous year, Martha had written, "We have all fallen in love with him." At Saratoga in 1855, Ellen apparently did. Ellen was also profoundly impressed with the women speakers. Martha used them as role models in one of her typical letters of maternal advice: "Be a good girl, & if you ever expect to take your place with such women as Mrs. Rose & Lucy Stone & Antoinette Brown it will only be attained by storing your mind with what is valuable—so do not I beg you spend your time in reading the worse than useless trash that the idlers round you supply."[48] When away at school, all of her children received similar advice about reading.

Saratoga was the first of many conventions at which Martha would preside. The next was the sixth National Woman's Rights Convention held that October in Cincinnati, which Martha opened with the following statement from the chair:

> The object of the Convention [is] to be to secure equality with man in social, civil, and political rights. It was only seven years since this movement commenced, since our first Convention was called, in timidity and doubt of our own strength, our own capacity, our own powers; now, east, west, north, and even south, there were found advocates of woman's rights. The newspapers which ridiculed and slandered us at first, are beginning to give impartial accounts of our meetings. Newspapers do not lead, but follow public opinion; and doing so, they go through three stages in regard to reforms; they first ridicule them, then report them without comment, and at last openly advocate them. We seem to be still in the first stage on this question.[49]

During this trip, which required another lengthy absence from home and husband, Martha again visited the Pelhams at their "old Kentucky home" in Maysville. After she had returned home to Auburn, Martha wrote to Susan B. Anthony about the convention:

> You don't know how much we missed you at the recent Convention, your practical business statements come in always so opportunely. . . . All went off very well at Cincinnati, Mrs. Rose, Mrs. Gage and Lucy, all speaking admirably, as usual. My sister too, took part, tho' she has suffered so much lately with Dyspepsia that she was not capable of much exertion. It was, I assure you, with many misgivings that I consented to serve as President, when she and Mrs. Rose were present, and would have been so much more suitable, but as they were needed as speakers, there seemed to be no choice left me, and I got along without committing any very material blunders.[50]

This letter was in response to a request from Anthony to collect signatures on a woman suffrage petition. In 1850, Martha had ducked a similar request from Elizabeth Cady Stanton. But the intervening five years, and attendance at several conventions, had deepened her commitment to the cause and convinced her that it was not quite as hopeless as it had earlier seemed. "I have been out lately," she wrote Ellen, "to get signers to a Petition for the Right of Suffrage for Women. Have had some refusals, & over a dozen signatures."[51] A local doctor refused on the grounds that "if he understood their aim, they would not stop short of being candidates for office, would seek to be senators, foreign ministers, &c. . . . I told him they certainly claimed, with the right to vote, the right to be voted for and he must be able to think of some women, quite as competent to fill the offices he mentioned, as some men."[52] She was luckier with a Methodist minister who had called at her house seeking contributions. Although she turned down his request, "He was not very importunate, avowed himself in favor of Woman's Rights and I gave him the opportunity of securing for himself a night of peaceful slumber resulting from the consciousness of having returned good for evil, that is, I got him to sign my petition which he willingly did." But she failed with David: "If you'll believe it, my husband will not sign the petition for Suffrage."[53] David was at that point willing to grant the right only to women who paid taxes.

That fall, David ran for justice of the state supreme court in an eight-county district with the support of a new political party. Seward and other antislavery Whigs had joined with other political groups to form the Republican Party (borrowing Thomas Jefferson's old party label).[54] David, although he had voted Democrat since the days of Jackson, had grown disillusioned with the strength of the proslavery forces in the party and ran as a Republican.[55] He lost in a very close race to the candidate of the Democrats and the American Party, commonly called the "Know-Nothings."[56] David's personal view of the contest was the choice between "temperance and freedom" and his opponent's support of "rum and slavery." The final tabulations showed David receiving 21,737 votes to his opponent's 21,756, losing by a margin of less than one vote per thousand. The *Cayuga Chief*, a local temperance and antislavery newspaper, had endorsed David's candidacy. When they announced the results, they added, "Does not this result show the importance of every man's discharging his duty at the polls?"[57]

In December 1855, Stanton invited Martha to her home in Seneca Falls to consult with her about an article on woman's rights she had written for publication. "I should like to take counsel with you," Stanton wrote, "& add any good things that you may have thought of. As I am rather larger than you [Stanton was then eight months pregnant], suppose you come to me instead of my going to you. Come over in the first train some morning this week & we will criticize together."[58] The ease of travel between Auburn and Seneca Falls led to many such consultations. Martha went, and worked with both Stanton and Anthony on the article.

A few months later, Martha passed on a question from Lucretia about Stanton's religious affiliation. Stanton replied, "I am a member of Junius meeting [Friends] & not of the Episcopal church. I have heard that infamous report [that she had become an Episcopalian] & feel about it very much as if I had been accused of petty larceny. I will write to Lucretia. If my theology could not keep me out of any church my deep & abiding reverence for the dignity of womankind would be all sufficient." But Stanton's hostility to the ideas of the church, and to its stance toward women, was tempered by practical considerations. "I go to the Episcopal church every Sunday morning. With four boys at home, I find Sunday a very noisy day. In church they must be still, I can think. I go simply & solely to keep the children still. All I enjoy is the organ music, always thrills my soul."[59] Although Martha could understand the practicality of that, she felt that it was very risky to expose children of an impressionable age to the teachings of an orthodox church. "I should question the wisdom of that," she wrote to her daughter Eliza, "unless she is willing to impose on them, the chains from which she is emancipated."[60]

Having successfully served as president of two conventions in 1855, the New York Convention in Saratoga and the National Convention in Cincinnati, Martha was approached the following summer by Susan B. Anthony to preside again at Saratoga. "Will you attend that convention & be the *President—*," Anthony wrote, "there is *nobody else* who can fill that office as nobly as you." Anthony was having trouble collecting enough speakers, so she also urged Martha to "get up a speech," but added "President you must be—speech or no speech."[61] Martha assured Anthony that "as regards preparing a speech, *that*, you know, would be to me, an impossibility," but she reluctantly agreed to preside again despite "distrust of my own ability to preside; as it by no means follows that one can act successfully a third time, because one chanced to avoid any material blunder, the first and second."[62] As it turned out, Anthony called off this meeting for lack of speakers, but Martha's response makes it clear that despite her enthusiasm for the cause, making a public speech was out of the question.

When the seventh national convention was scheduled to be held in New York City in late November 1856, Martha wrote to David, "It will be a good time for you to attend and correct some of your heresies on the Womans Rights subject."[63] He did not attend, nor did he ever fully rid himself of his "heresies." David shared Martha's views on abolition, temperance, capital punishment, and most political and religious questions, but she was never able to fully convert him to her views on woman suffrage and other woman's rights issues. Martha attended the convention without him and, as president of the national convention the previous year, called the seventh to order. As soon as Lucy Stone was appointed president, Martha returned to her preferred role as secretary.

Martha would be active in various capacities in many more woman's rights conventions and preside over several, but the nation's attention in November 1856 was becoming more and more focused on the conflict between North and South over the issue of slavery. In the election held that month, the Democrat James Buchanan ran on a platform of compromise. The Republicans nominated John C. Frémont for President. Buchanan was elected, but the newly formed Republicans behind Frémont, with a platform opposing the extension of slavery in the western territories, carried eleven of the free states, including New York. Martha wrote to a friend, "You don't know how proud we are of New York State, & especially of our own County, which gave Frémont a majority of 3300. Mr. Wright is confident that earnest work during the coming four years will ensure future victory & he writes me that Gov. Seward says he never went to Washington in better spirits."[64] Frémont won 55 percent of the popular vote in the North and West, while Buchanan won 56 percent of the vote in the South and carried all the slave states except Maryland (taken by Millard Fillmore and the American Party). This was the first of the presidential elections to reveal such a stark split between North and South and showed clear prospects of a Republican victory in 1860. The nation was heading toward disunion.

CHAPTER EIGHT

In January 1857, the death of David's sister Sarah led him to write Martha, who was then visiting in Philadelphia, a long and uncharacteristically intro-spective letter about his unhappy childhood and his long search for a suitable profession and happiness in life. The letter ended with happy recollections of the years "when we were young at Aurora." "I commenced the study of law and soon became acquainted with a young widow with one of the dearest and sweetest little girls you ever saw who lived at Aurora and how foolish I was to marry them and how many pleasant and happy days we have spent together since."[65] Martha responded:

> What an imprudent thing it was for you to join your fortunes to those of an almost portionless widow & her pretty little daughter—but she seems to have begun with a cheerful determination to share with her husband the difficulties that beset the path of the 'poor & proud' and her economy and diligence in doing what she could toward their mutual support, joined to your indefatigable industry & unswerving probity made that path as pleasant as life's paths usually are, and now here we are after 26 years [actually 27], with all the essentials to our own personal enjoyment, and ready 'hand in hand' to go this life."[66]

Although the United States was heading toward disunion, the union of David and Martha Wright remained strong.

9

Toward Disunion

Boys and Girls

IN THE latter half of the 1850s, as the nation moved inexorably toward war, Martha was able to devote more time and energy to the woman's rights and antislavery movements. With her three younger children away at boarding schools, she fulfilled her maternal responsibilities largely through letters, full of love but also full of advice and occasional criticism. Her letters reveal what a mother promoting woman's rights considered proper guidelines for preparing two adolescent boys and an adolescent girl for adult life in the mid-nineteenth century.[1]

Ellen and Willy went off in 1854 to Eagleswood, Theodore Weld's school in New Jersey, and Frank would soon be sent there as well. The school became a very popular place for abolitionist parents to send their children.[2] By the age of thirteen, Ellen had developed a strong interest in the piano. Martha wrote to David, "I feel very anxious to have a piano for her as soon as she comes home, and have her to learn—if it is a possible thing—as it will place in her power a means of earning something at a future time." A year later, she urged Ellen, "Find out if you can, what occupation your genius best suits you for, qualify yourself for that by earnest study and effort. . . . Why should it not be just as much a girl's study as a boy's how she can best secure her own independence."[3] Such advice was not typical mother-to-daughter advice in the 1850s, nor was it typical of Martha's letters to Marianna or Eliza, her older daughters, when they were Ellen's age. With Eliza, Martha had progressed only to the point of noting that Eliza would have made a good lawyer "if she had only been the boy."

Ellen had attended a Woman's Rights Convention in Saratoga in 1855, where she met and greatly admired Lucy Stone and Antoinette Brown, both graduates of Oberlin College. With them as role models, Martha advised her, later that year, to "learn as fast as possible to prepare yourself for such college as we decide upon for you after suitable arguing."[4] But very few girls then attended college, and David did not approve, even after "suitable arguing." His later correspondence makes it clear that he was very doubtful that a college education was useful even for boys. No future letters mention the possibility of college, but Martha urged Ellen to "prepare for whatever position you might be called upon to fill" and to "try to outgrow stories & read History. Lay the foundation now for the eminence you aspire to."[5]

When Ellen began to be distracted by the attentions of a series of boys, Martha warned her of "the danger of cultivating the affections at the expense of the reason."

> The devotion of the lover seldom survives the bridal, but where the wife has cultivated those qualities which will command lasting regard & esteem, there comes a quiet happiness, far more enduring . . . [I]f you would, by your own example, prove the equality of men & women, throw aside, resolutely and at once, all sentimental novel reading, and by severe mental and physical training, qualify yourself for that course. Prove your ability to make your own way in the world, and then, when a suitable time comes, if you chance to find any one with whom you can go happily thro' life, as Lucy Stone thinks she has done, you will be old enough to make a wise choice.[6]

In a later letter, she added, "The opponents of Woman's Rights say 'there! That's just the way—as soon as women begin *to be* anything, they are married.' But what they are aiming at is to *be something, after* they are married, as well as before."[7]

Martha's letters to Willy and Frank were different. They were full of admonitions to avoid smoking, drinking, and gambling, and to brush their teeth, make their clothes last, and exercise more frugality. She often stressed cleanliness. To Willy, she wrote, "By keeping your person as clean as it ought to be, your clothes will keep clean longer." To Frank, "What did you want of perfumery—cleanliness is the best perfume." "Above all things Willy," she once wrote, "do not allow yourself ever to touch tobacco in any shape. I think as young people become more enlightened as to its deadly effects, it will not be quite so easy for chewing and smoking young men to make themselves acceptable." She also warned Willy and Frank about too much billiards and card playing. When Frank developed an interest in boxing, she wrote to him, "What use it can be to learn the best way of mauling one another I can't see."[8]

Whereas Martha had challenged Ellen to "prove the equality of men & women," she challenged Willy to keep up with Ellen in learning Latin, adding, "Do you think the boys in your school are so much smarter than the girls, as they *think* they are?"[9] In another letter, she admonished him, "You must do your best, as boys have to, when they have an even start with girls, for all their fancied superiority—How is it with your classes, do you find your sex so very superior as some of you imagine?"[10] In many letters she corrected his spelling, and in one pointed out, "There are some young ladies who would quickly cut the acquaintance of an illiterate young gentleman who made such mistakes."[11] With Willy, she often used the need to produce a favorable impression on young ladies to motivate him to study. However, she usually gave both boys a more straightforward reason to study: "You will soon be obliged to earn your own living, and will then regret any wasted opportunities."[12]

In 1858, tuition and board at Weld's school was sixty dollars for a ten-week "quarter." Books, music, and other extras added at least another forty dollars a quarter, so that total expenses were approximately four hundred dollars a year for each child, an amount David considered excessive. With Willy and Frank at Theodore Weld's Eagleswood School and Ellen now boarding at a girls' school, the total costs of schooling ate up a large fraction of the family income. And an end was not yet in sight, because both Willy and Frank began to express interest in college, specifically Harvard. David wrote to Willy, "And you really desire to graduate at Harvard and become a lawyer! I don't think the latter need in any respect to depend upon the former."[13] David knew from his own experience that one could learn law without attending college. To Frank, he wrote, "I *think* you told me distinctly that you did not desire to go to College but would much rather come into my office and study law, which seemed to me, not only much better for you but a great comfort to me."[14] As he had earlier with Tallman, David hoped that at least one of his sons would choose to join him in his law office.

In early November 1859, Theodore Weld wrote a letter to Martha and David about Frank's and Willie's education at Eagleswood and the "question whether or not they shd. go to college." Weld's handwriting was very difficult to decipher, so Martha wrote a "translation of Mr. Weld's letter," to which she added a note: "Mr. Weld is mistaken in thinking I sd. the boys going to College depended on their improvement & their wish to go. I always told him that their father was strongly prejudiced against College & that their going depended on my being able to remove that prejudice—I wished them to go."[15] Martha apparently made rapid progress on removing David's "prejudice." Later that month, she wrote Frank, "Pa consents that you should prepare yourself for college, but he will not decide finally until the time comes—meantime you & Willy too will have to deny yourselves luxuries & form habits of economy, for I know he will never consent for either of you to go, unless you know the importance of economy."[16] The coming war would keep Willy from college, but Frank did go to Harvard. As had happened in many earlier family disagreements, Martha ended up having her way.

Martha continued also to correspond with her married daughters, Marianna and Eliza, and made a practice of helping out before the births of new grandchildren. She was in Philadelphia with Marianna in April 1858 when her third child, Maria Mott, arrived. (This was Marianna's third daughter. She and Thomas had hoped this time for a boy.) It was a very difficult delivery, and Martha's letter to Eliza, written when Maria was only four hours old, described the ordeal with unusual frankness for the time. "Marianna has had such a suffering time," she wrote, "what people generally call a favorable time. . . . Which means that she was not killed, and didn't suffer as many hours as some do—and is what is called *comfortable* now—which means racked & worn out, and sleeping, when severe after pains will let her." Marianna "insisted on taking ether, & that diminished the force of the pain, but prolonged the labor . . . she is glad she had it—says she did not know when the baby was born."[17] The birth was also hard on Martha, who told Eliza, "It is so exciting & so dreadful to witness such suffering."

Martha's maternal responsibilities still included making and repairing clothes for her younger children. That fall Martha took a step she had been considering for several years—she bought a sewing machine. She had first learned about domestic sewing machines in 1851, the year that Isaac Singer developed an improved model based on earlier machines designed by others. "If it is anything that I can manage I will have one," she wrote Lucretia, "and a sweeping & dusting machine too if any are in town—or one for housekeeping in general."[18] At first, Singer's sewing machine, Martha noted, could "only stitch" and was "entirely ignorant of the art of hemming or overseaming." But machines continued to improve, and five years later Martha wrote, "I am bound to have one, & only wish I had the time wasted in all these years, by the slow process of hand work."[19] She finally got her machine in late 1858, and it took some weeks to master. One day, the new machine shuddered and made noises that to Martha's imaginative mind sounded like a woman in labor: "It groaned and made such a fuss, you wd. have thought there wd. be a young machine." As it turned out, the problem with the machine was a lack of oil at a crucial joint. In describing the solution, she could not resist a characteristic pun. "I tho't I had oiled every joint, but at last I found it was the middle of the shoes, and a drop of oil was 'like water to the thirsty *soul*.'"[20] Her machine was of course pedal-driven. It would be many years before electricity would become available to further ease the work of sewing and other household tasks—not in time for Martha.

She later reported using her machine to make a flannel shirt for Frank that cost $4.00 in the store but, she bragged, "I can make one for $2.50, not counting my time (and who counts that?)." In the previous ten days, she had finished Frank's shirt and an "undershirt & pair of drawers, 4 aprons, new seated & mended a pr. of pantaloons for D., mended a pr. & two vests, run the heels of two pr. of stockings for Eliza & mended a lot for ourselves & a few for her, beside little mending of gloves &c.—and a big hole that I burnt in my morning dress, & had all right again before dinner."[21] With the money she saved by making and mending clothes at home, Martha indulged in the occasional luxury of buying clothes for herself in the Philadelphia stores. But she had her limits, aware that David sometimes thought her extravagant. "I am not willing to pay $40 for a shawl," she wrote Eliza in 1857, "unless it is something that will last forever. I got a lovely fuzzy angora for $6.50 and a chenile scarf for $2.50."[22] Martha was sensitive to cold and wore a warm shawl much of the year, especially during the long Auburn winters.

"No Union with Slaveholders"

Martha was always concerned about the progress of her children and grand-children, but in the 1850s her attention was being drawn more and more to the issue that was dividing the nation—slavery. From the time of the drafting of the Constitution, compromises with the South over the issue of slavery had been the guiding principle of the United States to "maintain the union" as it expanded westward.[23] The Missouri Compromise of 1820 allowed the admission of Missouri as a slave state with the proviso that slavery would be excluded from the remainder of the Louisiana Purchase north of the southern border of Missouri. Further states were gradually admitted as paired free and slave states to keep the balance of power in the Senate equal between North and South. The Compromise of 1850 involved, among other things, the admission of California as a free state, organization of the rest of the land acquired from Mexico into two territories (Utah and New Mexico) with no federal restriction on slavery, and passage of a stringent fugitive slave law, a revealing case where the interest of the South in defending "states' rights" clashed directly with its interest in defending slavery.[24] In fighting for the fugitive slave law, the South made clear that defending slavery was the higher priority, giving the federal government expanded powers and responsibilities to assist slaveowners in recovering their "property" that had escaped into the North. This law was especially hateful to the Northern abolitionists and led to numerous heated clashes involving the capture or rescue of fugitive slaves. Tempers heightened considerably on both sides of the Mason-Dixon Line.

Then came the Kansas-Nebraska Act of 1854, which essentially repealed the Missouri Compromise and left the question of slavery within the territories of Nebraska and Kansas to be decided by "popular sovereignty," that is, by the residents of the territory. This measure angered even the moderates in the North, who attempted to organize free-state settlers to move west into Kansas to counter the hordes of proslavery Missourians who were crossing the border to influence the vote. Violence ensued, a prelude to the much wider war that was now only a few years away.

Many abolitionists, following William Lloyd Garrison, had declared themselves to be "nonresistants," opposing violence in even as noble a cause as opposition to slavery.[25] The crisis in Kansas, however, severely tested this position. Martha and David discussed Kansas with their Universalist minister Rev. W. R. G. Mellen and even gave some consideration to the possibility of going to Kansas. After Mellen left Auburn for a pulpit in Massachusetts, Martha wrote to him that David "feels quite a strong interest in Kansas affairs, and says if any fighting is necessary for Freedom, he means to be *thar*. People exclaim 'Why Mr. Wright, I thought you were a non-resistant.' He replies that, like Theodore Parker [a prominent Unitarian minister and abolitionist], he never adopted *that* nonsense. I hope those who are there will maintain their ground manfully, and not be driven off by the idle threats of the Missourians."[26] In a later letter to Mellen, she added, "I have often thought if we had all participated in your enthusiasm and gone with you to Kansas to live, what would have been the result, and how *we women* would have borne ourselves in the difficulties & dangers that would have encompassed us. Do you think we could have held firmly to non-resistant principles—are you sure that *you* could?"[27]

To Lucretia, who remained firmly committed to nonviolence, Martha wrote, "I confess to a wish that a goodly number of those who *don't* think it wrong to fight, may be on the ground in time to aid those already there in holding their own, and driving back the aggressors. . . . One thing is certain, no one can be truly a *Christian*, unless he adopts the non resistant doctrine underlying all Christ's teachings, and the only course, for one who advocates a resort to force, under any circumstances, is to confess that he was mistaken in supposing himself one; that beautiful as the theory is, the practice is not always expedient or practicable."[28] Any traces of nonresistant principles in Martha would later be removed by the Civil War and her son's participation in it.

"No union with slaveholders" had become the official slogan of Garrison and the American Anti-Slavery Society. Most abolitionists still hoped that moral suasion would somehow gradually eliminate slavery without violence, but their efforts continued to polarize the North and the South. When Garrison visited Auburn in early 1856, Martha and David engaged the public hall for his speech, after finding the new Universalist minister very reluctant to allow the use of the church for the event. Later Martha reported to Lucretia, "There was quite a good audience" and "he boldly arraigned all parties and sects and advocated dissolution of the Union, and was listened to with earnest attention and frequent applause."[29] Although some did literally support "dissolution of the Union" into two separate nations, one slave and one free, most abolitionists did not, for that would not ease their moral concerns about the slaves in the South. For most, advocating "disunion" was merely a strategy to increase pressure on the federal government to change its priorities and put abolition of slavery above further concessions to the South.[30] It is deeply ironic that the efforts of Garrison and his "nonresistant" followers contributed to leading the nation into one of the bloodiest wars of human history.[31]

Not all abolitionists agreed with Garrison. Some felt that slavery was so evil that any means to combat it would meet God's approval and support. Such a man was John Brown. He had used extreme violence to combat proslavery violence in Kansas, and in 1859 planned a daring raid on the South that he dreamed would incite a slave revolt and lead to the final destruction of slavery. On October 16, he and a group of heavily armed white and black followers raided the federal arsenal at Harpers Ferry, Virginia, and took several hostages. But he was soon captured and sentenced to death and rapidly became a martyr to the antislavery cause.[32] At that time the Wrights had a pew in the Second Presbyterian Church, largely because the minister, Henry Fowler, was often outspoken in his support for abolition. On the Sunday before Brown was to be hanged, Fowler remembered him in his prayer. This offended a majority of the congregation, and a meeting was called to consider discharging Fowler; opposing slavery was one thing, but condoning armed intervention was another. David recalled in his memoirs that at the meeting, he "asked that the women should be allowed to vote, and was only laughed at." Fowler was discharged, "and my connection with any church or congregation ceased. I never believed in the dogmas of any orthodox church."[33]

Before their brief connection to the Second Presbyterian Church, the Wrights had a pew in the Universalist Church and were close friends with the minister, W. R. G. Mellen, and his wife. Mellen, like Fowler, was firmly antislavery; and he also preached on another topic of reform of special interest to David—temperance. However, like the Presbyterians, the Universalists in Auburn were not very reform-minded, and Mellen was asked to leave.

While Mellen was still in Auburn, Martha had many discussions with him, not only about antislavery but also about other religious issues. After one discussion, Martha referred to his reverence for the Bible. Mellen responded, "If I had been called upon to portray your character, I should say your greatest fault was a want of Reverence." Martha wrote to Lucretia that she "only smiled, not thinking it worth while to go into any defence, feeling rather pleased that he had discovered no greater fault."[34]

Among the many religious issues being widely debated at the time was the sanctity of the Sabbath. There were ardent "sabbatarians" who wanted all business, including the mails and public transportation, stopped on Sundays, and "antisabbatarians" who opposed such measures both on practical grounds and on the more fundamental issue of the separation of church and state. Garrison took a firm antisabbatarian stand in the *Liberator*, giving his critics another reason to call him "infidel."[35] Lucretia and Martha both supported Garrison's view. (Martha did not cease her household or other activities on Sundays. A friend once said to her, "How much you do, Mrs. Wright, and how much leisure you have!" to which she answered, "You forget that I have seven days a week, while you church people have only six.")[36] Mellen had preached on the importance of observing the Sabbath, so Martha felt compelled to send him antisabbatarian literature to convert him, accompanied by a letter conveying both her opinion on the issue and her more general views on majority versus minority rights and freedom of opinion and expression:

I have for several years been "fully persuaded in my own mind," and while I am willing to accord to others perfect freedom of opinion I must claim the same; according & claiming also perfect *freedom* of *expression* for I maintain that others have no more right to be shocked at what they consider *my* erroneous views, than I at theirs . . . in a question like this, where there is a constant disposition in the strong to oppose the weak by legislative enactments, it behooves the minority faithfully to speak their own convictions whether men will hear or whether they will forbear. Even error can do no harm when the truth is left free to combat it. There is a constant effort on the part of our religious denominations to influence public sentiment for the suppression of Sunday mails & the prohibition of all travelling on that day; so far as they have been successful they have often caused great inconvenience to many as conscientious in all respects as themselves.[37]

On this particular issue, Martha's opinion was influenced both by the importance of correspondence in her life and by her resistance to the dictates of orthodox religion. But beyond this particular issue, this letter reveals her firm belief in freedom of opinion and freedom of expression. In later debates over "freedom of the platform" at woman's rights meetings, she expressed the related thought that "liberty alone can cure the evils of liberty."

Freedom of the Platform

The publication of Harriet Beecher Stowe's *Uncle Tom's Cabin* in 1852, passage of the Kansas-Nebraska Act of 1854 and the resulting violence in Kansas, and the Supreme Court's *Dred Scott* decision of 1857 supporting slavery greatly widened support of the antislavery movement in the North. By 1858, woman's rights leaders decided to increase the already strong overlap between their movement and that of antislavery by coordinating their conventions with those of the American Anti-Slavery Society (AAS) in an effort to increase attendance and public interest. Thus, the eighth, ninth, and tenth national woman's rights conventions were held in New York City in May 1858, 1859, and 1860, respectively, following the national AAS meetings, and the New York State meetings on both topics were held sequentially in Albany early in the year. Martha had been among the few women who attended the 1833 organizational meeting of the AAS in Philadelphia and had participated in numerous antislavery conventions in Pennsylvania and New York over the intervening years. The new scheduling made it easier for her to participate more actively in the two reform movements to which she was most strongly committed.

Although Martha assumed more of a leadership role in woman's rights than in antislavery, she was active in both the state and the national AAS. Her service to the AAS included membership on the Business Committee of the national organization (the same committee to which Abby Kelley's election in 1840 led to the split of the abolitionists over "the woman question") and a major role in organizing and presiding over several state antislavery meetings. One of the methods by which many women supported AAS was through holding "fairs" to raise money for the cause. Martha participated in several antislavery fairs during her frequent visits to Philadelphia, and, when she could not attend, sewed items to be sold at the Philadelphia fairs. But apparently no such fairs were held in Auburn. "I doubt whether Auburn, with its Theological Seminary & Prison, cd. ever rise to the height of an Anti Slavery Fair," Martha wrote in 1859.[38] Her experiences with carrying petitions and with hosting the visits of reformist speakers had convinced her that her hometown was much too conservative for a successful antislavery fair.

Martha opened the eighth national woman's rights convention in New York in May 1858. "Lucy not being there, they wanted me to open the mg. wh. I did, and we had an unusually interesting morning session." But her official post was again secretary. "She [Ernestine Rose] asked me if I would be Secretary, and as there is nothing else I am good for, I am always willing to do that."[39] The issue of the "free platform" at woman's rights conventions became especially problematic when Stephen Pearl Andrews made a brief presentation. Andrews was an extremist in his zeal to reform society and had founded a community named Modern Times based on a philosophy that included "free love."[40] After the convention, Martha wrote to Lucretia, "I don't know who that dismal Pearl Andrews was, but as he did not press his views, I suppose there was no great harm done."[41] But there was. The press, always looking for the sensational and controversial, gave considerable coverage to Andrews. Martha later wrote to Elizabeth Cady Stanton about the convention, "the sweeping censure that has fallen upon it," and "the harm done by Andrews" but strongly supported Susan B. Anthony's unwillingness to close the convention platform to "unwelcome speakers."[42] "The Free Love intrusion on our platform seemed to me a matter of very little moment," she wrote to Anthony, "and I don't think there were many real friends of the movement who viewed it in any other light than as one of those trifling annoyances which are inseparable from a free platform."[43] The "Free Love intrusion" would become much more than a trifling annoyance to the woman's movement in the postwar years.

In January 1860, Martha organized an antislavery meeting in Auburn and presided over another in Albany the following month.[44] She also joined Stanton and Anthony in a visit to the state legislature that contributed to the passage of a state law increasing the property and custody rights of married women.[45] Woman suffrage was still sixty years away, but the many petitions and conventions promoting woman's rights were beginning to have some notable effects. From Martha's letter to Willy, it appears that she was not awed with the state legislature. "Some of us went to the Hall of representatives, and the Senate chamber, to see what we could learn from so much collective wisdom; the proceedings however were not particularly edifying, and conducted with no more wisdom than some meetings of common folk."[46]

A few months later in New York City, Martha took part in both the antislavery and woman's rights national conventions. She had begun to keep a diary sporadically, and her diary entries for that week reveal some of her activities.[47] May 8—"Arrived in N. Y. 1.30 PM . . . went to A. S. business meeting in the afternoon." (Although female membership of AAS committees was very controversial in 1840, it was common by 1860.) May 9—"Dined with Mrs. Rose in company with [William Lloyd] Garrison & [Wendell] Phillips—back to the meeting—heard a grand speech by Garrison."[48] May 10— "Woman's Rights Convention met—called to preside, home to lunch, helped S. B. Anthony and Mrs. Stanton copy resolutions."

This was the tenth national woman's rights convention, the last to be held before the war, and Martha presided over an audience of one thousand people. In her opening speech as president, she predicted, "After all that we demand has been granted, as it will be soon, *The New York Observer* will piously fold its hands and roll up its eyes, and say, 'This beneficent movement we have always advocated,' and the pulpits will say 'Amen!'"[49] *History of Woman Suffrage* records that the audience responded with laughter and applause. Martha had learned through her writing and private conversations, and now through her public speaking, that humor has great power to move an audience.

Later in her opening speech, Martha tackled a question that had become a controversial issue two years earlier and would later become one of the issues that led to disunion in the woman's rights movement—the question of a free platform.

There are those, too, who find fault with the freedom of our platform, who stand aloof and criticize, fearful of being involved in something that they can not fully endorse. Forgetting that, as Macauley says, "Liberty alone can cure the evils of liberty," they fear to trust on the platform all who have a word to say. But we have invited all to come forward and speak, and not to stand aside and afterward criticize what has been said. We trust that those present who have an opinion, who have a word to say, whether they have ever spoken before or not, will speak now. If they disapprove of our resolutions, if they disapprove of anything that is said on this platform, let them oppose if they can not unite with us.[50]

At this convention, Stanton herself became the center of controversy when she introduced several resolutions calling for the liberalization of divorce laws.[51] Stanton, Anthony, Rose, and others had become interested in this issue through their activities in the temperance movement and their sympathy with wives suffering from drunken husbands. However, at the time, many people considered marriage indissoluble, and support of liberalized divorce seemed little different from support of "free love." Stanton's resolutions were countered by a series of resolutions from Rev. Antoinette Brown Blackwell, the first of which stated that marriage "must be, from the nature of things, as permanent as the life of the parties." Heated discussion ensued, including a motion from Wendell Phillips to strike both sets of resolutions from the record because any discussion of divorce "unnecessarily burdened" woman's rights. (In his dealings with Stanton and Anthony, Phillips "was, for once, less radical than the company he kept," according to his biographer Irving Bartlett.)[52] His motion was defeated after a spirited speech by the unmarried Anthony, who argued that "nearly all the wrongs of which we complain grow out of the inequality, the injustice of the marriage laws, that rob the wife of the right to herself and her children—that make her the slave of the man she marries."

Press coverage was intense, and the press used the controversy over liberalized divorce as further proof of the connection between the woman's rights movement and free love. "This hue & cry about Free Love in New York, of all places in the world," Martha wrote to Anthony, "is too contemptible & hypocritical to be worth a moment's notice."[53] Although the intense disagreement over the topic of divorce had made her job as president more difficult than usual, Martha felt the topic was appropriate for a woman's rights convention. "Of course there will be difference of opinion as to the wisdom of introducing the subject of divorce yet awhile," she wrote Stanton, "but that it must come up eventually, in conventions met for the discussion of all the rights and *all the wrongs* of woman, cannot be disputed."[54] The issues of divorce and free love, however, did hurt the movement. Antoinette Brown Blackwell's close friend and sister-in-law, Lucy Stone, did not attend this convention, but these topics were among those that would split the woman's rights movement a decade later, with Stone and Blackwell in one camp and Stanton and Anthony (and Martha) in the other.[55] It was not only the United States that was heading toward disunion.

On the national political scene, the Republicans met in Chicago later that month to select their presidential candidate, and the favorite going into the convention was William Henry Seward. He had stepped aside in 1856 in favor of John C. Frémont, with the expectation that it would be his turn in 1860. But ever since his "higher law" speech during the debate on the Compromise of 1850, his public image had been strongly antislavery. He had strengthened that image in an 1858 campaign speech for the New York State Republican ticket, in which he declared that the issue of slavery created an "irrepressible conflict between opposing and enduring forces, and it means that the United States must and will, sooner or later, become either entirely a slave-holding nation or entirely a free-labor nation." This "irrepressible conflict" speech was widely reported and was taken by many to mean that a civil war between North and South was inevitable, an interpretation Seward disavowed. Nevertheless, many Republicans felt that they would attract more votes in 1860 with a figure less polarizing than Seward, such as the relatively unknown lawyer from Illinois, Abraham Lincoln. Seward was well ahead of Lincoln on the first ballot, but Lincoln pulled almost even on the second, and won on the third. Martha's disappointment was mitigated by knowledge that her friend Frances Seward, unhappy with her husband's political career and ambitions, had not been looking forward to becoming the wife of a presidential candidate.[56] The Democrats split, the northern wing nominating Stephen Douglas and the southern wing John Breckenridge. Lincoln was elected in November, and on December 20, South Carolina voted to secede from the Union.

Fugitives, Mobs, and War

In the years immediately preceding the Civil War, Martha often found herself in the midst of the increasing tension between abolitionists and anti-abolitionists. She and Lucretia were among a large group of abolitionists who attended an 1859 Philadelphia trial of a fugitive slave, with the hope that their continued presence would make it difficult for the judge to send the man back to slavery. The man, named Daniel Dangerfield, had been working on a farm near Harrisburg but was seized as a fugitive and brought for trial in Philadel-phia.[57] "They got the slave in amid the roars of the crowd," Martha wrote to David. "It was very evident that none but the claimants and their friends were to be admitted, but by going round to another door, we got in and were fairly lifted from our feet in the pressure of the crowd to the little jury room. The glass was broken from the door, but we got the places we wanted. Sister L. held on to the slave & kept close by him all the time." By the second day, Martha took ill, but she was "determined to go live or die," and all (except the slaveholder claimants) were pleased when the former slave was released on a minor technical error in the writ of accusation. As Martha wrote, "I have no doubt the determination of respectable people to witness the proceedings & to show their sympathy for the slave had a good effect. . . . I hope the ill success of the slaveholders in the recent case here, will discourage them from future attempts."[58]

A few days later, Martha and Lucretia, along with eighteen-year-old Ellen and two of Martha's nieces, attended an abolitionist meeting called "to resolve that no slave should ever be taken from Philadelphia." Abolitionist feelings were rising, but so were anti-abolitionist feelings, and order was maintained at the meeting only with the timely intervention of the police. As Martha reported to Eliza:

> The Hall soon filled, and then a disorderly multitude of sympathisers with the
> South crowded the lower part and by constant cheers and groans drowned the

voice of speakers. . . . It looked rather serious just before the police arrived. The mob voted themselves the citizens of Philadelphia, & repeatedly resolved that they would not associate with niggers, and there were many present, so designated, from Robert Purvis & family,[59] to the deepest shades, & some were much terrified. I told some who were hurrying to leave by a door near the platform, that they were much safer in than out, & they remained. . . . I sat next Harriet Purvis . . . on a seat near the platform.[60] . . . It was grand to see the police with their stars, step in & confront the mob just as they reached the platform.[61]

Martha's home was part of the Underground Railroad, a network organized by antislavery activists to provide safe houses for fugitive slaves. Through her work with this network, she became acquainted with Harriet Tubman, the most famous "conductor" on this "railroad," who acquired from Seward a home and property in Auburn. Tubman herself had escaped from slavery in Maryland in 1849, later returned to guide several family members north, and eventually led so many slaves to freedom in the 1850s that she became known as the "Moses of her people."[62] Martha described one of Tubman's trips in a letter written in December 1860 to her daughter Ellen.

> We have been expending our sympathies, as well as congratulations, on seven newly arrived slaves that Harriet Tubman has just pioneered safely from the Southern part of Maryland. One woman carried a baby all the way, & brought two other children that Harriet & the men helped along. They brought a piece of old comfort & blanket, in a basket with a little kindling, a little bread for the baby with some laudanum, to keep it from crying during the day. They walked all night, carrying the little ones, and spread the old comfort on the frozen ground, in some dense thicket, where they all hid, while Harriet went out foraging & sometimes could not get back till dark, fearing she would be followed. Then if they had crept further in, & she couldn't find them, she would whistle, or sing certain hymns, & they would answer.[63]

This group was the last that Tubman guided north before the war. It is not known whether they continued on to Canada, where Tubman had earlier delivered most fugitive slaves, or stayed in Auburn. But by December 1860 most of the North, including Auburn, was relatively safe from slave catchers. After the war, Tubman maintained her Auburn home for many years as a haven for freed blacks. Martha and her daughter Eliza Osborne became two of Tubman's most reliable friends and supporters.[64]

By January 1861, five southern states had followed the lead of South Carolina and seceded from the Union. Martha was busy that month painting pictures to decorate her parlor. "You know I like to paint birds, she wrote to Ellen, "but—picture it—think of it dissolute man—the country perishing by intestine war, and her patriots wasting six hours a day, painting."[65] After Peter Pelham's death in 1826, Martha had studied painting in Philadelphia. She taught painting in the Quaker girls' school in Aurora, later taught it to her own children and other children in her extended family, and continued to enjoy painting when time allowed. Her favorite subjects were birds, flowering plants, and other natural objects. (The few of her paintings that have been preserved reveal that she was fairly skillful.)[66] Within a week, her paintings were completed and she was again devoting her energies to the cause of abolition.

Anthony and Stanton had organized a tour of abolition speakers across upper New York State to rally antislavery sentiment and pressure Lincoln to avoid more concessions to the South, and Martha presided over two of these very controversial conventions. With the nation already on the brink of war, the tour stirred up intense emotions with slogans such as "No Compromise with Slave Holders." Anti-abolitionists countered with "Freedom of Speech, but not Treason," equating abolitionism with treason. Martha arranged a convention for January 31 and February 1 in Auburn, but earlier conventions in Buffalo, Rochester, and Syracuse were disrupted by angry mobs. On the twenty-seventh, she wrote to Ellen, "This will be my busy week, getting the notices for the Convention posted, putting one in the Dailies, seeing the Mayor to get him to send policemen to the Hall, & entertaining our guests."[67] She wrote to Willy on the thirtieth, "Our Anti Slavery Convention here begins tomorrow afternoon, & lasts through Friday, afternoon & evening—that is if it is not broken up by a mob, as it was in Syracuse yesterday & has been in several other places. I have taken such precautions as I could in arranging for the Convention & then if it is disturbed, the responsibility must rest on our public men, who are continually preaching up compromise & concession toward our *Southern brethren*. We are expecting Rev. Beriah Green, Saml. J. May, Aaron M. Powell, Mrs. Stanton & S. B. Anthony tomorrow morning."[68]

By January 1861, Martha had presided over numerous conventions, and maintaining order had not always been easy. The topics of woman's rights and abolition often drew many noisy hecklers, and the policy of a free platform occasionally drew controversial speakers, such as Stephen Pearl Andrews and his calls for "free love," that encouraged boos and catcalls from even the moderate members of the audience. But this time was different, and Martha was more nervous than usual. Abolition had been an inflammatory subject for many years, but feelings had greatly intensified with Lincoln's election and the secession of several Southern states. Based on reports about the mobs that had disrupted abolitionist conventions at Buffalo, Rochester, and Syracuse, Martha anticipated much more this time than heckling and catcalls. On the platform beside her was a local minister who attempted to calm her by passing her some lines of poetry by John Greenleaf Whittier: "Happy they whose inward ear / Angel comfortings can hear / O'er the rabble's laughter, / And while hatred's faggots burn, / Glimpses, thro' the smoke, discern / Of the good hereafter."[69] The afternoon session in Auburn was undisturbed, but by evening Martha would indeed hear the sounds of hatred and "the rabble's laughter" and feel the need for "angel comfortings."

According to an area newspaper, "In the evening a motley crowd of rowdies and loafers assembled, and broke up the meeting, taking possession of the room, and organizing a meeting of their own, and passed the same resolutions adopted by the Syracuse mob meeting." The paper estimated the mob to consist of "100 to 150 adult males and boys" and reported that "Miss Anthony leaned over the desk and said, 'Why, boys, you're nothing but a *baby mob*—you ought to go to Syracuse, and learn how to do it, and also learn how to get before the Grand Jury." Afterward, the article noted, "the Abolitionists held a meeting at the dwelling of a citizen of Auburn, where they were not molested."[70] That "dwelling" was Martha and David's house at 192 Genesee Street, where Anthony, Stanton, and the others completed their meeting peacefully.[71] The abolitionist leaders spent the night at the Wrights' home, gathering strength for their next confrontation. The commitment of Martha and her colleagues to woman's rights exposed them to much ridicule, but their commitment to abolition exposed them to physical danger as well.

The abolitionists met again on February 4 and 5 in Albany, with Martha again presiding (her brief opening address stressed "the religious nature of the antislavery cause"). This time Lucretia was among the speakers.[72] Here mob violence was largely held in check by a large and conspicuous police presence, and by the mayor himself appearing on stage with a loaded gun visible in his lap. As Martha wrote Ellen, "The roughs compelled to sit in the body of the hall, the whole police force in uniform sprinkled among them. . . . In Susan's address read just after the galleries were cleared there was a sentence about John Brown which they hissed. The mayor compelled quiet & she repeated— another uproar which was stilled & I said to her 'Repeat' & she repeated for the third time with better success. It was grand for those rough creatures to be compelled to hear so much for their edification & they really seemed interested—that is, those who had gone only for the fun of it, & not from any vicious *union saving* sentiment."[73] "I shall never forget," she wrote to a friend many years later, "that last convention we held in Albany, under the personal and active protection of the Mayor, amid the howling of a mob, furious to the last, and following us with hootings to the Delavan [hotel], the Mayor waiting on my sister Lucretia, Frederick Douglass with me, and quite a procession of members of the Convention. . . . I shall always remember the manly bravery of Frederick Douglass, as he stood on the edge of the platform with folded arms, and dared the mob to come on, as they threatened to attack him."[74]

After the Albany "mob convention," Martha presided over the state woman's rights convention immediately following, which she reported "was smaller than the other, & not a sign of a mob."[75] This was the last state convention before the war. Although the nation was focused on the threat of disunion over the issue of slavery, Martha and her colleagues continued to agitate for the rights of women. They delivered to the legislature a fiery petition that had been circulated around the state. It ended with the words:

> We now demand the ballot, trial by jury of our peers, and an equal right to the joint earnings of the marriage copartnership. And, until the Constitution be so changed as to give us a voice in the government, we demand that man shall

make all his laws on property, marriage, and divorce, to bear equally on man and woman.[76]

Challenging enough, but the petition also included an attack on the authority of the Bible and "the opinions uttered by a Jewish teacher, which, alas! the mass believe to be the will of God." Such phrases contributed to the "infidel" image of the woman's rights movement and antagonized not only the legislators and much of the general public but also many in the movement itself. The petition had been drafted by the five-person "New York State Woman's Rights Committee," consisting of Stanton, Anthony, Martha, Ernestine Rose, and Lydia Mott. Lydia Mott was a distant cousin of James Mott's who served in Albany as a local representative for the movement. Ernestine Rose had been agitating for woman's rights in New York State for many years before Seneca Falls. An avowed atheist with a Jewish background, Rose willingly accepted the label of "infidel," which led many of her colleagues in reform to distance themselves from her. But not Martha. "There are so few who dare to be friendly toward her," she once wrote to Lucretia. "She said to me in N.Y. 'It is so seldom that I see a face that expresses so much sympathy as yours.'"[77] Martha did not share Rose's atheism but felt "she should be judged by her fruits and not by her belief."[78] The convention speakers also had a hearing before the state Judiciary Committee on a pending bill designed to liberalize divorce. Afterward, Martha returned to Auburn and "called at Mr. Seward's & sat an hour, telling them abt. the Convention."[79] Seward would soon be heading to Washington to serve as Lincoln's secretary of state.

On April 10, Lucretia and James Mott celebrated their fiftieth wedding anniversary at their home outside of Philadelphia, and Martha was there. She wrote home to David that "there were only 5 of the signers of the [marriage] certificate 50 years ago, & I was one, my hand being guided." (She was only four when the Motts were married.) It apparently was a large celebration, because her description of the festivities ended with the comment, "By 10 o'clock all had left but the 39 who slept in the house (including the family)—and by 11 everybody had gone to bed."[80] Two days later, Confederate forces in Charleston, South Carolina, fired on federal troops occupying

Fort Sumter, and the Civil War had begun. Soon thereafter, Martha received a brief visit in Philadelphia from her nephew John Pelham, who was on his way from West Point to Alabama to join the Confederate Army. He was to become famous the following year through his battlefield exploits, and revered throughout the South as "gallant Pelham."

10

The Rebel Pelhams

The Slaveholding Pelhams

MARTHA'S WRIGHT'S correspondence with her slaveholding Pelham relatives in the months before the outbreak of war reflects the intensifying feelings of the national controversy over the issue of slavery. Her first husband, Peter Pelham, had died in 1826 when she was only nineteen years old and their daughter Marianna was only one, but Martha maintained contact with his relatives for many years, even into the 1870s. She corresponded with Peter's father, a Revolutionary War veteran, until his death, with Peter's brothers John, William, and Atkinson, and later with Atkinson's oldest son, Charles. From 1841 on, Marianna also corresponded with her Pelham relatives. Since Martha and Marianna were both ardent abolitionists, they of course differed strongly with their Pelham relatives on the issue dividing the nation. Martha characteristically supported their right to express their opinions, and maintained her right to express hers forcefully to them.

Peter's brother John had remained at the family homestead in Maysville, Kentucky, along with several of Peter's unmarried sisters, and Martha visited them there in 1853 and 1855. Marianna had visited on two earlier occasions. The letters John and his sisters wrote to Marianna and Martha dealt exclusively with family matters and discreetly avoided the delicate subject of slavery.

Although John was a slaveholder, Kentucky was one of the "border states" (along with Missouri, Delaware, and Maryland) that did not secede from the Union. Maysville, in northern Kentucky, just across the Ohio River from the free state of Ohio, was liberal enough on the topic to have responded favorably (for the most part) to Lucretia's antislavery speech there in 1853.

Peter's brother William, in his capacity as surveyor general of Arkansas, sometimes had business in Washington, allowing him several opportunities to visit Martha and Marianna in the 1840s and 1850s. The first was the 1841 visit to Auburn during which he won the approval of Martha to take Marianna to Kentucky and Arkansas to meet her other Pelham relatives. At that time, he had a farm of about five hundred acres in western Arkansas, but his job as surveyor general required him to live mostly in the state capital at Little Rock. Marianna and Martha both became very fond of William, and Martha's second son, William Pelham Wright, was named after him. William Pelham later moved from Arkansas to Texas, and in 1854 to the Territory of New Mexico, where he again held the post of surveyor general. When he visited Marianna and her husband, Thomas Mott, in Philadelphia in 1854, he also met with Lucretia and the rest of the Mott family, one of the most prominent abolitionist families in the country. After the visit, he wrote to Marianna, "I am fearful my dear Niece that if I were to make you another visit, your kindness, and the kindness of your Relatives would have the effect to weaken my opinion in regard to the Abolitionists. . . . How delicately they treated me, never in a single instance mentioning the subject of slavery except when brought up by myself."[1] William, however, was more ardent in his support of slavery than his brother John, and his federal position in New Mexico led to some unusual experiences in the war, when a Confederate army from Texas invaded the territory.

Martha knew Atkinson before she met Peter, when she was still a young girl in Philadelphia and Atkinson was a medical student and boarder in her mother's boarding house. After receiving his medical degree, Atkinson moved to North Carolina and later married and moved to Alabama, where his six sons and one daughter were born and grew up. All six sons served in the Confederate army, and one demonstrated so much skill and bravery on the battlefield that he was singled out by General Robert E. Lee as "gallant Pelham" and became a hero known throughout the South. The most interesting of the existing correspondence between Martha and Marianna and the slaveholding Pelhams was the correspondence with Martha's brother-in-law William, who for a short time became Confederate governor of New Mexico, and that with several of Atkinson's sons, including John, "gallant-Pelham," and Charles, who became a "reconstructed reb."

Governor Pelham

William Pelham's last visit with Marianna and Martha in Philadelphia was early in 1859. By then, the topic of slavery had become extremely sensitive, but he and Martha were still able to discuss it. As she wrote David, "I am very glad to have seen him. Have had some talks on Slavery, which he bears very well, not being one of the fierce & excitable kind, but I think the consciousness that we are diametrically opposite in sentiment throws a little restraint over his manner. When Ellen comes in from her Junior [antislavery] society, he says 'Well Miss Ellen, have you dissolved the Union yet?' "[2] About his job as surveyor general of New Mexico, she wrote, William "does not expect now to hold it after *Mr.* [William Henry] *Seward* is elected." Although William's (and the South's) fears of Seward being nominated for President turned out to be unfounded, Seward's Republican Party did win the White House in 1860 with Abraham Lincoln. Secession and the firing on Fort Sumter followed. By the summer of 1861, events had become so unpleasant for William in New Mexico that he had reason to be much more "fierce and excitable" than he had been with Martha two years earlier.

In 1861, the Territory of New Mexico included most of the present-day states of New Mexico and Arizona. It was very sparsely populated, and many of those living there were Mexicans or Indians with little direct interest in the issues that had split the North and South. However, the territory was under federal control, and officials in Santa Fé demanded that all prominent citizens take an oath swearing their allegiance to the Union. Texas had seceded in February, and William Pelham, a Texan and slaveholder, refused to take the oath. He was put in prison, and his next letter to his Northern relatives, written from prison, was very different from the many loving letters he had written them since meeting Martha and Marianna in 1841. Conditions in the nation and his personal situation had changed dramatically even since his last meeting with Martha in Philadelphia in 1859, when his discussions with her about slavery had been controlled and polite. In this revealing letter, written to Marianna but mailed to Martha, he released his anger at abolitionists like them whose opinions and actions had led the nation into what Seward had termed the "irrepressible conflict."

Santa Fé, N. M.
Aug. 11th 1861

My dear niece

It has been long since I have addressed you or you me and this perhaps is the last time. The "irrepressible conflict" is upon us. I see it and feel it. While I write, sentinels with their gay uniforms and bright arms reflect the light of the sun upon me as they pass my cell door. My Father was a prisoner in the war of 1776. My brother (your father) was a prisoner in the war of 1812 and I am now a prisoner in the war of 1861. I have not taken up arms against the government neither have I aided or abetted either party in the late irrepressible conflict, yet my house was invaded, my private papers overhauled after I had first been marched off the prison and I know not what for. It may be for the reason that I am one of those unfortunate individuals who is a rightful subject for the application of your principles of reform—a slaveholder. I am a Kentuckian as you are aware and was born in sight of a non slave-holding state [Ohio], while I have lived in this Territory a third longer than I did in the state of Texas, yet I am regarded as a Texan and treated as one in rebellion against the government. Let it be so: it is one of the results of the teachings of your doctrines. Oh! The blood which has been and will be spilt in consequence of the false sympathy for the negro and the Indians. I think it is a great misfortune to mankind that there is a large party who prize the negro blood more highly than that of their own intelligent country men. Had it not been for that accursed negro question peace and prosperity would now reign where blood flows in torrents and lives are taken by thousands. But such are the results of false and fanatical teachings. You are too tender hearted to see a deer killed for the necessities of man, which was intended by God for his use, but you can see hundreds of thousands of men go into a sister state and slay thousands of your countrymen and believe they are doing God's service because they happen to be the owners of property in slaves which you for the sake of lucre sold them. You may think you can conquer the people and keep states in the union which you *desired should leave it* only a few months since, but you cannot accomplish your purpose, there are too many Bull Runs to pass on the way. We cannot expect to win all of the battles, but I think we will win a majority of them even if you come forth with a million of men. . . . We love the constitution as it was, and only asked that it might be executed but we have long since lost all hope of seeing that done and have adopted the only alternative left to us in my belief, and that is separation, and we desire it in peace.

Like his father in the Revolution, and like his brother Peter in the War of 1812, William had become a prisoner of war. He was enraged at his situation and at the war, for which he blamed his abolitionist relatives. About the war, he was prophetic when he warned that "there were too many Bull Runs to pass on the way." The first major battle of the Civil War, Bull Run (Manassas), had been a victory for the Confederates the previous month, but there indeed would be another battle there the following summer, and Second Bull Run would also be a Confederate victory. He concluded his letter with his fears for the South and for his personal future, and with a final "affectionate" salutation:

Now I ask you if you intend to kill us all off, because you will not allow us to have equality in the union with you. I was only settling up my business preparatory to departing for Texas, but I was arrested and now it is impossible to say if I will ever be liberated. Before this may reach you my destiny will have been decided and I either acquitted or be *hanged*. I am in the hands of my enemies, who thirst for my blood. If this letter is not couched in language like my former ones, it is because I am in prison (as I believe) unjustly, and feel oppressed.

Give my love to Thomas, Mr. & Mrs. Wright, your daughters and all of your friends.

Your affectionate uncle
Wm Pelham[3]

After reading the letter, Martha wrote to her son Frank, "I had a letter from Wm Pelham from prison. You know he has been arrested in Santa Fé. He refused to take the oath. The letter is written to Marianna, & addressed to me. He wishes peaceable separation & thinks the present state of things is the result of abolition teachings."[4] To Ellen, she added, "He thought they were thirsting for his blood, but I guess they only mean to keep him from taking up arms against the Govt. He was preparing to leave Santa Fé for his home in Texas."[5]

Many Texans had dreamed of expanding slavery westward to the Pacific Ocean. That also now became a dream of Jefferson Davis, president of the Confederacy. Early in 1862, the Confederate general Henry Sibley led a force of thirty-seven hundred, mostly Texans, in an attempt to take New Mexico. For a while, they were successful. In early March, anticipating the advance of the Texans, the governor and Union troops evacuated Santa Fé. The Texans then occupied the capital, released William Pelham from prison, and established him as Confederate governor of New Mexico. Newspaper accounts called him "General William Pelham" through confusion over his former title as surveyor general. Martha followed the news from New Mexico with special interest and wrote to her son Willy, now a lieutenant in the Union army, "The papers say that the Texans (Rebels) have taken Santa Fé, New Mexico & that General William Pelham is appointed Governor. (They established a provisional Government there.)"[6] The new governor, who the previous year had refused to take an oath of allegiance to the Union, then took revenge by demanding that local officials take an oath of allegiance to the Confederacy.

William's term as governor of New Mexico was limited, however, to a few short weeks. After defeat in the Battle of Glorieta Pass,[7] Confederate troops left Santa Fé in early April and retreated south along the Rio Grande. In May, Martha wrote to Frank, "I saw by the paper that the Rebels had left Santa Fé, and Wm Pelham with them."[8] But by then William was already a prisoner again. He had escaped and traveled about one hundred miles south with the rebels, but there he and a group of thirty Texans surrendered to the Union army, about two weeks after his escape from Santa Fé. The others were paroled after taking the oath of allegiance to the Union, but William, being a civilian, was not eligible for parole and was made a political prisoner. He had gone from prisoner to governor back to prisoner again in less than a month.

The remainder of Sibley's army limped back to Texas, their dreams of a westward extension of the Confederacy shattered.[9]

The war brought William further sadness when his only son, Charles T. Pelham, serving in the Eighth Texas Cavalry, was killed in battle.[10] Since William's son had died without issue, the surname of one of his daughter's sons was changed from Ten Eyck to Pelham, by special act of the Texas legislature, to perpetuate the name of the fallen soldier.[11] In 1869, Martha learned from Atkinson's son Charles Pelham that the Civil War left William "ruined in health, fortune & happiness."[12] He spent the postwar years on his Texas farm a few miles south of Austin, participated in local Democratic politics, and died there in 1879 at the age of seventy-six, leaving a wife, a daughter, and four grandchildren.[13] But William's angry 1861 letter from the Santa Fé prison was his last direct communication to Martha or Marianna, his abolitionist kin.

Gallant Pelham

Another Pelham who visited Marianna and Martha was John, the third of Atkinson's six sons. In 1856, he left Alabama to enter West Point for a five-year program, with instructions from his parents to call on his cousin Marianna at her home outside of Philadelphia. He did so before April 1858, since his letter to her that month ends with, "Remember me to Mr. Mott also to my little cousins. Tell them not to forget me before I return. I am learning to ride well, that I may ride with them again on my return in June '61."[14] That was his scheduled date of graduation, but events beyond his control intervened.

In January 1861, John's state of Alabama and four other states followed South Carolina's example and seceded from the Union. West Point cadets from the South began to resign, but John had been studying there nearly five years, and was only a few months away from graduation. In March 1861, he wrote to Marianna again from West Point, "I suppose you will think it quite strange that I am still here—it appears strange even to me, yet it is nevertheless so. But how much longer I will remain is quite impossible for me to say—future events will decide what course I will pursue. I am very anxious to graduate, the family exceedingly so. Almost all the Cadets from the Seceding States have resigned."[15] However, he expressed a wish to visit her and her family again before heading South. Marianna responded quickly to this message, informing him that her mother, Martha, and her sister Ellen would be there on a visit in April, stimulating another letter from John.

West Point N.Y.
March 26th '61

Dear Cousin [Marianna]

I am just in receipt of your kind letter of the 23rd Inst. I would like above all things to meet your Mother [Martha] and Sister [Ellen] in Phila. It may be the only opportunity I will ever have of seeing them. I am most anxious to see them, but can not say when I will leave. If I remain to get my diploma I will have to wait till 15th June. But whether I will stay till then is the question. I am not master of my own acts at present. I have been appointed a 1st Lieutenant in the Army of the "Confederate States of America." My appointment has also been confirmed by the Congress. The appointment was made without my consent or knowledge. I cannot accept an appointment from them as long as I am a member of this Institution, but if I am recalled by the Authorities, I will obey it. I have thus far resisted every overture, on the part of my friends, to resign, disregarding their advice and braved their anger. My father and brothers alone wished me to graduate. I had no idea I was so well supplied with friends. All seemed to vie with each other in attempting to *force* me to resign. I have worked almost five years for my diploma, and it pains me to give up the undertaking now—besides all this, it chagrins me to be forced to leave an undertaking unfinished. I believe there is only two Cadets here at present from the Seceded States—Myself and a classmate from Texas. We will leave together in June—or before, as the fates will it. We have been living together for three or four years, and I feel like we are inseparable—like his presence is necessary to my happiness. If we leave before June, it will be in about two weeks. You must allow me to introduce him.

I suppose you have heard of Bro. Charles' marriage through Aunt Ann or some of our Kentucky kin. I believe Aunt Martha knew Bro. Chas.—if so, tell her, he married one of the nicest ladies in Ky. So they all write. I have never seen her.

I had a letter from Henry Pelham a few days since, he says all are well in

Ky. Sister is almost crazy about her sister—it is the first she has ever had. I think it would be doing her a kind and brotherly act to present her with another, but none of the girls will have me. It is the most unaccountable thing I ever heard of—don't you think so?

I can let you know definitely in a week or two whether I will have the pleasure of visiting you before you leave Phila.

If anything could compensate me for giving up my dearest object—graduating—it is the pleasure I could have in visiting your family, your Mother & Sister.

Tell Cousins Belle and Emily [Isabella Pelham Mott and Emily Mott, Marianna's two teenage daughters] we may get another ride together, and then I will teach them to ride like Cavalry officers. Give them my best love. Remember me kindly to Mr. Mott [Thomas].

Affectionately
Jn. Pelham[16]

In April, shortly after the Confederates fired on Fort Sumter, John finally resigned from West Point and headed home for Alabama. On his journey south, he made a brief visit to Marianna and her family in Philadelphia, and there met Martha and Ellen. John Pelham's several biographers give varying accounts of his return to Alabama from West Point, but none apparently was aware that his trip south started with a visit with his Aunt Martha and her daughters, all abolitionists.[17] Three months after Martha, Marianna, and Ellen met with the handsome young cadet from Alabama, John Pelham was in Manassas, Virginia, directing cannon fire at Union troops in the first Battle of Bull Run.

John performed so well at Bull Run that he was promoted to captain and transferred to the command of General J. E. B. ("Jeb") Stuart. Stuart had become convinced of the importance of having cannon that could be rapidly moved to strategic spots during battles and directed John to organize a mobile artillery unit, soon to become famous as Stuart's Horse Artillery. They were active in the Peninsula Campaign of 1862, in which Robert E. Lee's Army of Northern Virginia drove back the Federal army from the outskirts of Richmond, the Confederate capital. John and his horse artillery also fought with honor in the second Battle of Bull Run that August, and at Antietam (Sharpsburg, Maryland) the following month. John's skill and valor in battle earned him the admiration of Stuart and of General "Stonewall" Jackson and a promotion to major. Jackson reportedly said to Stuart, "If you have another Pelham, I would like to have him." But it was his exploits at the Battle of Fredericksburg in December that drew public praise from General Robert E. Lee and made John Pelham famous across the South.

Fredericksburg, Virginia, is about midway between Washington and Richmond and was the site of several major battles during the war. On December 13, 1862, Lee's army took a position on high ground behind Fredericksburg and faced the advance of many thousands of Union troops. Stuart's Horse Artillery was placed on the far right of the Confederate line, and John Pelham moved two of his guns down the hill to a hidden position from which he opened fire directly onto the flank of the Union troops. For over an hour, he inflicted heavy casualties despite receiving intense return fire from Union artillery. Lee, watching John's skill and bravery in action, is said to have remarked, "It is glorious to see such courage in one so young." Major John Pelham, then only twenty-four, contributed notably throughout the day to one of the worst defeats suffered by the Union army in the entire war. The North suffered over twelve thousand casualties that day, more than twice the Southern losses. The battle was such an overwhelming victory for the South that it greatly strengthened morale throughout the Confederacy. General Lee's official report of the Battle of Fredericksburg singled out "the gallant Pelham" for praise, his only report during the war in which he mentioned by name anyone below the rank of general. Martha too would read newspaper accounts of "the gallant Pelham" but could not confirm until after the war that he was the nephew she had met in 1861, a son of Atkinson Pelham, the medical student she had known in her mother's Philadelphia boardinghouse forty years earlier.

Three months later, John was killed in a minor cavalry encounter at a location on the Rapahannock River called Kelly's Ford. His promotion to lieutenant-colonel had not yet been confirmed by the Confederate Senate but was passed posthumously after Lee wrote to Jefferson Davis, "I mourn the loss of Major Pelham. I had hoped that a long career of usefulness and honor was still before him. He has been stricken down in the midst of both, and before he could receive the promotion he had richly won. I hope there will be no impropriety in presenting his name to the Senate that his comrades may see that his services have been appreciated, and may be inclined to emulate them."[18]

John's death so soon after his widely publicized recognition by Lee at Fredericksburg established him as a popular martyr to the Southern cause. His body was taken to Richmond and laid in state, where it was viewed by thousands. He was buried near his home in Jacksonville, Alabama, where a statue was erected in his honor. A city in southern Alabama was later named Pelham, and over a century after his death, a thoroughbred racehorse named Gallant Pelham, several biographies, and numerous memorials have kept his fame alive.[19] His Aunt Martha and her family certainly disapproved of his cause. But they admired his bravery and regretted the death of the handsome young cadet who, on his way south to answer the call of duty, had stopped in Philadelphia to visit his abolitionist aunt and cousins.

Reconstructed Reb

John was only one of the six sons of Atkinson Pelham who fought with the Confederate army. In January 1865, Marianna received a letter from John's brother William, written from the Union prison on Johnsons Island, Ohio. (This island lies in Sandusky Bay off Lake Erie, and the fifteen-acre prison held over twenty-five hundred men. Today it is the site of a Confederate cemetery with two hundred graves.) William was a second Lieutenant in the Fifty-first Alabama Cavalry, and his letter reported John's death, the wounding of his brother Charles, the capture of his brother Peter, and his own imprisonment. He had been captured in June 1863 in Shelbyville, Tennessee. After Marianna responded with a friendly letter, William requested her help in obtaining a parole. She responded, "How deeply I regret the unfortunate position of one so nearly related to me, I hardly need tell you—yet you must remember how much we have had to feel for the cruel suffering of our men confined in the South."[20] In a third letter, he suggested a prisoner exchange for any friend she may have in a Southern prison. To this she responded, "I have no longer any friends in southern prisons, those so unfortunate having died there."[21] (A close friend of Marianna's had died at Andersonville, the infamous Southern prison.) She did add, however, that her husband, Thomas Mott, had written to the secretary of war requesting that William's name be put on the roll for an early exchange. Thomas's letter seemed to have an effect, because William's military records show that he was paroled on February 24 and sent to Virginia for prisoner exchange. For a few years after the war, he lived in Texas and helped to work the farm of his uncle and namesake, the man who for a few weeks in 1862 had been Confederate governor of New Mexico. William was killed in a gunfight in Anniston, Alabama in 1889.[22]

The only son of Atkinson's who corresponded directly with Martha both before and after the war was Charles, the oldest. In 1856, he was twenty-one and studying law in Alabama when an incident on the floor of the United States Senate greatly inflamed feelings in both North and South. Senator Charles Sumner delivered a strong antislavery speech that included sharp criticism of South Carolina's senator Andrew Butler. The speech so enraged Butler's nephew, Congressman Preston Brooks, that two days later he invaded the Senate chamber and beat Sumner into unconsciousness with his gold-headed walking stick. Young Charles Pelham wrote to Martha expressing his approval of the attack. His letter generated a spirited reply, condemning his views and defending the vital importance of freedom of speech.

> I felt very sorry that you should justify the murderous attack on Sumner, & that you should be willing to endorse the sentiment, so unworthy an American citizen, that personal violence, under any circumstances, was allowable, for words uttered in debate. The cowardly mode of the attack, I believe you do not justify, but do you think it possible for liberty to exist where freedom of speech is restrained, by the fear of personal indignity, at the hand of every assassin who bases his claim to respectability on his skill in the use of the bowie knife & revolver? . . . [A]re you willing to admit, that for words spoken in the excitement of debate, the scholar, the gentleman, the statesman, is to be rudely assaulted & to find that he expresses his opinion at the risk of his life? I hope you will review your opinions, read what is written on both sides, & come to a less prejudiced judgment. . . . I shall always be happy to hear from you & I

trust that more mature reflection, & the generous impulses of youth, will lead you to judge wisely on this momentous question wh. is destined to shake the Union from centre to circumference.[23]

Charles completed his law studies and entered into practice in Talladega, Alabama, in 1858. On December 6, 1860, shortly after Lincoln's election, he wrote to Martha from Talladega.

As you are now probably rejoicing over yr. late victory, you will pardon me for writing to you—We don't feel mortified at our defeat. I for one rejoice that we have an oppy. for "precipitating the Cotton States into a revolution." I have tho't for a long time that we wd. get along more amicably as two independent nations. . . . If the S. had submitted to Lincoln's election, I intended to have sold what few negroes I now have, & have gone to the North West. But I am proud to say that our people have enough of the spirit of our forefathers, to resist oppression, & to throw off the chains wh. wd. make them the slaves of a tyrannizing majority. . . . I have not heard from you in a long time, & hope you have seen fit to change yr. opinions in regard to the institution of Slavery. . . . If any of my former letters offended you, I now ask yr. forgiveness. I had hoped to see you again, before this, & make an apology, but now, it is too late. If I ever go North now, it will not be on an errand of *love*. . . . Nothing wd. give me more pleasure than to see you & my cousin Marianna settled at the *South*—till then I must bid you a long farewell, for on the 3rd day of March next, the copartnership existing between the Sovereignty of Alabama & the Union, will be dissolved.

Your nephew
Chas. Pelham[24]

Martha responded that about slavery, "I must still differ from you in sentiment as earnestly as ever." But even on this topic, she supported freedom of expression, adding, "No apology is needed for the freedom of expression in your former letters, to which we both have the same undoubted right. I only regret that you do not see as clearly as [Thomas] Jefferson did, the inevitable result of conflict between wrong and injustice on the one hand, and the eternal and unchanging principle of right, on the other." To Martha, on the issue of slavery there was the simple and clear-cut distinction between right and wrong. "As to the election of Lincoln," she added, "I am not so much delighted as you imagine, because I do not feel at all sure that he has the courage to meet the present emergency, and that he will not by a temporizing policy, a mean spirit of compromise, put back the day of universal emancipation for *the masters* as well as the slaves of the south."[25] The future of slavery was still by no means clear in December 1860. Then and for several years to come, Martha would fear that what she considered Lincoln's "mean spirit of compromise" would delay abolition.

Alabama moved faster than Charles expected and seceded from the Union on January 11. South Carolina had led the way on December 20, and by February 1, had been joined by Mississippi, Alabama, Florida, Georgia, and Texas. Four other states—Virginia, Arkansas, Tennessee, and North Carolina—would follow a few months later. Martha's last letter from Charles before the war was written on March 12, a month before the attack on Fort Sumter. "Now Aunt Martha," he wrote, "just lay aside your abolition prejudices one moment & say if you don't like the bold stance the Cotton States have taken?" He then switched to family news, including his marriage in January and his brother John's decision to remain at West Point until graduation unless actual hostilities begin. "We boys are all secessionists but Pa & Lulie (my wife) are very conservative—we call them submissionists." Charles's wife and his father, Atkinson, were not so eager for war as the hot-headed young lawyer. Charles ended his letter with a mixture of political anger and family love:

You complain of the way abolitionists are treated in the South. We hung one to a china tree on the square last Oct. without a Judge or Jury—we tried three negroes by a jury of citizens & hung two of them before court. I had no hand [in] it but many of our best citizens did. Pa asked me to assure you of his continued love & esteem. Lulie sends her love.

Yr. nephew
C. Pelham[26]

A mixed message indeed. Soon after this letter, Charles, his brothers John and William and three other brothers all took up arms against the North. Martha lost contact with Charles during the war but wrote to him again in July 1869, asking for news of her various Pelham relatives. His letter of response first reveals his pride at the military record of his brother John and confirms Martha's suspicion that the "gallant Pelham" she had read about was indeed her nephew John, whom she had met in 1861 at Marianna's home.

Talladega, Ala.
12th July, 1869

My dear Aunt,

Your kind letter of the 7th was received yesterday; I had never learned one word, directly or indirectly, from you or cousin Marianna, since bro. John was in Philada. in 61. You are correct in supposing that the "gallant Pelham" was the young Cadet who called on you at Mr. Mott's. He was killed at the head of the 4th Va. Cavalry at Kelly's ford 17 March 1863, and if you would like to know something of the record he made, I will order (from New York) some of the histories and incidents of the war, which will give you an idea of what he did. If cousin Marianna comes back [Marianna was then traveling in Europe], I should like for her to see them. Now that the Government is safe & slavery abolished, it would seem that one could read of the courage and daring of a relative, though engaged in a cause that did not meet ones approval. Some day the world will recognize the difference between men "who precipitate a rebellion" and those who "go with their state."

Although Martha's views against the South became extreme during the war (see Chapter 11), by 1869, with the fevers of war behind her, she could appreciate that many young men like John could simply "go with their state" and not view themselves as fighting for slavery.

Charles continued his letter with further family news and an account of his own adaptation to the changes brought by the war.

"Cotton Bush" (the old home at Maysville) must be a lonely place *now*. Aunt Penelope is the only one there; Uncle John died soon after the close of the war. . . . Uncle William is ruined in health, fortune & happiness. . . . My father [Atkinson Pelham] and Mother are still living, both in fine health. They have two of the boys at home with them, and with a few hired hands, and the improved labor saving machines and farming implements, cultivate all the land they formerly cultivated with 30 negroes. When I was elected [to a federal judgeship] five of Pa's former slaves *voted* for me. Pa and the boys at home were inclined to joke me about it for a long time, but I believe every body is getting accustomed to the changed condition. . . . I am what you would call "a reconstructed reb." I voted for the adoption of the State Constitution, under the reconstruction measures of Congress, and for Genl [Ulysses S.] Grant, as the best means of restoring the country to peace and quiet. . . . I know a good many Ex Federal Officers in Florida, and have promised one of them to take a hunt with him in Escambria (Fla.) before a great while, and I shall certainly hunt up your son [Willy], when I go. I can & will offer him my sympathy and shall ask his for I languished on a bed of excruciating pain for 8 months, from a gunshot wound, received at the engagement at Kennesaw Mountain in June 64. I haven't fully recovered yet.

Mrs. Pelham (Lulu) sends her loving regards to you and all your family. She desires me to ask you to send her your Photograph. She has read your letters to me, many times, and has unbounded admiration for you and cousin M.

very affectionately
C. Pelham[27]

Charles was a first lieutenant in the Alabama Infantry and was wounded at the battle of Kennesaw Mountain, a Confederate victory that slowed William Tecumseh Sherman's advance toward Atlanta. Charles served as a federal judge from 1868 to 1873, and as a Representative in the United States Congress from 1873 to 1875. The "reb" who in 1861 had bragged to his Aunt Martha about the hanging of abolitionists and blacks in Alabama was now serving the Union as a "reconstructed" Republican Congressman who had voted for Grant for President.[28] Charles did not run for reelection but stayed in Washington to practice law. He later retired to Georgia, where he died in 1908, aged seventy-three.

Charles's letter above refers to a possible visit to Martha's son Willy in Florida. Willy, like his cousin John Pelham, had become an artillery officer, but in the Union army. Wounded in the war, he moved to Florida in 1869 to take up citrus farming. Whether Charles ever visited Willy in Florida to compare wounds and war stories, we have not learned. Whatever Martha may have thought of Charles's transformation from an angry "secessionist" to a "reconstructed reb," she continued to correspond with her nephew until her death. Her Pelham relatives gave Martha a glimpse into the war from a Southern perspective, but her heart was of course with the cause of abolition, with the Union troops, and especially with her son Willy, whose story we recount in the next chapter.

11

The Loyal Wrights

Willy Goes to War

WHEN CONFEDERATE guns fired on Fort Sumter in April 1861, Martha was in Philadelphia for Lucretia's fiftieth wedding anniversary. That month she and Marianna received a visit from John Pelham on his way south from West Point to Alabama to take up arms against the Union. A few days later, David arrived for a brief visit, also traveling south, but only to Washington and only on legal business with the Patent Office. However, when he applied at the railroad office for tickets to Washington, he was refused. With war fever gripping the nation, travel to the nation's capital was being severely restricted. Virginia, across the Potomac from Washington, had just seceded, and travel to Washington was through Maryland, a slave state that was bitterly divided over the possibility of secession. David was carrying a letter to William Henry Seward, President Abraham Lincoln's secretary of state, from Seward's wife, and on this basis, visited the governor of Pennsylvania in Harrisburg and was able to obtain a pass for travel to Washington.

As David rode south on a train carrying troops to defend the capital, he saw the newly enlisted soldiers harassing a black woman who was trying to sell them cakes. "I felt disgusted, outraged, and heartsore," he wrote. "And these were the men who were expected to fight against the slave power, beginning by grossly mistreating and abusing a woman, merely because she was a negress."[1] Most men who enlisted for the Union did not think of themselves as fighting for the emancipation of the blacks, and David later wondered, "Would they have enlisted had they known?" In Washington, after calling on Secretary Seward to deliver the letter, he watched Lincoln and his cabinet in front of the White House officially receiving several military regiments in the service of the United States. Although he was surprised to find the Patent Office building had been taken over by a Rhode Island regiment for temporary quarters, he was able to complete his business with the government attorneys and return to Auburn by early May.

Martha's two surviving sons, Frank and Willy, had studied together at Weld's school but their paths diverged during the war years. Frank, at sixteen, entered school at Phillips Exeter that fall to help him prepare for Harvard. Willy, at eighteen, contemplated enlisting in an artillery battery being organized in Auburn by two young men from the city who had become officers in the Union army, Captain Terrance Kennedy and Lieutenant Andrew Cowan. "Pa would be glad for him to give up all thought of [enlistment]," Martha wrote to Frank, "& assist him in the office, but still he would not withhold his consent if the right opportunity came."[2] The opportunity came in the form of a commission as second lieutenant, and Willy joined the "1st New York Independent Battery" in October. With a full complement of 156 men, Kennedy, Cowan, and Lieutenant William Pelham Wright set off toward Washington on December 2.[3] For many months thereafter, Martha and David would study the newspapers every day with intense anxiety for news of Willy's battery.

Martha worried not only that Willy might be wounded or killed in battle but also that he might succumb to disease. Events were to show this was a reasonable concern, since twice as many Civil War soldiers died of disease as were killed from combat.[4] There was little that Martha could do to improve Willy's chances of surviving in battle, but she could provide her expert advice for combating disease. As early as the 1820s, Martha had obtained from Atkinson Pelham, Peter's brother who studied medicine in Philadelphia, a treatise entitled "Diseases Most Prevalent in the US."[5] It included lists of appropriate medicines and doses to treat various diseases and physical complaints. With the help of her brother-in-law Solomon Temple, a druggist, she assembled a substantial medicine chest that she used over the years in doctoring her family.

She supplemented the recommendations of mainstream medicine with those of homeopathy, then a popular system of therapeutics and one for which Martha had great respect. She summarized her medical knowledge in a letter to Willy in January 1862, listing all the medicines she recommended for various diseases.[6] But it would not be disease that would fell Willy.

After training for several months in camps near Washington, Willy's battery departed in late March for Fort Monroe on the Virginia coast. They were to be part of General George McClellan's Army of the Potomac in his grand plan to attack Richmond, the Confederate capital, from the east. Willy saw his first military action here in what became known as the "Peninsula Campaign," which dragged on for several months and was ultimately unsuccessful. Terrance Kennedy resigned to join a different battery, Andrew Cowan was promoted to captain and assumed command, and Willy was promoted to first lieutenant. Cowan's unit received its first casualties in the Battle of Williamsburg on May 5, 1862, when counterfire from the confederate forces killed one private and wounded three others. Martha nervously followed accounts of the actions of the battery in the New York City and Auburn papers. When she read of these first casualties, and that her son Willy had a very close call in the same battle, she wrote to Frank, "Willy's horse was shot as he was leading him, think what a narrow escape!"[7] Martha apparently sent a newspaper account of the battle to Theodore Weld, Willy's former principal at Eagleswood School. Weld responded, "We all thank you heartily for the paper containing the report of Willie's admirably gallant bearing, in that desperate conflict at Williamsburg . . . [and] the testimony about W's coolness & courage, in the midst of perils & carnage. When you write him, send him my heartiest love, congratulations, All hail! & God speed."[8] McClellan's army continued westward and approached to within six miles of Richmond. Some had hoped that the capture of Richmond would end the rebellion, and Willy wrote home in June, announcing, "I am in hope that after the battle before Richmond we will be discharged."[9] But Robert E. Lee assumed command of the Army of Northern Virginia and soon was pushing the Union army back. By July, McClellan had retreated from Richmond, and the Peninsula Campaign was over. But the war was far from over for Willy or for the nation.

The next major battle in which the Auburn battery took part was the Battle of Antietam, near Sharpsburg, Maryland, on September 17. This was the single bloodiest day in American history, with total casualties over twenty thousand. Lee had invaded Maryland, but here he was successfully repulsed by the Union forces. J. E. B. Stuart's Horse Artillery was in action on the Confederate side, and since each army's artillery often directed fire toward the enemy artillery, William Pelham Wright and his cousin John Pelham were presumably firing at each other. And they were again that December at the Battle of Fredericksburg, where John earned recognition from Lee as "gallant Pelham."

Martha continued to write to Willy weekly throughout 1862. "We look forward fondly," she wrote in March, "to the time when this dreadful war will be ended, freedom forever established, and our dear son, once more with us. It seems to me you will feel that in these five months you will feel that you have lived years."[10] Like other abolitionists, Martha still feared that there might be some settlement between North and South that would fall short of emancipating the slaves. "My only hope for permanent peace," she wrote, "is in a decree of immediate & unconditional emancipation—under the War power. My great fear is that the War may be temporarily ended, by some hollow compromise, only to give time for new atrocities on the part of the slave power and its supporters. Stand firm to your Abolition principles, my dear boy."[11] "I open the paper every day with fear & trembling," she wrote to David from Philadelphia, but added, despite her fears for Willy, "I cannot say that I wish it to end, till Slavery is abolished."[12]

Although Martha and David and other abolitionists justified the Civil War in those terms, Lincoln and his government had originally described the purpose of the war to be preservation of the Union, not the abolition of slavery. The first official step toward abolition came that September, shortly after the costly Union victory at Antietam, when Lincoln issued his Emancipation Proclamation. The proclamation freed slaves only in those states still in rebellion on January 1, 1863. The President could do this much under his war powers but had no constitutional power to eliminate slavery in the border states still in the Union. Martha wrote to Willy, "The Emancipation Proclamation, tho' far less than we hoped, & had a right to demand, after the expenditure of so much of the best blood of the nation, is still an advance, which we hail with joy, as the forerunner of a proclamation of Liberty throughout *all* the land, to all the inhabitants thereof." She added, "We look forward to the time, proud as we can be, that you can be classed with the 'Veterans' in this holy war between Liberty and Slavery."[13] David wrote to Willy, "My dear son, you are fighting in the holiest cause in which any mortal ever drew sword."[14]

While Willy was fighting the "holy war between Liberty and Slavery," his younger brother, Frank, entered Harvard in 1862, and a cousin who had visited him there said to Martha, "Poor Frank—four long years." Martha did not see it that way. "To me, it seemed as if he were entering Paradise," she wrote to Willy. "I envy a young man this privilege more than almost any other."[15] Neither she nor her daughters had the opportunity to attend college, and she wanted one of her sons to have "four years of only intellectual responsibility." David approved only very reluctantly. He later wrote to Martha, "I never had much faith in sending boys to college and the more I know about it the less I like it. . . . As to preparing boys for the business of life, a college education does no such thing, but the reverse."[16]

Although antislavery conventions continued during the war, woman's rights conventions did not. When Susan B. Anthony proposed continuing them in 1862, David remarked, "Susan B. must be insane to think to interest people in Woman's rights at this time."[17] Martha was more tactful in a letter to Anthony:

As to calling a National Woman's Rights Convention, I have felt that it would be very unwise, at this time, when the nation's whole heart and soul are engrossed with this momentous crisis. It is true, as you say, that we "should not forget our principles, or fail to declare them because the majority do not, or cannot recognize them"; but it is useless to speak if nobody will listen. . . . I have hoped that it would be given up until the war is over, & the question of a revision of the Constitution, makes it necessary for us to assert our claim to a voice in the matter."[18]

Martha foresaw that a victory over the South would lead to Constitutional amendments eliminating slavery and giving the vote to freed blacks, and she hoped those changes would provide the opportunity to push for expanding suffrage to women as well. They would learn after the war, however, that most men were more willing to grant the vote to freed male slaves than to women.

Martha's diary entry for March 15, 1863 reads "spent day with Willy." Martha was visiting Philadelphia, and Willy was on a brief leave from his battery. He returned the next day, when she wrote, "Felt very sad to part with him, with all the dread possibilities of the future but proud that he appreciated & was willing to take part in the struggle for National life."[19] On the same day, she wrote to David, "Neither he, nor any one else knew the effort it cost me to bid him goodbye nor the heaviness of heart with which I think of the possibilities of the future—Still I would not have him anywhere else than at his post of duty."[20]

Martha continued to write to Willy every week. Although he was now twenty and had matured beyond his years through extended exposure to the horrors of war, her letters still occasionally contained maternal advice. In April, she wrote, "You mentioned drinking several glasses of Ale on your journey. I was sorry for that, because all those things are only a lure to a fatal craving for stronger drink. Therefore I hope you will never allow yourself to touch anything of the kind under any possible circumstances. The only safety is in total abstinence."[21] However, her letters usually focused on war news and on the doings of neighbors, friends, and family members, including news of Frank at Harvard. That spring Frank established himself in the college's history books by forming the first Harvard baseball team. He was captain and pitcher for this first team and remained captain and pitcher of the Harvard team throughout his college career.[22] Frank's letters to home recounted his baseball activities in great detail and seldom mentioned his studies. Martha wrote to Willy, "We are anxious lest he should be so absorbed in the ball contests as to neglect his lessons."[23] And she had other worries about Frank: "I hope he is strong enough in principle to escape the manifold temptations of College life."[24]

In May, Martha left Philadelphia for New York City, where she and her daughter Ellen attended conventions of the American Anti-Slavery Society and a new organization, the Women's National Loyal League.[25] Martha had convinced Susan B. Anthony that woman's rights conventions should be postponed until after the war, and so instead Anthony organized the National Loyal

League, with Elizabeth Cady Stanton as president. Lucy Stone, Antoinette Blackwell, Ernestine Rose, Martha, and other women abolitionists gathered in New York with Anthony and Stanton to pledge their "most earnest influence in support of the Government in its prosecution of the War for Freedom" and to initiate a petition to Congress to pass "an act emancipating all persons of African descent held to involuntary service or labor in the United States." Shortly after the meeting, Martha reported that she had received "half an acre of petitions that Miss Anthony sent for me," adding "I must see what I can do."[26] The league was in existence only a little more than a year, but in that brief time the women, Martha among them, collected four hundred thousand signatures supporting emancipation that Congress later used as evidence of nationwide support for the Thirteenth Amendment, which in 1865 finally abolished slavery.

Shortly before the conventions, Willy's artillery regiment was in action in the Battle of Chancellorsville, near Fredericksburg, Virginia. Lee's army triumphed there against superior Union forces, but the First New York Independent Battery performed well, receiving praise from General John Sedgwick, commander of the Sixth Corps. Most important to Martha, they incurred no casualties. She wrote to Willy from New York, "It was an inexpressible relief to get your letter, forwarded from Auburn this morning, & know that you had escaped all the perils of the battle." She added, "My heart is so constantly with you, and in this great struggle, that I find it difficult to interest myself in anything else."[27] Lee's success at Chancellorsville, and his earlier successes, emboldened him to once again invade the North. Willy would next face Lee's army outside a little town in southern Pennsylvania called Gettysburg.

Stopping Pickett's Charge

When the Battle of Gettysburg began on July 1, Sedgwick's Sixth Corps, including the Auburn battery, was about twenty miles away in northern Maryland. At dinner that evening, the men received orders to head for Gettysburg and were on the march by 9 P.M. It was a difficult march, and they did not reach the battlefield until late on July 2.[28] The first two days of battle produced heavy losses on both sides. At sunrise on July 3, Willy's battery was instructed to transfer to the First Corps, who, along with the Second Corps, were defending the federal center along Cemetery Ridge. They did not yet know this was the precise location that Robert E. Lee had chosen as the focus of the afternoon's attack.

Martha and David had lost two of their four sons—Charlie in his infancy and Tallman, at twenty-two, by drowning. Willy was twenty in 1863. His parents were very proud of his participation in what Martha called "the holy war between Liberty and Slavery," but they read the newspapers each day with great apprehension. On the morning of July 3, 1863, the same morning that Willy's battery was moving onto Cemetery Ridge, Martha was at home in Auburn writing to Ellen, "I wait as patiently as possible, but in great anxiety, for news from Willy—these forced marches are pretty hard for them."[29] Martha apparently had learned that the Sixth Corps was on the move but had no way of knowing that her son would, within a few hours, be at the center of one of the most famous battles of American military history—the repulsion of Pickett's Charge. Nor did she know that the news she would receive about her son three days later would be very troubling indeed.

At 1 P.M., the Confederate guns started a massive barrage against the troops along Cemetery Ridge, and shells began bursting around the battery, which at first had been stationed in reserve behind the troops. As Willy recorded later in his war diary, "most of the shells passed over the troops & came crashing all around us in the woods, numbers striking in front of us."[30] The battery then moved up and exchanged fire with the Confederate artillery on the opposite ridge. During the lengthy bombardment, the Rhode Island artillery unit to their right was especially hard hit, and Willy's unit was ordered to move over to replace them. Now they were even closer to the clump of trees that Lee had chosen as the center of his attack. As the battery moved into its new position, they were told to hold their fire for the enemy infantry. Across the fields below them, they now saw the rebel infantry, including a division of Virginians commanded by General George Pickett, beginning its march in parade formation toward Cemetery Ridge. As one historian describes it, "It was a magnificent mile-wide spectacle, a picture-book view of war that participants on both sides remembered with awe until their dying moment-which for many came within the next hour."[31] It was a spectacle, both grand

and terrifying, that Willy would recount to family and friends for many years to come.

Fourteen thousand soldiers marched toward the Union line, traversing the open fields at about a hundred yards a minute. Willy's battery and other artillery units opened fire. The advancing line came closer, and the battery switched from shells to canister, cans filled with metal balls that turned the cannons into deadly shotguns. But the confederates kept coming. When they were within rifle range, Union riflemen increased the deadly toll. Confederates were now about a hundred yards in front of the stone wall in front of the battery, behind which Pennsylvania troops were firing. Some rebels dropped prone and began firing at the battery. Near Willy, a private fell dead and the other lieutenant of the battery fell wounded. Now Willy and Captain Cowan were the only officers in the battery still with the guns. They had little ammunition left, but they ordered their five cannon loaded with double charges of canister for one last deadly round.

On the battery's right, a group from Pickett's division crossed the stone wall and drove the neighboring artillery unit from their guns. Another group of rebels stormed toward Willy's battery, screaming, "Take the guns!" Willy fell, with a bullet through his chest fired by a Confederate at the wall. Several others of the battery fell in the hail of bullets. Those who remained fired their cannons. Double canister from the five guns of the Auburn battery spewed deadly fire into the Confederates, some of whom by then were only ten yards away. None remained standing. To the right of the battery, Union troops in hand-to-hand fighting killed or captured all the remaining rebels who had crossed the wall, and "Pickett's Charge" was soon over. After the Confederates retreated across the fields covered with fallen comrades, Lee approached Pickett and ordered him to regroup his division against a possible Union counterattack. Pickett is said to have replied, "General Lee, I have no division now."[32]

The repulse of Pickett's Charge on July 3, 1863, was Lee's greatest defeat. Although the war dragged on for two more years, Lee's army never reached so far north again. Gettysburg has been called the High Tide of the Confederacy and the region on Cemetery Ridge where the Confederates briefly broke through the Union lines is called the High Water Mark. There is now a monument at High Water Mark, erected in 1887, to the battery from Auburn

in which Willy served. It is flanked by two cannon, and the face reads
"COWAN'S FIRST NEW YORK BATTERY ARTILLERY BRIGADE—SIXTH CORPS,
July 3, 1863, DOUBLE CANISTER AT TEN YARDS." The reverse side briefly
describes the role of the battery in the heat of the battle: "The Confederate
lines were advancing and continued their charge in the most splendid manner
up to our position. The artillery fire was continuous and did much execution.
Our last charge, double canister, was fired when some of the enemy were over
the defences and within ten yards of our guns. Our loss was four men and
fourteen horses killed, two lieutenants and six men wounded."[33] Although
Willy fell just before the final canister blast, he and the other members of
Cowan's battery played a central role in stopping Pickett's Charge, an important contribution to the Union's most notable victory of the war.

A Farmhouse at Gettysburg

It was not until Monday, July 6, that Martha and David read news of the First
New York Independent Battery and learned that Willy was "dangerously
wounded." Martha wrote to Frank at Harvard, "If you have chanced to see the
New York Times of Monday, you have seen Willy's name as severely wounded,
probably mortally, but we trust it is not so bad—and have reason to feel a
little encouraged, since receiving pencilled notes from Capts. Cowan & Birney
written on the field. . . . If his wound proves less serious than was at first
feared, I shall feel that it came to give him the rest that he was so much in
need of."[34] Martha was in serious need of such optimism. It helped a great deal
that she received hopeful notes from Willy's companions on the field on the
same day that she received the dreadful news in the *New York Times*.[35]

David left for Gettysburg the next day, stopping first in Philadelphia to
pick up Marianna. In Baltimore, they heard from a general that Lieutenant
Wright was dead, but they pressed on.[36] They arrived in Gettysburg on the
tenth, and after a lengthy search, David found Willy alive in a makeshift
hospital in a farmhouse several miles outside of town, sitting up in a bed with
a handkerchief over his chest to keep the flies from his wound. The rifle ball
had entered Willy's chest between the second and third ribs, passed upward
through his right lung and shoulder blade, and exited his back. As soon as the

action at High Water Mark subsided, several of his men had helped him to the rear. He later recorded in his diary, "At about sunset Cowan brought me some claret which tasted very good."[37] He was then moved to this Sixth Corps hospital about three miles from the battlefield. A male nurse assigned to the battery took care of him in the farmhouse hospital until David and Marianna arrived to assist. Willy had to remain sitting up for weeks, because the surgeon warned he could not live lying down until his wounds healed.

On the twelfth, Marianna wrote to Martha, "I am writing this Sunday morning from Willy's bedside. Father sits beside him, fanning away the flies and heat. . . . The doctors will not allow us any hopes notwithstanding the favorable progress of his wound, neither do they bid us despair. The chances are always against wounds in this most vital part, but his youth and health and good habits and temperament are all in his favor, and above all his strong determination to live."[38] Lying in the neighboring beds were a Confedente army captain who had lost an arm and a German who had lost a leg.[39] Many patients in the farmhouse died from their wounds while Willy was there. Marianna, who was sharing a small room in a Gettysburg hotel with four other women, wrote to Martha, "I found in my bed with me this morning a woman, a grasshopper, a spider, many smaller creatures which 'graze upon the human body,' and a moving canopy of flies."[40] Marianna was later relieved from her nursing duties by Frank, and he and David were later relieved by Eliza, who stayed with her brother until he returned home to Auburn on August 8.

Martha had packed her trunk with the expectation of traveling to Philadelphia to care for Willy once he was well enough to be moved there from Gettysburg. David had urged Martha not to go directly to Gettysburg herself, but she later wrote, "If I had not been over-ruled, I should have gone, & I shall always be sorry I didn't."[41] David returned from Gettysburg very ill himself, requiring Martha's care. And once Willy was home, Martha assumed responsibility for her wounded son during his many months of recuperation. For over a year, he had trouble breathing, but he eventually recovered full use of his lungs. Willy's later offer to return to the army in a staff position was rejected, but Martha was "proud for one so desperately wounded to be willing to give further service."[42]

By 1863, volunteers no longer filled the needs of the Union army, and Congress passed a conscription act that March. The first drawing of names came in July and led to widespread resistance. While Willy was recovering in the Gettysburg farmhouse, over a hundred people were killed in draft riots in New York City, which ended only when Union troops from Gettysburg arrived to preserve order. Martha and her friends in Auburn heard rumors that men angered by the draft had threatened to attack the homes and property of abolitionists, and she wrote to the mayor in mid-July:

> As I am about leaving town to be nearer my wounded son, I wish to ask of you protection for any property we have here, in case of a mob, during the enforcement of the Conscription Act.
>
> We have been informed that our house was to be attacked, as well as those belonging to other well-known Abolitionists, and tho' I comprehend little danger since the vigorous measures pursued in New York, I deem it best to notify you.[43]

Martha and her friends had required police protection from angry mobs at several antislavery conventions. Now she felt even her house was unsafe. Fortunately, after the draft riots in New York, other cities and towns made preparations to resist violence, and the draft passed off quietly in Auburn.

In November 1863, President Lincoln delivered a brief, but now famous, address at the dedication of the national cemetery at Gettysburg. In his opening sentence, he referred to "a new nation, conceived in Liberty, and dedicated to the proposition that all men are created equal." With this and his closing call for "a new birth of freedom," he provided support for the abolitionist view that the war was, as Martha described it, "a holy war between Liberty and Slavery," and not, as most Southerners saw it, simply a conflict between federal and states' rights. The eloquence of Lincoln's Gettysburg Address added immeasurably to the stature of the Battle of Gettysburg in the pages of American history.

Abolitionist Wedding

Martha's spirits were low throughout 1863 with worries about Willy, but they were lifted the following spring with news that Ellen had become engaged to

William Lloyd Garrison Jr.[44] Martha wrote to Ellen her enthusiastic approval, "not only on account of his own moral worth, but because he is the son of one whom we have so long regarded with reverence."[45] And Ellen's prospective father-in-law wrote to her, "I trust it will prove acceptable to your beloved parents, whom I have long been proud to reckon among my most esteemed friends."[46] (He had known Martha since 1833, when they met in Lucretia's home during the founding meeting of the American Anti-Slavery Society.) Lucretia also was very pleased with the news and wrote to the prospective bridegroom, "Your family has long seemed almost interwoven with ours, so closely allied in the Slave's cause, as well as in liberal Christianity."[47]

The wedding was held in September 1864 in Auburn, with Willy, well on the road to recovery, and Frank, home from Harvard, part of the wedding party. "You ask our plans," Martha wrote to Lucretia in August, "but they are not many. There will be about 125 counting the family, the Lord & Matthews are to provide sending dishes & waiters & loaves & fishes and it will all get through somehow. . . . I knew I couldn't make wedding cake, if the world came to an end for want of it."[48] Ellen invited Susan B. Anthony, who responded, "How can I say aught but yes I don't see. So expect me as per your orders."[49] Anthony had become very close to Ellen since meeting her in Saratoga in 1855. The service was performed by Rev. Samuel J. May, whom Martha had first heard speaking on abolition in Philadelphia in 1833. May had responded to William's invitation, "It will be indeed a delightful incident in my life, if I shall be permitted to officiate at the marriage of William Lloyd Garrison, jr., and Ellen his wife—as I did thirty years ago at the marriage of William Lloyd Garrison and Helen his wife."[50]

After the wedding, Ellen moved to a house in Boston that was only a few miles from Frank's dormitory at Harvard. Martha wrote to Ellen, "I hope by this time Frank has sufficiently rested from his multitudinous cares & responsibilities to visit you. He gave me a list of the various mental exercises required to qualify him for initiation into the Hasty Pudding Society—whatever that may be."[51] Frank continued to devote much of his time and energy to baseball, which worried Martha "unless he thinks to be a good pitcher is glory enough for one 'man'—as they call the college children." Frank's emphasis on sports added to David's continuing doubts about the value of college. Although Martha had her own reservations, to David she argued, "The exercise he has at ball

& boating will be the making of him, & prepare him for the future, far better than study alone would; as to the education there, he gets what nothing can ever take away, & I think if he only makes out to get honorably through you will yet be proud that we could give him that opportunity."[52] Martha's will prevailed, and Frank did complete his education and graduate. However, the major mark he made at Harvard was the initiation of intercollegiate baseball.

In the fall of 1864, Martha's attention was focused on Willy's convalescence, Ellen's wedding, and Frank's progress at Harvard, but she was also concerned about the coming presidential election. She had worried from the start that Lincoln was more interested in preserving the Union than in abolishing slavery. Despite the reverence with which he is viewed today, Lincoln was at the time very unpopular with many abolitionists.[53] In 1862, shortly before the Emancipation Proclamation was issued, Martha had referred to Lincoln as "the old fool who sits in [former President James] Buchanan's chair & pledges himself to slavery."[54] Lincoln's approach toward abolition was tempered by political realities, including his desire to keep the border states in the Union, that were not fully appreciated by committed abolitionists like Martha. As the question of his renomination approached, she wrote, "I am so sick of the two sided policy of Lincoln that almost any change wd. be preferable. I hope Fremont will be nominated. . . . It is a pity that Garrison committed himself to Lincoln—[Wendell] Phillips & other radical Abolitionists are for [John C.] Fremont."[55] Early in the war, Garrison had been highly critical of Lincoln for his lukewarm moves toward abolition, but he grew to believe that Lincoln was moving as fast as the public would allow and decided to support his renomination by the Republicans. Phillips continued to worry that Lincoln would allow the war to end without the abolition of slavery, and he instead supported Frémont.[56] The split between Garrison and Phillips, then the two most prominent antislavery leaders, caused dissension within abolitionist ranks, but the Democrats nominated McClellan and Frémont withdrew. "Now that the choice is narrowed down to McC. or Lincoln—there is nothing more to be said," Martha wrote to Ellen, "tho' I could have wished for a truer Anti-Slavery man than I take Lincoln to be."[57] Lincoln was easily re-elected.

By the spring of 1865, the tide of war had turned against the Confederacy, and General Ulysses S. Grant was closing in on Lee's weakened army in Virginia. On April 9, Lee surrendered at Appomattox Court House, and the remaining Confederate armies would soon follow suit. (Martha, still amused by the notion of college students being called "men," teased Frank, "Did they let you little boys out to rejoice over Lee's surrender?")[58] A few days after Appomattox, a special ceremony was held at Fort Sumter. The same U.S. flag that had been taken down four years earlier was once again raised over the fort. William Lloyd Garrison, once widely hated, was now viewed as a hero by many, especially by the freed blacks, and was guest of honor at the ceremony. He was also honored at several related events in Charleston, where he visited the grave of John C. Calhoun, the politician who, before his death in 1850, had been the most prominent and influential of those defending the institution of slavery. Standing before Calhoun's tomb, Garrison said, "Down into a deeper grave than this slavery has gone, and for it there is no resurrection."[59] Martha wrote to Garrison's son, now her son-in-law, "I hope your Father will derive benefit from his short voyage. We were very glad for him to have the journey & the rest, and above all, the glorious triumph. Down with the traitors, up with the Flag! . . . I dread any misplaced 'magnanimity' toward the leaders of the Rebellion, & the murderers of our prisoners. I would not have *one* hanged, but disfranchised & their land confiscated."[60] Throughout the war, Lucretia, a longtime pacifist, had chided Martha "for wishing too much harm to the rebels" and cherishing a "spirit of revenge." Having Willy nearly killed by the rebels made Martha far less forgiving of the South than Lucretia.[61] Martha consistently called for confiscation of property and disenfranchisement of confederate leaders, but a few days before the end of the war, she became even more extreme, writing to Willy, "I for one wd. rather the War wd. last till the South is depopulated."[62] Lincoln's second inaugural address had urged the nation to proceed "with malice toward none; with charity for all," but in the spring of 1865, Martha's heart was not full of charity for the South. Her hatred of slavery and the emotions stirred by the war had moved her far from the Quaker teachings of pacifism she had received as a child.

Shortly after the ceremony at Sumter, Lincoln was assassinated at Ford's Theatre in Washington by John Wilkes Booth. Simultaneously, a collaborator of Booth's attempted unsuccessfully to kill Seward, who was in his bedroom recovering from injuries incurred in a serious carriage accident nine days earlier. Martha wrote to Marianna about "the dreadful deed that so stunned &

shocked us all. . . . What stronger proof could we have, of the danger result-ing from the fatal policy of conciliation toward the infamous leaders of the rebellion. . . . I want all the rebels forgiven when they are thoroughly disabled from ever doing any more mischief, & deprived of political power, not be-fore."[63] Martha was shocked at Lincoln's assassination but hoped that his suc-cessor would be tougher on the South than she had expected Lincoln to be. She predicted that "the rebels would find the little finger of Andy Johnson heavier than the loins of the man they had murdered,"[64] but she soon learned that the Reconstruction policies of President Andrew Johnson, a Tennessee Democrat and former slaveholder, were also very lenient toward the South.

Controversy over the proper postwar treatment of the former rebels troubled national politics for some time. But the postwar granting of suffrage to the newly freed slaves—the freed *male* slaves—produced a controversy that would split the woman's rights movement, leaving Martha on one side and the man she had "so long regarded with reverence," William Lloyd Garrison, on the other. Since the 1830s, Martha had revered Garrison for his leadership role in the abolitionist movement, but she had not seen eye to eye with him on every issue. She had not shared his enthusiasm for spiritualism, for non-resistance, or for the renomination of Lincoln. In the postwar years, she would again part ways with Garrison in the controversy over the Fifteenth Amendment.

12

Aftermath

The Home Front

BY THE summer of 1866, Martha had eight grandchildren—Marianna and Thomas Mott's three daughters, Eliza and Munson Osborne's three daughters and one son, and Ellen and William Garrison's one daughter. Martha's two remaining sons, Willy and Frank, were now in their twenties but remained unmarried. Willy had largely recovered from his war wounds, but his future remained uncertain. He showed no interest in studying law in David's office, or in working on David's farm or sawmill, and had not yet developed any alternate plans. David wrote to him in frustration: "I wonder often why you can content yourself with playing ball, and rowing on the Lake and such amusements, which are certainly much more laborious than anything I ever asked you to do. . . . You are a good boy and did your whole duty during the war and have suffered much for us, and I will try not to expect too much from you. . . . There are so many pleasant opportunities open to you. I need help so much in my office and also in my outdoor matters. Munson [Osborne, Eliza's husband] also is in much need of help in his business. In fine, it is utterly inexplicable to me that you will not try to do *any thing*."[1] Responding to David's pressure, Willy decided to try working as a representative of Munson's farm machinery business in the Midwest and moved to Chicago.

June 1866 was the month of Frank's graduation from Harvard, and he also had not yet settled on his life's work. Martha attended the graduation ceremonies and met Fanny Rosalie Pell, whose engagement to Frank had recently become known. Martha met Fanny's mother and later wrote to David that Mrs. Pell liked Frank, but, "she said she did not think they ought to be married till Frank was in business."[2] Frank's most consuming interest was still baseball, and he at first tried to make a living selling baseballs and bats.[3] Frank and Fanny married in April and moved in with Martha and David. By then, Willy had given up his job with Munson and joined with Frank in his baseball business, sending him bats for shipping throughout the East. In May, Martha wrote to Ellen that "the barn is too full of bats and boxes & Fanny sits & watches him box them when he has orders, or unpack the ones Willy sends."[4] Willy once complained to Martha about a broken bat he had received, and she, displaying her practical mind, responded, "You say the river is the best place for it—I should say the stove, where it could be useful still." The baseball business never worked out for either Willy or Frank.

In January 1868, the family was saddened by the death of James Mott, Lucretia's husband for fifty-seven years. Martha entered in her diary, "Sat alone from 6 to 10—thinking of all we had lost, & the gradual breakup of our happy family circle—happy at the same time to think how soon we three sisters might meet one another & those who have gone, when partings are no more."[5] Despite Martha's liberal approach to religion, she found comfort in the thought of an afterlife where she would commune with lost family members.

One of Martha's closest friends had been Frances Seward, who died in June 1865, only two months after the unsuccessful assassination attempt on her husband. Still bearing the signs of the attack and his prior carriage accident, William Henry Seward returned to Auburn for his wife's funeral, at which David was one of the pall bearers. Frances had never been happy with her husband's political ambitions, and Martha wrote to Lucretia, "Poor Mrs. Seward sleeps well, untortured by the restless ambitions of others."[6] Martha remained close to Frances's sister, Lazette Worden, and she and David remained friendly with Seward, whom Andrew Johnson kept on as his secretary of state. (One of Seward's successes under Johnson was his purchase of Alaska from Russia, although at the time it was criticized by many as "Seward's folly.")[7] Seward attempted to improve U.S. relations with China, and in 1868 a delegation of thirty, the first mission from China to any Western country, arrived in Washington to negotiate a treaty. The Chinese delegation then traveled to Auburn, where Seward gave a grand party. Martha attended and later wrote to Stanton, "The chief Mandarin told Mrs. Worden that he admired the intelligence of American women. She answered that the women in China would be intelligent also, if they were allowed to come into the parlor, instead of being kept in the back part of the house."[8] Martha's letter, published in the *Revolution*, did not record the response of the Mandarin to this expression of American feminism.

There was further excitement in Auburn the following month when the celebrated actress Fanny Kemble gave a reading. Martha enjoyed the reading, but her Quaker sensibilities were shocked by Kemble's white silk dress with a "square neck—*inexpressibly* low, a thin worked lace underhandkerchief, which by no means concealed a remarkable fullness considering the over mature years."[9] Martha, radical in many ways, remained conservative with regard to female dress.

In summer 1868, David had an idea that finally settled Willy's future: "What do you think of going to Florida and buying a plantation on the St. Johns [a river in northern Florida] and make a fruit farm of it?"[10] That's just what Willy did, with financial help from David. In Florida, David met Flora McMartin, a niece of Elizabeth Cady Stanton, and in the fall of 1869, they were married in Johnstown, New York, Stanton's hometown. Martha wrote to Willy, "We can only pray that you may both be happy—'yr. dependence mutual, your independence equal, yr. duties reciprocal.'"[11] This symmetric relation between husband and wife was rare, but it was one that woman's rights supporters like Martha set as the ideal toward which to strive. About the wedding, she reported to Ellen that "Flora looked very pretty, and *didn't* promise to *obey*,"[12] an omission that was very appropriate for the niece of Elizabeth Cady Stanton and the daughter-in-law of Martha Coffin Wright.

Just as Ellen's marriage had strengthened Martha's ties to William Lloyd Garrison, Willy's marriage strengthened her ties to Stanton. After Willy and Flora's first child was born, and while Ellen was visiting Martha with her children, Stanton, who, like Martha, had borne seven children, wrote, "I suppose you are now in the full enjoyment of Ellen's children—the teazing, the tumbling, the feeding, &c. &c. Alas! for pap spoons & diapers—Oh!

Martha—Martha! Let us together sing Hallelujahs that we are thro' that dispensation . . . [and] tell Ellen there is a good time coming, when these little animals will be intelligent companions."[13] Martha agreed: "I feel very much as you express, in regard to the incessant cares inseparable from that time of life, & gladly welcome the added years . . . with the repose, following such toil."[14] Martha would ultimately have fifteen grandchildren, Stanton eight.

Martha returned to Auburn from Willy's wedding just in time for the birth of Frank and Fanny's first child, Mabel Channing Wright. Fanny's mother was a Channing, a first cousin of the well-known Unitarian minister William Ellery Channing. Fanny's delivery was long and painful. In a letter reminiscent of one she had written many years earlier after a difficult delivery of Marianna's, Martha wrote to Ellen, "She suffered dreadfully with ineffectual forcing pains. . . . It was too distressing to see her torture . . . I could not get her suffering out of my mind for hours." The delivery was also hard on the men: "Frank was entirely overcome, & had to go to his room. Your father hurried away as soon as he had eaten his dinner, saying he could not stay in the house." The "stronger sex" left, but Martha stayed. She later wrote to Lucretia that it was a "dreadful world" in which women endured such pain in childbirth. But as for the new mother, "Fanny bore her sufferings with wonderful heroism & seemed somewhat reconciled when all was over, & her pretty little black haired Mabel by her side."[15] Lucretia admonished Martha, "Think of thou calling this a 'dreadful world' when *Mabel* was ushered in."[16]

Harriet Tubman

Martha's circle of friends in Auburn included Harriet Tubman, foremost hero of the Underground Railroad.[17] The earliest reference to Tubman in Martha's existing correspondence is in the 1860 letter quoted in Chapter 9, describing the last group of slaves that Tubman guided from slavery to freedom before the war. During the war, she served the Union army as a scout and as a nurse. After the war, on a train trip north, she carried a pass for half fare that she had received as a former nurse. Unimpressed, the conductor had her forcefully dragged out of one car and into the smoking car. On her return to Auburn,

Tubman described her ordeal to Martha, who relayed the story to Marianna in November 1865:

> How dreadful it was for that wicked conductor to drag her out into the smoking car & hurt her so seriously, disabling her left arm, perhaps for the winter. She still has 'the misery' in her shoulder & side & carries her hand in a sling. It took three of them to drag her out after first trying to wrench her finger and then her arm. She told the man he was a copperhead scoundrel, for which he choked her. . . . She told him she didn't thank any body to call her cullud pusson. She would be called black or Negro. She was as proud of being a black woman as he was of being white.[18]

Tubman settled in Auburn and, on the property obtained from Seward, provided a home for numerous freed slaves. The Wrights, Osbornes, Sewards, and other sympathetic Auburn residents helped in a variety of ways, including making contributions of money, food, and clothes. William Lloyd Garrison, Wendell Phillips, and others sent financial help from afar. "She has a good deal of that honest pride," Martha wrote Lucretia, "which makes her unwilling to beg."[19] Tubman's Auburn supporters raised funds through the sale of food and a variety of contributed goods at her "Freedman's fairs," modeled after the antislavery fairs at which women earlier had raised money for the abolitionist cause. For one 1868 fair for which Martha sewed thirty-eight aprons, she reported that Seward's daughter Fanny was on "the begging committee, called, for shortness, 'Committee to solicit donations.'"[20] The fair took in over four hundred dollars. While there, Martha attempted to get signatures for a woman suffrage petition but got only six and found some people "disposed to be rather short. 'Suffrage? What's that? Women vote? No!! Perfect nonsense!!' I rather dread going round to fill up the petition, but will try."[21] Twenty years had passed since Seneca Falls, and woman suffrage still seemed like "perfect non-sense" to many.

Martha's diaries for the late 1860s and early 1870s contain many references to Tubman, such as "went in Eliza's buggy to see Harriet Tubman," "rode to HT's and left her the $10," "Harriet Tubman called—$5 from Gerrit Smith,

$2 from Mrs. Pomeroy, $3 from self," "Harriet Tubman called & got clothes for freedmen," "Harriet Tubman called for pears," "Harriet Tubman called. Wrote letter for her."[22] (Tubman was illiterate, and both Martha and Eliza wrote letters for her.) Tubman preferred working for money rather than begging, so "Harriet Tubman came to clean" is a frequent entry in the diaries. Tubman also sold Martha handmade items, probably made by some of the freed slaves: "Harriet Tubman came and bro't hoop basket. Pd. her 62½¢."

In the fall of 1867, Ellen visited Auburn with her new daughter and made a call on Tubman, but she was out. After Ellen had returned to Boston, Martha wrote to her, "Harriet Tubman came on Wednesday to see you & the baby. She didn't hear of your call till the evening before, & was so disappointed that her eyes filled with tears. She never shed a tear in telling me of all her troubles."[23] Tubman was especially interested in Ellen because of her connection to Garrison, one of Tubman's heroes.

Sarah Bradford, a woman from nearby Geneva, took down Tubman's tales of her life, especially her journeys on the Underground Railroad, and produced a book that was sold to raise money to support her home for freed slaves. The book sold well at the freedman's fairs, and Martha asked Ellen's husband to promote it in Boston circles. "We all owe you thanks," she later wrote to William, "for your efforts to make Harriet Tubman's book known. . . . I think Mrs. Bradford deserves credit for having done ever so well, almost impossible as it is to understand Harriet's desultory talk." Martha's letters provide interesting information on Tubman's view of the 1859 martyrdom of John Brown: "She told me that John Brown staid at her house in Canada, while he was there, & that he wanted her to go with him on his expedition, but when he sent a messenger for her, she was not at home. I asked her if she did not feel bad, when she heard of his death—She said 'Yes, at first, but he done more in dying, than 100 men would do, in living.'"[24]

"The Negro's Hour"

Congress had passed the Thirteenth Amendment to the Constitution, abolishing slavery, in January 1865, when the end of the war was in sight. The amendment was ratified and became law that December, and David remarked sarcastically that abolition was finally achieved "in this 19th century of the *Christian* era. Wonder how matters would have progressed if we had not been a Christian people!!"[25]

The ultimate success of the amendment was already clear in May 1865, when the American Anti-Slavery Society (AAS) gathered for its annual meeting in New York. Garrison, who had been a leader of the antislavery movement for over thirty years, had already announced that he would stop publication of the *Liberator* at the end of the year and now moved that it was time for the AAS to declare its goal accomplished and dissolve the organization. Wendell Phillips and others disagreed, arguing that their work was not complete until it became clear that the freed slaves would have full legal and voting rights (which would later be addressed by the Fourteenth and Fifteenth Amendments, respectively). Garrison's motion to dissolve the AAS was defeated soundly. Martha was there, one of the few who had also been present at the founding of the society in Philadelphia in 1833. Her description of the meeting in a letter to Marianna does not indicate how she voted, although she wrote, "I hoped he [Garrison] might be induced to continue a few months longer."[26] For another five years, the AAS would continue without its former leader.

Phillips was elected president, and in his inaugural address declared that winning the vote for former slaves would be a difficult enough task without trying to persuade both Democrats and Republicans also to support votes for women. Although he still supported the concept of woman suffrage, this, he said, was "the Negro's hour," and the hour for women had not yet arrived. The women would have to wait their turn. The woman's rights leaders had fought for abolition alongside the men since the 1830s, and, as the Women's National Loyal League, had collected thousands of petitions for the Thirteenth Amendment during the war. They had hoped and expected that "when the Constitutional door was open," abolitionist leaders would push for woman suffrage as well as for black suffrage. They were mistaken. For most male abolitionists, as well as for Congress and the general public, suffrage for black men took precedence over woman suffrage.[27] It was the Negro *man's* hour. Stanton and Anthony were incensed by the desertion of their abolitionist colleagues who had given lip service to woman suffrage for many years.

In the summer of 1865, a new amendment was drafted to define legal rights for freed blacks, and the draft included the word *male* to define citizens and voters. Sex discrimination that had been implicit in the Constitution was now threatening to become explicit. Stanton and Anthony rapidly generated a petition to eliminate sex discrimination in voting, but even Martha at first was hesitant to sign and wrote to Stanton that she wanted to "rest on her oars" for a time. Stanton blamed Phillips and wrote to him, "What good are our petitions so long as such women as Martha Wright . . . will not sign them? & why will they not? because they feel that our antislavery priesthood are opposed to them."[28] For four years, the Civil War and Willy's participation in it had focused Martha's attentions more on the issue of slavery than on woman's rights. She also had great admiration for Phillips. For several decades, she had found him to be the most compelling of the abolitionist speakers, and she had worked closely with him on AAS committees and on antislavery projects before and during the war. She also admired Frederick Douglass and Garrison and other members of what Stanton termed the "abolitionist priesthood," and had some sympathy for their argument that this was "the Negro's hour." Stanton wrote to her in January 1866, "Martha, what are you all thinking about that you propose to rest on your oars in such a crisis? I conjure you and Lucretia to be a power at this moment in taking the onward step."[29] Martha soon relented and indicated her support, to which Stanton replied, "Your letter shows you are sound at the core" and "your disease was only skin-deep."[30] Although Martha's ties to Phillips and Garrison were strong, her ties to Stanton and Anthony were stronger. She was still woman's rights "at the core."

The first woman's rights convention held after the war met in New York in May 1866, and the women attempted to merge the issues of black and woman suffrage by reincorporating as the American Equal Rights Association. The key motion, made by Susan B. Anthony and seconded by Martha, read, "Whereas, by the set of Emancipation and the Civil Rights bill, the negro and the woman now hold the same civil and political status, alike needing only the ballot: and whereas the same arguments apply equally to both classes, proving all partial legislation fatal to republican institutions, therefore Resolved, that the time has come for an organization that shall demand UNIVERSAL SUFFRAGE, and that hereafter we shall be known as the "AMERICAN EQUAL RIGHTS ASSOCIATION."[31] In the ensuing discussion, one man charged that the motive for the change was only "to get rid of the odious name Woman's Rights." Martha, her support for the cause now fully restored, denied that charge heatedly and declared, "I for one have always gloried in the name of Woman's Rights, and pitied those of my sex who ignobly declared they had all the rights they wanted."[32] Lucretia was chosen to be president of the new association.

The following month, Martha traveled to Boston, a visit that characteristically combined the personal and the political. She was there for the birth of Agnes Garrison, Ellen's first child and William Lloyd Garrison's first grandchild. But while in Boston, Martha also attended a meeting of the New England Anti-Slavery Society and presided over a meeting of the newly formed association dedicated to "equal rights," suffrage for both blacks and women. "I was rather taken aback," she wrote to David, "to find that I was expected to preside at the Equal Suffrage meeting but I got through with it tolerably well & had a very cordial congratulation at the close, from Wendell Phillips, who spoke well, several times."[33] A few male abolitionists supported the American Equal Rights Association. However, most concentrated their efforts on passage of the Fourteenth Amendment and later the Fifteenth Amendment, which gave the vote to black men.

In 1867, the citizens of Kansas were given the opportunity to vote on both black suffrage (the Fifteenth Amendment had not yet passed) and woman suffrage, and Lucy Stone, her husband, Henry Blackwell, Stanton, Anthony, and others toured the state in support of both black and woman suffrage. Martha provided some modest financial support.[34] In a move that later contributed to a split in the women's ranks, Anthony toured the state in company with a highly controversial figure—an eccentric millionaire Democrat named George Francis Train.[35] The Kansas Republicans had endorsed black suffrage but not woman suffrage, and Anthony and Stanton were willing to accept even controversial allies. Train's flamboyant dress and personality helped to attract audiences, and his money and speeches in support of woman suffrage were very welcome. But they came at a high price, because Train flavored his speeches and writings with racism. Many who supported both black suffrage and woman suffrage, including William Lloyd Garrison, were appalled by the association of Stanton and Anthony, and thereby the American Equal Rights Association, with a racist like Train.

Both black suffrage and woman suffrage were defeated in Kansas, and many blamed Train. Stanton told Martha that the cause was so important that she would accept support "from the devil himself." Martha wrote to Stanton,

"I am sorry for the idiosyncrasies of Mr. Train" but still declared, "count me now as your true & unswerving friend."[36] Although Martha felt that Train was "just as great a mountebank as represented" and "everybody is surprised that they accept such questionable aid," she continued to support Stanton, explaining, "I choose to stand by old friends, even if they do unwise things."[37] Problems deepened in 1868 when Stanton and Anthony, financially supported by Train, began publication of the *Revolution*, a fiery weekly devoted to woman's rights but that also featured numerous diatribes by Train.[38] Furthermore, it offended most abolitionists by opposing passage of the Fifteenth Amendment unless accompanied by a sixteenth granting women the vote.

The Split

The Fourteenth Amendment was ratified in 1868. It overturned the Dred Scott decision and established legal rights for blacks but also inserted the word *male* into the U.S. Constitution for the first time. Ratification was followed by consideration of another amendment, declaring that the right to vote should not be denied "on account of race, color, or previous condition of servitude." A variety of issues and personality clashes contributed to the split of the woman's movement, including Stanton's and Anthony's raising of controversial issues such as liberalized divorce, their past alliance with the racist Train, and Stanton's own flirtations with racism, including her use of the term *Sambo* when speaking of freed black males.[39] But foremost among the issues was the Fifteenth Amendment. Stanton and Anthony opposed passage unless the word *sex* was added, or unless the amendment was accompanied by a sixteenth amendment specifically granting woman suffrage. Most male abolitionists attached themselves to the Republican Party, which supported black male suffrage now, with the expectation that the party would support woman suffrage later.[40] But Stanton and Anthony felt that women had already waited long enough and chose to fight against the Fifteenth Amendment unless women were included. Abolitionists who for decades had been radical and uncompromising with regard to antislavery now found themselves in conflict with women who remained radical and uncompromising with regard to woman suffrage.

In October 1868, Stanton and Anthony made plans for a January meeting in Washington to lobby Congress to accept their views. In November, a host of male and female abolitionists, including Lucy Stone and Abby Kelley Foster, met in Boston to form the New England Woman Suffrage Association. This association, differing from the views of Stanton and Anthony, supported eventual woman suffrage but passage of the Fifteenth Amendment now. Julia Ward Howe, author of "Battle Hymn of the Republic," was elected president and clearly stated the policy of the new association: "I am willing that the negro shall get [the ballot] before me."[41]

Martha wrote to Lucretia, "Lucy says if she has not infinite patience, she has infinite faith in the success of our cause. I think she makes too many mountains out of molehills. So long as Mrs. Stanton & Susan . . . are doing such a good work with their paper, what need she take Train so to heart."[42] In several other letters that year, Martha expressed her frustration with the increasing alienation between Stanton and Stone. "I am utterly disgusted & disheartened," she stated in one, "to find what Kilkenny cats the best of friends can become."[43]

Martha and Lucretia had long admired both Stanton and Stone, but their ties to Stanton were longer and stronger. Lucretia's dated to the 1840 antislavery conference in London, Martha's to Seneca Falls. Both sisters were radicals who, like Stanton, felt that tradition could be challenged only by continued agitation, and both doubted the sincerity of the Republican commitment to woman suffrage. The sisters supported Stanton and Anthony by attending their January 1869 woman suffrage conference in Washington, and Martha chaired one of the sessions. Stanton spoke forcefully against giving the ballot to any more men until women got the vote. As Martha reported to David:

We had a spirited debate which gave interest to the Convention. Susan [B. Anthony] told them they were fighting a man of straw, for there should be no antagonism—all we asked was *equal* suffrage, not that one should precede the other, taking the broadest ground & leaving the politicians to wrangle over expediency. Edward [M. Davis, son-in-law of Lucretia and a long-time abolitionist] insisted, & some of the best friends in Congress agreed with him, that abolitionists were recreant, who asked for anything, at this juncture, but negro suffrage. They all ignore the negro woman. I think we hold the right ground, & that justice can be secured, only by maintaining it.[44]

The women were surprised and pleased to receive support from Robert Purvis, a prominent black abolitionist.

Mr. Purvis came forward, & said that deeply as he felt the wrongs of his race, & anxious as he felt for that long delayed measure of his justice, he could not help feeling the justice of our demand, & seeing the danger of much added ignorance & bigotry, to weigh down our cause, therefore he must stand with us. You can imagine the vehement applause. . . . Noble & handsome as he is, & devoted to the interests of his race, his speech was very effective & his magnanimous declaration warmly received by audience & platform."[45]

Purvis explained that his position was based on his concern for the rights of his daughter and sister. As Martha noted in the preceding letter, abolitionists arguing only for black male suffrage "all ignore the negro woman."

While in Washington for the woman suffrage convention, Martha and Lucretia visited the Capitol and listened to some of the debates in the House. They also dined with Secretary Seward and Lazette Worden, sister of the late Frances Seward. Worden was now a widow and often served her brother-in-law as hostess for his Washington social events. "He had been reading the Report of the Convention the day we dined there," Martha wrote, "& he said he didn't understand why reformers were always pitching into each other." Worden showed them the room where Seward had been attacked at the time of Lincoln's assassination, and Martha said Seward "thought it rather hard that the only really peaceable ones of his family, who never got angry with any body, should have their throats cut & heads battered."[46] Like Martha, both Worden and Frances Seward had been ardent abolitionists and feminists, less "peaceable" than Seward, whose antislavery views had been moderated by the practicalities of politics.

The conflict over the Fifteenth Amendment came to a head at the May 1969 meeting of the American Equal Rights Association.[47] Lucretia, respected by both sides of the conflict, chaired the meeting. (Martha was busy in Boston, aiding Ellen in the care of her two small children. Martha's family responsibilities, now largely focused on her grandchildren, often came into conflict with her reform activities.) In the keynote speech, Stanton called for vigorous support of a sixteenth amendment providing woman suffrage. Anthony proposed a motion in opposition to the Fifteenth Amendment without a sixteenth, but it was soundly defeated. Discussion on this and related topics was heated. One of the most effective speakers arguing for black suffrage now, woman suffrage later, was Frederick Douglass, who had been a strong supporter of woman suffrage since Seneca Falls. "When women, because they are women, are hunted down through the cities of New York and New Orleans; when they are dragged from their houses and hung upon lamp-posts; when their children are torn from their arms and their brains dashed to the pavement," argued Douglass, "then they will have an urgency to obtain the ballot equal to our own." When someone called, "Is that not all true about black women?" he replied that it was true, "but not because she is a woman, but because she is black."[48] Feelings were high on both sides, and the gap could not be satisfactorily closed. The meeting was effectively the end of the American Equal Rights Association. Stanton and Anthony and their supporters held a rump session on the following day to form the National Woman Suffrage Association (NWSA), a name that Stanton had already applied to the group that met in January in Washington. Stone and her husband, Henry Blackwell, announced a November meeting to found the rival American Woman Suffrage Association (AWSA).

At a July meeting in Saratoga, the New York Woman Suffrage Association was formed as an auxiliary of the NWSA, with Martha as its first president.[49] Both in this capacity, and as an individual prominent in the movement, she received an invitation to represent New York at the founding meeting of the AWSA in Cleveland. Martha felt strongly that the cause of woman suffrage would be hurt by a split into two competing organizations, and replied to Stone:

Auburn Aug. 22nd, 69

My dear Lucy—I received your letter & circular, proposing an American Woman Suffrage Association but as there is already a National Association I cannot agree with you, that the cause will be better served by two. In *union* there is strength & I feel persuaded that our cause will be weakened, & the day of our success postponed by unwise dissension, or the attempt to ostracise some of the truest & noblest pioneers of the cause, & the most energetic & indefatigable workers.

It may be wise to meet in Convention, with a view of making the present organization "more comprehensive, & more truly representative" if it is lacking in those essentials.

There was an honest difference of opinion as to wisdom of giving the ballot to the black man, before the black woman, but have we not always claimed the fullest freedom of opinion, & does not the attempt to control it lead inevitably to petty feuds, & final disorganization & defeat?

Let us now work *in unison* for the passage of the 16th Amendment, & in our final triumph, forget all past differences.

> Very truly
> Yr. Friend
> M. C. Wright[50]

Henry Blackwell next wrote Martha, personally urging her to attend the Cleveland convention, or send delegates from her New York Society, stressing that "no one is excluded, nor proscribed. We want to form a Society so broad that it cannot be controlled by any individual, clique, newspaper, or locality."[51] She responded, "I would gladly meet you at the Cleveland Convention if it were practicable, if only to see whether we could have as pleasant meetings as we had in 1853, so many years ago, when you & I were Secretaries. . . . Whatever differences of opinion as to methods may exist, I trust they may be amicably arranged, lest the daughters of the Philistines rejoice, & the enemies of our cause triumph." But she closed with the reminder, "Our State Society is auxiliary to the existing National Association" and it was inappropriate to send delegates "to help form what would seem to be a rival Association."[52] Blackwell followed with a long and argumentative letter detailing all of his objections to Stanton and Anthony and their National Association.[53] "Your reasons for forming a new Society," Martha answered, "are not satisfactory to me. If there were, as you aver, errors in the formation & the conduct of the existing one, they were errors of judgment that could have been remedied." She ended with "Wishing for *the cause*, whether through one organization or another, every possible success, for yourself & Lucy every possible happiness, for Mrs. Stanton & Miss Anthony all the love & honor that their untiring devotion deserves, & hoping that we all may meet soon on a common ground."[54] (Parker Pillsbury, a long-time abolitionist who was working with Anthony and Stanton on the *Revolution*, saw the correspondence between Martha and Blackwell, and wrote to Martha, "Your treatment of Mr. Blackwell was better, a good deal, than his impudence deserved.")[55] Unfortunately, the "common ground" that Martha longed for would not return to the woman suffrage movement until long after her death.

Both the NWSA and the AWSA had members from many states, and both organizations worked actively to widen their membership, but the National leadership was largely from New York, the American leadership largely from Boston. Martha remained loyal to the National, but Garrison, who had been shocked and offended by Stanton's and Anthony's past alliance with Train, aligned with the American. This left Ellen in the awkward position of having her mother on one side of the dispute, her father-in-law on the other. (Martha told Ellen, "I will love him just the same.")[56] Martha's choice to align with the National was influenced by her long and close friendship with Stanton and Anthony. However, it was also consistent with her interest in the advance of woman's rights in the broadest sense, to which Stanton and Anthony remained committed. Blackwell and Stone proposed instead to narrow their focus to woman suffrage and to avoid more controversial subjects such as liberalization of divorce laws. Many historians have characterized the split between the NWSA and the AWSA as a split between the radicals and the moderates.[57] With regard to woman's rights, Martha was a radical.

The Fifteenth Amendment was ratified in 1870—without an accompanying sixteenth. Another half-century would pass before woman suffrage was established with the Nineteenth Amendment.

13

Free Platform, Free Love, Free Lust

Informing the Nation

For MANY years, Elizabeth Cady Stanton and Susan B. Anthony, with help from Martha Wright and others, had lobbied in Albany, the capital of New York, to improve state laws pertaining to women, such as married women's property rights, child custody, and liberalized divorce. Starting in January 1869, they focused on Washington, lobbying Congress for a sixteenth amendment establishing woman suffrage.[1] A description of the prominent participants in the 1869 Washington Convention includes "Mrs. Wright, of Auburn, a woman of strong, constant character, and of rare intellectual culture."[2]

The National Woman Suffrage Association (NWSA) met again in Washington in January 1870, as it would every January for many years to come.[3] Stanton presided, except for one session when Martha replaced her (while Stanton attended a White House reception hosted by Mrs. Ulysses S. Grant). "The Convention was a great success," Martha reported, "the interest was so great, that a third days session was decided on."[4] Encouraged by the 1869 adoption of woman suffrage in the Territory of Wyoming, part of the NWSA strategy became to persuade Congress to institute woman suffrage in the District of Columbia as a step toward passage of the Sixteenth Amendment.

Anthony, whom Martha described as "the leading spirit of the Convention," presented a resolution to that effect that was passed by the Convention.

A deputation of eleven NWSA women, including Martha, was granted a joint hearing on January 22 with the District Committees of the House and Senate. The hearing was arranged by Senator Samuel Pomeroy of Kansas, who was a prime supporter of woman suffrage, both in the District of Columbia and in the nation. (In 1868 he had proposed to Congress a fifteenth amendment for universal suffrage, and in 1869 a sixteenth amendment for woman suffrage. Speaking at the 1870 NWSA Convention, Pomeroy declared, "The negro's hour is passed, and it is woman's hour now.")[5] With about a dozen members of the House and Senate in attendance, Senator Hannibal Hamlin, chairman of the Senate Committee (and Abraham Lincoln's vice president from 1860 to 1864) called the meeting to order and introduced Stanton. Her speech arguing for woman suffrage in the District was later published in the *Revolution*, along with a list of the women and Congressmen in attendance.[6] Anthony also spoke at the two-hour hearing, and Paulina Wright Davis, organizer of the 1850 Worcester Convention, and Isabella Beecher Hooker, a relative newcomer to the movement, "ventured a few timid words," according to Martha. She reported proudly to David, "This hearing marked an era in the history of our movement & of course in the nation. It may still be long, before the demand for suffrage is acceded to, but it is evident that thinking people everywhere are considering the matter, instead of ridiculing." Among those at the hearing was Senator Charles Sumner of Massachusetts, who "said he had never, among all the exciting questions of the last 20 years, attended a meeting so full of interest."[7] Despite supportive statements from Sumner and others, the committees took no action in support of woman suffrage.

Martha also wrote to David, "We were invited to sit for Photographs in Brady's Gallery."[8] Mathew Brady, the best-known of nineteenth-century American photographers, had made it a practice of photographing as many of the famous people of his time as he could. His invitation to the women is itself an indication that by 1870 Stanton, Anthony, and other NWSA leaders, including Martha, were achieving a significant degree of public recognition.

On March 24, the weekly newspaper the *Nation* carried the first of a series of articles on woman suffrage entitled "The Vexed Question" signed by "M." The author was J. Miller McKim, one of the editors of the *Nation* and a longtime friend of Lucretia's who argued with her over numerous issues, including woman suffrage. Starting with the point that "there is almost, if not quite, as much opposition to woman's voting among women as there is among men," M went on to claim, "Not an instance is known in the country's history in which women, duly authorized to speak for their sex, have asked for legislation and been denied." Martha knew McKim and respected his earlier efforts in the abolition cause but his arguments against woman suffrage, she proclaimed to Lucretia, were "not worthy such a man as Miller."[9]

McKim's article angered Martha, and her diary entry for March 28 included the brief comment "wrote answer to Nation." Her answer, published in the April 7 issue over the initials M.C.W., did not mince words. "An article headed 'The Vexed Question' demands some notice," she began, "though evidently written by one who has not kept pace with the history of the times or with the question which has claimed his reluctant attention." She answered his opening point about "the opposition to woman's voting among women" with, "Was it any argument against emancipation that the slaves were contented and did not wish for their freedom?" She also quoted a speech of Lucretia's delivered at the 1852 convention in Syracuse: "The woman who is satisfied with her inferior condition, averring that she has all the rights that she wants, does but exhibit the enervating effects of the wrongs to which she is subjected." Then she pointed out: "For more than twenty years 'women duly authorized to speak' have reiterated their demands, which, except in a few instances, have been denied or ignored. He who denies or ignores this fact reads our country's history to little purpose." She went on to quote various resolutions from the 1848 Seneca Falls Convention and the 1850 and 1851 Worcester conventions, mentioning by name leaders of both woman suffrage organizations. M's third and final article responded with disdain to Martha's letter, but Martha's eloquent defense of the woman suffrage movement in the *Nation*, a widely read paper, was much appreciated by all who supported the movement.[10] The *Nation* would soon hear from her again.

Martha also attended that October the "Decade Meeting" in New York called by Paulina Wright Davis. The *New York Times* described the meeting as "the 20th anniversary of the founding of the female suffrage movement as a national one" (the 1850 Worcester Convention, which was organized by Davis). It also recognized Seneca Falls by adding, "and the 22nd anniversary of the holding of the first public meeting in aid of that projected measure."[11] Stanton and Anthony, and Lucretia and Martha, were in attendance, but Lucy Stone and most of the American Woman Suffrage Association (AWSA) were not. The headquarters hotel was the St. James, at which rooms, European plan, were two dollars a night. Martha's charges for three nights, including meals, was ten dollars, but as one of the honored pioneers of the woman's movement, her bill was paid by the convention. Davis presented a history of the movement and in her report of the convention paid tribute to various long-time workers for the cause. About Martha, she wrote, "Mrs. Martha Wright, sister of Lucretia Mott, of Auburn, has presided in most of the NY State Conventions, and in some of the National, and her pen has always been sharpened in ready defence of the cause and the active workers. A woman of rare good sense and large sympathies, she is to be trusted in emergencies."[12]

In keeping with the policy of a "free platform," the organizers of the Decade Meeting allowed many letters to be read to the group on a wide variety of subjects, including some only remotely related to woman suffrage. One was from an Emilie J. Meriman proposing that she proceed to France on behalf of the women of America to plead with the King of Prussia and the foreign minister of France to maintain peace in Europe. The *New York Times* mistakenly reported this idealistic letter as a resolution adopted by the convention. Based on the *Times* report, the *Nation* ridiculed the "impertinent gabble" of "reforming geese" who should "not meddle with things they do not understand."[13] Martha, consummate counterpuncher, once again picked up her sharpened pen to defend the cause. She first wrote to Stanton, "The *Nation* alludes, with its usual discrimination and amiability, to our convention, mistaking the mere reading of Mrs. Meriman's letter for the decided action of the convention, and characterizes its members as 'reformatory geese!' 'Be sure you're right, then go ahead' is not one of the *Nation's* rules." Stanton published Martha's letter in the *Revolution*, leading the *Nation* to quote it and correct her, again citing the *Times* report as its authority.[14] "Isn't the Nation lovely," she wrote to Ellen, "I sent an answer but told some truths wh. they may not choose to publish."[15] The *Nation* published only a brief excerpt of her letter to them, now admitting the possibility that the *Times* report might have been in error but expressing doubt that there was much difference "between reading anything so silly and passing it."[16] The women's policy of providing a "free platform" had often contributed to ridicule in the press, even when the topic treated was unrelated to the main business of the convention. The policy would produce much more negative press in the years ahead.

Isabella Beecher Hooker was chosen to lead the January 1871 NWSA convention in Washington. "It would be a fine thing for her to preside over the Washington Convention," Martha wrote to Stanton, "while her sister Miss Catharine Beecher was inveighing against Suffrage."[17] Catharine Beecher was an influential writer on woman's domestic responsibilities (despite herself being unmarried) and had come out publicly against woman suffrage. Other members of the prominent Beecher family included Harriet Beecher Stowe, the author of *Uncle Tom's Cabin* (whom Abraham Lincoln had called "the little woman who started this great war"), and Henry Ward Beecher, a well-known preacher and first president of the AWSA.[18] Hooker had helped to form the New England Suffrage Association, and after the split, AWSA leaders tried to persuade her to work with them. Hooker instead chose the NWSA but hoped to soften its radical image.

Hooker planned to improve press coverage by limiting speeches strictly to the topic of woman suffrage, keeping away from more sensitive issues, such as marriage and divorce. "Suffrage Conventions shd. deal with suffrage chiefly," she wrote to Stanton.[19] Later she wrote that she would work "by every means known to an honest woman, and I fully expect to accomplish far more by a Convention devoted to the purely political aspect of the whole woman question, than by a W. R. Con. [woman's rights convention]."[20] In a letter to Stanton, Martha disagreed: "It was the freedom of our platform to all subjects bearing on Woman's Rights that gave our Conventions their charm. . . . I have never ceased to regret that we gave up the good old name of Woman's Rights."[21] She also doubted that Hooker's "means known to an honest woman" would sway Congress but suggested, "Perhaps the means known to *the other kind* would meet a readier response!"[22] Despite Hooker's plans to make the NWSA meetings less controversial, even worse press coverage was ahead. A colorful but extremely controversial figure was about to insert herself into the woman suffrage movement—Victoria Woodhull. And she would decidedly not limit her speeches to the topic of woman suffrage.

FREE PLATFORM, FREE LOVE, FREE LUST

Victoria Woodhull

Many in the woman suffrage movement had never heard of Victoria Woodhull before January 1871. In little more than a year, most wished that they never had. During her brief fling with the cause, Woodhull deepened the differences between the NWSA and the AWSA, temporarily damaged the relation between Stanton and Anthony, and gave the press and public ample reason to tar the woman suffrage movement with the brush of "free love." Yet at first Martha, and many of her colleagues, welcomed Woodhull to the cause of woman's rights.

Woodhull and her sister Tennessee Claflin arrived in New York in 1868 with a checkered history as "psychic healers." They developed a close relationship with the wealthy but aging Cornelius Vanderbilt, who helped Woodhull amass a small fortune on the stock market and, in January 1870, open a Wall Street brokerage firm with her sister. This was the first such firm ever operated by women and it generated much publicity. Reveling in her new celebrity status, Woodhull announced in April her candidacy for President of the United States and the following month launched *Woodhull and Claflin's Weekly* to advance her candidacy and a wide variety of issues, including spiritualism, communism, and free love. Stanton, Rose, and others had long argued for liberalized divorce laws, which many conservatives attacked as "free love." As would soon become very clear, however, Woodhull's concept of free love often extended far beyond the liberalization of divorce laws.[23]

Woodhull was intelligent, attractive, and charming. Among those she charmed was Congressman Benjamin Butler of Massachusetts, who arranged for Woodhull to appear in January 1871 before the House Judiciary Committee and present a "memorial" on woman suffrage, probably written by Butler. Many sources cite this as the first occasion in history when a woman addressed a committee of Congress, overlooking the appearance of Stanton, Anthony, and others (including Martha) before Congress's joint District Committee the previous January. However, the NWSA leaders had failed to obtain a hearing before the more powerful Judiciary Committee, an honor that now fell to Woodhull, a newcomer to the woman suffrage movement.

Woodhull's memorial, based partly on an earlier argument of Stanton's, claimed that the Constitution and the Fourteenth Amendment already implicitly allowed woman suffrage, and all that was required was a confirmatory act passed by Congress. There was no need, she argued, for an amendment specifically approving of woman suffrage. This argument was unlikely to win much support in Congress, since that certainly was not the understanding of Congress when it passed the amendment, nor of the states when they ratified it. But the committee listened politely, and Woodhull spoke well. Anthony and Hooker were in Washington for their January meeting, attended the hearing, and also spoke before the committee. Impressed with Woodhull, the women invited her to speak on the same subject at their convention, where she was well received. A new star, with a striking new message, had arrived to stimulate excitement in a movement that very much needed a lift.

Martha and Lucretia met Woodhull in Philadelphia on March 15. "We were all charmed with her beauty & grace & knowledge & enthusiasm," Martha wrote to Ellen.[24] Woodhull was "young & pretty, short curly hair, the only peculiarity a Mother Goose steeple hat—dress very simple—black silk—no hoops—graceful in every motion but no airs & graces & little affectations. . . . She scorns the innuendos against her character & challenges any one to point to a single act of her life that would not bear scrutiny."[25] A few days later, Martha listened to Woodhull lecture in Philadelphia on her Constitutional argument and reported to David, "No one could doubt, or help respecting & admiring her."[26] She wrote to Anthony in April, "I am sorry for any women to lend themselves to the ungracious office of casting stones at Mrs. Woodhull. . . . No one can be with her, without believing in her goodness & purity, but with her past we have nothing to do."[27] Woodhull had clearly charmed Martha, but persistent rumors circulated that "goodness and purity" were not the dominant features of Woodhull's past—or of her present.

Both the NWSA and the AWSA held meetings in New York that May. Martha and Lucretia, who had close friends in both associations and who still deplored the split, attended sessions of both conventions. In her diary and letters, Martha referred to the AWSA meeting as "the Lucy Stone Convention" or "the Boston Convention." "The division is so senseless," she wrote, "all thinking so nearly alike, all working for the same end, nearly all loving one another, that I have no patience with it."[28] At the NWSA Convention, Woodhull supporters in the spiritualist and labor movements helped to swell the crowd. A few women, concerned about the "free love" image associated with Woodhull, did not want to sit near her on the platform. She was given respectability by being placed between Stanton and Lucretia. By now, Lucretia's public image was almost saintly, and the audience responded fervently when Anthony introduced her as "the Mother of us all." When her turn came, Woodhull gave a fiery speech, declaring a "war upon marriage, . . . the most terrible curse from which humanity now suffers. . . . [S]anctioned and defended by marriage, night after night there are thousands of rapes committed, under cover of this accursed license." "I have asked for equality nothing more," she declared. "Sexual freedom means the abolition of prostitution both in and out of marriage, means the emancipation of woman from sexual slavery and her coming into ownership and control of her own body."[29] She proposed elimination of the double standard not by limiting men to the standards applied to women but by giving women the same sexual freedom enjoyed by men.

Martha wrote to Ellen that "Mrs. Woodhull was affectionately welcomed & listened to with the greatest interest."[30] But Woodhull's speech had not been limited to the relatively tame topic of woman suffrage; she had attacked marriage in extreme terms and called for sexual freedom. Her speech was followed by the reading of a series of resolutions written by Stephen Pearl Andrews, a close associate of Woodhull's and founder of a community that openly practiced free love. One of his resolutions stated that the government had no right to interfere "with the rights of adult individuals to pursue happiness as they may choose." The resolutions were not endorsed by the convention, but, as on earlier occasions, this distinction was ignored in the press accounts. Woodhull's speech and Andrews's resolutions encouraged the *Tribune* to headline their critical article on the NWSA convention, "Free Love Is Free Lust." The same extrapolation had been used a few months earlier by AWSA's *Woman's Journal*. Associating Elizabeth Cady Stanton's calls for liberalized divorce laws with free love, the *Journal* warned, "be not deceived—*free love means free lust*."[31]

"Nobody paying the least attention to the Tribune's Free love nonsense," Martha wrote to Eliza. "You'd think, from the howling of the Press, that there had not been free love in New York all the time. . . . When they talk so glibly about the wretched prostitutes, they seem to forget that there are as many men who share their crime."[32] Despite Martha's wishful thinking, people did pay attention to the "Free love nonsense." Martha later wrote to Anthony that Andrews's "foolish mistimed Resolutions have done harm in giving the Philistines such a chance to rejoice."[33] And she wrote to Stanton, "No harm could have been done, if it hadn't been for that that ridiculous string of Resolutions which the Tribune falsely says were adopted by the Convention. . . . No action at all was taken on them, but the omnivorous Reporters got hold of them."[34] At the AWSA convention, the members further distanced themselves from the NWSA by passing a resolution against free love, and Martha claimed to Ellen, "The free love Resolution of the other party, intended as an insult, had the opposite effect from the one intended."[35] Despite her brave claims to her daughters, Martha surely realized that the free love issue had done damage to the NWSA and to the cause of woman suffrage. It did not help that Woodhull received more negative publicity later that year in a trial that drew attention to her unconventional private life and from her declaration at a widely attended lecture, "Yes! I am a free lover!" Lucy Stone and the AWSA were more convinced than ever that they should limit their conventions to the topic of woman suffrage and disassociate themselves as much as possible from Stanton, Anthony, and the NWSA. But Martha continued to defend freedom of opinion and freedom of expression, admitting to Stanton, "One's taste is inevitably outraged at times on a free platform, but is it not better than the cut & dried affair that our Mentors in Boston have ordained?"[36]

After the convention, Stanton and Anthony traveled west on a lecture tour. Anthony wrote to Martha from Iowa about the AWSA effort "to save themselves from contamination from touch even of the hem of the Woodhull garment. It is too sick!!"[37] Stanton enclosed her own message to Martha. "Boston has not killed us yet," she declared and assured Martha that she and Anthony "talk of you beloved strong minded ones often."[38] Their trip would carry them to California and Yosemite, where most visitors toured the park on horseback. In her letter from Iowa, Anthony had suggested that Martha ask Eliza "if she thinks Mrs. Stanton's 180 Avoirdupois will break the back of the Yosemite mustang?"[39]

Like Stanton, Martha had been gaining substantial weight over the years. In 1838 she reported, "my present weight is 127—quite enough for all useful purposes."[40] By 1845 she weighed 148 ("don't like to be so heavy and large")[41] and in 1866 she weighed 178 ("there's majesty for you")[42]. During a visit to Auburn by Lucretia in August 1871, Martha wrote in her diary, "stopping at Munson's shop to be weighed. Sister L 82 & 1/2, my own weight 183 & 1/2."[43] Martha was also taller than her older sister, and the two must have presented quite a contrast in appearance as they strolled side by side along the streets of Auburn. Lucretia remained tiny throughout her life, partly a result of chronic digestive problems. By the time she died in 1880 at the age of eighty-seven, Lucretia had accumulated more years than pounds, a rare achievement.

January 1872 brought another Washington NWSA convention and another congressional hearing, this time before the Senate Judiciary Committee. Once again, Martha was present and convinced that history was being made. Stanton, Anthony, and Hooker addressed the committee, and Martha reported, "All were excellent, & listened to with the closest attention. . . . We lunched at the Senate Restaurant—finding our bill paid, & then went back to the meeting." The committee was hospitable enough to provide the women with lunch, but not enough to provide them with the vote. "Of course, they will not report favorably," Martha wrote, "but they are gradually being *educated* up to that point. We could see a marked change in public opinion since 2 years ago." About the press, "the Washington papers gave very full reports & respectful notices. They said it was 'evident the brain of the movement' was in this division of the Woman Suffrage party." Woodhull this time maintained a lower profile. She "was at the Convention but quiet & retiring. She made a good speech & was well received."[44]

Woodhull was far from "quiet & retiring," however, at the May meeting in New York, which would turn out to be her last with the NWSA. (Martha was ill and unable to attend.) With the presidential election only a few months away, Woodhull attempted to turn the convention into a joint meeting with her "People's Party," which was about to nominate her for the presidency. Stanton supported her plan, but Anthony was enraged and refused to yield the floor to Woodhull. Woodhull and her supporters completed their nomination process in another hall, though the controversy seriously strained the longstanding close relationship between Stanton and Anthony and thereby threatened the cohesiveness of the NWSA.

Place of Refuge

After the debacle in New York over the Woodhull nomination, Anthony confided to her diary, "I *never* was so *hurt with folly of Stanton*. . . . Our movement as such is so demoralized by the letting the helm of the ship to Woodhull—though we rescued it—it was as by a hair breadth escape."[45] She wrote to Martha, "*Victoria & her Peoples Party* seceded from us—& we are left alone."[46] Feeling desperately in need of the support of some longtime friends, Anthony arranged to meet in Auburn with Martha and Matilda Joslyn Gage, writing, "So much do I want to talk over everything with you & Mrs. Gage—*two sane women I do hope*—I tell you I am thrown half off my own feet—really not knowing whether it is *I* who have gone *stark mad* or some other people. . . . I tell you Mrs. Wright I am feeling today that *life doesn't pay*—the way seems so blocked to me on all sides."[47]

Since she first visited in 1855, Anthony had enjoyed many more visits to 192 Genesee Street. According to Anthony's authorized biographer Ida Harper, "Martha Wright's home was one of Miss Anthony's most precious places of refuge."[48] Anthony herself would later record in her diary, "[Martha's home] was my home, always so restful and refreshing."[49] As was her custom for houseguests, Martha laid flowers on the bed pillows of both Anthony and Gage in anticipation of their arrival. Anthony arrived late Friday morning, and she and Martha took a horse-drawn hack to the station to meet Gage on the one o'clock train. The three women spent the weekend discussing the problems and future of the women's movement, including the differences between Anthony and Stanton over the issue of Woodhull and her People's Party.

The meeting at Martha's "place of refuge" seemed to calm Anthony. Afterward, she reported to Stanton, "Home from Mrs Wrights—good pow wow with her & Mrs. Gage."[50] Martha, eager to do whatever else she could to heal the breach between her two friends, also wrote to Stanton about the visit.

I enjoyed the visit from them exceedingly, from Friday to Monday morning, the only drawback being that you were not here also. We wished for you all the time—for of course no effective programme of future measures to convulse the world could be satisfactorily evolved, without your aid. Susan [B. Anthony] mournfully came to the conclusion after we had had the best of times

& much comparing of notes, that after all for positive practical aid and wise suggestion Mrs. Stanton was the one to go to. I told her of course she was— she had the largest brain, had given the most thought to the subject, & was— oh well—never mind—I need not tell you all that—but I have always said that you & Susan were the complement of each other.[51]

With the help of Martha, Anthony's breach with Stanton was soon healed, and the Stanton-Anthony partnership remained the driving force of the woman's movement for thirty more years. Martha had been charmed from the beginning by Elizabeth Cady Stanton, who was a cheerful, witty conversationalist. "We all fell in love with Mrs. Stanton," Martha wrote in 1854 after a visit from Stanton, "the merry twinkle of her eye and her genuine hearty laugh."[52] During her years living in nearby Seneca Falls, Stanton was a frequent visitor to 192 Genesee, and Martha often visited her in return. As Stanton wrote in her autobiography, Martha "was a frequent visitor at the center of rebellion, as my sequestered cottage on Locust Hill was facetiously called."[53] Martha's feelings toward Stanton remained warm and positive throughout her life, but she had not at first been drawn to Anthony. In her letter to Lucretia describing Anthony's first visit to 192 Genesee Street, Martha had referred to Anthony's "hammer and anvil style" of lecturing and classed her among "people of the Gradgrind stamp."[54] Over the years, however, Anthony's untiring efforts for woman's rights and woman suffrage had won more and more of Martha's respect and admiration. By the 1870s, she referred to her as "Susan, dear indefatigable, indomitable, self-sacrificing Susan."[55] Frequent personal contacts at conventions and in Martha's home made that respect and admiration grow into affection. Her letters were at first formally addressed to "My dear Miss Anthony" but soon were addressed to "dear Susan." In her letters to others, Martha's references to Anthony changed from a joking "Banthony" to "Susan" to "dear Susan." In contrast, she always referred to Stanton as "Mrs. Stanton" or "Mrs. S.," never "Elizabeth."[56] Martha remained charmed with Stanton throughout her life, but her letters indicate that by the 1870s she felt personally closer to Anthony.

After the disorderly NWSA meeting in May 1872, Victoria Woodhull ended her brief fling with the woman suffrage movement. However, her name was now associated in the public mind with the NWSA, and more bad press associated with Woodhull would follow. Late that year, she revealed in her *Weekly* an adulterous affair involving Henry Ward Beecher. She criticized Beecher not for practicing free love but for hypocrisy—a minister pretending to be a faithful husband while carrying on a secret affair with a married parishioner. Woodhull and her sister were briefly thrown into jail on charges of sending obscenity through the mails, and the ensuing legal actions on this and the Beecher affair received generous coverage in the press for many months. It would be years before the woman suffrage movement would recover from Victoria Woodhull.

In her letters Martha always referred with disdain to what she called Andrews's "ridiculous string of Resolutions."[57] But she had been won over by Woodhull's personality and intelligence and genuinely liked her. Furthermore Woodhull's ideas on free love had been presented in terms that resonated with Martha's deeply held views. As a supporter of woman's rights she could hardly disapprove of Woodhull's concept of a woman "coming into ownership and control of her own body"[58]

The most revealing expression of Martha's views on the issue is perhaps in a letter written to Ellen in March 1873, when Woodhull was still in the news but no longer associated with the NWSA. Martha started writing "I don't believe" but then crossed out "believe" and substituted "understand," resulting in "I don't understand Mrs. Woodhull's theories, but she has a right to her opinions & the expression of them."[59] To Martha, freedom of opinion and freedom of expression were core values. (In 1859, she had written to her nephew Charles Pelham that he had a right to his pro-slavery opinions, even though she strongly disagreed with them.) There was often ambiguity, however, about exactly what Woodhull meant by free love, which explains Martha's substituting "understand" for "believe." Martha once referred to Woodhull's "refined and incomprehensible idea of Free love."[60]

Whatever Woodhull meant by free love, which seemed to vary with the occasion, it is clear that Martha did not believe in free love in the form of unlimited sexual freedom. But she did believe in Woodhull's right to express her opinions, and sympathized with a woman whom she liked personally and who was allied with her on woman suffrage and other woman's rights issues. Furthermore, she recognized the hypocrisy of many of Woodhull's critics, men and women, who practiced free love in secret while attacking Woodhull in public. Martha had been championing woman's rights and woman suffrage for twenty-five years and had become accustomed to ridicule and attacks in the press, often on unjustified grounds and on side issues. The current hue and cry over free love was just the most recent example. As she wrote to Ellen, "People who have not argument at command are glad to avail themselves of the mad dog cry of Free-love to frighten innocent men out of their wits."[61]

14

Final Years

Prepared for Death

IN JANUARY 1870, after participating in the National Woman Suffrage
Association (NWSA) convention and congressional hearing in Washington,
Martha traveled to Philadelphia and spent several days caring for her sister
Eliza Yarnall, who was nearing death. "I seldom left her during her illness," she
wrote to Ellen, "& was very thankful to have been with her from the first."[1] In
one conversation held in Eliza's final days, we get some evidence that Martha's
conversations were as frank as her letters. Eliza said, "I know what thee *says* is
thy opinion," but, Martha wrote, "I told her I always said what I meant."[2]
Eliza, age seventy-five, died on February 4, leaving Martha, age sixty-three,
and Lucretia, seventy-seven, as the only surviving children of Thomas and
Anna Coffin. Eliza had always lived near Lucretia and had maintained a close
sisterly relationship with her throughout her life. But unlike Martha, Eliza had
never joined with Lucretia in the fights for abolition and woman's rights.

Martha, who had suffered the death of two sons, Charley and Tallman,
would, within a few years after Eliza's death, suffer the death of her oldest
daughter, Marianna Pelham Mott. Marianna, not quite one when her father,
Peter Pelham, died in Florida in 1826, had spent most of her childhood in
Aurora and her adolescent years in boarding school or in Auburn with her

mother and stepfather. After she married her first cousin Thomas Mott in 1845, she settled in the Philadelphia area but remained in close touch with her mother through correspondence and frequent visits. Marianna and Thomas visited Europe before the war and traveled there extensively after the war with their three daughters. By 1871, Marianna had grown very ill from a gyneco-logical disorder and wrote to Martha from Newport, Rhode Island, "I have not strength or courage to go through another Northern winter here if I am able to get away—we should get to Rome as soon as possible."[3] They sailed for Europe in October, but Marianna grew worse. They moved from Rome to Switzerland the following spring, in the hope that the mountain air would improve her health, but she died there in July. She was buried in a churchyard in Samedan, a small Alpine town near St. Moritz. Martha's diary entry for July 22: "D came up bringing letter from Anna Hopper telling of our precious suffering Marianna's death on the 4th July."

Lucretia rushed to Auburn to console Martha in her grief. It was deeply shared grief, since Marianna had been Lucretia's daughter-in-law since 1845 and had lived in the Philadelphia area near Lucretia most of her married life. "My dear sister, despite her 80 years hastened to us," Martha reported to Susan B. Anthony, "and it has been a great comfort to have her."[4] She received condolence letters from Elizabeth Cady Stanton, Anthony, and many other friends, including Thomas Wentworth Higginson, whom she thanked for his "tender remembrance of my precious Marianna" and added, "You cannot know how much we miss her, ever cheerful & beautiful and lovely as she was, amid all her intense suffering."[5]

A few months after Marianna's death, Martha would also learn of the deaths of two of her Auburn friends. William Henry Seward had been a friend of Martha and David's since the 1830s, although they had frequently disagreed with his political actions. They had viewed Seward, like Abraham Lincoln, too willing to compromise with the South, more interested in saving the Union than in abolishing the evils of slavery. In 1870, Martha had called on Seward with her house guest Parker Pillsbury, one of the few male abolitionists who allied himself with the NWSA. (Martha considered Pillsbury "one of the truest & best, one of the clearest in vision, & most unselfish of the A. S. [antislavery] apostles.")[6] She reported that they "were politely and kindly received, shown through his [Seward's] labyrinth, partly of his mind, but mainly of his garden."[7]

As a former governor, U.S. Senator, Republican presidential hopeful in 1860, and finally, secretary of state under Lincoln and Andrew Johnson, Seward was by far the best-known resident of Auburn, but apparently Martha was not in awe of her famous neighbor.

Martha learned about Seward's death in October 1872 in the midst of writing a letter to Ellen. Early in her letter she noted that Seward was "not well," but three pages later she wrote, "Frank came in, & told me of Mr. Seward's death at 2 p.m. They were not expecting it. He was taken with a chill about a week ago, but they did not consider him very sick."[8] Martha had remained close to Seward's wife, Frances, until her death in 1865, and even closer to Frances's sister Lazette Worden, who helped care for Seward during his brief fatal illness. Seward's funeral brought politicians and other dignitaries from afar to pay their last respects to Auburn's favorite son. He was laid in state in his home on South Street, and Frank was one of the three young men asked to guide the long lines of viewers past the coffin. David, Seward's partner in his most famous case, the 1846 Freeman trial, delivered a eulogy to Seward at a meeting of the Cayuga County Bar Association.[9] Like Martha, David had often wished his famous neighbor to be stronger in support of abolition. However, his eulogy warmly praised Seward's two best-known antislavery speeches, his 1850 "higher law" speech in the Senate and his 1858 Republican campaign speech on the "irrepressible conflict" between slavery in the South and the free-labor system of the North.

Also in October 1872, Martha learned of the suicide of a good friend and neighbor, Harriet Hall (widow of Dr. Edward Hall), who had grown "so utterly wretched" from financial worries and fears of hereditary insanity that she killed herself with an overdose of morphine.[10] Martha wrote to Ellen that she was pleased that her troubled friend was finally at rest. Ellen, influenced by her early exposure at an Episcopal seminary to orthodox ideas about the eternal fires of hell, expressed doubt that someone who took her own life would find peace in the afterlife. "I do not know where you get your information or belief that she is *not* at rest, that she has not escaped her difficulties" responded Martha. "We only know or take for granted that she has left her suffering body, that she is no longer tortured with head aches, with homesickness, with fears of poverty that distressed her here. That her emancipated spirit finds at last repose & happiness unspeakable, I am willing to take on trust." Martha followed with a clear and revealing expression of her attitude toward the teachings of orthodox religion and her views of life after death.

> No living mortal knows any more than you or I know. As to the teachings of the pulpit or the Bible, they come only from fallible mortals like ourselves, & their opinion is worth just as much as yours & mine—neither more nor less—less if it seems less rational. . . . As to the Laws which govern another world, we may guess what we please & one opinion is as good as another. . . . I believe in no jealous & revengeful God, but a tender & loving Father . . . no hell fire or "boiling water," but I wait with the most serene faith, that whatever is best for us in the future, we shall have, that the wearied spirit will find rest, whatever the untoward circumstances that may have surrounded us here. That is my guess, and I wait the solution, sometimes impatiently, always hopefully.[11]

Death was very much on Martha's mind in 1872, as it had been in 1844 following the death of her mother. Then she had written to Lucretia, "It is long since I came to the conclusion that sudden death was preferable to protracted illness. Few agree with me, however, in that sentiment, but when I advance it, they say 'how dreadful not to have any time *to prepare*' As if one's whole life was not the time to prepare."[12] By living fully, Martha felt prepared for death, and awaited it "sometimes impatiently, always hopefully." When death finally came for Martha, it would not be as sudden as she might have wished, but her final illness would be fairly brief, like Seward's, not protracted, like Marianna's.

Postwar Politics

Despite distractions in her personal life, Martha in the postwar years remained keenly interested in any public evidence of progress, however slight, toward acceptance of woman's rights. In 1869, she wrote to Ellen about a local homeopathy convention at which "a resolution was passed, that qualification, not sex, should decide admission to their Association—So the world is slowly moving."[13] The world was indeed moving, but slowly. Three years later, she wrote to Stanton, "Eliza recd. a letter from Mr. Cornell, informing her that the C. University was opened to woman."[14] Cornell became in 1872 the first major university in the East to admit women, and "qualification, not sex" already decided admission in many other institutions of higher education as well.[15] But most of the demands made at Seneca Falls in 1848 remained largely unmet, including woman suffrage. Some in the movement placed their hopes in the political parties, particularly the Republicans. However, as the 1872 presidential election approached, Martha was unconvinced that either side would help the women's cause. Ulysses S. Grant was running for re-election on the Republican ticket, and a group of dissident Republicans formed the Liberal Republican Party and nominated Horace Greeley, editor of the *New York Tribune*, to run against Grant. The Democrats also chose Greeley, but only reluctantly, since he had been strongly antislavery before the war. Martha wrote to Stanton:

> I have been anxious to talk with you amid this turmoil of parties, as to the wisdom of taking any active part in a strife, where one can only "choose the least of two evils." A very grave question with me is which *is* the least, and whether we should not injure rather than aid our cause by the support of a party that only *pretends* to be friendly while secretly despising the aid it solicits, or the one whose contempt is open & undisguised. It would be amusing to watch the various political complications, if one had not quite so deep an interest in them.
>
> Our family is quite divided. Will is an earnest, out & out Greeley man, Frank a staunch believer in Grant, David inclining rather to Greeley, & I on those serene heights (higher than any *fence*) where I can survey the turmoil & try to find out, if possible, which side *deserves* to win. As it now seems to me, I should say—*neither!*[16]

Martha's reference to "our cause" is, of course, to the cause of woman suffrage. The American Woman Suffrage Association (AWSA), led by Henry Blackwell and Lucy Stone, was firmly attached to the Republican Party and sought help from Stanton, Anthony, and the NWSA to drum up support for Grant among their followers. Blackwell and others put considerable effort into urging the Republicans to support woman suffrage in their campaign platform, but the only result was their fourteenth plank: "The Republican Party is mindful of its obligations to the loyal women of America for their noble devotion to the cause of freedom. Their admission to wider fields of usefulness is viewed with satisfaction, and the honest demand of any class of citizens for additional rights should be treated with respectful consideration."[17] As Martha wrote to Anthony, "As to the 14th plank, it is so cunningly worded, to mean anything or nothing, that I think the political wire pullers must believe we are easily cheated."[18]

Since Greeley had in recent years opposed woman suffrage, Anthony agreed to campaign for Grant. Her decision prompted Blackwell to send her a letter of advice. He opened in a tone of Boston snobbishness: "You work with a somewhat different class of women from ours." He went on to advise that "women can *persuade* men, can reason with them, can appeal to their sense of *justice* and *chivalry;* they cannot scold them into compliance." Anthony, he suggested, should "do nothing and say nothing to antagonize the sexes," "let woman suffrage be *incidental*," and end meetings "in a glow of patriotic and religious fervor."[19] This gratuitous advice was sent to a woman who for twenty years had been one of the most effective speakers and organizers in the abolition and woman's rights movements. Anthony showed Blackwell's letter to Martha, who responded sarcastically, "As the sense of Justice & the Chivalry of men never have been relied on, or appealed to, it might be a good idea to try it, but 'let woman suffrage be incidental' by all means. Among that 'different class of women,' you find the mature *fruit* of 20 years training. . . . Get up a due amount of religious fervor, of course."[20]

Grant won re-election handily, and Martha wrote to Ellen, "I could not feel much enthusiasm about the election, & I was surprised to see how many men felt the same indifference—Still I was rather glad for Greeley to have to go back to his Trib a sadder & a wiser & no doubt a poorer man."[21] He was also a sicker man, and he died a few weeks after the election. One candidate for President, Victoria Woodhull, was in jail on election day, charged with sending obscenity through the mails. Although she probably received some votes, none appeared in the official tallies. (She was an ineligible candidate anyway, since she was only thirty-four in 1872, one year younger than the required age.) Martha was staying with Lucretia, and David wrote to her, "You will have seen by the papers that Mrs. Woodhull and sister Tennie have come to grief." As a lawyer, he doubted the legal basis of the case. "I don't believe that Congress has any authority to exclude matter from the mail upon any such plea, any more than they had to exclude the Anti-slavery papers because they were deemed incendiary." As he and Martha remembered well, Southern post offices before the war had refused to distribute abolitionist literature. He had another reason to disapprove of the government action against Woodhull: "It will only tend to make these women martyrs."[22] Martha had been charmed with Woodhull when she first met her the previous year and continued to support her right to express her controversial opinions. But her enthusiasm had waned as Woodhull's public statements and actions became more and more provocative, damaging the image of the woman suffrage cause.

David also commented to Martha, "You will also see by the papers that Susan B. Anthony and many others have voted in Rochester, but I doubt the truth of the reports." But it was true. Anthony wrote to Stanton on election day, "Well I have been & gone & done it!!—positively voted the Republican ticket."[23] She and nearly fifty other women had registered to vote a few days earlier. When told she and the others could not register, Anthony read the inspectors the Fourteenth Amendment and an article from the New York Constitution, which contained no sex qualification for voting. She then threatened to sue them for damages if they refused to permit her to register. They registered her, and she returned to vote on election day. This was not the first time that women had tried to vote, but this time it was Susan B. Anthony, and it received national publicity. A government marshal soon arrived at her home to arrest her for voting illegally. "I never dreamed of the U. S. officers prosecuting me for voting," she wrote to Martha, "thought only that if I was refused I should bring action against inspectors. But 'Uncle Sam' waxes wroth with *holy indignation* at such violation of his laws!!"[24] Martha recorded in her diary, "wrote to Miss Anthony enclosing $5 for lawyers."[25] Anthony was convicted and fined $100, but she refused to pay the fine. The Government never collected. Her trial for the "crime" of voting became the subject of many of her lectures, and increased her renown and her audiences. It also increased Martha's respect for her indomitable friend.

Martha and Lucretia participated in the May 1873 NWSA meeting in New York, billed as the twenty-fifth anniversary of Seneca Falls. (Perhaps partly because Lucy Stone and the AWSA downplayed the importance of the Seneca Falls Convention, preferring to cite the 1850 Convention in Worcester as the origin of the woman suffrage movement, Anthony put more and more emphasis over the years on the historical importance of Seneca Falls.) "The Convention went off very well," Martha wrote to Ellen, "Sister L. spoke several times, Mrs. Stanton better than ever, Anna Brown [a niece] thought, & Susan's account of her voting and arrest was interesting and very well received." But she continued to be disheartened by the split between the Stanton-Anthony and Stone-Blackwell wings of the woman suffrage movement and continued to work for compromise. "I always deplore the unwise policy of the Boston seceders," she told Ellen, "& long for their presence,"

> because in union there is strength, and there is no good reason, & never was, for their separate action. When anything particularly good is said, I always wish that Lucy & the others could hear it, & I feel that there is mutual loss in the want of co-operation. But it will always be so, I suppose, to the end of time. The large endowment of combativeness needed to make a reformer inevitably finds exercise in the house of his friends. Who ever would have thought that dear little Lucy would have flown straight in the face of Providence, & endangered *the cause*, to fight poor Susan?[26]

The abolitionist movement split in 1840 over the woman issue, although personality conflicts between Garrison and other leaders played a role. The woman's movement split in 1869 over the issue of "the Negro's hour," but personality conflicts between Stone and Stanton and their allies played a role. Several eminent scholars have put forth different explanations of the basic source of such splits in reform movements,[27] but none is better or more succinct than Martha's: "The large endowment of combativeness needed to make a reformer."[28]

Martha considered the split in the woman's movement to be a serious problem, yet in the letter to Ellen quoted above, she characteristically turned to humor. Immediately after her discussion of the difference of opinion between "dear little Lucy" (Stone) and "poor Susan" (Anthony), Martha inserted a conundrum: "What's the difference between a bird with one wing & a bird with two? A mere difference of a *pinion*."[29] Martha's sense of humor and her fascination with words show up often in her letters. In the midst of discussing serious issues, she would often insert puns and wordplay. After writing in one letter at great length about a minor incident, she added, "For all my short-comings, let my long-goings be my apology."[30] Her usage extended even to bilingual puns, for in one letter she concluded her description of the burial of a deceased cat with a twist on the Latin prayer for the dead: "Requies-*cat*!"[31] But she had a special fondness for conundrums and compiled a long list of them in one of her diaries.[32] One example from her list: "What food did Noah take on the Ark? Preserved *pairs*."

In contrast to Martha, many of her reformist colleagues, including Lucretia, tended to be overly serious. An exception was Elizabeth Cady Stanton, who knew the power of humor in moving audiences. One day in 1868, Stanton was looking through some old letters and wrote to Martha, "I found nine amusing ones from you which I laughed over. You are certainly guilty of being a wit."[33] Martha's wit apparently enlivened her conversation as well as her letters, for Stanton later wrote, "her pungent wit and satire, without a ripple on the surface, burst forth at unexpected moments to the surprise and delight of all of us."[34] Similarly, Martha's friend Rev. W.R.G. Mellen once wrote to her, picturing her in conversation, "I cd see the merry twinkle of your eye, & the expressive smile about the lips wh I have often noticed when they were about to drop any thing particularly pleasant & pungent."[35]

Lucretia, ever serious, once charged Martha that she "had cultivated Mirthfulness at the expense of other faculties."[36] Martha responded that "the reproof did not benefit me so much as her counsels always ought to" and later wrote, "People love to laugh. . . . If it were not for the blessed organ of Mirthfulness, what would become of us all."[37] Martha once advised a relative who was downcast over a setback, "Just make fun of it that is the best way—just get hold of life's reverses & disappointments in a ridiculous point of view, & it helps along wonderfully—there is a great deal of fun, among all the annoyances, if one can only find it."[38]

FINAL YEARS

Boston and Florida

In her earlier years, most of Martha's travels were to Lucretia and the Philadelphia family circle or to woman's rights conventions. In the postwar years,
her younger children became more and more dispersed, Auburn seemed more
isolated to her, and other travel destinations beckoned. Frank had gone to
Europe to represent Munson Osborne's farm machinery business, but Martha's
shipwreck in Florida during her teens, and her general vulnerability to seasick-
ness, made a trip across the Atlantic unappealing. She did foresee that such
trips might become easier in the distant future and wrote Marianna in 1865,
"The improvement in the next 100 years commensurate with the inventions
of the past century, must be in greater possibilities of locomotion—flying for
instance. There must be some better way of reaching those from whom it is
so dreadful to be separated."[39] Transatlantic flights would indeed come in the
next century, but not in time for Martha. More feasible in her day, facilitated
by the growth of the railroads, were frequent visits to Ellen and William
Garrison in Boston, the city of her birth, and a visit to distant Florida, where
Willy had settled.

The Garrisons often spent part of their summers in the seaside town of
Swampscott, north of Boston. While visiting them there, Martha very much
enjoyed watching the waves, which she proclaimed "as good as a book."[40]
There was little that Martha enjoyed more than reading a good book, and she
held authors, especially successful woman authors, in very high esteem. Once
when her daughter Eliza, traveling in England, had written to Martha about
the sights, Martha responded, "You don't say anything of Haworth." Surely
you will see where Charlotte Bronte [author of one of Martha's favorite novels,
Jane Eyre] lived, & endured, & died. I wd. rather see her home than that of
fifty dead Emperors."[41]

When Martha visited the Garrisons at their home in the Roxbury section
of Boston, they often took her to cultural events in the city. Some she enjoyed
very much, but she was put off by the meetings of Boston's Radical Club,
where "the Boston literary Lords" discussed what she called their "transcenden-
tal nonsense." "Just between ourselves," she wrote, "I think those radical
meetings a great humbug. Each essayist, in turn, trying to see how obscure he
can make his meaning, by wrapping it, like a mummy, in spiced cloths, and

then aping Emerson in the reading." She seemed especially unimpressed with an abstruse speech by the philosopher Bronson Alcott: "What do you think of Alcott's question? 'Is *is*, is, or is it isn't?"[42]

November 1873 was a snowy month in upstate New York, so Martha and David were especially pleased to leave Auburn and head south for a visit to Willy's plantation in north central Florida. Both were eager to see his property on the St. Johns River, where he had begun growing oranges, bananas, and a variety of other crops, including cotton. But Martha had another reason for making the trip. Willy's wife, Flora, niece of Elizabeth Cady Stanton, was expecting a second child in February, and Martha had a practice of being on the scene, whenever possible, for the birth of each of her growing collection of grandchildren, assisting with household chores during the final weeks of pregnancy and the first weeks after the birth.

Martha had first traveled to Florida forty-nine years earlier as the new wife of Peter Pelham on a trip that ended in shipwreck of the sloop *Hope*. Her trip in 1873, by railroad and steamboat, went much more smoothly. On the journey between Charleston and Savannah, she met a "pretty Southern lady" and later recounted to Lucretia the woman's description of changes the war had brought to the South, an account reminiscent of Tara and Scarlett O'Hara:

> You should have seen the trees before the War. The soldiers destroyed so many—cut them down & burn them & after the war cut them & sent them North for timber. I had to leave my home, with a beautiful avenue of them, & when I went back I cried to see them all destroyed. [Here Martha inserted, "I could sympathize with her there."] . . . There were ladies who had never done anything but ride on horseback & play on the piano & read—never wore a thimble in their lives, who now had to wash & cook & work & her own hands had bled from the washing she had to do.[43]

Despite Martha's sympathy for some of the woman's complaints, when her subject turned to the blacks, Martha was moved to challenge her. "She said the blacks were very idle—lounging around, refusing to work & attributed the desolation of the country to that—I asked her if she could not go further back & trace it directly to slavery." The letter was sent from Jacksonville, where, Martha reported, "the negros [are] so jolly, enjoying the laziness they had so long pined for."

From Jacksonville, Martha and David traveled by steamboat for about sixty miles south on the St. Johns, reaching the wharf at Willy's Mount Royal plantation (their neighbors called it "the Yankee wharf") just before midnight. David stayed little more than a week, of which Martha said he "enjoyed every minute," and left before Christmas to return to his law office in Auburn. "You cannot think how much I miss you," Martha wrote. After forty-four years of marriage, she was still very much in love with her husband.

Martha's conversation with the "pretty Southern lady" was complemented by one David had with a "Virginia Gentleman" during his return trip. Whereas the women discussed the effects of the war on the landscape and the people, the men focused instead on political issues. David and his companion had very different views of slavery but found several areas of agreement. As he reported to Martha, David's companion was

> a very large land holder and had been a large slave owner. Slavery he believed to be a divine institution sanctioned by our Saviour, yet he accepted the situation and we agreed fully that the only safety for the South in the future was to educate the colored citizens and make them as intelligent as possible that they might understand political matters, and not vote as bidden or coerced by demagogues. He went into the rebellion for state rights and not for slavery. He believed the U. S. Government was not intended by the *Fathers* as a concentrated and consolidated Government of the People, but rather a confederation of States having one common Government in regard to *certain* specified matters, in which I think he was right. As to the slavery difficulty, that he said was entirely by reason of the cowardice of the leading men of the revolution. They dared not carry out their sentiments and crystallize freedom into the constitution, and there we agreed exactly.[44]

Arriving back home on December 31, David proudly told his neighbors in frigid Auburn about the wonders of his brief stay in Florida—the six-pound flounder he caught in the St. Johns, the ripe banana he ate from the tree, and the ripe tomatoes he picked on the day before Christmas. Martha's letters to

David and her family told of the beauty of the St. Johns ("as beautiful as the Owasco Lake & in many places wider"), the sunsets, the weather, and the Florida birds. "I want so much to know their names," she wrote. "Next time we come we will bring our bird book."[45] (Although some of Florida's birds were new to her, Martha was very familiar with the birds that arrived each spring in Auburn. One year, she announced to Ellen, "The orioles came the very day after I got home. I said so, & that positive man [David] said 'O no— you have mistaken some other bird for it. Orioles never come till the blossoms come!' as though I didn't know an Oriole's clear whistle, & the sort of plaintive call with which they announce their coming. But I let him call it Pigeon or Widgeon as he preferred, & before we were up next morning he heard it & was satisfied—& so was I. The wrens & cat-birds too have come.")[46] Martha's letters over the years frequently noted the arrival of various birds, the blooming of flowers and trees, the arrival of berries and fruits. She once noted to Willy, "most people see & hear little more of what is going on around them, than if they had neither eyes nor ears."[47] Martha's eyes and ears were always open.

In a letter to David, Martha recounted a conversation she had with a local schoolteacher during her visit with Willy. The teacher told Martha that she had invited a neighboring planter to send his children to her school, but "he said 'me & my wife had no eddication, nor any of my gals, but I would rather they never would have any, than to go to school with niggers.' So he had his druther!"[48] Although Martha was enchanted with the natural beauty of Florida, she was disturbed by the attitudes of many Floridians toward blacks. The Civil War had changed the legal status of blacks, but did little to change attitudes.

Much of Martha's pleasure in Florida seems to have been provided by her one-year-old granddaughter Anne, whom she describes with great tenderness, including her outburst when Martha was preparing to return home: "Grandma I like you and I love you, what makes you go?" One day Flora heard Anne say, "Open the door boobyhead." When Flora said she should not use that word, Anne replied, "Grandma did." Martha had to plead guilty. After a cat killed Anne's pet rabbit, Martha wrote, "Her first lesson in cruelty—poor child— she will have so many more before she dies."[49] Flora and Willy's second daughter, Edith Livingston Wright, was born in late February, and Martha remained at Mount Royal until late March. (Edith's middle name was in memory of Flora's grandmother and Elizabeth Cady Stanton's mother, Margaret Livingston.)

New York and Auburn

On her return trip from Florida, Martha visited Lucretia in Philadelphia and Ellen in Boston and, soon after reaching Auburn, left again for the May 1874 meeting of the NWSA in New York. She had been away from home so long that she had not planned to attend the convention, but Susan B. Anthony, now recognized by most as the NWSA leader, urged her to attend and sit by her on the platform to give her courage, which she often found lacking when Stanton was not by her side. Martha arrived in New York the evening before the opening of the convention and immediately made a point of confirming her presence to Anthony, "because I felt that you would sleep better if you knew I had come."[50] Anthony wrote to Ellen the following year about how pleased she was when Martha arrived. "What a tower of strength I always felt her to be on the platform with us—And never more so than last May, when she went to New York, as she said, just to sit by me."[51]

History of Woman Suffrage records that at this meeting, "Martha C. Wright, one of the most judicious and clear-sighted women in the movement, was elected president."[52] It was only with great reluctance that Martha accepted the NWSA presidency. As she later wrote to Stanton, "I dreaded inexpressibly the greatness thrust upon me, knowing so well my own limitations on the matter of speech making, when that seems to be considered one of the essentials for a Presiding officer, & I knew that you were so much more suitable, & Susan had filled the place so well, but my protests were unheeded."[53] By that time, Martha had successfully presided over many woman's rights and abolitionist conventions and had received many compliments on her officiating skills, but she never fully lost her fear of public speaking. Only a few months earlier, she had written to Anthony that she "could not speak if the world was coming to an end."[54] But to continue her support of "the great cause" of woman suffrage, and of Anthony and Stanton and the NWSA, Martha accepted the "greatness thrust upon me."

After the NWSA meeting in New York, Martha went to Boston for another visit with Ellen and her family. While there, the new NWSA president attended a meeting of the rival AWSA. She still mourned the split and continued to argue for compromise. She urged Lucy Stone and her allies in the Boston group to forget past differences and reunify the woman suffrage movement, but to no avail. The past associations of Stanton and Anthony with George Francis Train and Victoria Woodhull, their opposition to the Fifteenth Amendment, and other conflicts between the two camps had led to personal animosities that would take many years to abate. Stanton and Anthony continued to favor a "free platform," allowing a variety of woman's rights issues to be raised at their conventions, including divorce laws and gender-based salary inequalities. In contrast, AWSA leaders took pains to limit themselves to the single issue of woman suffrage, ironically the one issue that had seemed most revolutionary at Seneca Falls in 1848. While in Boston in May, Martha learned that Ellen, already the mother of three, was expecting another child late in the year, and Martha promised to return in December. Whether traveling or at home, Martha's life was an intimate blend of the personal and the political.

In June 1874, a prohibition convention was held in Auburn, and Martha was in attendance along with her friend Matilda Joslyn Gage, who had started working with Anthony and Stanton on a history of the woman's movement. When Martha and Gage arrived at the meeting hall, they found themselves to be the only women there. Martha remained firmly against alcohol and had recently chastised her daughter Eliza for drinking champagne, but her commitment to the woman's rights movement was much more intense than her commitment to the temperance movement. She and Gage therefore made an effort to maneuver the convention into passing a resolution endorsing woman suffrage. The men resisted a direct endorsement but were sympathetic and eventually adopted a compromise resolution: "Resolved—that we hail with devout thankfulness to God the great uprising among the women of our land to put away the liquor nuisance from among us, and that we renew our pledge to put the ballot into the hands of women when we shall have power to do so, thus enabling them to vote as well as pray against the giant curse of the world."[55] As Martha noted to Ellen, "How much more powerful *votes* are, than prayers."[56]

Martha was also pleased that summer to receive visits in Auburn from Ellen and her children and Will and Flora and their two daughters. Martha was charmed by the antics of two of the cousins, Frank Garrison, age three, and Anne Wright, age two. One day Frank whispered something into Anne's ear and they immediately ran off together as fast as they could. When Anne was asked why she ran away with Frank, she replied, "I didn't run away with him—he runned away his self, & I runned away my self." As Martha reported to Stanton, "You see Anne put it on independent woman's rights ground."[57]

In November, Lucretia traveled to Auburn for a weeklong visit. In 1843, her mother, Anna Coffin, had worried about Lucretia's fragile health and feared that Martha's visit to Philadelphia that year would be the last time the three remaining sisters and their brother would be together. But thirty years later, Lucretia was still very active. Anna, her son Thomas, and her daughter Eliza Yarnall were gone, and only Lucretia and Martha remained. The two sisters had always been close, but they grew ever closer over the years as they grieved together over family deaths and worked side by side for abolition and for woman's rights. Lucretia's health still seemed fragile, but she was nearly eighty-two and described by Martha as "active as a grasshopper."[58] When Lucretia left Auburn on November 16 after a pleasant visit, it was the last parting of two loving sisters, longtime partners in family life and in public reform.

Christmas with the Garrisons

Martha wrote to her son-in-law William Lloyd Garrison Jr. in the fall of 1874, reporting, "[David] says I am always 'anxious' & who wouldn't be, with 13 grandchildren all to have teeth & mumps & Scarlet fever & measles & whooping cough & lovers & weddings & things!"[59] Martha's thirteen grandchildren that fall included three children of Marianna's, four of Eliza's, three of Ellen's, two of Willy's, and one of Frank's. Marianna's oldest daughter, Isabel Mott Parrish, had also provided Martha with three great-grandchildren. On December 5, 1874, Ellen delivered Martha's fourteenth grandchild—William Lloyd Garrison III—and Martha was in Boston with her to help.

"I arrived here last Tuesday," Martha wrote to Anthony, "and on Saturday (yesterday) morning another scion of the House of Garrison was born. Ellen would have preferred another daughter, the 2nd and 3rd being sons."[60] (Ellen's daughter Agnes, then eight, was already feeling the limitations imposed on her by her sex. As Martha wrote to David, "She wishes she was a boy & could sit on a fence & put her hands in her pockets & whistle.")[61] When Ellen learned that her fourth child was a boy, she complained, "Another horrid boy," to which William responded, "But he can vote."[62] Martha reported to David that Ellen was doing well, and planned to name the baby William Lloyd Garrison III, even though his father "demurs a little fearing he may not bear up the standard" set by the new baby's famous grandfather. The family debate continued for over a week, but Ellen finally had her way.

A week after the baby's arrival, Martha and her son-in-law visited the home of his father, the first William Lloyd Garrison, to help him celebrate what Martha was told was his seventieth birthday. (He is now recognized as having been born in December 1805, making this birthday, by normal accounting, his sixty-ninth.)[63] "Mr. G. does not look so old as some people do at 60," Martha wrote, "Not a wrinkle to be seen, & so genial & pleasant. He still is confined to the house by his lameness, but for that he said he should be young as anybody."[64]

On December 21, Martha wrote to Lucy Stone, asking her to post a notice for the forthcoming Washington NWSA meeting in *Woman's Journal*, the weekly newspaper the Boston group started publishing in 1870 (and which had helped to drive Stanton and Anthony's *Revolution* out of business). Still upset about the split in the woman suffrage ranks, Martha added:

> I only wish, as I told you last Spring, that we could all meet together, as of old, in the interest of a cause that we all have equally at heart, and are trying to forward by the same means, but I fear with doubtful success, until we are once more united. Why we should not be, passes my understanding. The reasons you gave were not convincing, for in a cause so momentous, petty or personal differences should have no place.
>
> Nothing would give me more pleasure, than to see you on our platform in Washington, and all those whom I listened to in Boston last spring. . . .

Ellen is doing well, better perhaps than ever before, at two weeks. Another irrepressible *voter*, instead of the little girl she had hoped for.

With regards to Mr. Blackwell

Ever your friend
M. C. Wright[65]

Martha and her son-in-law William joined his parents for their family
holiday celebrations on Christmas Eve. As William Lloyd Garrison Sr. later
wrote to his son Wendell, referring to Martha, "On Christmas Eve she was
with us, apparently in excellent health, to enter with the grandchildren and
our family circles into the festivities of the occasion around our beautiful
Christmas tree. As we gave the parting hand to each other that night, little did
either of us imagine that it was to be a final parting here."[66]

Martha's diary entry for December 25, 1874 was her last: "Christmas—
68 years old. Beautiful bright day." It was her sixty-eighth birthday, and two
letters she wrote that day have also been preserved. One was to Anna Davis
Hallowell, a granddaughter of Lucretia's. It is a cheerful letter recounting
Christmas activities but mentions "a slight indisposition for a day or two."
Sadly prophetic, she added, "I hope it may be possible for me to see you all
again in the Spring but I seldom plan far ahead."[67]

Her other Christmas letter was to David. Ellen was by then largely recovered from childbirth, and Martha planned to leave Boston on the twenty-ninth
and return to Auburn to prepare for her second trip with David to Florida,
interrupted with a brief stop in Washington to preside over the NWSA meeting. David had thoroughly enjoyed his visit to Florida the previous year and
had arranged his business so that he could make a much longer visit this time.
However, he had recently been taken ill, and Martha was torn between her
responsibilities to her daughter and those to her husband. She wrote to him, "I
need not say how hard these divided duties are to me, & how much I wished
to be with you while you were suffering." But she also was not completely
well herself:

Ellen & the baby sleep, & despairing of ever finding an uninterrupted moment to write by day, I write in my room by gas light. Going out to mail my last letter to you the day after snow, I took cold & was threatened with rheumatism—Ellen insisted on having Dr. Jackson sent for & he left medicines. I do not believe but my own box would have done just as well & my precious $3 dollars saved. I wanted them for Christmas—but I consented thinking he might possibly save me from a disabled arm as I had even in lovely Florida. Being 68 today, I have probably reached the age that Sydney Smith [English preacher and writer] had, when he said he had 37 distinct aches & pains.[68]

On Saturday the twenty-sixth, Martha went with William to the Museum Theatre to see a new play. Ellen described the subsequent days in a lengthy letter to her cousin Maria Davis, one of Lucretia's daughters. "Sat. evening before she was taken sick, she sat in my room knitting & sewing just as usual tho' not talking any. . . . She had been with Wm to the Museum in the pm, but didn't like the play & said it didn't pay. As soon as I got tired, she bid me goodnight, & went to bed complaining of nothing." On Sunday, Martha became ill, but described her illness to Ellen as "only a sick stomach." She was worse on Monday and, realizing that she might not be able to leave on Tuesday for Auburn to care for her sick husband as she had planned, said, "How can I ever get there—poor David!"[69] News of Martha's sudden illness reached Auburn, and David wrote to Martha, "I doubt if we shall, either of us, be in fit condition to risk a day and night journey to Florida this winter. . . . I have come to the conclusion that we had better remain quietly at home. . . . I will play that I am a gentleman of leisure this winter . . . so just remain quietly in Boston until you shall feel fully equal to the travel home."[70]

Despite visits from the doctor and attempts at treatment, Martha continued to deteriorate, and on Wednesday Ellen telegraphed Eliza to come to Boston. She and David arrived on Friday, but by then Martha was delirious, unable to carry on a conversation beyond short utterances such as, "What will become of me?" and "He giveth his beloved sleep." David, Eliza, and Ellen took turns holding Martha's hand during her final hours. "She seemed to want her hand held all the time," Ellen recalled, "even at the very last, when it was almost cold, she raised it & laid it across my lap." Martha Coffin Pelham

Wright died on Sunday morning, January 4, 1875, with a form of pneumonia then called typhoid pneumonia. Her descent from having "took cold" to her death took only a week, long enough to allow David and Eliza to come and be with her when she died, but not the protracted illness that she had long feared. According to Eliza, Martha's last words were, "It's almost time for Marianna to come for me."[71]

Martha was buried in Auburn's Fort Hill Cemetery,[72] only a few hundred yards behind 192 Genesee Street, the house that had been her home since 1841. When Elizabeth Cady Stanton once addressed a letter to her as "Martha Coffin Wright," her response was "it looked so funny." She had become accustomed to Martha C. Wright. And when Lucy Stone kept her maiden name after marriage, Martha judged it "an absurd whim that she will outlive." But it somehow seems appropriate that the name engraved on her gravestone, in prominent raised letters, is MARTHA COFFIN. Although the stone goes on to read "Wife of DAVID WRIGHT," she was much more than that. Martha was very much her own person, with her own strong opinions and her own significant accomplishments. And she rests beneath a stone bearing her own name.

15

Martha Coffin Pelham Wright

After Martha

As PRESIDENT of the National Woman Suffrage Association, Martha was expected to chair its January 1875 meeting in Washington. Elizabeth Cady Stanton, then first vice president, replaced her, and reported to the press that the convention honored Martha "with a fitting tribute to the departed friend who signed the call for the first convention in '48, took an active part in its proceedings, and has been a steadfast advocate of woman's enfranchisement during all these years, attending nearly every meeting, presiding frequently, and giving generously to the treasury of the association."[1] In a memorial to Martha written in the 1890s, Stanton wrote, "In all the usual frictions, jealousies and antagonisms between members of committees, Martha Wright never had a personal grievance or complaint. Her voice was always for peace, except against the common enemy, there she was ever ready for uncompromising resistance. Though she loved peace, she was firm as the rock of Gibraltar in defense of principle."[2]

Susan B. Anthony was deeply shocked by Martha's death. "It struck me dumb," she recorded in her diary. "I could not believe it; clear-sighted, true and steadfast almost beyond all other women! Her home was my home, always so restful and refreshing, her friendship never failed; the darker the hour, the brighter were her words of encouragement, the stronger and closer her support. I can not be reconciled."[3] To Ellen, Anthony wrote:

> How good & true she always was—and what a tower of strength I always felt
> her to be on the platform with us—And never more so than last May, when
> she went to New York, as she said, just to sit by me—because Mrs. Stanton
> was in Michigan—and she knew how *weak* I would feel without her presence.
> Well—there is none other to fill her place—unless it shall be one of her
> daughters—So calm—So self-poised—so equal to every emergency.[4]

To Eliza, she wrote: "I always felt sure Mrs. Stanton's and my plannings were right when Mrs. Wright gave them her sanction. Her calm, cool judgment was safe. . . . Every word was to the point and we all felt that her opinion on every question carried decisive weight, not only with the platform, but with the audience as well."[5] Ellen and Eliza also received condolence letters from Wendell Phillips, Parker Pillsbury, and other leaders of the abolition and woman's rights movements, each praising Martha and her contributions.

In her *Woman's Journal*, Lucy Stone wrote about Martha: "She was the constant friend of the slaves, and one of the earliest advocates of woman Suffrage. She was firm and decided in her opinions, and clear in her support of them. The friends of every good cause, by the death of this estimable woman, have lost a dignified, earnest and indefatigable co-worker."[6] As president of the NWSA, Martha had visited Stone, president of the American association, the previous May in an unsuccessful attempt to reunite the two woman suffrage organizations. Only two weeks before her death, Martha had written to Stone urging reunification. Despite Martha's efforts, the New York—based and Boston-based groups would remain apart until fifteen years after Martha's death. Lucy Stone and her allies finally agreed to rejoin Stanton and Anthony, and the two groups merged to form the National American Woman Suffrage Association in 1890. Stone died three years later.

The same issue of *Woman's Journal* also carried a lengthy obituary written by William Lloyd Garrison. He provided a rare description of her physical appearance: "She had a stately and commanding presence, with rare modesty; being above the medium height in stature, and finely developed in form, with most intelligent and striking features." Garrison had known Martha for over forty years and could provide authoritative confirmation of her credentials as an antislavery activist: "In company with her sister, she was an interested witness of the proceedings of the first National Anti-Slavery Convention held at Philadelphia in 1833, and to the last had her sympathies drawn out to the millions of a proscribed race, whose emancipation she had nobly done her part to secure." After citing also her leadership in the woman's rights movement, he noted a defining characteristic of Martha's that went unmentioned in other obituaries. "Beneath an habitual gravity there lurked a keen sense of the ludi-crous, her wit and humor being always at command."[7] Garrison, nearly lynched by anti-abolitionists in 1835, had lived long enough to see the scourge of slavery abolished. He died in 1879 at the age of seventy-three.

In Stone's account, she was Martha C. Wright, in Garrison's, Martha Coffin Wright. To the mainstream press, however, following contemporary standards, she was Mrs. David Wright. The *New York Tribune* noted, "In the death of Mrs. David Wright we lose another of that valiant Anti-Slavery army of forty years ago, which contained so many names illustrious for devotion and nobility of character,"[8] and then quoted extensively from Martha's obituary in Auburn's *Daily Advertiser*. In her hometown paper, she was knowingly and accurately described: "Always independent in asserting her convictions, she was fearless in maintaining them. . . . Her earnestly expressed belief in the mercy and goodness of an All-Wise God, and her readiness either to live or to die, characterized her last conversations, and she said when speaking of the dread of death so natural to some persons, 'I thank God I know nothing of that. I trust in the life beyond.' "[9] Martha felt that she knew neither more nor less than anyone else—including the orthodox ministers who preached about heaven and hell. Her logic told her that God would be higher and better than the best of humans and would be merciful, not vengeful and punishing.

Martha's sudden death of course had its greatest impact on her family. Lucretia was already ill when she heard the news and was inconsolable for some time. Her daughter Maria Davis represented her at the burial in Auburn and represented the Philadelphia family circle in writing about Martha, "There was no other one who came here, who came with such zest, & how pleasant the visits were! And her letters! How welcome ever was the sight of an envelope with her beautiful hand-writing."[10] Lucretia added condolences to "poor, dear, stricken David" and the children, and a plaintive, "How sad it all is!"[11] After some months, Lucretia's remarkable spirit eventually returned, and for several years she appeared as an honored guest at various gatherings of reform groups, including an 1878 meeting to commemorate the thirtieth anniversary of the Seneca Falls Convention. She died in November 1880 at the age of eighty-seven.

David continued to live at 192 Genesee Street for a few years, broken by winter visits to Willy and Flora in Florida. He then moved to live with Eliza and Munson Osborne in their home on South Street, where he lived until his death in February 1897.[12] He was buried beside Martha in Fort Hill Cemetery. Martha's first two loves, Peter Pelham and Julius Catlin, had each died young, but David outlived Martha by twenty-two years and almost reached his ninety-first birthday.

Martha's son Willy remained in Florida, growing oranges and other fruits and vegetables until his death in 1902. Frank lived in Europe for several years, representing Munson's farm machinery business, but later returned to New York and then to Florida to try his hand, along with Willy, at citrus farming. There he founded the Harvard Club of Florida and served for several years as County Clerk of Putnam County. He was separated from his wife, Fanny, who became romantically involved with Charles Longfellow, son of the famous poet. Fanny died in Boston in 1892. Frank went in 1898 to St. Louis as local auditor for AT&T, and married Julia Floyd-Jones, a widow, two years later. He died in St. Louis in 1903.

Eliza and Ellen continued their interest in the woman suffrage movement but never to the same degree of commitment as their mother. In 1898, they were honored guests at the fiftieth anniversary of the Seneca Falls Convention and were formally recognized from the platform by Susan B. Anthony as the daughters of one of the organizers of the 1848 convention. Eliza continued to live in Auburn, and her home, like Martha's, was frequently visited by Stanton, Anthony, Harriet Tubman, and other reformers. After one meeting with Eliza in 1891, Stanton humorously chided her for continually knitting throughout their conversation. Eliza responded with a poem that Stanton reprinted in her autobiography, one stanza of which asked:

CHAPTER FIFTEEN

> In retrospective vision bright,
> Can you recall dear Martha Wright
>   Without her work or knitting?
> The needles flying in her hands,
> Or washing rags or baby's bands,
>   Or other work as fitting?[13]

Martha often wrote rhymes to amuse her children and, at various family gatherings, to entertain everyone.[14] Occasionally her verses appeared in print. These included her "Recollections of Vienna" in Auburn's *Daily Advertiser* in 1852 and a brief testimonial to Susan B. Anthony in the *Revolution* in 1870.[15] Eliza had inherited the rhyming habit as well as Martha's tendency to keep her hands busy with knitting during social occasions. She also inherited Martha's love of literature and became an avid book collector, assembling a large library.[16] Eliza died in 1911, nine years before women finally gained the right of suffrage. The graves of Eliza, her husband, Munson, and other Osbornes are adjacent to the graves of Martha and David on Fort Hill. One of Eliza's sons, Thomas Mott Osborne, carried on the family's reform tradition and became a prominent prison reformer.[17] One of Thomas's sons, Lithgow, became ambassador to Norway and helped to place many of the Osborne and Wright family papers in the Syracuse University library. The collection contains many of Martha's and David's letters, as well as early correspondence and papers of Peter Pelham.

Martha's youngest daughter, Ellen Garrison, lived until 1931 and was able to vote in several national elections. Ellen voted in a school election as early as 1879, after which she reported proudly to Eliza, "Today the women of Boston vote with their lords & masters, & right after breakfast I went with Wm to the polls. The room was neatly swept, no smoking was allowed until 12 o.c.—the men were perfectly quiet, & it was as easy as falling off a log—I do believe it won't be long before we shall have a chance at the law makers, as well as the school makers."[18] One of Ellen's daughters, Eleanor Garrison, studied at Smith College and, with the help of her brother Frank, contributed to Smith an extensive collection of Garrison and Wright family papers, including most of Martha's letters that were preserved.

After the deaths of Martha and Lucretia, who had helped to initiate the fight for woman suffrage in 1848, Stanton and Anthony continued the effort until their deaths in 1902 and 1906, respectively. Another generation of women added massed marches and public protests to the tactical mix and finally brought to fruition the task started in Seneca Falls in 1848. Only one signer of the Declaration of Sentiments lived long enough to see the passage of the Nineteenth Amendment granting woman suffrage: Charlotte Woodward Pierce of Philadelphia, who was only nineteen at Seneca Falls.[19] "I was at the first meeting held at Seneca Falls," she wrote to Lucretia in 1871, "when I was but a young girl, little knowing the broad field awaiting laborers."[20] Of the prominent laborers in the early woman's movement, only Rev. Antoinette Brown Blackwell, whom Martha first met at the 1852 Woman's Rights Convention in Syracuse, survived long enough to gain the vote. Nearly ninety-five, she cast her hard-earned ballot in 1920 and died the following year.

Martha knew that the opposition to woman suffrage was deep and that it would be a long fight. She wrote to Ellen in 1869, "These younger & untried ones who are coming forward, full of energy & enthusiasm, can carry it forward & even tho' perilled by unwise antagonisms, I suppose it is bound to succeed—in time for Agnes & Ethel & Mabel."[21] Her granddaughter Mabel had just been born, and the vote was indeed won in time for her and for all of Martha's granddaughters.

In September 1962, when Mabel was nearly ninety-three, she was asked what memories she had of her grandmother Martha Wright. Mabel was only five when Martha died and had not seen her grandmother since she was three. Her description of Martha is therefore based on memories formed at three, viewed from the perspective of ninety-three. She wrote, "I remember visiting my Grandma, who was an adorable person who painted paper dolls and their dresses for me and gave me strings of gay buttons to play with and string to entangle."[22]

"Dangerous" Martha

The same person remembered by her granddaughter as "an adorable person" was considered a "very dangerous woman" and an "infidel" by her Auburn neighbors, as recorded by her daughter Eliza.[23] The reasons included Martha's openly expressed support for women's rights and for the abolition of slavery, and her rejection of the authority of the pulpit and the Bible. Although there were other women of the period with more extreme opinions on such topics, Martha was the most prominent woman in conservative Auburn associated with such liberal views. As the wife of a successful and respected lawyer and the mother of a large family, she was hard to discount as a social misfit. Her knowledge obtained from wide reading, coupled with her natural intelligence, made her arguments hard to refute. Her personal charm and infectious humor made her hard to dislike. All these factors made her ideas, which challenged the status quo at a very basic level, hard to ignore. Although Martha's views may look rather moderate to us today, it is telling that they seemed "dangerous" to most men and women of Auburn and elsewhere in the mid-nineteenth century.

Martha's espousal of women's rights challenged the relative roles of men and women both inside and outside the home. Although the term *feminist* was not used in her time, Martha was certainly a feminist as the term is used today. She believed that women should have the same opportunities and political, legal, educational, economic, and social rights as men. She argued not only for the vote for women but also for equal access to higher education and the professions, equal pay for equal work, property rights in marriage, easier access to divorce, and custody rights in divorce. All these ideas were considered extreme in the mid-nineteenth century.

Women with these beliefs were a tiny minority among the women of Martha's day. What made her into a feminist? Her mother, Anna Coffin, set an example as a strong and independent woman who supported her family by managing a store and a boardinghouse. Her sister Lucretia became a highly respected Quaker preacher and another powerful woman who would continue to inspire Martha throughout her life. Another influence in Martha's early years was the Quaker emphasis on the Inner Light of God within each individual, whether male or female. This philosophy extended to Quaker schools, so that Martha, when she left Westtown at fifteen, had received essentially the same education as the Quaker boys of her age, and considerably more than most non-Quaker girls.

Martha brought her intelligence, sense of humor, and high spirits to the job of being a wife and mother, tackling year after year the daily drudgery of household tasks. At first, she relieved some of her frustrations by exercising her "Spirit of Mischief" through family letters and writings, such as her "Hints for Wives" that was read at Seneca Falls. However, the organized woman's rights movement that initiated there gave her the opportunity to talk and work with other intelligent women dissatisfied with current views of "woman's sphere." She participated actively in the movement until her death, and in her later years, Martha became in many ways a more ardent feminist than her famous older sister. When Lucretia told her, "I never like to ask men to do errands, their time's so valuable," Martha retorted, "indeed! As if our time wasn't valuable too!"[24]

Martha has been relatively neglected in historical treatments of the woman's rights movement largely because, as Robert Riegel points out in *American Feminists,* "The eminence of Lucretia Mott threw the career of her sister Martha C. Wright into the shadow."[25] Lucretia was for many years the most widely known and respected woman in America; the title of one biography is *The Greatest American Woman.* Lucretia indeed cast a long shadow. However, from the 1848 Seneca Falls Convention, which Martha helped to organize, to the 1874 NWSA Convention in New York City, where she was elected president, Martha participated in dozens of women's rights conventions in various capacities and presided over many. The British historian Christine Bolt accurately and succinctly describes Martha as bringing to the women's movement "an attractive blend of judgment, humour, and practicality,"[26] three qualities effective in any movement attempting to sway public opinion. Although Lucretia remained a respected senior figure in the movement until her death, from 1855 on Martha played a more active role than her older sister. Beyond her extensive convention activities, Martha carried petitions, drafted resolutions, wrote convention reports and memorials for state legislatures, appeared before legislatures and congressional committees, and defended and promoted the women's cause in articles published in the *Nation,* the *Revolution, North Star,* and other newspapers.

Hampered by a lifelong fear of public speaking, she did much of her work out of the spotlight. She became a close friend, confidant, and adviser to both Elizabeth Cady Stanton and Susan B. Anthony; volumes 1 and 2 of Ann D. Gordon's *Selected Papers of Elizabeth Cady Stanton and Susan B. Anthony* contain more correspondence with Martha than with any other person. Blanch Glassman Hersh wrote that Martha's "personal charm and warmth enabled her to act as a respected intermediary between hostile factions of feminist-abolitionists."[27] In May 1872, her efforts healed the serious breach between Susan B. Anthony and Elizabeth Cady Stanton over the issue of Victoria Woodhull's presidential candidacy. Her approaches to Lucy Stone and others to resolve the controversies between the two woman's rights association helped to decrease the hostility between the warring camps.

Despite her fervent commitment to the woman's rights movement, Martha realized that the changes she and others were calling for would not come soon enough to significantly affect her life or even those of her daughters, and she continued to fulfill her responsibilities to her large family, remaining always a devoted wife, mother, and grandmother. Her major activities in the women's cause were delayed until her children had grown and gone off to school. In later years, when the arrival of a grandchild conflicted with an important convention, Martha was often with her son and daughter rather than on the convention platform. As memorialized by her statue at Seneca Falls, she helped to organize the 1848 convention that launched the women's movement while she was six months pregnant with her seventh child. Despite continual conflict between her public and private commitments, Martha remained a major figure in the women's movement from Seneca Falls until her death over a quarter-century later.

Although Martha's major public contributions were in the woman's rights movement, she also worked many years for the abolition of slavery. This was another cause viewed as "dangerous" to the majority of her contemporaries, since it threatened the stability of the Union. In her home and in her Quaker schools, she had been exposed to antislavery values from an early age. Although she never directly observed the evils of slavery in the South, through Lucretia she met many of the freed blacks of Philadelphia and heard their stories. In Aurora, she saw the scars a neighbor's cook retained on her back from the many whippings she had endured when she was a slave. (Slavery in New York was not formally abolished until 1827.) As a result of Martha's early experiences, she was already strongly opposed to slavery when she met William Lloyd Garrison in Philadelphia in 1833 and attended several sessions of the founding meeting of the American Anti-Slavery Society (AAS). Through

the talks she heard there, and through discussions with Garrison and his followers, she became a committed abolitionist. David Wright did also, so that they
shared this cause (unlike woman's rights and woman suffrage, about which he
remained largely unconvinced).

Martha's 1843 letter to Lucretia describing the harboring of a fugitive
slave in her kitchen overnight is a rare contemporary account of this illegal
activity, and it can be assumed that this was not an isolated incident. By the
1840s, the AAS had voted to accept women members and Martha became an
active member. She served on AAS committees and presided over several state
abolitionist conventions, including two just before the war that were attacked
by angry mobs. She warmly welcomed black friends, including Frederick
Douglass and Harriet Tubman, to 192 Genesee Street, although they were
unwelcome at the hotels and most homes in Auburn. During the Civil War,
she held office in the Women's National Loyal League and carried petitions for
the abolition of slavery. With abolition accomplished, Martha continued to
participate in the AAS after the war, when the focus of the organization turned
to securing full citizenship and voting rights for the freed slaves. She was
instrumental in the 1866 formation of the American Equal Rights Association,
which attempted to unite the questions of black suffrage and woman suffrage.
On her death, AAS leader William Lloyd Garrison proclaimed Martha "a
pronounced, outspoken, uncompromising abolitionist."[28]

In the literature and sermons of Martha's time, women were judged
against the ideal of True Womanhood, which historian Barbara Welter has
described as "divided into four cardinal virtues—piety, purity, submissiveness
and domesticity."[29] A True Woman was expected to leave the worlds of business and politics to men and confine herself to "woman's sphere"—the home.
Although Martha met contemporary standards on purity and domesticity (David later wrote, "she was a model housekeeper, and took careful charge of all
home matters"),[30] she fell short on piety and submissiveness. Martha believed
in God and considered herself a Christian, but her critical attitude toward
organized religion and the authority of the Bible and the pulpit, and her
infrequent church attendance, led many of her neighbors to consider her an
"infidel." And she certainly was not submissive. She often disagreed with David, with her sister Lucretia, and with her colleagues in reform. Stanton knew
both sisters well and made an interesting and somewhat surprising comparison

after their deaths. She wrote that Martha "was naturally a much stronger and more independent character than Lucretia."[31] The term "strong-minded" was used to disparage women in the nineteenth century.[32] Rather than identify Martha as a True Woman by nineteenth-century standards, we judge her instead to have been a Strong-minded Woman.

One characteristic that seems best to describe Martha's general outlook on life was her love of, and desire for, freedom. As in other reformers of the time, the "Spirit of 1776" lived on in Martha. As an abolitionist, she worked for the freedom of slaves from their masters. As a pioneer for women's rights, she worked for women to be free from male domination, free to vote, free to seek higher education, and free to enter any profession of their choosing and receive equal pay. In religion, she wanted freedom of thought and freedom from the dogmas of orthodox churches. She believed strongly in freedom of opinion and freedom of expression, even of the pro-slavery opinions of her nephew Charles Pelham and the free-love theories of Victoria Woodhull. This outlook extended to her support for freedom of the platform at woman's rights conventions, even though the ideas of Woodhull and others resulted in bad publicity for the cause. Martha felt deeply that in the free debate of ideas, Truth would eventually win out over Error. In 1856, she wrote to Charles Pelham, "Do you think it possible for liberty to exist where freedom of speech is restrained?"[33]

Martha lived long enough to see some progress in the reforms to which she committed herself. In the Thirteenth, Fourteenth, and Fifteenth Amendments, she saw slavery abolished and the citizenship and voting rights of the freed slaves sanctioned by law. However, the white power structure of the South, with the complicity of the North, soon found ways other than slavery to limit the rights and opportunities of blacks. In woman's rights, there was modest progress during Martha's lifetime toward increased property rights for married women, and women gained more access to colleges and some professions. The Nineteenth Amendment, approved many years after Martha's death, finally achieved woman suffrage, but many of the other demands made at Seneca Falls remained unmet. Progress in rights for blacks and for women continued to be slow until the 1960s, when the civil rights and women's liberation movements once again moved such issues to the forefront. Racism is still not dead, but the situation for blacks in the United States today is far better than it was in 1833, when Martha attended the founding meeting of the American Anti-Slavery Society. Sexism is also not dead, but the situation for women in the United States today is far better than it was in 1848, when Martha helped to organize the world's first Women's Rights Convention.

George Bernard Shaw once wrote, "The reasonable man adapts himself to the world, the unreasonable one persists in trying to adapt the world to himself. Therefore all progress depends on the unreasonable man."[34] (He would probably accept the addition of "or woman.") It was perhaps not reasonable for Garrison and his followers to agitate for abolition in the decades preceding the Civil War, or reasonable for Martha and her colleagues to agitate for sexual equality at Seneca Falls and beyond. But agitate they did, and progress toward their goals eventually resulted. Later generations benefited from their unreasonableness. In a letter written to Martha in 1874, David reported reading a magazine article about the early abolitionists. He ended with a statement that seems appropriately applied both to the abolitionists and to the pioneer workers for woman's rights, including Martha: "The world is and will be the better that such men and women have lived and acted out their convictions."[35]

So when you visit Seneca Falls, pause in front of the statuary in the Visitors Center and pay homage to the "unreasonable" pioneers of 1848 who started the organized movement towards gender equality. And pay special attention to the statue representing a forty-one-year-old woman six months pregnant with her seventh child. She does not look very dangerous, but in her time and to most of her contemporaries, she was. That's Martha Coffin Pelham Wright— a strong-minded, unreasonable, "very dangerous" woman.

Appendix

Family of Martha Coffin Pelham Wright, 1806–1875

Parents

Thomas Coffin, 1766–1815
Anna Folger, 1771–1844

Siblings and Their Children

Sarah Coffin, 1790–1824, unmarried
Lucretia Coffin, 1793–1880, married James Mott
    Anna Mott, married Edward Hopper
    Maria Mott, married Edward Davis
    Thomas Mott, married Marianna Pelham
    Elizabeth Mott, married Thomas Cavender
    Martha Mott, married George Lord
Elizabeth (Eliza) Coffin, 1794–1870, married Benjamin Yarnall
    three sons and four daughters
Mary Coffin, 1796–1797
Thomas Mayhew Coffin, 1798–1849, unmarried

Mary Coffin, 1800–1824, married Solomon Temple
    Anna Temple, married Walter Brown
Lydia Coffin, 1804–1805

Husbands

Peter Pelham, 1785–1826, married Martha Coffin 1824
David Wright, 1806–1897, married Martha Coffin Pelham 1829

Children and Grandchildren

Marianna Pelham, 1825–1872, married Thomas Mott
    Isabel, Emily, Marian
Eliza Wright, 1830–1911, married David Munson Osborne
    Florence, Emily, Thomas Mott, Helen
Matthew Tallman Wright, 1832–1854, unmarried
Ellen Wright, 1840–1931, married William Lloyd Garrison Jr.
    Agnes, Charles, Frank, William Lloyd III, Eleanor
William Pelham Wright, 1842–1902, married Flora McMartin
    Anne, Edith
Frank Wright, 1844–1903, married (1) Fanny Rosalie Pell (2) Isabel Floyd-Jones
    Mabel, daughter of Fanny
Charles Edward Wright, 1848–1849

Brothers of First Husband, Peter Pelham

Atkinson Pelham, 1797–1880
William Pelham, 1803–1879
John Pelham, 1805–1866

APPENDIX

Nephews (sons of Atkinson Pelham)

Charles Pelham, 1835–1908
William Pelham, 1836–1889
John Pelham, 1838–1863

Notes

Abbreviations

SOURCES

GFP   Garrison Family Papers, Sophia Smith Collection, Smith College, North-ampton, Massachusetts.

HWS   Elizabeth Cady Stanton, Susan B. Anthony, and Matilda Joslyn Gage, eds. *History of Woman Suffrage.* 2 vols. 1881. Reprint (6 vols.), Salem, N.H.: Ayer, 1985. All quotations that appear in the text are from the reprint edition.

OFP   Osborne Family Papers, Department of Special Collections, Syracuse University Library, Syracuse, New York.

S/A 1   Elizabeth Cady Stanton and Susan B. Anthony. *In the School of Anti-Slavery, 1840–1866.* Vol. 1 of *The Selected Papers of Elizabeth Cady Stanton and Susan B. Anthony.* Edited by Ann D. Gordon. New Brunswick: Rutgers University Press, 1997.

S/A 2   Elizabeth Cady Stanton and Susan B. Anthony. *Against an Aristocracy of Sex, 1866 to 1873.* Vol. 2 of *The Selected Papers of Elizabeth Cady Stanton and Susan B. Anthony.* Edited by Ann D. Gordon. New Brunswick: Rutgers University Press, 2000.

S/A 3   Elizabeth Cady Stanton and Susan B. Anthony. *National Protection for Na-
tional Citizens, 1873 to 1880*. Vol. 3 of *The Selected Papers of Elizabeth Cady
Stanton and Susan B. Anthony*. Edited by Ann D. Gordon. New Brunswick:
Rutgers University Press, 2003.

S/A-MF   Elizabeth Cady Stanton and Susan B. Anthony. *The Papers of Elizabeth Cady
Stanton and Susan B. Anthony*. Edited by Patricia G. Holland and Ann D.
Gordon. Wilmington, Del.: Scholarly Resources, 1991. Microfilm.

PEOPLE

DW   David Wright
ECS   Elizabeth Cady Stanton
EWG   Ellen Wright Garrison
EWO   Eliza Wright Osborne
FW   Frank Wright
FPW   Fanny Pell Wright
LCM   Lucretia Coffin Mott
MCW   Martha Coffin (Pelham) Wright
MPM   Marianna Pelham Mott
PP   Peter Pelham
SBA   Susan B. Anthony
WLG   William Lloyd Garrison
WLG Jr.   William Lloyd Garrison Jr.
WPW   William Pelham Wright

Introduction

1. The historic Seneca Falls Declaration of Sentiments is quoted in *HWS*, S/A 1:
78, and numerous other sources.

2. The official *Report of the Woman's Rights Convention, Held at Seneca Falls, N.Y.,
July 19th and 20th, 1848* was published in Rochester in 1848. The full text also
appeared in the *Seneca County Courier*, Aug. 4, 1848. It was reprinted in 1870 and
appears in S/A 1:75.

3. MCW to LCM, Oct. 1, 1848, GFP.

4. Memoir of MCW written by her daughter Eliza Wright Osborne, GFP and OFP.

5. S/A 1:75.

6. Judith Wellman, "The Seneca Falls Women's Rights Convention: A Study of Social Networks," *Journal of Women's History* 3 (Spring 1991): 1071.

7. Robert E. Riegel, *American Feminists* (Lawrence: University Press of Kansas, 1968), 23–24.

8. MCW to LCM, Jan. 29, 1854, GFP.

9. Gerda Lerner, *The Female Experience: An American Documentary* (Indianapolis: Bobbs-Merrill, 1977); Jeanne Boydston, *Home and Work: Housework, Wages, and the Ideology of Labor in the Early Republic* (New York: Oxford University Press, 1990); Nancy F. Cott et al., eds., *Root of Bitterness: Documents of the Social History of American Women* (Boston: Northeastern University Press, 1996).

10. MCW to LCM, Sept. 8, 1855, GFP.

11. ECS to MCW, Mar. 2, 1868, GFP, and S/A-MF.

Chapter 1

1. See Anthony's biographical entry of Martha Wright in *Johnson's New Universal Cyclopedia* in S/A-MF, and Stanton's unpublished memorial of Martha in OFP. Martha probably seldom spoke of her Boston birthplace, since most of her childhood was spent in Philadelphia, where the family moved before her third birthday.

2. The history of the Coffin family on Nantucket, including Thomas Coffin's eventful journey on the *Trial,* is told in Will Gardner, *The Coffin Saga* (Cambridge, Mass.: Riverside Press, 1949), and in Louis Coffin, *The Coffin Family*, Nantucket Historical Society (1962). See also Margaret Hope Bacon, *Valiant Friend: The Life of Lucretia Mott* (New York: Walker, 1980); and Otelia Cromwell, *Lucretia Mott* (Cambridge: Harvard University Press, 1958).

3. For a history of the Quakers in America, see Hugh Barbour and J. William Frost, *The Quakers* (New York: Greenwood Press, 1988). For their role in the early antislavery movement, see James Brewer Stewart, *Holy Warriors: The Abolitionists and American Slavery* (New York: Hill and Wang, 1976). In *Mothers of Feminism* (San Francisco: Harper & Row, 1986), Margaret Hope Bacon explores the pioneer role that many Quaker women played in the woman's movement in America.

4. The American Revolution had left Spain very concerned about its ability to defend its American colonies and also about contraband trade being carried on in South America by some British and American ships. It is unlikely, however, that Thomas Coffin's ship was involved in such trade.

5. For the life of the Coffin family after their move to Boston, see Bacon, *Valiant Friend*, and Cromwell, *Lucretia Mott*.

6. The purchase by Thomas Coffin of "a new brick dwelling house" for "Five thousand six hundred dollars" in Boston in December 1806 is documented in Cromwell, *Lucretia Mott*, based on real estate records found in Boston City Hall. The seller was William Sutton Skinner.

7. The Puritans of Massachusetts Bay Colony famously banished Roger Williams in 1635 and Anne Hutchinson in 1638. The four Quakers they hanged later in that century included one woman. Her statue now stands in Boston over an inscription that reads, "Mary Dyer, Quaker, witness for religious freedom, hanged on Boston Common 1660." See Bacon, *Mothers of Feminism*. Boston was much more tolerant of religious diversity by the time the Coffins arrived in 1804, but Quakers remained a small minority.

8. Westtown school records show that Thomas was enrolled there from 1807 to 1811, Eliza and Mary only from 1809 to 1810.

9. LCM to MCW, Apr. 10, 1846, GFP.

10. MCW to LCM, Mar. 1, 1844, GFP.

11. Lucretia first spoke in the 12th Street Meeting House of Philadelphia in 1818. See Cromwell, *Lucretia Mott,* and Bacon, *Valiant Friend.*

12. Martha Coffin's will, Apr. 17, 1821, obtained from Erik Osborne, Auburn, N.Y. Copies have been deposited in both GFP and OFP.

13. The Westtown records show that Martha Coffin was enrolled there from June 1821 to June 1822. Martha's daughter Eliza, in her memorial of her mother (in OFP; typescript in GFP) written in the 1890s, reports that Martha attended Westtown for three years, but this report is not consistent with the school records. It is also not consistent with Martha's own statement in one letter (MCW to EWG, Apr. 17, 1856, GFP), in which she writes about Westtown, "where I spent a year." Paul Messbarger ("Martha Coffin Pelham Wright [1806–1875]," in *Notable American Women: A Biographical Dictionary* [Cambridge: Harvard University Press, Belknap Press, 1971], 684–85) states that she attended Kimberton School, but this is unlikely. Although her

letters often refer to her time at Westtown, she never mentions attending Kimberton, even in her letters to her daughter Marianna when Marianna attended Kimberton.

14. Details about the education at Westtown are from Kevin Gallagher, Archives Assistant at Westtown, personal communication, 2000.

15. Book titles are as they appear in the booklist (ca. 1800) kindly sent to us by Kevin Gallagher.

16. Although some Quakers owned slaves in colonial America, and a few were even involved in the slave trade, by the late eighteenth century the overwhelming majority of Quakers were antislavery.

17. Enoch Lewis taught mathematics at Westtown and elsewhere. He started publishing the *African Observer* monthly in 1827, but it lasted for only one year. Kevin Gallagher (personal communication, 2000) described Lewis to us as "one of the school's great teachers."

18. In contrast, Anthony had a rather sloppy hand, and Stanton's letters are extremely difficult to read.

19. MCW to DW, Mar. 24, 1871, GFP.

20. MCW to EWO, Apr. 5, 1871, GFP.

21. Swarthmore College was founded in 1864 by the Hicksite body of the Society of Friends. It opened in 1869, only two years before this visit. James and Lucretia Mott had been influential in founding the college, which became nonsectarian in 1911.

22. MCW to DW, Mar. 24, 1871, GFP.

23. MCW to Anna Mott, Aug. 25, 1826, GFP.

24. MCW to LCM, Feb. 3, 1843, GFP.

25. MCW to LCM, Apr. 5, 1841, GFP.

26. MCW to LCM, Nov. 25, 1845, GFP.

Chapter 2

1. Peter Pelham's books discussed in PP to MCW, May 3, 1824, OFP.

2. Pelham genealogy in William Pelham to MPM, June 25, 1854, GFP, and "A Genealogical account of the Pelham family," GFP. See also two articles by William Whitmore: "The Copleys and Pelhams of New England," *Heraldic Journal* 4 (1868):

175–82, and "Who Was Thomas Pelham?" *New England Historic Genealogical Register* 26 (1872): 399–402.

3. This Peter Pelham (1721–1803) served as organist in Williamsburg's Bruton Parish Church. His career is described in Parke Rouse Jr., " 'The Modern Orpheus': Peter Pelham," *The Iron Worker* (Lynchburg Foundry Co., Lynchburg, Va.) 39, no. 1 (Winter 1975).

4. Information on Charles Pelham's military career from William Pelham to MPM, June 25, 1854, GFP.

5. Charles Pelham wrote to his brother in April 1785 (published in *William and Mary Quarterly* 8, no. 1 [1928]: 45) that he had been injured the preceding year when his horse fell on him during his first attempt to reach Kentucky. "I am now preparing for a second attempt," he added, "& if I succeed I shall I hope move there the ensuing fall; had I not been disappointed last fall by this time in all probability I should now have been setting off with my family." This letter suggests that it was fall 1786, when Peter Pelham was less than one year old, that Charles and Isabella Pelham moved to Kentucky.

6. The National Register of Historic Places lists a "Charles Pelham House" on Taylor Mill Road, a stone house that may have been an early residence. The wooden house along the Ohio River where Peter Pelham grew up and where Martha visited in the 1850s is believed to have been farther east, near where Cabin Creek reaches the river (about three miles east of the town center). For this information, local maps, and other documentation pertinent to Charles Pelham from the Mason County Museum, Maysville, Ky., we are grateful to Thomas H. Hubert of St. Louis, Mo.

7. Julius Gordon, *Letters of Capt. Peter Pelham in the Territory of Florida, 1821–1826* (privately published, 1989), 166. We are grateful to the author for providing us with a copy of this book, which contains two photographs of Cottonwood, one of which purportedly shows the slave quarters. According to Gordon, "the place was sold for a brick yard in 1888" (166).

8. Information on Peter Pelham's military service was drawn largely from his correspondence, from as early as 1814, preserved in OFP. Deanne Blanton of the National Archives, Washington, D.C., provided us his dates of service from the Historical Register of the U.S. Army: appointed second lieutenant of the Twenty-first Infantry on Mar. 12, 1812; first lieutenant Apr. 16, 1813; captain Feb. 28, 1814; transferred to Fifth Infantry May 17, 1815; honorably discharged June 1, 1821.

9. See Donald E. Graves, *Field of Glory: The Battle of Crysler's Farm, 1813* (Toronto:

Robin Brass, 2000); C. P. Lucas, *The Canadian War of 1812* (Oxford: Oxford University Press, 1988).

10. Certification of disability and eligibility for invalid pension for PP by Dr. J. Everett, June 1, 1821, OFP.

11. Information on Peter Pelham's experiences in Florida was drawn primarily from his correspondence in OFP, supplemented by Gordon, *Letters of Capt. Peter Pelham.* Gordon's information was drawn largely from correspondence of Peter Pelham found in the National Archives.

12. For example, in one letter concerning the Indians, Peter wrote, "As the Government will provide for the protection of their property it is very desirable that they should not sell any part of their Negroes horses or cattle to unauthorized [by the government] persons." PP to H. Dexter, Mar. 24, 1822, OFP.

13. PP to John Calhoun, May 14, 1822, OFP.

14. This and the quoted phrases in the subsequent paragraph are from a series of undated letters, PP to MCW, [1823], OFP.

15. MCW to LCM, Apr. 25, 1855, GFP.

16. John Calhoun to PP, Apr. 12, 1823, OFP.

17. John Calhoun to PP, June 13, 1823, OFP.

18. The Treaty of Moultrie Creek was signed in Florida Sept. 18, 1823.

19. PP to MCW, Nov. 21, 1823, OFP.

20. For the early history of Fort Brooke, see Donald Chamberlin, "Frontier Outpost, 1824–42," *Tampa Bay History,* (spring/summer 1985): 5–29, available online at <http://www-scfn.thpl.lib.fl.us/bbs/tbhessays2.txt>.

21. PP to MCW, Oct. 5, 1824, OFP.

22. Martha and Peter's simple marriage certificate, signed by the minister Henry White, is in GFP. Martha's mother and family had become accepting of her marriage to Peter, a non-Quaker, but we have found no evidence that they attended the wedding. Perhaps they did not, because Quakers could be expelled from membership even for attending such a wedding.

23. PP to Charles Pelham, Nov. 28, 1824, OFP.

24. PP to Atkinson Pelham, partial letter, ca. 1824, GFP.

25. Soc. of Friends to MCW, Jan. 7, 1825, GFP.

26. For a more extensive discussion of Quaker discipline, see Barbour and Frost, *The Quakers.*

27. MCW to Soc. of Friends, Apr. 25, 1825, GFP.

28. MCW to Flora McMartin Wright (Mrs. WPW), Oct. 13, 1869, GFP.

29. MCW to EWG, Aug. 10, 1872, GFP, MCW to WPW, June 19, 1868, GFP.

30. MCW to PP, May 4, 1825, GFP.

31. MCW to PP, May 8, 1825, GFP.

32. Ibid.

33. MCW to PP, Aug. 21, 1825, GFP.

34. MCW to PP, May 8, 1825, GFP.

35. PP to MCW, July 4, 1825, OFP.

36. Atkinson Pelham to MCW, Aug. 15, 1826, OFP.

37. MCW to Anna Mott, Aug. 25, 1826, GFP.

38. Lt. Newcombe to Julius Catlin, n.d., GFP.

Chapter 3

1. The classic broad treatment of the various religious and reform movements, including the "fires of evangelism," that swept upstate New York in the early nineteenth century is Whitney Cross, *The Burned-Over District: The Social and Intellectual History of Enthusiastic Religion in Western New York, 1800–1850* (New York: Octagonal Books, 1981). More recent and more focused analyses include Michael Barkun, *Crucible of the Millennium: The Burned-Over District of New York in the 1840s* (Syracuse, N.Y.: Syracuse University Press, 1986), and Judith Wellman, *Grass Roots Reform in the Burned-over District of Upstate New York: Religion, Abolitionism, and Democracy* (New York: Garland, 2000).

2. Information on Brier Cliff School and the early history of Aurora taken from Temple Rice Hollcroft, *Aurora, Village of Constant Dawn* (Ovid, N.Y.: W. E. Morrison, 1976), and Hollcroft, "A Brief History of Aurora," *Wells College Alumnae News*, January 1954, both provided to us by Judy Furness, historian of the Town of Ledyard (which contains Aurora).

3. MCW to Charles Pelham, Feb. 10, 1828, GFP.

4. MCW to Atkinson Pelham, Oct. 23, 1828, GFP.

5. School account book of Anna Coffin, 1827–28, OFP.

6. MCW to Atkinson Pelham, Oct. 23, 1828, GFP.

7. Julius Catlin to MCW, undated scrap, GFP.

8. Information about Julius Catlin and his family is taken from Marjorie Catlin

Roehm, ed., *The Letters of George Catlin and His Family* (Berkeley: University of California Press, 1966). Several letters written by Julius to his brother George are in the Morgan Papers, Bancroft Library, University of California Berkeley.

9. *Rochester Daily Advertiser*, Sept. 22, 1828, reprinted in Roehm, *Letters of George Catlin*. A copy is in the Catlin folder in GFP.

10. According to Roehm, *Letters of George Catlin*, this poem appeared in the *Rochester Republican* the day after Julius Catlin was buried.

11. MCW to Mary Catlin Hartshorne, Oct. 3, 1828, GFP.

12. Putnam Catlin to MCW, Oct. 2, 1828, GFP.

13. MCW to Mary Catlin Hartshorne, Mar. 6, 1829, GFP.

14. Diary of unknown student, copied by Sheila Edmunds, historian of the Village of Aurora, and forwarded by Judy Furness.

15. DW autobiography, GFP. David Wright's early life is also recounted in an article by his law partner, Theodore Pomeroy, GFP.

16. The danger to standing passengers from low bridges across the Erie Canal was featured in the chorus of a popular folk song: "Low bridge, everybody down. Low bridge, for we're going through a town." Travel on the Erie Canal was very slow, and delays at the locks, of which there were eighty-two, were frequent. Passenger business became very limited after 1842, when the railroads offered through service from Albany to Buffalo.

17. David worked in the law office of Seneca Wood for over three years. Ordinarily, seven years of work in the office of a practicing lawyer were required before one could be admitted to practice as an attorney. The justice of the state supreme court, however, had the authority to deduct up to four years for educational or scientific attainment. On the basis of an exam David took, the justice "struck off three and a half years from the seven, saying that was the utmost ever allowed without a college diploma." DW autobiography.

18. MCW to LCM, Jan. 7, 1842, GFP.

19. The Wright marriage certificate, dated Nov. 18, 1829 and signed by William Thomas, Justice of the Peace, is in GFP.

20. Information on the Wright house in Aurora provided by Judy Furness from an unpublished manuscript, Lewis Himrod [?], "Samuel D. Mandell's History of the Houses in Aurora," 1906. One page reproduces a listing (date unknown) of about fifty early houses along the lake that includes "next E. B. Morgan, next David Write [*sic*], next Samuel Brush." This listing, plus the known locations of the Morgan and Brush

houses at that time, enabled Judy Furness to establish the approximate location of David and Martha Wright's first house at the north end of the village. The location of the house between the houses of Morgan and Brush is also confirmed in EWO memoir of MCW, GFP and OFP.

21. DW to MCW, Oct. 9, 1832, GFP.

22. MCW to DW, Oct. 19, 1832, GFP.

23. Ibid.

24. DW to MCW, Dec. 24, 1833, GFP.

25. Ibid.

26. DW to MCW, winter 1833—34 (undated scrap), GFP.

27. Ibid.

28. MCW to DW, Nov. 17, 1833, GFP.

29. Ibid.

30. Margaret Hope Bacon, *Valiant Friend: The Life of Lucretia Mott* (New York: Walker, 1970), 37.

31. MCW to DW, Dec. 30, 1833, GFP.

Chapter 4

1. The founding meeting of the American Anti-Slavery Society, held in Philadelphia December 4–6, 1833, is described in Henry Mayer's vibrant and comprehensive biography of William Lloyd Garrison, *All on Fire: William Lloyd Garrison and the Abolition of Slavery* (New York: St. Martin's, Griffen, 1998).

2. Some of the arguments of the period for and against colonization, for gradual emancipation, and for immediate emancipation, are presented in William H. Pease and Jane H. Pease, eds., *The Antislavery Argument* (Indianapolis: Bobbs-Merrill, 1965).

3. *Liberator* 1, no. 1 (Jan. 1, 1831).

4. MCW to DW, Dec. 5, 1833, GFP.

5. For more on the history and influence of these images, see Jean Fagan Yellin, *Women and Sisters: The Antislavery Feminists in American Culture* (New Haven: Yale University Press, 1989), chap. 1; and Phillip Lapsansky, "Graphic Discord: Abolitionist and Antiabolitionist Images," in *The Abolitionist Sisterhood: Women's Political Culture in Antebellum America*, ed. Yellin and John C. Van Horne (New Haven: Yale University Press, 1989). First developed by British abolitionists, the image of the kneeling

woman in chains appeared in the United States in 1830, and by 1832, Garrison had adopted it for his "Ladies Department" of *The Liberator*. It added a sexual component to the antislavery argument, depicting female innocence vulnerable to the power of the slaveholder.

6. MCW to DW, Dec. 5, 1833, GFP.

7. Ibid.

8. MCW to DW, Dec. 8, 1833, GFP.

9. MCW to DW, Dec. 22, 1833, GFP.

10. Article 1, section 2 of the Constitution apportioned the number of Representatives from each state "according to their respective numbers, which shall be determined by adding to the whole number of free persons, including those bound to service for a term of years, and excluding Indians not taxed, three fifths of all other persons." The three-fifths clause was removed in 1868 by the Fourteenth Amendment.

11. The composition of anti-abolitionist mobs is discussed by Leonard Richards in *Gentlemen of Property and Standing* (Oxford: Oxford University Press, 1970).

12. The 1838 burning of Pennsylvania Hall during the Second Anti-Slavery Convention of American Women is discussed in Margaret Hope Bacon, *Valiant Friend*, Otelia Cromwell, *Lucretia Mott,* and in numerous accounts of the antislavery movement.

13. Names and dates of the various members of the Coffin/Mott extended family and their offspring are listed in the Biographical Directory of *Selected Letters of Lucretia Coffin Mott*, Beverly Wilson Palmer (Urbana: University of Illinois Press, 2002).

14. Anna Coffin to DW, inserted in MCW to DW, Jan. 12, 1834, GFP.

15. Most of Martha Wright's family letters are in GFP and OFP. Lucretia Mott's family letters are in GFP and the Mott Manuscripts of the Friends Historical Library of Swarthmore College, Swarthmore, Pa. Numerous family letters written by Martha and Lucretia were burned or otherwise lost to posterity, resulting in frustrating gaps in the record.

16. Visit to phrenologist described in MCW to DW, Oct. 13, 1838, GFP.

17. Elizabeth Mott to MCW, Mar. 28, 1844, multi-authored letter in Anna Coffin folder, GFP.

18. MCW to LCM, Dec. 21, 1844, GFP.

19. From collection of MCW poems, GFP.

20. MCW to MPM, n.d. [1830s], GFP, Dec. 24, 1837, GFP.

21. MCW to MPM, June 19, 1838, GFP.

22. MCW to MPM, June 29, 1841, GFP.

23. William Pelham to MCW, Apr. 27, 1838, GFP.

24. MCW to William Pelham, copied in MCW to LCM, Mar. 11, 1841, GFP.

25. MCW to LCM, Apr. 5, 1841, GFP.

26. Ibid.

27. Ibid.

28. MCW to LCM, Feb. 7, 1847, GFP.

29. MCW to DW, Apr. 17, 1844, GFP.

30. Quoted in ibid.

31. DW to MCW, Apr. 23, 1844, GFP.

32. MCW to LCM, Dec. 21, 1844, GFP.

Chapter 5

1. Information on nineteenth-century Auburn was obtained from Henry Hall, *The History of Auburn* (Auburn, N.Y.: Dennis Brothers, 1869; reprint, Union Springs, N.Y.: Tallcot Bookshop, 1989); and Elliot G. Stocke, *History of Cayuga County, New York* (Syracuse: D. Mason, 1879). Also very helpful were the two volumes of *Images of America: Around Auburn*, a compilation of period photographs from the collections of the Cayuga Museum (203 Genesee Street, Auburn).

2. The railroad line from Auburn to Rochester was completed in 1841, but after 1852, when a direct line between Syracuse and Rochester was opened, the main road from Albany to the West no longer went through Auburn. See David M. Ellis et al., *A History of New York State* (Ithaca: Cornell University Press, 1957), chap. 20, for a review of the history of New York's transportation network.

3. EWO memoir of MCW, 1890s, OFP and GFP.

4. The Wright house at 192 Genesee Street was torn down about 1880 and replaced by a Victorian house, which in turn was torn down in 1975 and replaced with a ranch house, occupied in 2001 by a doctor's office. Information obtained from material in the History Room of Auburn's Seymour Library, with the help of librarian Mary Gilmore.

5. From the 1850s through the 1870s, David Wright's office was listed variously in the Auburn City Directory at numbers 87, 131, 99, and 57 Genesee Street. His

residence remained listed at 192 Genesee Street until the 1878–79 directory, when he was listed as a boarder at South Street and Fitch Avenue (home of his daughter Eliza and her husband, David Munson Osborne). The city directories were found in the History Room, Seymour Library, Auburn.

6. MCW to LCM, Nov. 7, 1841, GFP.

7. EWO memoir of MCW.

8. SBA to EWO, Jan. 1875, quoted in ibid.

9. MCW to LCM, Nov. 19, 1841, GFP. Much of this letter and other MCW letters of late 1841 describing her household chores and daily life appear in Nancy Cott et al., eds., *Root of Bitterness: Documents of the Social History of American Women* (Boston: Northeastern University Press, 1996).

10. Martha's visit to Philadelphia in 1833, after the births of Eliza and Tallman, would have given her ample access to information about birth control and relevant material. On the history of birth control in America, see Linda Gordon, *The Moral Property of Women: A History of Birth Control Politics in America* (Urbana: University of Illinois Press, 2002) (an update of her earlier work, *Woman's Body, Woman's Right: A Social History of Birth Control in America* [New York: Grossman, 1976]); Norman Himes, *Medical History of Contraception* (New York: Gamut Press, 1963); and Andrew Sinclair, *The Emancipation of the American Woman* (New York: Harper & Row, 1966). Abortion practices in the early nineteenth century are discussed in James C. Mohr, "Abortion in America," in *Women's America*, ed. Linda Kerber and Jane Sherron De Hart (New York: Oxford University Press, 2000), 183–92.

11. MCW to LCM, Feb. 17, 1848, GFP.

12. MCW to LCM, Apr. 23, 1846, GFP.

13. MCW to LCM, Nov. 13, 1845, GFP.

14. MCW to LCM, Mar. 17, 1847, GFP.

15. MCW to LCM, Jan. 7, 1842, GFP.

16. EWO memoir of MCW.

17. MCW to EWG, June 2, 1870, GFP.

18. MCW to LCM, Feb. 7, 1847, GFP. In this letter, part of which appears in Gerda Lerner, *The Female Experience: An American Documentary* (Indianapolis: Bobbs-Merrill, 1977), Martha Wright also describes making candles in "three moulds which make 32 candles in all which expedites the process, tho' it takes ten times longer to mould than to dip them, but they are so much neater that it compensates one for the labor."

19. MCW to LCM, Jan. 6, 1846, GFP.

20. MCW to LCM, Mar. 2, 1846, GFP.

21. Auburn State Prison, considered at the time a model for other U.S. prisons, was visited in 1831 by Alexis de Tocqueville and Gustave de Beaumont, two French noblemen who were touring the country to study the American penal system. Although they published a joint report on the prisons, the most lasting result of Tocqueville's journey was his *Democracy in America* (1835–40), an insightful analysis of the effects of democracy on individuals and on society. Auburn Theological Seminary, one of the nation's first seminaries, moved to New York City in 1939 and is now associated with Union Theological Seminary.

22. Of the numerous biographies of Seward, the one that treats his wife, Frances, in the greatest depth is Earl Conrad, *The Governor and His Lady: The Story of William Henry Seward and His Wife Frances* (New York: G. O. Putnam, 1960). Despite Seward's national reputation as an antislavery politician, Frances Seward and her sister Lazette Worden were more radical in their support of abolition than was Seward himself.

23. MCW to LCM, Dec. 18, 1841, GFP.

24. MCW to LCM, July 13, 1846, GFP.

25. Ibid.

26. MCW to LCM, Jan. 18, 1843, GFP.

27. EWO memoir of MCW. Martha's close connection with Harriet Tubman before and after the war (see Chapters 9 and 12) and the following letter about Rev. Eastup also indicate an involvement of the Wrights with the Underground Railroad.

28. MCW to EWG, Nov. 28, 1857, GFP.

29. MCW to LCM, Feb. 3, 1843, GFP.

30. In a letter to the 1850 Ohio Women's Convention (S/A 1, 166) Elizabeth Cady Stanton argued that if women had a voice in government, "that relic of barbarism, the gallows" would be abolished. Frederick Douglass, Wendell Phillips, and other reformers of the period also often spoke in favor of the abolition of capital punishment.

31. The Wyatt and Freeman trials are discussed in various biographies of Seward and at greatest length in George E. Baker, *The Life of William Henry Seward with Selections from His Works* (New York: Redfield, 1855).

32. MCW to LCM, June 25, 1845, GFP.

33. In New York State, execution was by hanging until 1890, when it was

replaced by electrocution. The electric chair was first used that August in Auburn State Prison and soon was adopted as the means of execution of criminals in many other states.

34. MCW to LCM, Feb. 20, 1846, GFP.

35. MCW to LCM, Aug. 15, 1846, GFP.

36. MCW to LCM, June 25, 1845, GFP.

37. David Wright's book, published in Auburn by J. C. Derby & Co., summarizes the laws of New York State. It was printed in several editions and remains available in many law libraries. Written as an aid to laymen, it "immediately became a standard text book on the practice in Surrogate's courts in every law office," according to an account written after David's death (Theodore Pomeroy, "Sketch of the Life and Character of David Wright," 1898, GFP).

38. MCW to LCM, Dec. 21, 1844, GFP.

39. Pomeroy, "Sketch." See also DW autobiography, GFP.

40. MCW to LCM, Jan. 6, 1846, GFP.

41. DW autobiography, GFP.

42. MCW to LCM, undated 1846, GFP.

43. The full text of the Supreme Court decision on the Freeman trial, which concluded, "This verdict was defective," was published in the *Auburn Daily Advertiser,* Feb. 11, 1847.

44. MCW to LCM, Jan. 9, 1849, GFP.

45. MCW to LCM, Jan. 17, 1846, GFP.

46. Ibid.

47. MCW to LCM, Dec. 11, 1845, GFP.

48. MCW to LCM, July 16, 1839, GFP.

49. MCW to LCM, May 13, 1846, GFP.

50. As listed in the Feb. 11, 1847 issue of the *Auburn Daily Advertiser*, found in the American Antiquarian Society, Worcester, Mass. Copies of this paper on microfilm are available in the library of the Cayuga County Community College, Auburn.

51. MCW to LCM, Oct. 29, 1848, GFP.

52. MCW to LCM, Feb. 17, 1848, GFP.

53. Alexander Pope, *An Essay on Man*, epistle 3, lines 303, 304.

54. MCW to LCM, undated scrap, ca. 1847, GFP.

55. "Infidelity—The Reforms of the Age," *The Liberator*, June 4, 1847.

56. Bacon, *Valiant Friend*, 37.

57. Garrison certainly agreed. In an article published in 1860 entitled "The 'Infidelity' of Abolitionism," he defends the American Anti-Slavery Society (and himself) against charges of "infidelity" and churches and ministers that defend or condone slavery, concluding that abolitionism "is an essential part of Christianity" and "is the spirit of Jesus." Anti-Slavery Tracts, no. 10, n.s., reprinted in William H. Pease and Jane H. Pease, eds., *The Antislavery Argument* (Indianapolis: Bobbs-Merrill, 1965).

58. MCW to LCM, Dec. 14, 1845, GFP.

Chapter 6

1. The Women's Rights National Historical Park in Seneca Falls, authorized by Congress in 1980, is administered by the National Park Service. There is considerable information on the park and on the Seneca Falls Convention on its Web site at <www .nps.gov/wori/home.htm>. As Gerda Lerner points out, "Until very recently, the Seneca Falls convention of 1848 was not recognized as significant by historians. . . . It was only due to the resurgence of modern feminism and the advances of the field of Women's History that the convention has entered the nation's consciousness. . . . Still, it took decades of struggle . . . to rescue the building at Seneca Falls and finally to persuade the National Park Service to turn it into a historic site." "The Meanings of Seneca Falls, 1848–1998," in *Women's America; Refocusing the Past*, ed. Linda K. Kerber and Jane Sherron De Hart, 5th ed. (New York: Oxford University Press, 2000), 201–2.

2. The most complete and historically accurate presentation of the 1848 convention is Judith Wellman, *The Road to Seneca Falls: Elizabeth Cady Stanton and the First Woman's Rights Convention* (Urbana: University of Illinois Press, forthcoming). See also Judith Wellman, "The Seneca Falls Women's Rights Convention: A Study of Social Networks," *Journal of Women's History* 3 (Spring 1991): 9–37; *HWS*, vol. 1; Eleanor Flexner, *Century of Struggle: The Woman's Rights Movement in the United States* (New York: Atheneum, 1959); Miriam Gurko, *The Ladies of Seneca Falls* (New York: Schocken Books, 1974).

3. Abigail Adams to John Adams, May 7, 1776. L. H. Butterfield et al., eds. *The Book of Abigail and John: Selected Letters of the Adams Family 1762–1784* (Cambridge: Harvard University Press, 1975), 127.

4. Mary Wollstonecraft, quoted in Barbara Taylor, *Mary Wollstonecraft and the Feminist Imagination* (Cambridge: Cambridge University Press, 2003), 246.

5. MCW to LCM, undated two-page typescript, starting "I have a perfect recollection," probably 1852 (from internal evidence), GFP.

6. Anne M. Boylan has discussed how the involvement of women in various benevolent societies in the early nineteenth century set the stage for their later involvement in the antislavery movement. Boylan, *The Origins of Women's Activism: New York and Boston, 1797–1840* (Chapel Hill: University of North, Carolina Press, 2002). For discussion of the evolution of the woman's rights movement from the antislavery movement, see Kathryn Kish Sklar, *Women's Rights Emerges Within the Antislavery Movement, 1830–1870: A Brief History with Documents* (Boston: Bedford/St. Martin's, 2000); Ellen Carol Dubois, *Feminism and Suffrage: The Emergence of an Independent Woman's Movement, 1848–1869* (Ithaca: Cornell University Press, 1978); Gerda Lerner, *The Grimké Sisters from South Carolina: Pioneers for Woman's Rights and Abdition* (New York: Shocken Books, 1971); Andrea Moore Kerr, *Lucy Stone: Speaking Out for Equality* (New Brunswick, N.J.: Rutgers University Press); and the biographies of Lucretia Mott listed under "Lucretia Mott" in the "Biographies" section of the Bibliography. For some women, other factors helped to draw them into woman's rights. For Susan B. Anthony, her experiences with gender bias as a teacher and as a worker in the temperance movement were important. Ernestine Rose was strongly influenced by Owenism and "the freethinking tradition," as discussed in Carol A. Kolmerten, *The American Life of Ernestine L. Rose* (Syracuse, N.Y.: Syracuse University Press, 1999). For Martha Wright, her experiences in marriage, including the burdens of raising children and maintaining a household, were clearly a major influence. And not all women active in antislavery were sympathetic to the woman's rights movement. For example, see Amy Swerdlow, "Abolition's Conservative Sisters," in *The Abolitionist Sisterhood: Women's Political Culture in Antebellum America*, ed. Jean Fagan Yellin and John C. Van Horne (Ithaca: Cornell University Press, 1994), 31–44.

7. Lerner, *Grimké Sisters*; Sklar, *Women's Rights Emerges*.

8. This convention is described in more depth by Kathryn Kish Sklar, "Women Who Speak for an Entire Nation" in Yellin and Van Horne, *Abolitionist Sisterhood*, 301–33. Sklar's article is based in part on Lucretia Mott's diary of her trip to England and compares the responses of the British and the Americans to "the woman question."

9. Elizabeth Cady Stanton, *Eighty Years and More: Reminiscences, 1815–1897* (New York: Schocken Books, 1971).

10. MCW to LCM, Mar. 11, 1841, GFP.

11. For more on the early efforts to establish married women's property rights in New York see Judith Wellman, "Women's Rights, Republicanism, and Revolutionary Rhetoric in Antebellum New York State," *New York History* 69 (July 1988): 353, and "The Seneca Falls Women's Rights Convention: A Study of Social Networks," *Journal of Women's History* 3 (Spring 1991): 9–37. See also S/A 1: 406; *HWS*, 1: 63–67, 686–87, and (since Ernestine Rose was an early proponent of women's property rights) Kolmerten, *American Life of Ernestine L. Rose*. According to Elizabeth Bowles Warbasse in *The Changing Legal Rights of Married Women, 1800–1861* (New York: Garland, 1987), 205, this 1848 act made New York into a leader in this area of reform; see also ibid., 262, concerning the 1860 expansion of this act and "Married Women's Property Acts, New York State, 1848, 1860", in Kerber and De Hart, *Women's America*, 210.

12. MCW to LCM, Dec. 1841, GFP. Much of this letter is reproduced in Nancy Cott et al., eds., *Root of Bitterness: Documents of the Social History of American Women* (Boston: Northeastern University Press, 1996).

13. MCW to LCM, Aug. 29, 1855, GFP.

14. MCW to LCM, May 13, 1846, GFP.

15. The Hunt home in Waterloo was recently purchased by the National Park Service and has become part of the Women's Rights National Historical Park.

16. A copy of the page of the *Seneca County Courier* including this announcement is available at the Seneca County Historical Society in Seneca Falls and at the Women's Rights National Historical Park. We are grateful to Judith Wellman, former historian at the park, and to Anne Derousie, current historian there, for confirming that the correct date of this announcement is July 11.

17. Stanton, *Eighty Years and More*, 148–49.

18. Wellman, "Seneca Falls Women's Rights Convention," 10–11.

19. *HWS*, 1: 68. The M'Clintock home is part of the Women's Rights National Historical Park, and the mahogany table on which the documents were reportedly written is now in the Smithsonian Institution in Washington, D.C.

20. ECS to Elizabeth M'Clintock, July 14, 1848, in S/A 1: 69.

21. LCM to ECS, July 16, 1848, S/A 1:74.

22. MCW to LCM, Jan. 6, 1856, GFP.

23. *HWS*, 1: 68.

24. MCW's abridgement of B. L. Rayner, *Life of Thomas Jefferson* (Boston: Lilly,

Wait, Colman & Holden, 1834) is discussed in MCW to LCM, July 13, 1846, GFP. It was written "with a view of having it printed in a little pamphlet to tack into the corner of Jefferson's Letters, as so little of Biography is contained there."

25. LCM to ECS, July 16, 1848, S/A 1: 74.

26. *Report of the Woman's Rights Convention held at Seneca Falls, N.Y., July 19th & 20th, 1848* (Rochester, N.Y.: printed by John Dick at the North Star Office, 1848), in S/A 1: 75.

27. The Stanton home is a short walk from the Visitors Center of the Women's Rights National Historical Park, and tours of the home are offered by the park.

28. *HWS*, 1:70. A possible explanation for some of the opposition to the woman suffrage resolution at Seneca Falls is that a large number of delegates were Quaker, and many Quakers believed that no one, man or woman, should participate in voting. Although many sources cite the Seneca Falls resolution as the first call for woman suffrage, an earlier appeal for woman suffrage in New York was in the form of a petition to the 1846 state constitutional convention, signed by six women from Jefferson County. This petition argued that "the present government of this state has widely departed from the true democratic principles upon which all just governments must be based by denying to the female portion of community the right of suffrage." Cited in Jacob Katz Cogan and Lori D. Ginzberg, "1846 Petition for Women's Suffrage, New York State Constitutional Convention," *Signs* (Winter 1997): 439.

29. *North Star* (Rochester, N.Y.), July 28, 1848. Other quotations from press reports on the 1848 Seneca Falls and Rochester Conventions are taken from *HWS*, vol. 1, appendix to chap. 4.

30. Press response to the 1848 Seneca Falls and Rochester Conventions is reproduced in *HWS*, 1: 802–5.

31. MCW to LCM, Oct. 1, 1848, GFP.

32. See Introduction, n. 2. *History of Woman Suffrage*, written several decades after the fact, states instead that "Martha Wright read some satirical articles she had published in the daily papers answering the diatribes on woman's sphere." *HWS*, 1:69. This error, presumably resulting from Stanton's faulty memory, has been repeated in several other sources. It is clear from Martha's correspondence that the official convention report is correct—it was Lucretia, not Martha, who read Martha's article at the convention.

33. MCW to LCM, Feb. 17, 1848, GFP.

34. *North Star*, Aug. 11, 1848; *United States Gazette*, Sep. 23, 1846. The full

article appears and is discussed in Sherry H. Penney and James D. Livingston, "Hints for Wives—and Husbands," *Journal of Women's History* 15 (Summer 2003): 180–87. A draft of this article in Martha's hand is in GFP, in a folder labeled "answers to mistaken editors." The published articles differ very slightly from Martha's draft, the few changes probably made by the editor of the *Gazette*. For example, missing in the published articles is a brief quotation Martha had used from *Eothen*, a travel book by Alexander W. Kinglake published in 1844. The editor probably realized that many of his newspaper's readers were not as widely read as Martha.

35. MCW to LCM, Mar. 11, 1844, GFP.

36. MCW to LCM, Aug. 21, 1848, GFP.

37. This quotation is from the text of *New England Primer* accompanying a woodcut picturing the martyrdom in 1555 of John Rogers, a London minister burned at the stake for preaching an anti-Catholic sermon. The text reads, "his wife with nine small children and one at her breast following him to the stake," and the woodcut shows "Mrs. Rogers" and her children watching Rogers burn. The *Primer*, designed to instill Protestant Christianity while teaching reading, was first published in the late seventeenth century, but later, more secular editions were widely read in Martha Wright's day. One edition that Martha and her siblings may have been exposed to in their youth, and which contains the woodcut and text describing the martyrdom of John Rogers, is *The New England Primer for the more easy attaining the true reading of English to which is added The Assembly of Divines, and Mr. Cotton's Catechism* (Boston: Edward Draper, 1777).

Chapter 7

1. MCW to LCM, Oct. 16, 1848, GFP.

2. Probably Phebe Hussey Gardner, a Nantucket Folger cousin of Martha and Lucretia's, or Phebe Earle Gibbons, another cousin.

3. MCW to LCM, June 28, 1847, GFP.

4. *Childe Harold's Pilgrimage*, canto 3, stanza 32.

5. She once wrote to David, "I never can *help loving* Byron when I read of him." MCW to DW, Oct. 19, 1832, GFP.

6. MCW to LCM, Nov. 29, 1848, GFP. (Letter is dated October 29, but contents suggest it was written November 29.)

7. MCW to LCM, Dec. 6, 1848, GFP.

8. MCW to LCM, Nov. 7, 1841, GFP.

9. MCW to LCM, Aug. 23, 1868, GFP. The importance of reading to women in antebellum America is explored by Mary Kelley in "Reading Women/Women Reading: The Making of Learned Women in Antebellum America," *Journal of American History*, September 1996, 401–24. For a discussion of the reading and writing of Martha's daughter Eliza and her friends, see Claire White Putala, "Reading and Writing Ourselves into Being—Then What? The Literacy of Certain Nineteenth-Century Women (Ph.D. diss., Syracuse University, 1997).

10. MCW to DW, Oct. 26, 1856, GFP.

11. MCW to LCM, Jan. 9, 1849, GFP.

12. MCW to LCM, Jan. 12, 1849, GFP.

13. Mary Watkins of the Cayuga and Owasco Lakes Historical Society, Moravia, New York, provided information on the location of David Wright's farms in Moravia. An 1853 town map shows the farms situated on the west side of the plank road, just south of the lake.

14. MCW to LCM, June 20, 1858, GFP.

15. In the first two years after the passage of this act, over 180 companies were formed to build plank roads in New York State, but most failed. See David M. Ellis et al., *A History of New York State* (Ithaca: Cornell University Press, 1957), 253–54. Some of the financial records of the Auburn-Moravia plank road company are in the David Wright Papers, Manuscripts and Special Collections, New York State Library, Albany.

16. David's obituary in the *Auburn Daily Advertiser*, Feb. 25, 1897, records that he built up "the leading law practice in the county," and that "he has the proud record of arguing twelve cases before the supreme court of the United States and winning nine of them." It also describes him as a "man of method." Among his rules was "never to leave the office earlier or later than 9 p.m." A biographical sketch of David, written in 1898 for the Cayuga County Historical Society by his former law partner, Theodore Pomeroy, is included in GFP. Pomeroy writes that David's law offices "were always neat and orderly, devoted entirely to professional work, and in them he spent nine or ten hours every work day."

17. MCW to LCM, Oct. 16, 1848, GFP.

18. MCW to LCM, Jan. 12, 1849, GFP.

19. 1849 catalogue for Auburn Female Academy, GFP.

20. MCW to LCM, Sept. 4, 1848, GFP.

21. MCW to LCM, Jan. 27, 1846, GFP. Three years later, Elizabeth Blackwell graduated at the head of her class at nearby Geneva College and became the first woman to receive a regular medical degree in the United States.

22. MCW to LCM, Mar. 5, 1849, GFP.

23. MCW to LCM, Feb. 13, 1849, GFP.

24. D. M. Osborne & Co. quickly became very successful, and by the time of the Civil War, was supplying harvesting machines to most of the Northern states. It merged with International Harvester in 1903. Information on the company available in OFP; see also Rudolph W. Chamberlain, *There Is No Truce: A Life of Thomas Mott Osborne* (New York: Macmillan, 1935). As noted in later chapters, Martha's sons Willy and Frank were each briefly employed by Osborne & Co.

25. MCW to LCM, Feb. 13, 1849, GFP.

26. MCW to LCM, Oct. 31, 1844, GFP.

27. For an excellent and comprehensive biography of Frederick Douglass, see William S. McFeely, *Frederick Douglass* (New York: Norton, 1991). Douglass was thirty-one when Martha first met him at Seneca Falls.

28. MCW to LCM, Aug. 21, 1848, GFP.

29. Ibid.

30. MCW to LCM, Apr. 2, 1849, GFP.

31. MCW to LCM, Sept. 29, 1854[?], GFP.

32. MCW to LCM, Nov. 7, 1841, GFP.

33. MCW to LCM, Nov. 19, 1841, GFP.

34. MCW to LCM, May 13, 1851, GFP.

35. MCW to LCM, May 6, 1849, GFP.

36. Noel Ignatiev examines how Irish immigrants to America in the nineteenth century established their place in society and includes their association with the Democratic Party and description of various Irish-led riots against blacks, with whom they competed for low-level jobs. Most notable were the 1863 draft riots in New York City, mentioned in Chapter 11. Ignatiev, *How the Irish Became White* (New York: Routledge, 1995).

37. MCW to LCM, Feb. 6, 1852, GFP.

38. Ibid.

39. Ibid.

40. MCW to EWG, Jan. 27, 1859, GFP. On this occasion, Emerson stopped by

192 Genesee Street for tea before his lecture, and Martha and David rode to the lecture with him.

41. Lucretia Mott's disappointment with Kossuth's unwillingness to condemn slavery is discussed in Otelia Cromwell, *Lucretia Mott* (Cambridge: Harvard University Press, 1958). William Lloyd Garrison condemned Kossuth's choice as "dishonorable." See Henry Mayer, *All on Fire: William Lloyd Garrison and the Abolition of Slavery* (New York: St. Martin's, Griffen, 1998).

42. William Ingraham Kip (1811–1893) became the first Episcopal bishop of California in 1854, two years after his Auburn lecture.

43. MCW to LCM, Feb. 6, 1852, GFP.

44. "Recollections of Vienna" in the collection of MCW poems, GFP, was published twice in the *Auburn Daily Advertiser* in February 1852.

45. MCW to LCM, Feb. 26, 1852, GFP.

46. The words "life protracted is protracted woe" are actually from Samuel Johnson, *The Vanity of Human Wishes* (1749).

47. LCM to MCW, Nov. 1849, quoted in Anna Davis Hallowell, *James and Lucretia Mott: Life and Letters* (Boston: Houghton, Mifflin, 1884).

48. MCW to LCM, Jan. 21, 1850, GFP.

49. MCW to LCM, May 13, 1851, GFP. In contrast to Martha's skepticism, several women in the early women's movement became devotees of this form of spiritualism. See Barbara Goldsmith, *Other Powers: The Age of Suffrage, Spiritualism, and the Scandalous Victoria Woodhull* (New York: Knopf, 1998); and Ann Braude, *Radical Spirits: Spiritualism and Women's Rights in Nineteenth-Century America* (Boston: Beacon Press, 1989). Braude wrote, "While not all feminists were Spiritualists, all Spiritualists advocated woman's rights" (3).

50. MCW to DW, Dec. 8, 1853, GFP.

51. Eliab Wilkinson Capron, *Modern Spiritualism: Its Facts and Fanaticisms, Its Consistencies and Contradictions* (New York: Bela Marsh, 1855; reprint, New York: Arno Press, 1976). Although Capron was generally a believer in various "manifestations of the spirits," he itemizes numerous cases where he finds reason to suspect fraud or delusion. In 1848, Capron had been one of the thirty-two male signers of the Seneca Falls Declaration of Sentiments.

52. MCW to LCM, Dec. 9, 1850, GFP.

53. 1849 catalogue for Auburn Female Seminary, GFP.

54. MCW to LCM, Dec. 9, 1850, GFP.

55. MCW to Tallman Wright, June 29, 1851, GFP.
56. Tallman Wright to MCW, Apr. 17, 1853, GFP.
57. MCW to DW, Nov. 18, 1853, GFP.
58. Tallman Wright to MCW, July 14, 1854, GFP.
59. MCW to LCM, Jan. 14, 1854, GFP.
60. MCW to LCM, Feb. 17, 1848, GFP.
61. MCW to Mrs. Clarke, Mar. 25, 1873, GFP.

Chapter 8

1. The most complete description of the early woman's rights conventions, and of Martha's contributions to them, can be found in *HWS*, 1.
2. ECS to LCM, Sept. 26, 1849, GFP and S/A, 1: 147.
3. "Drama by ECS and Elizabeth W. McClintock," dated November 1849, S/A 1: 152–160. The cast list includes Martha's son Tallman, who was living in Philadelphia with Lucretia at the time.
4. MCW to Elizabeth M'Clintock, Jan. 8, 1850, GFP.
5. MCW to LCM, Dec. 9, 1850, GFP.
6. *Syracuse Standard,* Sept. 13, 1852, quoted in *HWS*, 1: 520.
7. MCW's reading of the declaration is recorded in *HWS*, 1: 522; the text of the declaration starts on 1: 360.
8. *HWS*, 1: 535.
9. Amelia Bloomer started publishing the *Lily* in January 1849, six months after the Seneca Falls Convention, and by 1853 it had a circulation of more than four thousand. Ann Russo and Cheris Kramarae argue the importance of the *Lily* and other antebellum women's newspapers, and assemble a interesting collection of provocative writings on women's rights taken from their pages. Russ and Kramarae, eds., *The Radical Women's Press of the 1850s* (New York: Routledge, 1991). Bloomer's promotion in the *Lily* of dress reform for women consisting of full-length trousers covered by a mid-calf skirt led the mainstream press to label it the "bloomer" costume.
10. This historic meeting is commemorated on a street in Seneca Falls with a life-size group of statues representing Anthony, Stanton, and Amelia Bloomer.
11. Opened in 1833, Oberlin welcomed the first women into its collegiate program in 1837. The board of trustees also voted in 1835 to admit students "irre-

spective of color." Stone and Brown both graduated from Oberlin in 1847, but Brown stayed to complete its theological course in 1850. By the time of the 1852 convention in Syracuse, there were several other coeducational colleges, mostly in the Midwest. For the history of Oberlin and coeducational colleges in the United States, see Linda Eisenmann, ed., *Historical Dictionary of Women's Education in the United States* (Westport, Conn.: Greenwood Press, 1998).

12. Brown was ordained by the Congregational Church in August 1853 but left the church the following year to become a freelance lecturer, writer, and preacher. When she lectured in Auburn in 1859, Brown stayed overnight with Martha, and Martha wrote her candid opinion of her houseguest to her daughter Ellen: "Antoinette never interested me so much as some others. She is very lovely, and gentle and dignified, and her lecture was good & sensible, but wanting in brilliance and power." MCW to EWG, Jan. 27, 1859, GFP.

13. Blackwell's reading of "Marriage Protest" is described in Andrea Moore Kerr, *Lucy Stone: Speaking Out for Equality* (New Brunswick, N.J. Rutgers University Press, 1995). Chris Dixon analyzes the Stone-Blackwell marriage and several other "antislavery marriages," including the Motts. Such marriages tended to be more egalitarian than most, even though the husband was often still the primary wage earner and the wife still bore responsibility for housekeeping, as with David and Martha Wright. See Dixon, *Perfecting the Family: Antislavery Marriages in Nineteenth-Century America* (Amherst: University of Massachusetts Press, 1997).

14. Eleanor Flexner judges Lucretia Mott "the moral force of the movement," Elizabeth Cady Stanton "its outstanding philosopher," Susan B. Anthony "its incomparable organizer," and Lucy Stone "its most gifted orator." Flexner, *Century of Struggle: The Woman's Rights Movement in the United States* (New York: Atheneum, 1959), 84.

15. The *Standard*, Sept. 13, 1852, and the *Daily Journal*, Sept. 13, 1852, are quoted in *HWS*, 1: 542.

16. These comments are from the *Star*, Sept. 10, 1852 and Sept. 11, 1852, quoted in *HWS*, 1: 852.

17. *HWS*, 1: 535. Nancy Isenberg examines attacks on woman's rights based on religious grounds and argues that the church should be viewed as a political institution with an internal structure that reinforced traditional gender relations in society. See Isenberg, " 'Pillars in the same Temple and Priests of the same Worship': Women's Rights and the Politics of Church and State in Antebellum America," *Journal of American History* 85 (June 1998): 98–128.

18. *HWS*, 1: 852–53.

19. MCW to DW, Oct. 23, 1853, GFP.

20. Ibid. This visit to Maysville was also reported by Lucretia Mott to her Philadelphia family in a letter dated Oct. 17, 1853, that is reproduced in Beverly Wilson Palmer, ed., *Selected Letters of Lucretia Coffin Mott* The original letter is in the Mott Papers at Swarthmore. In the letter Lucretia reported, about the Pelhams, "We were made so entirely at home by their Kentucky hospitality, that we soon felt like old acquaintances."

21. William Pelham to MPM, Mar. 5, 1854, GFP.

22. Described in Otelia Cromwell, *Lucretia Mott* (Cambridge: Harvard University Press, 1958).

23. MCW to DW, Nov. 18, 1853, GFP.

24. MCW's description of the debate in her letter to DW, Dec. 4, 1853, GFP, was published in the *Liberator*, Dec. 16, 1853, 198.

25. MCW to DW, Dec. 25, 1853, GFP.

26. Elizabeth Cady Stanton, *Eighty Years and More: Reminiscences, 1815–1897* (New York: Arno and New York Times, 1969), 194.

27. MCW to LCM, July 30, 1854, GFP.

28. The history of dress reform in the nineteenth century and its relationships to gender and power are reviewed by Gayle V. Fischer in *Pantaloons and Power: A nineteenth-century Dress Reform in the United States* (Kent, Chio: Kent State University Press, 2001).

29. MCW to DW, Oct. 26, 1856, GFP.

30. MCW to LCM, Nov. 10, 1858, GFP.

31. In this respect Martha was more conservative than many of her fellow reformers and many Quaker women, who, like Stanton, used their maiden name as a middle name.

32. MCW to DW, Oct. 18, 1854, GFP.

33. MCW to DW, Oct. 23, 1854, GFP.

34. MCW to DW, Oct. 26, 1854, GFP.

35. Theodore Weld in 1834 became a highly effective agent for the newly formed American Anti-Slavery Society (AAS), recruiting and training people to work for the cause. His pamphlet put out by the AAS in 1839, *American Slavery as It Is: Testimony of a Thousand Witnesses*, widely publicized the horrors of slavery. In the 1850s, he founded a school to which many abolitionists sent their children. Weld's career and

school are described in Benjamin P. Thomas, *Theodore Dwight Weld: Crusader for Freedom* (New Brunswick, N.J.: Rutgers University Press, 1950); Robert H. Abzug, *Passionate Liberator: Theodore Dwight Weld and the Dilemma of Reform* (New York: Oxford University Press, 1980); and Gerda Lerner, *The Grimké Sisters from South Carolina: Pioneers for Women's Rights and Abolition* (New York: Schocken Books, 1971). For details about the school, see Chapter 9, n. 2.

36. MCW to EWG, Oct. 20, 1854, GFP.

37. MCW to LCM, Mar. 15, 1855, GFP.

38. Ibid.

39. *Auburn Daily Advertiser*, Mar. 15, 1855, reprinted in *Cayuga Chief*, Mar. 20, 1855.

40. As noted earlier, that an Auburn neighbor described Martha as a "very dangerous woman" is recorded in EWO's memoir of MCW, OFP and GFP.

41. *Daily Saratogian*, Aug. 15, 1855. We are grateful to Barbara Livingston for locating and copying issues of this newspaper.

42. MCW to EWG, Aug. 4, 1855, GFP. *HWS*, 1: 628, mistakenly reports that Martha Wright presided at a convention in Albany in February 1855. However, Martha's diaries and correspondence indicate that she was in Auburn at the time of that convention, and that the Saratoga convention in August was the first at which she presided. She would later preside at numerous conventions, including several state conventions in Albany.

43. MCW to Rev. W. R. G. Mellen, Oct. 10, 1855, GFP.

44. MCW to LCM, Sept. 8, 1855, GFP.

45. MCW to Rev. Mellen, Oct. 10, 1855, GFP.

46. Ibid.

47. Ellen pleaded with her mother, "Cant I go to the Convention? I want awful dreadful much to hear Lucy, and T. W. Higginson. . . . Do let me." EWG to MCW, Aug. 3, 1855, GFP. After resisting Ellen's entreaties in an earlier letter because of her health, Martha finally relented, writing, "as you are so anxious to go, I make no further objection." MCW to EWG, Aug. 8, 1855, GFP. Harriet Alonso writes that Martha permitted Ellen to attend this convention "in order to impress upon her daughter the wonderful aspects of the woman's rights movement," citing this as an example of Martha's pressure on her daughter to develop an interest in the movement. Alonso, *Growing Up Abolitionist: The Story of the Garrison Children* (Amherst: University of Massachusetts Press, 2002), 184. The August 1855 letters show that Martha gave

permission to fifteen-year-old Ellen to attend this convention only very reluctantly. There nevertheless is little doubt that Martha hoped that her daughters would eventually become interested in the woman's rights movement.

48. MCW to EWG, Aug. 27, 1855, GFP. Anne L. Hoblitzelle uses this letter as evidence that Martha was implicitly promoting marriage as Ellen's life role. Hoblitzelle writes, "The examples Martha Wright cited—Antoinette Brown, Ernestine Rose, Lucy Stone—were all married. Martha Wright mentions Susan B. Anthony's activities to Ellen, but Miss Anthony was not used directly as a model." Hoblitzelle, "The Ambivalent Message: Sex Role Training in Mid-Nineteenth-Century United States as Reflected in the Correspondence of Martha Coffin Wright to Ellen Wright Garrison" (master's thesis, Sarah Lawrence College, 1974), 28. The flaw in Hoblitzelle's argument is that at the time of this letter, Antoinette Brown was not yet married. (She married the following year.) The absence of Susan B. Anthony from Martha's list of role models may stem more from Martha's negative initial impressions of Anthony in 1855 as a "Gradgrind" than from Anthony's status as a single woman.

49. *HWS*, 1: 164.

50. MCW to SBA, Nov. 2, 1855, GFP.

51. MCW to EWG, Nov. 27, 1855, GFP.

52. MCW to LCM, Nov. 17, 1855, GFP.

53. MCW to LCM, Dec. 13, 1855, GFP.

54. The formation of the Republican Party, triggered in large part by the passage in 1854 of the proslavery Kansas-Nebraska Act, is described Hans L. Trefousse, *The Radical Republicans: Lincoln's Vanguard for Racial Justice* (New York: Knopf, 1969).

55. Martha referred to David as a "Jackson man" in 1832 (MCW to DW, Oct. 19, 1832, GFP). David's obituary in the *Auburn Daily Advertiser*, Feb. 25, 1897, reports, "Mr. Wright was originally a Democrat but ever since the passage of the Fugitive Slave law he has been a staunch Republican and never failed to vote in the fall elections."

56. When asked by outsiders about the party's organization, members of the American Party were supposed to respond that they "know nothing." Formed as an outgrowth of anti-immigrant and anti-Catholic sentiment in the late 1840s, the Know-Nothings had become a significant political party by 1852 but had disappeared by 1860, largely because of a split over the issue of slavery. In David's local race the Know-Nothings allied with the Democrats, but more typically they opposed the Democrats. The activity of the Know-Nothings in New York State is described in

David M. Ellis et al., *A History of New York State* (Ithaca: Cornell University Press, 1957). A more general discussion of their role in the politics of the 1850s can be found in Trefousse, *Radical Republicans*.

57. *Cayuga Chief*, Nov. 27, 1855.

58. ECS to MCW, Dec. 17[?], 1855, GFP and S/A 1: 305.

59. ECS to MCW, Apr. 1856, GFP and S/A-MF. Many reformers of the region, including Mary Ann M'Clintock and Jane Hunt, were members of Junius Monthly Meeting, which met in Waterloo. Its role in promoting women's rights in the Genesee Yearly Meeting is described in Christopher Densmore, "The Quaker Tradition: Sustaining Women's Rights" (paper prepared for National Women's Studies Association Annual Meeting, Oswego, N.Y., 1998), available at <http://ubib.buffalo.edu/libraries/units/archives/urr/NWSA.html>.

60. MCW to EWO, Feb. 9, 1857, OFP.

61. SBA to MCW, June 6, 1856, GFP and S/A-MF.

62. MCW to SBA, June 14, 1856, GFP.

63. MCW to DW, Oct. 26, 1856, GFP.

64. MCW to Rev. Mellen, Nov. 14, 1856, GFP.

65. DW to MCW, Jan. 6, 1857, OFP.

66. MCW to DW, Jan. 11, 1857, GFP.

Chapter 9

1. Anne Hoblitzelle, "Ambivalent Message: Sex-Role Training in Mid-Nineteenth-Century United States as Reflected in the Correspondence of Martha Coffin Wright to Ellen Wright Garrison" (master's thesis, Sarah Lawrence College, 1974), is based on a study of Martha's letters to her daughter Ellen and focuses on the conflict between Martha's feminist beliefs and the reality of current life options to a young woman like Ellen. Martha's correspondence with Ellen is also discussed in Harriet Alonso, *Growing Up Abolitionist: The Story of the Garrison Children* (Amherst: University of Massachusetts Press, 2002); and her earlier letters to her older daughter Eliza are quoted in Claire Putala, "Reading and Writing Ourselves into Being—Then What? The Literacy of Certain Nineteenth-Century Women" (Ph.D. diss., Syracuse University, 1997).

2. The Welds started a small school in Belleville, New Jersey, in the early 1850s

and in 1854 moved to open a new and somewhat larger school in Raritan Bay Union, a newly formed cooperative community near Perth Amboy. A brochure describing the program and principles of Weld's Eagleswood School on Raritan Bay is in the GFP. (Weld used blank portions of the brochure to write a letter to Frank Wright on Sept. 15, 1860.) The school had a limit of fifty-six boarding pupils and admitted "youth of both sexes" because "their education together, under a wise supervision, gives symmetry to mental and moral development . . . and general elevation and equilibrium to character." The curriculum and nature of Eagleswood are discussed in Alonso, *Growing Up Abolitionist*, 180–82.

3. MCW to EWG, Feb. 8, 1855, GFP. Part of this letter is reproduced in Gerda Lerner, *The Female Experience: An American Documentary* (Indianapolis: Bobbs-Merrill, 1977).

4. MCW to EWG, Aug. 7, 1855, GFP.

5. MCW to EWG, Sept. 1, 1855, GFP.

6. MCW to EWG, Jan. 13, 1856, GFP.

7. MCW to EWG, Jan. 7, 1857, GFP.

8. MCW to FW, Apr. 11, 1860, GFP.

9. MCW to WPW, Nov. 12, 1856, GFP.

10. MCW to WPW, Apr. 15, 1858, GFP.

11. Ibid.

12. MCW to WPW, Oct. 15, 1857, GFP.

13. DW to WPW, Mar. 28, 1859, GFP.

14. DW to FW, Nov. 1, 1859, GFP.

15. MCW "translation" of Theodore Weld to DW and MCW, Nov. 6, 1859, GFP.

16. MCW to FW, Nov. 23, 1859, GFP.

17. MCW to EWO, Apr. 6, 1858, OFP.

18. MCW to LCM, Mar. 14, 1851, GFP.

19. MCW to EWO, Aug. 2, 1856, OFP.

20. MCW to LCM, Dec. 3, 1858, GFP.

21. MCW to LCM, Feb. 11, 1865, GFP.

22. MCW to EWO, Jan. 3, 1857, OFP.

23. William W. Freehling, in *The Road to Disunion: Secessionists at Bay, 1776–1854* (New York: Oxford University Press, 2000), discusses the various controversies and compromises over slavery through 1854 and their effect on secessionist feelings in the

South. James M. McPherson, in *Battle Cry of Freedom: The Civil War Era* (New York: Oxford University Press, 1988), summarizes the final stages of the "road to disunion" from the Compromise of 1850 to the Civil War.

24. McPherson argues that the fugitive slave law "gave the national government more power than any other law yet passed by Congress" (*Battle Cry of Freedom*, 78). He goes on to describe some of the incendiary incidents that followed the passage of this law, which are also discussed in Henry Mayer, *All in Fire: William Lloyd Garrison and the Abolition of Slavery* (New York: St. Martins, Griffen, 1998), and by many other works on the antislavery movement.

25. For the role of nonresistance (or nonviolence, as the approach is termed today) in the activities of abolitionist women, see Margaret Hope Bacon, "By Moral Force Alone," in *The Abolitionist Sisterhood: Women's Political Culture in Antebellum America*, ed. Jean Fagan Yellin and John C. Van Horne (Ithaca: Cornell University Press, 1994), 275–97. For the response of Garrison and other nonresistants to the violence in Kansas, see Henry Mayer, *All on Fire*. A recent collection of articles edited by John R. McGivigan and Stanley Harrold, reexamines the roles of violence and nonresistance in the antislavery movement. See McGivigan and Harrold, eds., *Antislavery Violence: Sectional, Racial, and Cultural Conflicts in Antebellum America* (Knoxville: University of Tennessee Press, 1999). Martha appeared torn between the teachings of Jesus and the seeming need in Kansas to oppose violence with violence. The coming of the Civil War, and her son's participation in it, would lead Martha to discard entirely any sympathy for nonresistance.

26. MCW to Rev. Mellen, June 6, 1855, GFP.

27. MCW to Rev. Mellen, Nov. 14, 1856, GFP.

28. MCW to LCM, Feb. 14, 1856, GFP.

29. MCW to LCM, Mar. 1, 1856, GFP.

30. For the complex and differing views of Garrison, Douglass, and other abolitionists with regard to "disunion," see Mayer, *All on Fire*.

31. For Garrison's strained attempts to reconcile his philosophy of nonresistance with his eventual support of the war, see ibid. Mayer also points out that, "It was easy to show that the South fought *for* slavery, but it was difficult to show that the North fought *for* abolition, since the administration and a substantial portion of the Republican party denied such a purpose" (524).

32. Four of Brown's raiders, including two blacks, were also hanged. Eight of his men, including two of his sons, were killed during the raid. Brown and his sons

and several of his collaborators were buried on Brown's farm near Lake Placid, New York.

33. DW autobiography, GFP.

34. MCW to LCM, Jan. 29, 1854, GFP.

35. Lucretia Mott was among the speakers at Garrison's three-day "Anti-Sabbath Convention" held in Boston in 1848, a convention that drew much interest and much criticism. See Mayer, *All on Fire*; and Margaret Hope Bacon, *Valiant Friend: The Life of Lucretia Mott* (New York: Walker, 1980).

36. Quoted in Anna Davis Hallowell, *James and Lucretia Mott: Life and Letters* (Boston: Houghton Mifflin, 1884), 380.

37. MCW to Rev. Mellen, undated, ca. 1855, GFP.

38. MCW to EWG, Jan. 27, 1859, GFP.

39. MCW to LCM, May 15, 1858, GFP.

40. The term *free love* is today most commonly associated with complete sexual freedom, unencumbered by any marital restraints. Some in Andrews' community, Modern Times, appear to have approached this behavior, but many at the time employed the term for much less extreme positions, including the right of a wife to refuse her husband on occasions. For those who firmly believed that marriage bound husband and wife exclusively to each other until death, even support of modest liberalization of divorce laws was attacked as endorsing "free love." For more discussion of Andrews and the issue of "free love," see Barbara Goldsmith, *Other Powers: The Age of Suffrage, Spiritualism, and the Scandalous Victoria Woodhull* (New York: Knopf, 1998); Mary Gabriel, *Notorious Victoria: The Life of Victoria Woodhull, Uncensored* (Chapel Hill, N.C.: Algonquin Books, 1998); Joanna Johnson, *Mrs. Satan: The Incredible Saga of Victoria C. Woodhull* (New York: Putnam, 1967); M. M. Marberry, *Vicky: A Biography of Victoria C. Woodhull* (New York: Funk & Wagnall's, 1967); Eminie Sachs, *The Terrible Siren: Victoria Woodhull, 1838–1927* (New York: Harper, 1978); Lois Beachy Underhill *The Woman Who Ran for President: The Many Lives of Victoria Woodhull* (Binghamton, N.Y.: Bridge, 1995).

41. MCW to LCM, May 17, 1858, GFP.

42. MCW to ECS, Sept. 12, 1858, GFP, S/A-MF.

43. MCW to SBA, Oct. 4, 1858, GFP, S/A-MF.

44. The January 1860 antislavery meeting in Auburn is recorded in the *Auburn Daily Advertiser*, Jan. 14, 1860.

45. The 1860 New York bill on married women's property rights, described in

HWS, 1: 686–88, enlarged upon rights that had been granted in the groundbreaking 1848 act. Elizabeth Bowles Warbasse, in *The Changing Legal Rights of Married Women, 1800–1861* (New York: Garland, 1987), writes that this 1860 act "again made New York the leader in this area of reform" (262). However, parts of this act were repealed in 1862 (see *HWS*, 1: 747–48). For a general treatment of the history of married women's property rights in America, see Marylynn Salmon, *Women and the Law of Property in Early America* (Chapel Hill: University of North Carolina Press, 1986). Carole Shammas, in "Re-Assessing the Married Women's Property Acts," *Journal of Women's History* 6 (Spring 1994): 9–30, argues that historians have understated the importance of these acts. Hendrik Hartog examines how various nineteenth-century legal cases reshaped gender roles, not always to the advantage of women. See Hartog, *Man and Wife in America: A History* (Cambridge: Harvard University Press, 2000). Parts of both the 1848 and 1860 acts are reprinted in Linda Kerber and Jane Sherron De Hart, eds., *Women's America: Refocusing the Past*, 5th ed. (New York: Oxford University Press, 2000).

46. MCW to WPW, Feb. 8, 1860, GFP.

47. MCW diaries, May 8–10, 1860, GFP.

48. Wendell Phillips was a very popular lecturer and abolitionist leader. Most notable among several biographies is Irving H. Bartlett, *Wendell Phillips: Brahmin Radical* (Boston: Beacon Press, 1961).

49. *HWS*, 1: 689.

50. Ibid.

51. Stanton's speech at the 1860 convention appears in S/A 1: 418–29. For more details of the convention debate, see *HWS*, 1: 716–35.

52. Bartlett, *Wendell Phillips*.

53. MCW to SBA, July 17, 1860, GFP.

54. MCW to ECS, May 26, 1860, GFP and S/A 1: 432–33.

55. Andrea Moore Kerr, in *Lucy Stone: Speaking Out for Equality* (New Brunswick, N.J.: Rutgers University Press, 1995), writes that in the postwar years, "where Stanton had grown increasingly radical in her thinking on marriage, Stone had grown more conservative" (156) and that "The outraged press response to Stanton's divorce speeches intensified Stone's determination to keep the two associations separate" (157)

56. Frances Seward's unhappiness with her husband's political ambitions is most extensively treated in Earl Conrad, *The Governor and his Lady: The Story of William Henry Seward and His Wife Frances* (New York: G.O. Putnam, 1960).

57. This trial is discussed in Otelia Cromwell, *Lucretia Mott* (Cambridge: Harvard University Press, 1958).

58. MCW to DW, Apr. 7, 1859, GFP.

59. Robert Purvis, a Philadelphia abolitionist of mixed parentage, was very light-skinned.

60. Harriet (Hattie) Forten Purvis, wife of Robert, was one of the black women who were among the founding members of the Philadelphia Female Anti-Slavery Society. The group was organized by Lucretia Mott in December 1833 a few days after the founding of the American Anti-Slavery Society. See Janice Similar-Lewis, "The Forten-Purvis Women of Philadelphia and the American Anti-Slavery Crusade," *Journal of Negro History* 66 (Winter 1981): 281–88.

61. MCW to EWO, Apr. 9, 1859, GFP.

62. In the most recent biography of this remarkable woman, Jean Humez separates the established facts of Tubman's life from the legends that have evolved over the years. See Humez *Harriet Tubman: The Life and the Life Stories* (Madison: University of Wisconsin Press, 2003).

63. MCW to EWG, Dec. 30, 1860, GFP.

64. See Humez, *Harriet Tubman*.

65. MCW to EWG, Jan. 14, 1861, GFP.

66. Two of her paintings, decorative depictions of flowering plants, birds, and insects, are in GFP. Two others we have located are in the possession of Helen Osborne Fuller, a descendant of Martha Wright's.

67. MCW to EWG, Jan. 27, 1861, GFP.

68. MCW to WPW, Jan. 30, 1861, GFP. Beriah Green and Aaron Powell were both Quaker abolitionists. Powell led the New York State Anti-Slavery Society.

69. The following words appear with the poetry in the back of one of Martha's diaries in GFP: "Lines from Whittier handed me by D. K. Lee, on the platform, during the mob at Auburn." The lines are from Whittier's "Barclay of Ury," a poem honoring a Quaker who suffered religious persecution in Scotland. Whittier, a Quaker and an active abolitionist, was a favorite poet of abolitionists. The poem was appropriate, since most abolitionists felt their cause was a religious one.

70. *Onondaga Standard*, Feb. 6, 1861, reprinted in the *Liberator*, Feb. 15, 1861.

71. The movement of the meeting to the Wrights' house was reported in twenty-eighth Annual Report of the American Anti-Slavery Society (1861), 187.

72. The convention was reported in the *Albany Evening Journal*, Feb. 5 and 6,

1861, in the *Liberator*, Feb. 15, 1861, and in the *National Anti-Slavery Standard*, Feb. 23, 1861.

73. MCW to EWG, Feb. 10, 1861, GFP.

74. MCW to Matilda Joslyn Gage, Feb. 15, 1871, GFP.

75. MCW to EWG, Feb. 11, 1861, GFP.

76. *HWS*, 1: 742.

77. MCW to LCM, Oct. 26, 1858, GFP.

78. MCW to LCM, Mar. 2, 1855, GFP.

79. MCW to EWG, Feb. 11, 1861, GFP.

80. MCW to DW, Apr. 13, 1861, GFP.

Chapter 10

1. William Pelham to MPM, Apr. 28, 1854, GFP.

2. MCW to DW, Feb. 18, 1859, GFP.

3. William Pelham to MPM, Aug. 11, 1861, GFP.

4. MCW to FW, Sep. 6, 1861, GFP.

5. MCW to EWG, Sep. 9, 1861, GFP.

6. MCW to WPW, Apr. 5, 1862, GFP. An account in the *New York Times*, Apr. 4, 1862, p. 8, reports "The Texans hold Santa Fé, where they have organized a provisional Government, with Gen. PELHAM as Governor."

7. For a discussion of this battle that turned the tide against the Confederates, called by some historians "the Gettysburg of the West," see Thomas S. Edrington and John Taylor, *The Battle of Glorieta Pass* (Albuquerque: University of New Mexico Press, 1998).

8. MCW to FW, May 22, 1862, GFP.

9. The Civil War campaign in New Mexico is described in Martin Hardwick Hall, *Sibley's New Mexico Campaign* (Austin: University of Texas Press, 1960); and Robert Lee Kerby *The Confederate Invasion of New Mexico and Arizona, 1861–1862* (Los Angeles: Westernlore Press, 1958). William Pelham is mentioned briefly in these accounts and in Ralph Emerson Twitchell, *The Leading Facts of New Mexico History* (Cedar Rapids, Mich.: Torce Press, 1912), vol. 2. A brief biography of William Pelham, entitled "Surveyor of the Public Domain: A Portrait of William Pelham," was published by Wilfried Roeder in his "Antepasados" column published in the

newsletter of the New Mexico Professional Surveyors. (A copy complete with citations is filed in the Chavez History Library, Santa Fe, New Mexico.) We are grateful to him for sharing with us the further results of his research on William Pelham.

10. L. B. Giles reports the death near Dalton, Georgia, on May 9, 1864, of "Charles T. Pelham of Company D, an educated young man, of good family and fine promise, a civil engineer by profession." Giles, *Terry's Texas Rangers,* (Austin: Pemberton Press, 1867). Martha first learned of the death of William's son in an 1869 letter from another nephew named Charles Pelham, the oldest son of Atkinson Pelham, who referred to Charles Thomas Pelham as "the most reckless and daring soldier I ever saw." Charles Pelham to MCW, July 12, 1869, typescript in GFP, original in OFP.

11. Charles C. TenEyck, born in 1861, was the son of William's daughter Isabella Ann Pelham and Edward TenEyck. An act to change the name of Charles C. TenEyck to Charles Thomas Pelham was approved by the Texas Legislature on November 3, 1864.

12. Charles Pelham to MCW, July 12, 1869, typescript in GFP, original in OFP.

13. Information on William Pelham's postwar life was obtained from Wilfried Roeder of Tularosa, New Mexico, and from Wendy Wright of Austin.

14. John Pelham to MPM, Apr. 1, 1858, GFP.

15. John Pelham to MPM, Mar. 18, 1861, GFP.

16. John Pelham to MPM, Mar. 26, 1861, GFP.

17. William W. Hassler, *Colonel John Pelham: Lee's Boy Artillerist* (Chapel Hill: Univeristy of North Carolina Press, 1960); Philip Mercer, *The Life of the Gallant Pelham* (Kennesaw, Ga.: Continental Book, 1958); and Charles G. Milham, *Gallant Pelham: American Extraordinary* (Washington, D.C.: Public Affairs Press, 1959).

18. Quoted in Hassler, *Colonel John Pelham,* 167. This biography and those by Mercer and Milham (see n. 17) were consulted for information on John Pelham's military career.

19. The John Pelham Historical Association, formed in 1982, has held numerous conventions at historic sites related to John Pelham and continues to produce a bimonthly newsletter, *The Cannoneer.* An article in the May 1988 issue by Peggy Vogtsberger, "The Monuments to John Pelham," reported there were then thirteen monuments to him throughout the South, mostly in Virginia and Alabama. In addition to Pelham, Alabama, towns in Georgia and North Carolina were named after him.

20. MPM to William Pelham, copy of response to Jan. 28, 1865 letter, GFP.

21. MPM to William Pelham, copy of response to Feb. 14, 1865 letter, GFP.

22. For information about John Pelham's brother William, we are grateful to his descendant, William Pelham of Houston. Some correspondence of William Pelham (1836–1889) can be found in the Southern Historical Collection of the University of North Carolina at Chapel Hill.

23. MCW to Charles Pelham, [1856], copied for EWO, OFP.

24. Charles Pelham to MCW, Dec. 6, 1860, OFP.

25. MCW to Charles Pelham, Dec. 20, 1860, GFP.

26. Charles Pelham to MCW, Mar. 12, 1861, OFP.

27. Charles Pelham to MCW, July 12, 1869, typescript in GFP, original in OFP. This letter and the previous two letters of Charles Pelham (nn. 24, 26) and two letters of John Pelham (nn. 15, 16) appear in James D. Livingston, "The Gallant Pelhams and Their Abolitionist Kin," *Civil War Times* (October 2003): 20–21, 59–65. These five letters and other correspondence of Martha Wright and her daughter Marianna Mott with the Pelhams discussed in Chapter 10 appear in Sherry H. Penney and James D. Livingston, "How Did Abolitionist Women and Their Slaveholding Relatives Negotiate Their Differences over the Issue of Slavery?," in *Women and Social Movements in the United States 1775–2000*, Center for the Historical Study of Women and Gender at State University of New York, Binghamton, at <http://womhist.binghamton.edu/mcw/doclist.htm>.

28. Considering the strong secessionist and pro-slavery views that Charles expressed in his letters to Martha just before the war, it is interesting that he became a Republican politician during Reconstruction. Some of his postwar political activities in the Republican party appear in Sarah Woolfolk Wiggins, *The Scalawag in Alabama Politics, 1865–1881* (University: University of Alabama Press, 1977).

Chapter 11

1. DW autobiography, GFP.

2. MCW to FW, Oct. [?], 1861, GFP.

3. For the story of the First New York Independent Battery in the Civil War, see R. L. Murray, *"Hurrah for the Ould Flag": The True Story of Captain Cowan at the First New York Independence Battery at Gettysburg* (Wolcott, N.Y.: R. L. Murray, 1998). Willie Wright's wartime diaries are in GFP and OFP.

4. James M. McPherson, *Battle Cry of Freedom: The Civil War Era* (New York: Oxford University Press, 1988), 485.

5. Copy in OFP.

6. List of recommended medicines in MCW to WPW, Jan. 31, 1862, GFP.

7. MCW to FW, May. 15, 1862, GFP.

8. Theodore Weld to MCW, June 2, 1862, GFP.

9. WPW to MCW, June 13, 1862, GFP.

10. MCW to WPW, Mar. 25, 1862, GFP.

11. Ibid.

12. MCW to DW, Apr. 5, 1862, GFP.

13. MCW to WPW, Sept. 26, 1862, GFP.

14. DW to WPW, Apr. 13, 1862, GFP.

15. MCW to WPW, Sep. 26, 1862, GFP.

16. DW to MCW, Apr. 6, 1864, GFP.

17. DW to MCW, Mar. 27, 1862, GFP.

18. MCW to SBA, Mar. 31, 1862, GFP and S/A 1: 473.

19. MCW diary, Mar. 1863, GFP.

20. MCW to DW, Mar. 17, 1863, GFP.

21. MCW to WPW, Apr. 4, 1863, GFP.

22. The eleventh Secretary's report (1901–6) of Harvard's class of 1866 states that Wright and his classmate George A. Flagg "organized the first baseball nine at Harvard, and with Wright as captain and pitcher and Flagg as catcher played the first collegiate game, and established baseball as one of the permanent college athletic sports." This report, published by Harvard, is accessible in the University Archives, Pusey Library, Harvard.

23. MCW to WPW, Apr. 30, 1863, GFP.

24. MCW to WPW, May 7, 1863, GFP.

25. Activities of the Women's National Loyal League are detailed in Wendy Hamand Venet, *Neither Ballots nor Bullets: Women Abolitionists and the Civil War* (Charlottesville: University Press of Virginia, 1991).

26. MCW to EWG, June 22, 1863, GFP

27. MCW to WPW, May 14, 1863, GFP.

28. Details of the movements of Willy's battery drawn from his wartime diaries in OFP and GFP, and from Murray, *"Hurrah for the Ould Flag."*

29. MCW to EWG, July 3, 1863 (letter started July 2), GFP.

30. Wartime diary of WPW, OFP (portions of his wartime diary are also in the GFP).

31. McPherson, *Battle Cry of Freedom*, 662.

32. There are many accounts of the Battle of Gettysburg. Pickett's Charge and the role of Cowan's battery are discussed in detail in George R. Stewart, *Pickett's Charge: A Microhistory of the Final Attack at Gettysburg, July 3, 1863* (Boston: Houghton Mifflin, 1959), and Murray, *"Hurrah for the Ould Flag."*

33. The inscription on the Gettysburg monument honoring Cowan's battery is recorded in New York Monuments Commission, *Final Report on the Battlefield of Gettysburg*, (Albany: J.B. Lyon Ca., 1902), 3: 1268. According to the historical sketch that follows the words of the inscription, "Lieutenant Wright was shot through the body at Gettysburg, when the Confederates were less than twenty yards from the section he commanded." We are grateful to John Heiser, park ranger and historian at Gettysburg, for sending us this material.

34. MCW to FW, July 8, 1863, GFP.

35. Stanton and Anthony had also seen Willy's name listed among the wounded and had expressed their concern and sympathy to Martha's niece Anna Temple Brown. Anna reported, "Mrs. Stanton said she had noticed that Aunt Martha had never been herself since Willy had been in the Army. That she had not seemed to be a moment free from anxiety." Anna Brown to MCW, July 10, 1863, GFP.

36. This account is based in part on David Wright's autobiographical notes on the Civil War, GFP.

37. WPW war diary, OFP.

38. MPM to MCW, July 12, 1863, GFP.

39. One Union regiment, the Forty-fifth Regiment Infantry of New York, consisted almost entirely of Germans, and had "about 100 wounded" at Gettysburg. New York State Monuments Commission, *Final Report*, 1: 381.

40. MPM to MCW, July 12, 1863, GFP.

41. MCW to LCM, June 25, 1865, GFP.

42. MCW to EWG, Dec. 11, 1864, GFP.

43. Quoted in MCW to EWG, July 26, 1863, OFP.

44. The courtship of Ellen Wright and William Lloyd Garrison Jr. and several of Ellen's earlier romances are described by Harriet Alonso, *Growing Up Abolitionist: The Story of the Harrison Children* (Amherst: University of Massachusett Press, 2002). Alonso notes that early in their relationship, William expressed concern that Ellen,

with her brother Willy in the army, might not appreciate his nonresistant position, but that Ellen responded that it seemed "unnatural for a Garrison to wield a sword." EW to WLG Jr., June 13, 1863, GFP. Of the four adult sons of William Lloyd Garrison, only one served in the army, while the other three followed their father's principles of nonviolence. About the Garrison sons, Martha wrote in 1863, "They have been bro't up in the strictest principles of non resistance, but the Anti-slavery work they are doing, by assisting their father in the Liberator is perhaps quite as effective as anything *they* cd. do, in the Army. . . . Where wd. the nation have been, but for Mr. Garrison's persistent Anti-Slavery teaching for 30 years." MCW to FW, Apr. 30, 1863, GFP.

45. MCW to EWG, Mar. [?], 1864, GFP.

46. William Lloyd Garrison to EWG, Feb. 19, 1864, in *Let the Oppressed Go Free, 1861–1867*, ed. Walter M. Merrill, vol. 5 of *The Letters of William Lloyd Garrison*, (Cambridge: Harvard University Press, Belknap Press, 1979), 188.

47. LCM to WLG Jr., Mar. 4, 1864, GFP (copy by MCW).

48. MCW to LCM, Aug. 20, 1864, GFP.

49. SBA to EWG, Aug. 9, 1864, GFP.

50. Samuel J. May to WLG Jr., Aug. 1864, GFP.

51. MCW to EWG, Oct. 13, 1864, GFP. The Hasty Pudding Society was formed at Harvard in 1795 and started producing its annual theatrical productions in 1844.

52. MCW to DW, Apr. 9, 1864, GFP.

53. For the attitude of abolitionists toward Lincoln, see James M. McPherson, *The Struggle for Equality: Abolitionsts and the Negro in the Civil War and Reconstruction* (Princeton: Princeton University Press, 1964); Bartlett, *Wendell Phillips*; Mayer, *All on Fire*.

54. MCW to EWO, Aug. 10, 1862, OFP.

55. MCW to DW, Mar. 27, 1864, OFP.

56. For discussion of the split in abolitionist ranks over the reelection of Lincoln, see sources listed in n. 50. For the response of Stanton and Anthony, see by Wendy Hamand Venet, *Neither Ballots nor Bullets: Women Abolitionists and the Civil War* (Charlottsville: University Press of Virginia, 1991).

57. MCW to EWG, Oct. 13, 1864, GFP.

58. MCW to FW, Apr. 11, 1865, GFP.

59. Quoted in Mayer, *All on Fire*.

60. MCW to WLG Jr., Apr. 12, 1865, GFP.

61. The varying responses of abolitionist women to the Civil War have been described in Mary Elizabeth Massey, *Bonnet Brigades* (New York: Knopf, 1966). and Venet, *Neither Ballots nor Bullets*. Both books include several references to Martha Wright's letters.

62. MCW to WPW, Apr. 1, 1865, GFP.

63. MCW to MPM, May 4, 1865, GFP.

64. Ibid.

Chapter 12

1. DW to WPW, June 9, 1866, GFP.

2. MCW to DW, July 20, 1866, GFP.

3. Among the papers in GFP is a flyer headed "BASE BALL!" It announces, "The undersigned has been appointed Sole Agent, in Central and Western New York, for the celebrated ROSS BALL. The careful manner in which these Balls are made, and the wonderful elasticity they possess, have given them the place they rightly deserve among first-class clubs." After listing various clubs using these balls, the flyer concludes, "All orders will be promptly attended to by Yours Truly, F. WRIGHT."

4. MCW to EWG, May 12, 1867, GFP.

5. MCW Diary, Jan. 27, 1868, GFP.

6. MCW to LCM, July 5, 1865, GFP.

7. The treaty for the acquisition of Alaska was signed by Seward in March 1867. Although the price of $7.2 million amounted to only $.02 an acre, there was widespread opposition, and the treaty was approved by Congress in July 1868 only after extensive political maneuvering. See Glyndon Y. Van Deusen, *William Henry Seward* (New York: Oxford University Press, 1967); and John M. Taylor, *William Henry Seward: Lincoln's Right Hand* (New York: HarperCollins, 1991).

8. MCW to ECS, *The Revolution*, Aug. 27, 1868, S/A-MF.

9. MCW to EWG, Sept. 24, 1868, GFP.

10. DW to WPW, June 4, 1868, GFP. David argued about Florida: "It is going to be profitable to raise oranges, lemons, limes etc. for the City markets. The territory within which such fruits can be raised is so limited and the market so large and increasing that there can be no danger of low prices *ever*."

11. MCW to WPW, July 14, 1869, GFP. This wedding blessing is commonly attributed to Lucretia Mott, which accounts for Martha's use of quotation marks.

12. MCW to EWG, Oct. 31, 1869, GFP.

13. ECS to MCW, June 19, 1872, GFP and S/A 2: 513.

14. MCW to ECS, June 21, 1872, GFP.

15. MCW to EWG, Oct. 31, 1869, GFP. Much of this letter appears in Gerda Lerner, *The Female Experience: An American Documentary* (Indianapolis: Bobbs-Merrill, 1977).

16. LCM to MCW, Nov. 12, 1869, GFP.

17. We are grateful to Jean Humez, author of *Harriet Tubman: The Life and the Life Stories*, (Madison: University of Wisconsin Press, 2003), for discussions about the close relationship between Martha Wright and Harriet Tubman.

18. MCW to MPM, Nov. 9, 1865, GFP.

19. MCW to LCM, Apr. 16, 1866, GFP.

20. MCW to WLG Jr., Nov. 24, 1868, GFP.

21. MCW to EWG, Dec. 16, 1868, GFP.

22. MCW diaries, various dates in late 1860s and early 1870s, GFP.

23. MCW to EWG, Sept. 6, 1867, GFP.

24. MCW to WLG Jr., Jan. 10, 1869, GFP.

25. DW to MCW, Dec. 16, 1865, GFP.

26. MCW to MPM, May 13, 1865, GFP.

27. "Abolitionists' commitment to women's rights was a casualty of their new political strategy and relationship to the Republican party." Ellen Carol DuBois, *Feminism and Suffrage: The Emergence of an Independent Woman's Movement*, 1848–1869 (Ithaca: Cornell University Press, 1978), 59.

28. ECS to Wendell Phillips, Jan. 12, 1866, S/A 1: 570.

29. ECS to MCW, Jan. 6, 1866, quoted in Theodore Stanton and Harriott Stanton Blatch, eds., *Elizabeth Cady Stanton* (New York: Arno and New York Times, 1969).

30. ECS to MCW, Jan. 20, 1866, quoted in Stanton and Blatch, *Elizabeth Cady Stanton*.

31. *HWS*, 2: 171.

32. Ibid., 175.

33. MCW to DW, June 3, 1866, GFP.

34. Martha sent "a draft for $30—ten from our daughter Eliza, ten from Wil-

liam and Ellen, and ten from myself." MCW to Parker Pillsbury, Sept. 17, 1867, *HWS*, 2: 240.

35. Kathleen Barry presents evidence that the decision to use Train originated not with Anthony but with Lucy Stone's husband, Henry Blackwell, and Kansas senator Samuel N. Wood. This evidence is important, since Blackwell later used Anthony's alliance with Train as a major argument for forming a second woman suffrage association in competition with the one led by Anthony and Stanton. Barry, *Susan B. Anthony: a Singular Feminist* (New York: New York University Press, 1988), chap. 8.

36. MCW to ECS, Feb. 20, 1868, GFP.

37. MCW to DW, Dec. 12, 1867, GFP.

38. S/A-MF includes the complete run of the *Revolution*.

39. For example, in a letter to the editor of the *National Anti-Slavery Standard* in December 1865, Stanton attacked the idea that this was only "the negro's hour." She wrote, "The representative women of the nation have done their uttermost for the last thirty years to secure freedom for the negro, and so long as he was lowest in the scale of being we were willing to press *his* claims; but now, as the celestial gate to civil rights is slowly moving on its hinges, it becomes a serious question whether we had better stand aside and see "Sambo" walk into the kingdom first." S/A 1: 564.

40. The role of the Republican Party in this controversy is discussed in Melanie Susan Gustafson, *Women and the Republican Party* (Urban: University of Illinois Press, 2001).

41. "Woman Suffrage," *New York World*, Nov. 21, 1868, 5, quoted in DuBois, *Feminism and Suffrage*, 188. Frederick Douglass's citing of Howe's statement appears in *HWS*, 2: 382, and in Geoffrey C. Ward and Ken Burns, *Not for Ourselves Alone* (New York: Knopf, 1999), 119. Howe and her allies supporting Negro suffrage now, woman suffrage later, had no idea that women would have to wait another fifty-two years for woman suffrage.

42. MCW to LCM, May 30, 1868, GFP.

43. MCW to Anna Brown, Aug. 1, 1868, GFP. The "Kilkenny cats" are proverbial cats in Ireland who fought each other until their mutual destruction. One form of the traditional limerick:

> There once were two cats in Kilkenny
> Each thought that was one cat too many

They fought and they hit, they scratched and they bit
Till, excepting their nails and the tips of their tails,
Instead of two cats, there weren't any.

44. MCW to DW, Jan. 27, 1869, GFP.

45. Ibid.

46. MCW to EWG, Jan. 25, 1869, GFP.

47. This divisive 1869 meeting is described in most accounts of the nineteenth-century woman suffrage movement, including *HWS*, 2: 378–98.

48. Douglass's famous remarks on this controversy appear in numerous sources, including *HWS*, 2: 382; Ward and Burns, *Not for Ourselves Alone*, 119; and Eleanor Flexner, *Century of Struggle: The Woman's Rights Movement in the United States* (New York: Atheneum, 1959), 144.

49. Limited records of the New York Woman Suffrage Association, including related newspaper clippings, exist on microfilm. The years covered are 1869, 1870, and 1876–93. The officers listed for 1869 include Martha as president, Matilda Joslyn Gage as secretary and treasurer, and thirty vice presidents, including Eliza Wright Osborne. We are grateful to Sally Roesch Wagner, executive director of the Matilda Joslyn Gage Foundation, for loaning us this film.

50. MCW to Lucy Stone, Aug. 22, 1869, GFP.

51. Henry Blackwell to MCW, Nov. 6, 1869, GFP.

52. MCW to Henry Blackwell, Nov. 13, 1869, GFP.

53. Henry Blackwell to MCW, Dec. 16, 1869, GFP.

54. MCW to Henry Blackwell, Jan. 1, 1870, GFP. The letters between Martha Wright and Henry Blackwell on reasons for the split are quoted and discussed by Robert Riegel in "The Split of the Feminist Movement in 1869," *Mississippi Valley Historical Review* 49 (1962): 485–96.

55. Parker Pillsbury to MCW, Nov. 24, 1869, GFP.

56. MCW to EWG, Apr. 14, 1870, GFP.

57. Eleanor Flexner (*Century of Struggle*, 153) argues that the reason for the split was simply "deeply opposing social viewpoints—the conservative and the radical—which clashed, not on whether women should vote, but on *how* that vote should be won." Although many historians suggest that the split hurt the suffrage cause, Ellen Carol Dubois (*Feminism and Suffrage*, 200–201) argues instead that it "significantly advanced the movement, liberated it from its subservience to abolitionism, and pro-

pelled it into political independence." Robert Riegel, ("Split of the Feminist Movement 493)," discusses in depth the various issues that divided the women's movement, including the unfortunate prior association of Stanton and Anthony with the racist Train, which offended many. He concludes, however, that "most basically—and sadly—the split arose from personal frictions, which involved a struggle for power," and that "Mrs. Stone was the center of disaffection, and that she felt more than a little hurt at not being consulted more frequently about the management of the movement, and resented her lack of power."

Chapter 13

1. For details of the January 1869 Washington convention, see the *Revolution,* Jan. 28, 1869, S/A-MF.

2. *Revolution,* Feb. 4, 1869, 66, S/A-MF.

3. The January 1870 convention is described in the *Revolution,* Jan. 27, 1870, 52–55, S/A-MF, which includes several remarks made from the chair by Martha Wright. When Martha introduced Anthony as "one of the hardest workers for the cause," Anthony "objected to the manner of introduction, remarking that she would prefer to have her obituaries spoken after her demise."

4. MCW to EWG, Jan. 26, 1870, GFP.

5. *HWS,* 2: 420.

6. The hearing before the Joint District Committees of the Senate and House is described in the *Revolution,* Jan. 27, 1870, 58, S/A-MF

7. MCW to DW, Jan. 24, 1870, GFP.

8. Ibid. We have not located this group photograph, which is probably among the many early Brady plates that were lost.

9. MCW to LCM, Apr. 4, 1870, OFP.

10. "The Vexed Question" by "M" appeared in the *Nation,* Mar. 24 and 31 and Apr. 14, 1870, and Martha Wright's reply on Apr. 7, 1870.

11. *New York Times,* Oct. 22, 1870.

12. Account of 1870 Decade Meeting in Paulina Wright Davis, comp., *A History of the National Woman's Rights Movement for Twenty Years* (1871; reprint, New York: Source Book Press, 1970), 26.

13. *Nation*, Oct. 27, 1870, based on article in *New York Times*, Oct. 22, 1870.

14. MCW to ECS, *Revolution*, Nov. 24, 1870, S/A-MF, quoted and responded to in the *Nation*, Dec. 1, 1870.

15. MCW to EWG, Dec. 14, 1870, GFP.

16. MCW's letter to the *Nation* quoted and responded to in the *Nation,* Dec. 22, 1870.

17. MCW to ECS, Dec. 14, 1870, GFP and S/A 2: 386. Martha is amused that Isabella Beecher Hooker is becoming prominent in the woman suffrage movement because her better-known half-sister, Catharine Beecher, publicly opposed woman suffrage. Despite her opposition to suffrage for women, Catharine Beecher strongly encouraged women's education and an expansion of women's role in society. See Kathryn Kish Sklar, *Catharine Beecher: A Study in American Domesticity* (New York: W. W. Norton, 1976).

18. The interesting differences in the approaches of the three Beecher sisters to woman suffrage and women's rights is the focus of Jeanne Boydston, Mary Kelley, and Anne Margolis, *The Limits of Sisterhood: The Beecher Sisters on Women's Rights and Woman's Sphere* (Chapel Hill: University of North Carolina Press, 1988). The Beecher sisters are also featured prominently in Barbara Goldsmith, *Other Powers: The Age of Suffrage, Spiritualism, and the Scandalous Victoria Woodhull* (New York: Knopf, 1998).

19. Isabella Beecher Hooker to ECS, Nov. 25, 1870 (copy by MCW) GFP and S/A 2: 380.

20. Isabella Beecher Hooker to ECS, Dec. 21, 1870 (copy by MCW), GFP.

21. MCW to ECS, Dec. 14, 1870, GFP and S/A 2: 386.

22. MCW to ECS, Dec. 29, 1870, GFP and S/A-MF.

23. The colorful life of Victoria Woodhull has been the subject of many biographies, most recently Goldsmith, *Other Powers*. See also Woodhull biographies listed in Chapter 9, n. 40. The adjectives applied to Woodhull in the titles of these biographies include "notorious," "scandalous," "terrible," and "incredible." The title *Mrs. Satan* (by Joanna Johnston) is based on a famous cartoon by Thomas Nast published in *Harper's Weekly* picturing Woodhull with wings and horns, holding a banner reading "be saved by FREE LOVE," and the caption reading "Get thee behind me, Mrs. Satan." The conflicts around Woodhull were recently discussed in Amanda Frisken, "Sex in Politics: Victoria Woodhull as an American Public Woman, 1870–1876," *Journal of Woman's History* 12 (Spring 2000): 89–110; and Helen Lefkowitz Horowitz, "Victoria

Woodhull, Anthony Comstock, and Conflict over Sex in the United States in the 1870s," *Journal of American History* 87 (September 2000): 403—4.

24. MCW to EWG, Mar. 15, 1871, GFP.

25. MCW to EWO, Mar. 16, 1871, GFP.

26. MCW to DW, Mar. 24, 1871, GFP.

27. MCW to SBA, Apr. 6, 1871, GFP.

28. MCW to WLGJr., May 16, 1871, GFP.

29. Woodhull speech quoted in Goldsmith, *Other Powers*, 274.

30. MCW to EWG, May 14, 1871, GFP.

31. *Woman's Journal*, Nov. 5, 1870.

32. MCW to EWO, May 18, 1871, GFP.

33. MCW to SBA, May [?], 1871, S/A-MF

34. MCW to ECS, May 27, 1871, GFP.

35. MCW to EWG, May 14, 1871, GFP.

36. MCW to ECS, Mar. 3, 1872, GFP.

37. SBA to MCW, June 17, 1871, GFP.

38. ECS to MCW, June 19, 1871, GFP.

39. SBA to MCW, June 17, 1871, GFP.

40. MCW to DW, Sept. 9, 1838, GFP.

41. MCW to DW, May 18, 1845, GFP.

42. MCW to DW, June 13, 1866, GFP.

43. MCW diary, Aug. [?], 1871, GFP.

44. MCW to DW, Jan. 15, 1872, GFP.

45. SBA diary, May 11 and May 12, 1872, S/A 2: 494.

46. SBA to MCW, May 17, 1872, GFP and S/A 2: 495.

47. SBA to MCW, May 22, 1872, GFP and S/A 2: 496.

48. Ida Husted Harper, *The Life and Work of Susan B. Anthony* (Indianapolis: Hallenbeck Press, 1898), 1270.

49. Ibid., 467.

50. SBA to ECS, May 29, 1872, S/A 2: 497.

51. MCW to ECS, May 30, 1872, S/A 2: 499.

52. MCW to LCM, July 30, 1854, GFP.

53. Stanton, *Eighty Years*, 194.

54. MCW to LCM, Mar. 15, 1855, GFP.

55. MCW to EWG, May 14, 1873, GFP.

56. In this respect, Martha was like most of Stanton's other colleagues in reform, including Anthony. An exception was Lucretia, who usually addressed Stanton as "Elizabeth."

57. MCW to ECS, May 27, 1871, GFP.

58. From Woodhull's speech at the 1871 NWSA convention, quoted earlier and in Goldsmith, *Other Powers*, 274.

59. MCW to EWG, Mar. 26, 1873, GFP.

60. MCW to ECS, Mar. 22, 1872, GFP and S/A 2: 486.

61. MCW to EWG, May 23, 1873, GFP.

Chapter 14

1. MCW to EWG, Nov. 2, 1870, GFP. Much of this letter appears in Gerda Lerner, *The Female Experience: An American Documentary* (Indianapolis: Bobbs-Merrill, 1977).

2. MCW to EWG, Feb. 11, 1870, GFP.

3. MPM to MCW, Sept. 24, 1871, GFP.

4. MCW to SBA, July 27, 1872, GFP, and S/A-MF.

5. MCW to Thomas Wentworth Higginson, July [?], 1872, GFP.

6. MCW to LCM, June 25, 1865, GFP.

7. MCW to EWG, June 2, 1870, GFP.

8. MCW to EWG, Oct. 10, 1872, GFP.

9. David's eulogy to Seward, citing Seward's "higher law" and "irrepressible conflict" speeches as evidence of his importance in the antislavery movement, appears in the Oct. 14, 1872 issue of the *Auburn Daily Advertiser*, found in the American Antiquarian Society, Worcester, Mass.

10. MCW to EWG, Oct. 10, 1872, GFP. Harriet Hall was the wife of Dr. Edward Hall of Auburn, who had died two years earlier. Martha frequently refers to her in her letters, but only as "Mrs. Hall."

11. MCW to EWG, Nov. 8, 1872, GFP.

12. MCW to LCM, Mar. 11, 1844, GFP.

13. MCW to EWG, June 15, 1869, GFP.

14. MCW to ECS, Mar. 3, 1872, GFP.

15. "By 1870, 169 of America's 582 colleges and universities had become coed-

ucational." Jean V. Matthews, *Women's Struggle for Equality: The First Phase, 1828–1876* (Chicago: Ivan R. Dee, 1997), 176.

16. MCW to ECS, Sept. 4, 1872, GFP.

17. S/A 2: 505. For the reaction of various woman suffrage leaders to the Republican platform in 1872 and in subsequent elections, see Melanie Susan Gustafson, *Women and the Republican Party* (Urbana: University of Illinois Press, 2001). Although some took hope from the mention of "additional rights" for women in the 1872 platform, the Republican Party in future platforms continued to resist explicit support for woman suffrage.

18. MCW to SBA, July 27, 1872, GFP, and S/A-MF.

19. Henry Blackwell to SBA, Sept. 7, 1872, GFP.

20. MCW to SBA, Sept. 17, 1872, GFP.

21. MCW to EWG, Nov. 8, 1872, GFP.

22. DW to MCW, Nov. 5, 1872, GFP.

23. SBA to ECS, Nov. 5, 1872, S/A 2: 524.

24. SBA to MCW, Jan 1, 1873, GFP and S/A 2: 547.

25. MCW diary, Jan. 4, 1873, GFP.

26. MCW to EWG, May 14, 1873, GFP.

27. The 1840 split in the abolitionist movement is discussed briefly in Chapter 6, and the 1869 split in the woman's movement is discussed in depth in Chapter 12. Both splits are discussed by Kathryn Kish Sklar in *Women's Rights Emerges Within the Antislavery Movement 1830–1870: A Brief History with Documents* (Boston: Bedford/St. Martin's, 2000).

28. MCW to EWG, May 14, 1873, GFP

29. A "pinion" is a bird's wing.

30. MCW to LCM, Jan. 6, 1846, GFP.

31. MCW to LCM, June 12, 1865, GFP.

32. Martha's list of conundrums is in the back of a diary labeled 1872–1873, GFP.

33. ECS to MCW, Mar. 2, 1868, S/A-MF.

34. ECS memoir of MCW, 1890s, OFP.

35. Rev. Mellen to MCW, June 25, 1855, GFP.

36. MCW to LCM, September 8, 1855, GFP.

37. MCW to LCM, Jan. 14, 1858, GFP.

38. MCW to LCM, Dec. 3, 1858, GFP.

39. MCW to MPM, June 6, 1865, GFP.

40. MCW to DW, Aug. 7, 1873, GFP.

41. MCW to EWO, Aug. 10, 1862, GFP.

42. MCW to MPM, Jan. 1, 1868, GFP. Amos Bronson Alcott of Concord, Massachusetts, was an abolitionist, a supporter of woman's rights, founder of a short-lived utopian community (Fruitlands), and the father of the author Louisa May Alcott.

43. MCW to LCM, Dec. 11, 1873, GFP.

44. DW to MCW, Dec. 13, 1873, GFP.

45. MCW to DW, Jan. 10, 1874, GFP.

46. MCW to EWG, May 8, 1874, GFP.

47. MCW to WPW, May 25, 1867, GFP.

48. MCW to DW, Feb. 16, 1874, GFP.

49. MCW to DW, Jan. 10, 1874, GFP.

50. MCW quoted in EWO sketch of MCW life, GFP and OFP.

51. SBA to EWG, Jan. 22, 1875, S/A-MF.

52. *HWS* 2: 545.

53. MCW to ECS, Oct. 3, 1874, S/A 3: 113-15.

54. MCW to SBA, Nov. 29, 1873, GFP.

55. MCW to SBA, June 25, 1874, GFP, also in MCW diary, June 22, 1874, GFP.

56. MCW to EWG, June 27, 1874, GFP.

57. MCW to ECS, Oct. 3, 1874, S/A-MF.

58. MCW to EWG, Nov. 13, 1874, GFP.

59. MCW to WLG Jr., Oct. 20, 1874, GFP.

60. MCW to SBA, Dec. 6, 1874, GFP.

61. MCW to DW, Dec. 20, 1874, GFP.

62. WLG Jr. 2 to Wendell Garrison, Dec. 6, 1874, GFP.

63. Garrison's uncertainty about his birth year is noted by Henry Mayer in *All on Fire: William Lloyd Harrison and the Abolition of Slavery* (New York: St. Martin's Griffen, 1998), 36.

64. MCW to EWO, Dec. 15, 1874, GFP.

65. MCW to Lucy Stone, Dec. 21, 1874, GFP.

66. WLG to Wendell Garrison, Jan. 4, 1875, Garrison Collection, Boston Public Library.

67. MCW to Anna Davis Hallowell, Dec. 25, 1874, GFP.

68. MCW to DW, Dec. 25, 1874, GFP.

69. EWG to Maria Davis, Jan. 28, 1875, GFP.

70. DW to MCW, Dec. 29[?], 1874, GFP.

71. MCW quoted in EWO to Rev. Thomas Hartshorne, Jan. 26, 1882, GFP.

72. Martha's grave is in the eastern portion of Fort Hill Cemetery, in a region labeled "6" (Morning Side) on the map accessible on the Web at <www.rootsweb .com/~nycayuga/cem/cem1/fhmap.html>. The graves of William Henry Seward and Harriet Tubman are also in Fort Hill.

Chapter 15

1. ECS report of NWSA Washington convention, *Golden Age* (New York), Jan. 22, 1875, S/A-MF.

2. ECS memoir of MCW, 1890s, OFP.

3. SBA diary, January 1875, quoted in Ida Husted Harper, *The Life and Work of Susan B. Anthony,* (Indianapolis, Ind. Hallenbeck Press, 1898), 467.

4. SBA to EWG, Jan. 22, 1875, GFP, S/A-MF.

5. SBA to EWO, Nov. 3, 1875, GFP, S/A-MF, and quoted in EWO sketch of MCW's life, OFP and GFP.

6. MCW obituary by Lucy Stone, *Woman's Journal,* Jan. 9, 1875.

7. MCW obituary by WLG, *Woman's Journal*, Jan. 9, 1875.

8. MCW obituary, *New York Tribune*, Jan. 10, 1875.

9. MCW obituary, *Auburn Daily Advertiser*, Jan. 6, 1875.

10. Maria Davis to EWO, Jan. 12, 1875, GFP.

11. LCM to EWO, Jan 12, 1875, GFP and Beverly Wilson Palmer, ed., *Selected Letters of Lucretia Coffin Mott*, (Urbana: University of Illinois Press, 2002), 493.

12. A copy of David Wright's obituary in the *Auburn Daily Advertiser*, Feb. 25, 1897, was found in a vertical file in the county historian's office in Auburn. It describes his law business and his political and religious leanings and quotes an 1896 interview in which David remarked, "Lucretia Mott, the famous Quaker preacher and anti-slavery and woman's rights advocate was my wife's sister."

13. Quoted in Elizabeth Cady Stanton, *Eighty Years and More: Reminiscences, 1815–1897* (New York: Schocken Books, 1971), 437–38.

14. Margaret Hope Bacon records parts of two of Martha's poems read at an

1857 family party in Philadelphia and cites other books in which they were published. Bacon, *Valiant Friend: The Life of Lucretia Mott,* (New York: Walker, 1980), 165–66. A collection of Martha's poems, some clearly written for her children, can be found in a folder marked "poems" in GFP.

15. *Auburn Daily Advertiser,* Feb. 1852, MCW poems, GFP, *Revolution,* Feb. 24, 1870, S/A-MF.

16. An obituary of Ellen Wright Osborne called her a "lover of books and a woman of wide reading" and said "her home is filled with books and every chink and cranny contains a volume." *Auburn Citizen,* July 19, 1911, cited in Claire White Putala, "Reading and Writing Ourselves into Being—Then What? The Literacy of Certain Nineteenth-Century Women" (Ph.D. diss., Syracuse University, 1997), 3.

17. Rudolph W. Chamberlain spotlights Thomas Mott Osborne's work in prison reform. See Chamberlain, *There Is No Truce: A Life of Thomas Mott Osborne* (New York: Macmillan, 1935).

18. EWG to EWO, Dec. 9, 1879, GFP.

19. However, she was too ill to vote in 1920 and died soon thereafter. One female signer at Seneca Falls did live to vote. New York had granted woman suffrage in 1917, and on the first Tuesday in November 1918, 102-year-old Rhoda Palmer was driven to the polls to vote. She died in August 1919, two weeks before Congress passed the Nineteenth Amendment and a year before its ratification. Her local newspaper noted, "Her one wish that she would live to vote was realized." *Geneva Daily Times,* Aug. 11, 1919. We are grateful to Judith Wellman for information on Charlotte Woodward Pierce and Rhoda Palmer.

20. Charlotte Woodward Pierce to LCM, Oct. 18, 1871, Mott Manuscripts, Friends Historical Library, Swarthmore College, Swarthmore, Pa.

21. MCW to EWG, Nov. 25, 1869, GFP.

22. Mabel Channing Wright Livingston to James Gould, Sept. 22, 1962, GFP.

23. EWO memoir of MCW, OFP and GFP.

24. MCW to LCM, Nov. 28, 1867, GFP.

25. Robert E. Riegel, *American Feminists* (Lawrence: University Press of Kansas, 1968), 23–24.

26. Christine Bolt, *The Women's Movement in the United States and Britain from the 1790s to the 1920s* (New York: Harvester Wheatsheaf, 1993), 82.

27. Blanch Glassman Hersh, *The Slavery of Sex: Feminist-Abolitionists in America* (Urbana: University of Illinois Press, 1978), 162.

28. MCW obituary by WLG, *Woman's Journal*, Jan. 9, 1875.

29. Barbara Welter, *Dimity Convictions: The American Woman in the Nineteenth Century* (Athens: Ohio University Press, 1976), 21.

30. DW autobiography, GFP.

31. ECS memoir of MCW, 1890s, OFP.

32. As Jean Matthews notes, the use of "strong-minded" as an epithet for women in Martha's day suggests that men felt the true feminine woman should be weak-minded! see Matthew, *Women's Struggle for Equality: The First Phase, 1828–1876* (Chicago: Ivan R. Dec., 1997.

33. MCW to Charles Pelham, 1856, copied for EWO, OFP.

34. George Bernard Shaw, *Nine Plays*. New York: Dodd, Mead & Co., 1947: 739. (From "The Revolutionist's Handbook," in *Man and Superman*).

35. DW to MCW, Mar. 1, 1874, GFP.

Bibliography

Primary Sources

An important resource that contains much primary material is the six-volume *History of Woman Suffrage* (*HWS*), edited by Elizabeth Cady Stanton, Susan B. Anthony, and Matilda Joslyn Gage. Another important source is the papers of Elizabeth Cady Stanton and Susan B. Anthony edited by Ann D. Gordon (S/A 1; S/A 2; S/A 3) and the more inclusive microfilm (S/A-MF).

The Garrison Family Papers (GFP) in the Sophia Smith Collection of Smith College include over fifteen hundred letters written by Martha Coffin Wright and most of her diaries, as well as poems, photographs, paintings, letters written to Martha, correspondence of family members, an autobiography and a biography of David Wright, a twenty-one-page typescript of a sketch of Martha's life written in the 1890s by her daughter Eliza Wright Osborne, and a four-page handwritten sketch of Martha's life by an unknown author. Many of the letters written to Martha Wright by her sister Lucretia Mott are included in the collection, but many others are in the Mott Manuscripts, Friends Historical Library, Swarthmore College, Swarthmore, Pennsylvania.

Also very important to our research were the Osborne Family Papers (OFP) in the Department of Special Collections, Syracuse University Library. This collection includes extensive correspondence of the Osbornes, of Martha and David

Wright, and of Peter Pelham (with letters and other documents from as early as 1814), as well as one diary of Martha's, David's account book, an account book of the Aurora school managed by Anna Coffin, handwritten copies of Eliza Wright Osborne's sketch of Martha's life, and a four-page memoir of Martha written by Elizabeth Cady Stanton. Among the many photographs in the collection is one of the Wright home at 192 Genesee Street, Auburn, New York. Many legal and financial papers of David Wright's are in David Wright Papers, Manuscripts and Special Collections, New York State Library, Albany, and in the Cayuga Museum in Auburn.

OTHER MANUSCRIPT COLLECTIONS

Caroline Dall Papers, Massachusetts Historical Society, Boston
Edward Dromgoole and William Pelham Papers, Southern Historical Collection, University of North Carolina at Chapel Hill.
Abby Kelley Foster and Wendell Phillips Papers, American Antiquarian Society, Worcester, Massachusetts
Matilda Joslyn Gage and Alma Lutz Collections, Schlesinger Library, Cambridge, Massachusetts
William Lloyd Garrison and Antislavery Collections, Boston Public Library
Isabella Beecher Hooker Papers, Stowe-Day Library, Hartford, Connecticut
Dale L. Morgan Papers, Bancroft Library, University of California, Berkeley
Isaac and Amy Post Papers and William Henry Seward Papers, Rush Rhees Library, University of Rochester, New York
Gerrit Smith Papers, Syracuse University, Syracuse, New York.

NEWSPAPERS

Albany (N.Y.) Argus
Albany (N.Y.) Evening Journal
Auburn (N.Y.) Daily Advertiser
Auburn (N.Y.) Democrat
Cayuga (N.Y.) Chief
The Liberator
The Nation

National Anti-Slavery Standard
New York Times
New York Tribune
New-York World
North Star
The Revolution
United States Gazette
Woman's Journal

SOURCES CONTAINING MARTHA WRIGHT CORRESPONDENCE

Cott, Nancy F., Jeanne Boydston, Ann Braude, Lori D. Ginzberg, and Molly Ladd-Taylor, eds. *Root of Bitterness: Documents of the Social History of American Women.* Boston: Northeastern University Press, 1996.

Lerner, Gerda. *The Female Experience: An American Documentary.* Indianapolis: Bobbs-Merrill, 1977.

Merrill, Walter M., ed. *Let the Oppressed Go Free, 1861–1867.* Vol. 5 of *The Letters of William Lloyd Garrison.* Cambridge: Harvard University Press, Belknap Press, 1979.

Palmer, Beverly Wilson, ed. *Selected Letters of Lucretia Coffin Mott.* Urbana: University of Illinois Press, 2002.

Secondary Sources

ARTICLES ON MARTHA WRIGHT

Cuddy, Michael J. Jr. "Martha Coffin Wright and Eliza Wright Osborne: Mother and Daughter Helped Launch Woman's Rights Movement." In *Bicentennial Portraits: Noteworthy Sons and Daughters of Auburn, New York.* Auburn: Jacobs Press, 1993.

Hoblitzelle, Anne L. *The Ambivalent Message: Sex-Role Training in Mid-Nineteenth-Century United States as Reflected in the Correspondence of Martha Coffin Wright to Ellen Wright Garrison.* Master's thesis, Sarah Lawrence College, 1974.

Livingston, James D. "The Gallant Pelhams and Their Abolitionist Kin." *Civil War Times,* October 2003, 20.

Messbarger, Paul. "Martha Coffin Pelham Wright (1806–1875)." In *Notable American Women: A Biographical Dictionary,* edited by Edward T. James, 3:684–85. Cambridge: Harvard University Press, Belknap Press, 1971.

Nutter, Kathleen Banks. "Martha Coffin Pelham Wright." In *American National Biography,* edited by John A. Garrity and Mark C. Carnes, 4:44–45. Oxford: Oxford University Press, 1999.

Penney, Sherry H., and James D. Livingston. "Expectant at Seneca Falls." *New York History,* Winter 2003, 32–49.

———. "Hints for Wives—and Husbands." *Journal of Women's History* 15 (Summer 2003): 180–87.

———. "How Did Abolitionist Women and Their Slaveholding Relatives Negotiate Their Differences over the Issue of Slavery?" *Women and Social Movements in the United States, 1775–2000.* Center for the Historical Study of Women and Gender at State University of New York, Binghamton <http://womhist.binghamton.edu/mcw/doclist.htm> (July 2003).

Putala, Claire White. "Reading and Writing Ourselves into Being—Then What? The Literacy of Certain Nineteenth-Century Women." Ph.D. diss., Syracuse University, 1997. This thesis is based on family letters, including Martha's, in OFP.

———. *Reading and Writing Ourselves into Being: The Literacy of Certain Nineteenth-Century Young Women.* Greenwich, Conn.: Information Age Publishing, forthcoming 2004.

Shosa, Martha J. "Martha Coffin Wright: Auburn's Pioneer in Women's Rights." *Local History Notes, Newsletter of Cayuga Museum, Auburn,* August–September 1995.

BIOGRAPHIES

Lucretia Mott

Bacon, Margaret Hope. *Valiant Friend: The Life of Lucretia Mott.* New York: Walker, 1980.

Cromwell, Otelia. *Lucretia Mott.* Cambridge: Harvard University Press, 1958.

BIBLIOGRAPHY

Hallowell, Anna Davis. *James and Lucretia Mott: Life and Letters*. Boston: Houghton, Mifflin, 1884.

Hare, Lloyd C. M. *The Greatest American Woman: Lucretia Mott*. New York: American Historical Society, 1937.

Sterling, Dorothy. *Lucretia Mott: Gentle Warrior*. Garden City, N.Y.: Doubleday, 1964.

Elizabeth Cady Stanton

Banner, Lois W. *Elizabeth Cady Stanton: A Radical for Woman's Rights*. Boston: Little, Brown, 1980.

Griffith, Elisabeth. *In Her Own Right: The Life of Elizabeth Cady Stanton*. Oxford: Oxford University Press, 1984.

Lutz, Alma. *Created Equal: A Biography of Elizabeth Cady Stanton*. New York: John Day, 1940.

Stanton, Elizabeth Cady. *Eighty Years and More: Reminiscences, 1815–1897*. New York: Schocken Books, 1971.

Stanton, Theodore, and Harriot Stanton Blatch, eds. *Elizabeth Cady Stanton*. New York: Arno and New York Times, 1969.

Susan B. Anthony

Anthony, Katherine. *Susan B. Anthony*. Garden City, N.Y.: Doubleday, 1954.

Barry, Kathleen. *Susan B. Anthony: A Singular Feminist*. New York: New York University Press, 1988.

Dorr, Rheta C. *Susan B. Anthony*. New York: Stokes, 1928.

Harper, Ida Husted. *The Life and Work of Susan B. Anthony*. Indianapolis, Ind.: Hallenbeck Press, 1898.

Harper, Judith. *Susan B. Anthony: A Biographical Companion*. Santa Barbara: ABC-CLIO, 1998.

Lutz, Alma. *Susan B. Anthony: Rebel, Crusader, Humanitarian*. Boston: Beacon Press, 1959.

Sherr, Lynn. *Failure Is Impossible: Susan B. Anthony in Her Own Words*. New York: Random House, 1995.

Other Woman's Rights Leaders

Blackwell, Alice Stone. *Lucy Stone, Pioneer of Woman's Rights*. Boston: Little, Brown, 1930.

Brammer, Leila R. *Excluded from Suffrage History: Matilda Joslyn Gage, Nineteenth-Century American Feminist*. Westport, Conn.: Greenwood Press, 2000.

Coté, Charlotte. *Olympia Brown: The Battle for Equality*. Racine, Wis.: Mother Courage Press, 1988.

Gabriel, Mary. *Notorious Victoria: The Life of Victoria Woodhull, Uncensored*. Chapel Hill, N.C.: Algonquin Books, 1998.

Goldsmith, Barbara. *Other Powers: The Age of Suffrage, Spiritualism, and the Scandalous Victoria Woodhull*. New York: Knopf, 1998.

Hays, Elinor Rice. *Morning Star: A Biography of Lucy Stone, 1818–1893*. New York: Harcourt, Brace, 1961.

Johnston, Joanna. *Mrs. Satan: The Incredible Saga of Victoria C. Woodhull*. New York: Putnam, 1967.

Kerr, Andrea Moore. *Lucy Stone: Speaking Out for Equality*. New Brunswick, N.J.: Rutgers University Press, 1995.

Kolmerten, Carol A. *The American Life of Ernestine L. Rose*. Syracuse, N.Y.: Syracuse University Press, 1999.

Lerner, Gerda. *The Grimké Sisters from South Carolina: Pioneers for Woman's Rights and Abolition*. New York: Schocken Books, 1971.

Marberry, M. M. *Vicky: A Biography of Victoria C. Woodhull*. New York: Funk & Wagnall's, 1967.

Million, Joelle. *Women's Voice, Women's Place: Lucy Stone and the Birth of Women's Rights*. Westport, Conn.: Praeger, 2003.

Parton, James, et al. *Eminent Women of the Age, being narratives of the lives and deeds of the most prominent women of the present generation*. Chicago: Betts, 1868.

Sachs, Eminie. *The Terrible Siren: Victoria Woodhull, 1838–1927*. New York: Harper, 1978.

Sklar, Kathryn Kish. *Catharine Beecher: A Study in American Domesticity*. New York: W. W. Norton, 1976.

Suhl, Yori. *Eloquent Crusader, Ernestine Rose*. New York: Julian Messner, 1970.

———. *Ernestine L. Rose and the Battle for Human Rights*. New York: Reynal, 1959.

Underhill, Lois Beachy. *The Woman Who Ran for President: The Many Lives of Victoria Woodhull*. Binghamton, N.Y.: Bridge, 1995.

BIBLIOGRAPHY

Antislavery Leaders

Abzug, Robert H. *Passionate Liberator: Theodore Dwight Weld and the Dilemma of Reform.* New York: Oxford University Press, 1980.

Baker, George E. *The Life of William Henry Seward with Selections from His Works.* New York: Redfield, 1855.

Bartlett, Irving H. *Wendell Phillips: Brahmin Radical.* Boston: Beacon Press, 1961.

Clinton, Catherine. *Harriet Tubman: The Road to Freedom.* Boston: Little, Brown, 2004.

Conrad, Earl. *The Governor and His Lady: The Story of William Henry Seward and His Wife Frances.* New York: G. O. Putnam, 1960.

————. *Harriet Tubman.* Washington: Associated Publishers, 1943.

Humez, Jean. *Harriet Tubman: The Life and the Life Stories.* Madison: University of Wisconsin Press, 2003.

Larson, Kate Clifford. *Bound for the Promised Land: Harriet Tubman, Portrait of an American Hero.* New York: Ballantine Books, 2004.

Mayer, Henry. *All on Fire: William Lloyd Garrison and the Abolition of Slavery.* New York: St. Martin's, Griffin, 1998.

McFeely, William S. *Frederick Douglass.* New York: Norton, 1991.

Robertson, Stacey M. *Parker Pillsbury: Radical Abolitionist, Male Feminist.* Ithaca: Cornell University Press, 2000.

Taylor, John M. *William Henry Seward: Lincoln's Right Hand.* New York: HarperCollins, 1991.

Thomas, Benjamin P. *Theodore Dwight Weld, Crusader for Freedom.* New Brunswick, N.J.: Rutgers University Press, 1950.

Van Deusen, Glyndon G. *William Henry Seward.* New York: Oxford University Press, 1967.

Wells, Anna Mary. *Dear Preceptor: The Life and Times of Thomas Wentworth Higginson.* Boston: Houghton Mifflin, 1963.

Winch, Julie. *A Gentleman of Color: The Life of James Forten.* Oxford: Oxford University Press, 2002.

Yacavone, Donald. *Samuel Joseph May and the Dilemmas of the Liberal Persuasion, 1797–1871.* Philadelphia: Temple University Press, 1991.

98

BIBLIOGRAPHY

John Pelham

Hassler, William W. *Colonel John Pelham: Lee's Boy Artillerist*. Chapel Hill: University of North Carolina Press, 1960.

Mercer, Philip. *The Life of the Gallant Pelham*. Kennesaw, Ga.: Continental Book, 1958

Milham, Charles G. *Gallant Pelham: American Extraordinary*. Washington, D.C.: Public Affairs Press, 1959.

WOMAN'S RIGHTS AND ABOLITION MOVEMENTS

Alonso, Harriet. *Growing Up Abolitionist: The Story of the Garrison Children*. Amherst: University of Massachusetts Press, 2002.

Bacon, Margaret Hope. *Mothers of Feminism: The Story of Quaker Women in America*. San Francisco: Harper & Row, 1986.

Blockson, Charles L. *The Underground Railroad*. New York: Prentice Hall, 1987.

Bolt, Christine. *The Women's Movement in the United States and Britain from the 1790s to the 1920s*. New York: Harvester Wheatsheaf, 1993.

Boydston, Jeanne. *Home and Work: Housework, Wages, and the Ideology of Labor in the Early Republic*. New York: Oxford University Press, 1990.

Boydston, Jeanne, Mary Kelley, and Anne Margolis. *The Limits of Sisterhood: The Beecher Sisters on Women's Rights and Woman's Sphere*. Chapel Hill: University of North Carolina Press, 1988.

Boylan, Anne M. *The Origins of Women's Activism: New York and Boston, 1797–1840*. Chapel Hill: University of North Carolina Press, 2002.

Braude, Ann. *Radical Spirits: Spiritualism and Woman's Rights in Nineteenth-Century America*. Boston: Beacon Press, 1989.

Butterfield, L. H., et al. *The Book of Abigail and John: Selected Letters of the Adams Family, 1762–1784*. Cambridge: Harvard University Press, 1975.

Chammas, Carole. "Re-Assessing the Married Women's Property Acts." *Journal of Women's History* 6 (Spring 1996): 9–30.

Cogan, Jacob Katz, and Lori D. Ginzberg. "1846 Petition for Women's Suffrage, New York State Constitutional Convention." *Signs* 22 (Winter 1997): 427–38.

Davis, Paulina W., comp. *A History of the National Woman's Rights Movement for Twenty Years*. 1871. Reprint, New York: Source Book Press, 1970.

BIBLIOGRAPHY

Densmore, Christopher. "The Quaker Tradition: Sustaining Women's Rights." Paper prepared for National Women's Studies Association annual meeting, Oswego, N.Y., 1998. Available at <http://ubib.buffalo.edu/libraries/uinits/archives/urr/NWSA.html>.

Dixon, Chris. *Perfecting the Family: Antislavery Marriages in Nineteenth-Century America.* Amherst: University of Massachusetts Press, 1997.

DuBois, Ellen Carol. *Feminism and Suffrage: The Emergence of an Independent Woman's Movement, 1848–1869.* Ithaca: Cornell University Press, 1978.

———. *Woman Suffrage and Woman's Rights.* New York: New York University Press, 1998.

Fischer, Gayle V. *Pantaloons and Power: A Nineteenth-Century Dress Reform in the United States.* Kent, Ohio: Kent State University Press, 2001.

Flexner, Eleanor. *Century of Struggle: The Woman's Rights Movement in the United States.* New York: Atheneum, 1959.

Frisken, Amanda. "Sex in Politics: Victoria Woodhull as an American Public Woman, 1870–1876." *Journal of Woman's History* 12 (Spring 2000): 89–110.

Ginzburg, Lori. *Women in Antebellum Reform.* Wheeling, Ill.: Harlan Davidson, 2000.

Gurko, Miriam. *The Ladies of Seneca Falls.* New York: Schocken Books, 1974.

Gustafson, Melanie Susan. *Women and the Republican Party.* Urbana: University of Illinois Press, 2001.

Hartog, Hendrik. *Man and Wife in America: A History.* Cambridge: Harvard University Press, 2000.

Hawke, Andrea Constantine. "'Feeling a Strong Desire to Tread a Broader Road to Fortune': The Antebellum Evolution of Elizabeth Wilson McClintock's Entrepreneurial Consciousness." Master's thesis, University of Maine, 1995.

Hersh, Blanche Glassman. *The Slavery of Sex: Feminist-Abolitionists in America.* Urbana: University of Illinois Press, 1978.

Hewitt, Nancy. *Women's Activism and Social Change: Rochester, New York, 1822–1872.* Ithaca: Cornell University Press, 1984.

Hoffert, Sylvia D. *When Hens Crow: The Woman's Rights Movement in Antebellum America.* Indianapolis: Indiana University Press, 1995.

Horowitz, Helen Lefkowitz. "Victoria Woodhull, Anthony Comstock, and Conflict over Sex in the United States in the 1870s." *Journal of American History* 87 (September 2000): 403–4.

Isenberg, Nancy. "'Pillars in the Same Temple and Priests of the Same Worship':

Woman's Rights and the Politics of Church and State in Antebellum America."
Journal of American History. 85 (June 1998): 98–128.

―――――. *Sex and Citizenship in Antebellum America.* Chapel Hill: University of North Carolina Press, 1998.

Kerber, Linda K., and Jane Sherron De Hart, eds.. *Women's America: Refocusing the Past.* 5th ed. New York: Oxford University Press, 2000.

Massey, Mary Elizabeth. *Bonnet Brigades.* New York: Knopf, 1966.

Matthews, Jean V. *Women's Struggle for Equality: The First Phase, 1828–1876.* Chicago: Ivan R. Dee, 1997.

McKivigan, John R. *The War Against Proslavery Religion: Abolitionism and the Northern Churches, 1830–1865.* Ithaca: Cornell University Press, 1984.

McKivigan, John R., and Stanley Harrold, eds. *Antislavery Violence: Sectional, Racial, and Cultural Conflict in Antebellum America.* Knoxville: University of Tennessee Press, 1999.

McPherson, James M. *The Struggle for Equality: Abolitionists and the Negro in the Civil War and Reconstruction.* Princeton: Princeton University Press, 1964.

Pease, William H., and Jane H. Pease, eds. *The Antislavery Argument.* Indianapolis: Bobbs-Merrill, 1965.

Quarles, Benjamin. *Black Abolitionists.* Oxford: Oxford University Press, 1969.

Richards, Leonard L. *"Gentlemen of Property and Standing": Anti-Abolition Mobs in Jacksonian America.* Oxford: Oxford University Press, 1970.

Riegel, Robert E. *American Feminists.* Lawrence: University Press of Kansas, 1968.

―――――. *American Women: A Story of Social Change.* Rutherford: Fairleigh Dickinson University Press, 1970.

―――――. "The Split of the Feminist Movement in 1869." *Mississippi Valley Historical Review* 49 (December 1962): 485–96.

Ruchames, Louis. *The Abolitionists: A Collection of Their Writings.* New York: Capricorn Books, 1964.

Russo, Ann, and Cheris Kramarae, eds. *The Radical Women's Press of the 1850s.* New York: Routledge, 1991.

Salmon, Marylynn. *Women and the Law of Property in Early America.* Chapel Hill: University of North Carolina Press, 1986.

Simler-Lewis, Janice. "The Forten-Purvis Women of Philadelphia and the American Anti-Slavery Crusade." *Journal of Negro History* 66 (Winter 1981): 281–88.

Sinclair, Andrew. *The Emancipation of the American Woman*. New York: Harper & Row, 1966.

Sklar, Kathryn Kish. *Women's Rights Emerges Within the Antislavery Movement, 1830–1870: A Brief History with Documents*. Boston: Bedford/St. Martin's, 2000.

Stewart, James Brewer. *Holy Warriors: The Abolitionists and American Slavery*. New York: Hill and Wang, 1976.

Taylor, Barbara. *Mary Wollstonecraft and the Feminist Imagination*. Cambridge: Cambridge University Press, 2003.

Terborg-Penn, Rosalyn. *African American Women in the Struggle for the Vote, 1850–1920*. Indianapolis: Indiana University Press, 1998.

Venet, Wendy Hamand. *Neither Ballots nor Bullets: Women Abolitionists and the Civil War*. Charlottesville: University Press of Virginia, 1991.

Walters, Ronald G. *American Reformers, 1815–1860*. New York: Hill andWang, 1978.

Warbasse, Elizabeth Bowles. *The Changing Legal Rights of Married Women, 1800–1861*. New York: Garland, 1987.

Ward, Geoffrey C., and Ken Burns. *Not for Ourselves Alone*. New York: Knopf, 1999.

Weatherford, Doris. *A History of the American Suffragist Movement*. Santa Barbara: ABC-CLIO, 1998.

Wellman, Judith. *Grass Roots Reform in the Burned-Over District of Upstate New York: Religion, Abolitionism, and Democracy*. New York: Garland, 2000.

————. *The Road to Seneca Falls: Elizabeth Cady Stanton and the First Woman's Rights Convention*. Urbana: University of Illinois Press, forthcoming.

————. "The Seneca Falls Women's Rights Convention: A Study of Social Networks." *Journal of Women's History* 3 (Spring 1991): 9–37.

————. "Women's Rights, Republicanism, and Revolutionary Rhetoric in Antebellum New York State." *New York History* 69 (July 1988): 353–84.

Welter, Barbara. *Dimity Convictions: The American Woman in the Nineteenth Century*. Athens: Ohio University Press, 1976.

Wheeler, Marjorie Sproull, ed. *One Woman, One Vote: Rediscovering the Woman Suffrage Movement*. Troutdale, Ore.: New Sage Press, 1995.

Wollstonecraft, Mary. *A Vindication of the Rights of Woman with Strictures on Political and Moral Subjects*. London: Joseph Johnson, 1792. Reprint, New York: Norton, 1967.

Yellin, Jean Fagan. *Women and Sisters: The Antislavery Feminists in American Culture.* New Haven: Yale University Press, 1989.

Yellin, Jean Fagan, and John C. Van Horne, eds. *The Abolitionist Sisterhood: Women's Political Culture in Antebellum America.* Ithaca: Cornell University Press, 1994.

GENERAL HISTORY

Barber, Hugh, and J. William Frost. *The Quakers.* New York: Greenwood Press, 1988.

Barkun, Michael. *Crucible of the Millennium: The Burned-over District of New York in the 1840s.* Syracuse, N.Y.: Syracuse University Press, 1986.

Capron, Eliab Wilkinson. *Modern Spiritualism: Its Facts and Fanaticisms, Its Consistencies and Contradictions.* New York: Bela Marsh, 1855. Reprint, New York: Arno Press, 1976.

Chamberlain, Rudolph W. *There Is No Truce: A Life of Thomas Mott Osborne.* New York: Macmillan, 1935.

Chamberlin, Donald L. "Fort Brooke: Frontier Outpost, 1824–42." *Tampa Bay History* 7 (Spring/Summer 1985): 5–29.

Coddington, Edwin B. *The Gettysburg Campaign.* New York: Scribner's, 1968.

Coffin, Louis. *The Coffin Family.* Nantucket Historical Society, 1952.

Cross, Whitney. *The Burned-over District: The Social and Intellectual History of Enthusiastic Religion in Western New York, 1800–1850.* New York: Octagon Books, 1981.

Edrington, Thomas S., and John Taylor. *The Battle of Glorieta Pass.* Albuquerque: University of New Mexico Press, 1998.

Eisenmann, Linda, ed. *Historical Dictionary of Women's Education in the United States.* Westport, Conn.: Greenwood Press, 1998.

Ellis, David M., James A. Frost, Harold C. Syrett, and Harry J. Carman. *A History of New York State.* Ithaca: Cornell University Press, 1957.

Freehling, William W. *The Road to Disunion: Secessionists at Bay, 1776–1854.* New York: Oxford University Press, 1990.

Gardner, Will. *The Coffin Saga.* Cambridge, Mass.: Riverside Press, 1949.

Giles, L. B. *Terry's Texas Rangers.* Austin: Pemberton Press, 1867.

Gordon, Julius. *Letters of Capt. Peter Pelham in the Territory of Florida, 1821–1826.*

Privately published, 1989. Available from Tampa Bay History Center, Tampa Bay, Fla.

Gordon, Linda. *The Moral Property of Women: A History of Birth Control Politics in America*. Urbana: University of Illinois Press, 2002.

————. *Woman's Body, Woman's Right: A Social History of Birth Control in America*. New York: Grossman, 1976.

Graves, Donald E. *Field of Glory: The Battle of Crysler's Farm, 1813*. Toronto: Robin Brass, 2000.

Hall, Henry. *The History of Auburn*. Auburn, N.Y.: Dennis Brothers, 1869. Reprint, Union Springs, N.Y.: Tallcot Bookshop, 1989.

Hall, Martin Hardwick. *Sibley's New Mexico Campaign*. Austin: University of Texas Press, 1960.

Himes, Norman. *Medical History of Contraception*. New York: Gamut Press, 1963.

Hollcroft, Temple Rice. *Aurora, Village of Constant Dawn*. Ovid, N.Y.: W. E. Morrison, 1976.

Ignatiev, Noel. *How the Irish Became White*. New York: Routledge, 1995.

Jones, Peter Lloyd, and Stephanie E. Przybylek. *Around Auburn*. Images of America. Charleston, S.C.: Arcadia, 1995.

Kelley, Mary. "Reading Women/Women Reading: The Making of Learned Women in Antebellum America." *Journal of American History* 83 (September 1996): 401–24.

Kerby, Robert Lee. *The Confederate Invasion of New Mexico and Arizona, 1861–1862*. Los Angeles: Westernlore Press, 1958.

Lucas, C. P. *The Canadian War of 1812*. Oxford: Oxford University Press, 1906.

McPherson, James M. *Battle Cry of Freedom: The Civil War Era*. New York: Oxford University Press, 1988.

Murray, R. L. *"Hurrah for the Ould Flag": The True Story of Captain Cowan and the First New York Independent Battery at Gettysburg*. Wolcott, N.Y.: R. L. Murray, 1998.

New York State Monuments Commission. *Final Report on the Battlefield of Gettysburg*. Albany: J. B. Lyon, 1900–1902.

Pelham, Caroline Creese. "William Pelham." *William and Mary Quarterly* 8, no. 1 (1928): 42–45.

Przybylek, Stephanie E. *Around Auburn*. Vol. 2. Images of America. Charleston, S.C.: Arcadia, 1998.

Roehm, Marjorie Catlin, ed. *The Letters of George Catlin and His Family*. Berkeley: University of California Press, 1966.

Rouse, Parke Jr. "'The Modern Orpheus': Peter Pelham." *Iron Worker* (Lynchburg Foundry Co., Lynchburg, Va.) 39, no. 1 (Winter 1975): 2–9.

Stewart, George R. *Pickett's Charge: A Microhistory of the Final Attack at Gettysburg, July 3, 1863*. Boston: Houghton Mifflin, 1959.

Stocke, Elliot G. *History of Cayuga County, New York*. Syracuse: D. Mason, 1879.

Trefousse, Hans L. *The Radical Republicans: Lincoln's Vanguard for Racial Justice*. New York: Knopf, 1969.

Twitchell, Ralph Emerson. *The Leading Facts of New Mexican History*. 5 vols. Cedar Rapids, Iowa: Torch Press, 1911–17.

Whitmore, William. "The Copleys and Pelhams of New England." *Heraldic Journal* 4 (1868): 175–82.

———. "Who Was Thomas Pelham?" *New England Historic Genealogical Register* 26 (1872): 399–402.

Wiggins, Sarah Woolfolk. *The Scalawag in Alabama Politics, 1865–1881*. University: University of Alabama Press, 1977.

Index

temperance, 101, 129, 214
Temple, Anna. *See* Brown, Anna
 Temple
Temple, Mary Coffin, 9, 10, 12, 25,
 234
Temple, Solomon, 10, 12, 156
Ten Eyck, 144
Texas, 139, 140, 143, 144
theater, 37, 105, 218
Thirteenth Amendment, 161, 176, 230
Thompson, George, 94
"three-fifths clause," 42
tobacco, 119
Train, George Francis, 179–80, 214
Trial, 8–9
True Womanhood, 229
Truth, 38, 125, 230
Tubman, Harriet, 3, 132–33, 174–76,
 223, 229, *illus.*

Uncle Tom's Cabin, 105, 126, 190
Underground Railroad, 56–58, 132,
 174
Unitarians, 65
United States Gazette, 78
Universalist Church, 64, 89, 124

Van Buren, John, 58
Van Buren, Martin, 58
Vanderbilt, Cornelius, 191
Van Nest, John, 60
Virgin Mary, 68

Wampanoag Indians, 8
War of 1812, 18
Washington conventions, 181, 186–
 87, 190, 192, 195, 220
Waterloo, New York, 71–72
weight, 194–95
Weld, Angelina Grimké, 68, 108
Weld, Theodore, 108, 117, 119, 120,
 157, 262–63n35

Wellman, Judith, 3
Wells College, 29
Welter, Barbara, 229
Wesleyan Chapel, Seneca Falls, 74,
 76
West Point, 30, 137, 144, 146, 151
Westtown School, 12–15, 226
whaling, 7
Wharton, Rodman, 48
Whitman, Walt, 83
Whittier, John Greenleaf, 134
will (of MCW), 11–12
Williamsburg, battle of, 157
Williamsburg, Virginia, 18
Wollstonecraft, Mary, 67–68
Woman's Journal, 193, 216, 221
woman suffrage, 76, 100, 177, 179–
 83, 214, 225, 255n28
Women's National Loyal League, 160–
 61, 177, 229
women's rights conventions: Albany,
 135; Auburn, 109–10; Boston, 179;
 Cincinnati, 112; Cleveland, 103,
 183–84; New York, 115, 126–30,
 178, 192, 195, 213; Philadelphia,
 108; Rochester, 76–77; Salem, 98;
 Saratoga, 110–12; Seneca Falls, 1–
 2, 71–79, 188–89, 204, 207; Syracuse, 100–102, 188; Washington,
 181, 186–87, 190, 192, 195, 220;
 Worcester, 98, 188, 207
women's rights movement, precur-
 sors, 67–68, 253n6
Women's Rights National Historical
 Park, Seneca Falls, 1, 67, 76, 231,
 252n1
Woodhull, Victoria, 190–99, 205–6,
 282–83n23
Woodhull and Claflin's Weekly, 191, 198
Woodward, Charlotte. *See* Pierce,
 Charlotte Woodward
Worcester conventions, 98, 188, 207

Worden, Lazette, 55, 106, 172, 173, 182, 202
World Anti-Slavery Convention (London), 69
Wright, Amos, 34
Wright, Anne, 212, 215
Wright, Charley, 81, 88, 92–93, 234
Wright, David, 34–37, 113, 234, *illus.*; book, 60; and college, 120, 159, 167; death, 223; farms, 84; finances, 36–37; to Gettysburg, 164–65; law career, 34, 35, 37, 60–61, 84, 245n17, 257n16; marriage, 35, 116: plank road, 84; politics, 113; and Quakers, 34; to Washington, 155–56; on women's rights, 70–71, 113, 115; youth, 34, 116
Wright, Edith Livingston, 212–13
Wright, Eliza. *See* Osborne, Eliza Wright
Wright, Ellen. *See* Garrison, Ellen Wright
Wright, Fanny Rosalie Pell, 172, 174, 223
Wright, Flora McMartin, 173, 210
Wright, Frank, 87, 95, 234, *illus.*: baseball, 160, 167–68, 172; birth, 52; daughter, 174; death, 223; Florida, 223; Harvard, 156, 159, 160, 167–68; marriage (first), 172; marriage (second), 223; MCW letters to, 119; school, 85, 95, 117, 119, 156; work, 172, 209, 223
Wright, Mabel Channing. *See* Livingston, Mabel Channing Wright
Wright, Martha Coffin (MCW), *illus.*: and abolition, 39–41, 228–29; advice to children, 45–46, 117–20; birth, 7; children, 234; clothes, 121–22; death of, 218–19; death, attitude toward, 202–3, 222; expulsion from Quakers, 23–24; freedom of

thought and expression, 150, 198, 230; friendified, 37; grandchildren, 81, 171, 183, 210, 215, 234; home, 51–52; housework, 54, 82, 229; humor, 2, 4–5, 46, 207–8, 222; in Kentucky, 103–5, 112; marriage (first), 21–22; marriage (second), 35; obituaries, 221–2; painting, 29, 133; penmanship, 14; poems, 44–45, 91–92, 224; president of NWSA, 213; presiding at conventions, 110–12, 128, 134–36, 179, 186; public speaking, 100, 114–15, 213; reading, 14, 83, 85, 209; religion, 38, 61–66, 95, 203; schools, 11, 12–16, 240n13; shipwreck, 23; teaching, 29–30; women's rights, 69–70, 80, 98, 178–79, 190; writings, 65–66, 78–80, 91–92, 100, 110, 187–90, 227
Wright, Sarah. *See* Kniffen, Sarah Wright
Wright, Tallman (Matthew Tallman), 234: birth, 35, 52; in California, 95–96; death, 96–97; and fugitive slave, 57; and guns, 53; in Philadelphia, 84
Wright, William Pelham, 85, 87, 234, *illus.*: birth, 52; children, 212–13, 215; Civil War, 47, 156–64; death, 223; Florida, 154, 173, 210–11, 223; marriage, 173; MCW letters to, 119, 160; school, 85, 95, 108, 117, 119; work, 171–72; wounded, 163–65
Wright Avenue, Auburn, 84
Wyatt, Henry, 59
Wyoming, 186

Yarnall, Benjamin, 10, 12, 42
Yarnall, Eliza Coffin, 9, 10, 12, 20, 25, 38, 42, 200, 233

SHERRY H. PENNEY (LIVINGSTON) is the Sherry H. Penney Professor of Leadership in the College of Management, University of Massachusetts Boston. She has a doctorate in American history from the State University of New York in Albany and has taught history at Union College, Yale University, SUNY Albany, and the University of Massachusetts Boston. She served as associate provost at Yale, as vice chancellor for academic programs, policy, and planning for the sixty-four-campus SUNY system, and as acting president of SUNY Plattsburgh. From 1988 to 2000 she was chancellor of University of Massachusetts Boston, except for 1995, when she served as interim president of the five-campus University system. She is the author of *Patrician in Politics: Daniel Dewey Barnard of New York* and articles on leadership, higher education, and American history.

JAMES D. LIVINGSTON is a senior lecturer in the Department of Materials Science and Engineering of the Massachusetts Institute of Technology. He has a doctorate in applied physics from Harvard University, and he worked from 1956 to 1989 as a physicist in materials research and development for the General Electric Company. He is a member of the National Academy of Engineering, a General Electric Coolidge Fellow, and a Fellow of the American Physical Society and ASM International. His books include *Driving Force: The Natural History of Magnets* and *Electronic Properties of Engineering Materials*, and he has published several articles on New York State history.